MACROECONOMICS AND THE WAGE BARGAIN

Macroeconomics and the Wage Bargain

A Modern Approach to Employment, Inflation, and the Exchange Rate

Wendy Carlin and David Soskice

Oxford University Press
1990

Oxford University Press, Walton Street, Oxford OX2 6DP

Oxford New York Toronto
Delhi Bombay Calcutta Madras Karachi
Petaling Jaya Singapore Hong Kong Tokyo
Nairobi Dar es Salaam Cape Town
Melbourne Auckland

and associated companies in
Berlin Ibadan

Oxford is a trade mark of Oxford University Press

Published in the United States
by Oxford University Press, New York

© Wendy J. Carlin and David W. Soskice 1990

British Library Cataloguing in Publication Data
Carlin, Wendy
Macroeconomics and the wage bargain: a modern approach to
employment, inflation and the exchange rate.
1. Macroeconomics
I. Title   II. Soskice, David
339
ISBN 0-19-877245-9
ISBN 0-19-877244-0 pbk

Library of Congress Cataloging in Publication Data
Carlin, Wendy.
Macroeconomics and the wage bargain: a modern approach to
employment, inflation, and the exchange rate/Wendy Carlin and David Soskice.
Includes bibliographical references and index.
1. Labor market.   2. Employment.   3. Competition, Imperfect.
4. Foreign exchange.   5. Keynesian economics.   6. Macroeconomics.
I. Soskice, David W., 1942–   .   II. Title.
HD5706.C285   1990 339.5–dc20 90-7601
ISBN 0-19-877245-9
ISBN 0-19-877244-0 pbk

Typeset by KEYTEC, Bridport, Dorset
Printed and bound in Great Britain by
Biddles Ltd, Guildford and King's Lynn

Preface

In the last decade, an approach to macroeconomics which is coming to be known as the 'New Keynesian Macroeconomics' has been constructed. This approach roots macroeconomics in the microfoundations of imperfectly competitive labour and product markets. Bargaining between unions and oligopolistic employers matches the institutional context of Western European economies, and the approach lies behind the analysis of changing equilibrium rates of unemployment (NAIRUs) and the persistence of high unemployment in Europe. Among the leading economists who have been developing and applying the new approach are Blanchard, Dreze, Layard, Nickell, Rowthorn, Sachs, and Summers.

Most of the work by these authors has been written in journals or graduate textbooks. Notable books are the MIT graduate textbook *Lectures on Macroeconomics*, by Blanchard and Fischer, and *Unemployment*, by the LSE economists Jackman, Layard, Nickell, and Wadhwani, setting out the theoretical and applied work associated with the Centre for Labour Economics. Our major motivation has been to make this increasingly central literature accessible to undergraduates, as well as to economists not working in the field or outside academic life.

The book is based on a course of lectures which we developed together and have been giving for several years to second- and third-year economics undergraduates at Oxford University and University College London. These lectures have been successful, we believe, because from beginning to end they have been organized—as the book is—around a core diagram and around the central concept of the resolution of competing claims on the economy's output. The key models and results are presented in verbal and graphical terms using a common core of diagrams. Often the argument is repeated algebraically. Readers can choose whichever mode of presentation best suits them. Shaded boxes are used to present more detailed explanation of some of the material in the text and to provide background information on key concepts. Asterisks are used to identify more difficult passages or extensions of arguments which can be omitted without loss of continuity.

The book also follows the lectures in making clear the genesis of the New

Keynesìan Macroeconomics in shortcomings of both the 'Keynes-reappraisal' school (Clower, Malinvaud) and the New Classical Macroeconomics (Lucas, Sargent). The shortcomings of the former are inadequate microfoundations; and those of the latter, failure to provide convincing explanations for the key stylized facts of macroeconomic performance. Part I of *Macroeconomics and the Wage Bargain* reviews the development of macro theory to provide the link to the new macroeconomics based on imperfect competition.

Part II of the book sets out imperfect competition-based macro analysis for a closed economy and Part III, that for the open economy. More detailed discussion of the microfoundations is provided in Part IV, as the basis for reviewing the most recent literature on hysteresis and persistence of unemployment, and for showing how the key stylized facts are explained by the imperfect competition model. These discussions are summarized in the first chapter of Part IV, which at the same time provides an overview of the book as a whole. The interested reader might turn to this chapter after reading the Introduction to get an overall idea of what we have tried to do.

The book is intended both as a text and as a general introduction to this important area. As a text it is designed to be used for intermediate macroeconomics courses which concentrate on employment, inflation, and exchange rates. But it can be used flexibly. Our experience has been that it is useful for students to have a good grasp of the background set out in Part I. However, the other parts do not depend on it, just as the open economy part can be used largely independently of the closed economy part. For example, combining Chapter 6 with Part III creates a coherent course on open economy macroeconomics. Similarly, Part II and the bulk of Part IV can be used for the macro theory section of a labour economics course.

Throughout the book, lower-case letters denote real magnitudes and upper-case letters denote nominal magnitudes; e.g., $w \equiv$ real wage; $W \equiv$ nominal wage.

Our success in completing this book owes much to Andrew Glyn, who read and commented on countless drafts of the manuscript and who has supported the project from the outset in practical as well as intellectual ways. V. Bhaskar made substantive contributions which have improved key parts of the book. Others who have read and commented, often extensively, on draft chapters are Deborah Mabbett, Andrew Oswald, Lloyd Ulman, and two anonymous readers. We also want to thank the following for their contributions: Chris Allsopp, Michael Bacharach, Clair Brown, Andrew Graham, Steve Nickell, Bob Rowthorn, Michele Salvati, Andrew Trigg, and Donald Verry. The enthusiasm and support of our students and colleagues has been important in seeing the project through to the end. We have been particularly lucky in both our editor Andrew Schuller and our copy editor Sue Hughes. Finally, we have each had the most enormous help and encouragement in every way from the people we live with, Andrew Glyn and Niki Lacey.

W.J.C. and D.W.S.

Contents

Introduction

Inflation and Unemployment in Contemporary Economies

The aim of this introductory chapter is to set the scene empirically and theoretically for the rest of the book. We begin by identifying the changes in economic performance in the major advanced economies which occurred in the 1970s and 1980s and prompted a reassessment of macroeconomic theory. We argue that three important lines of research were stimulated by the inadequacies of the consensus model of the 1950s and 1960s (the so-called Keynesian–neoclassical synthesis) to cope with the applied problems of recent years. One was the reassertion of the classical tradition of macroeconomics in the form of the New Classical model. The second was the school that developed out of the reappraisal of Keynes's theory: the fixed-price approach to macroeconomics. The third line of research sought to base macroeconomic analysis firmly on imperfectly competitive microeconomic foundations. Much of this book presents and extends the third approach. The central concept that characterizes the imperfect competition approach is that of the competing claims on the economy's output per head which are exercised by the holders of monopoly power: unions and price-setting firms. In this chapter, we introduce the competing-claims approach by presenting the core diagram and defining the equilibrium rate of unemployment.

The Context

The emergence in the 1970s of concurrent inflation and unemployment created a challenge not only to economic policy-makers but also to theorists. Figure I1 shows the sharp change in the performance of the major industrialized economies as between the 'Golden Age' of the 1950s and 1960s and the less brilliant 1970s and 1980s. Growth was virtually halved, unemployment more than doubled, and inflation had accelerated. In addition, although all economies experienced a marked weakening of performance on the conventional criteria of unemployment, inflation, and growth, there has been a great diversity in performance. Figure I2

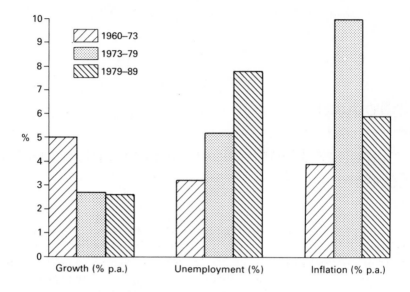

Fig. I1 Growth, unemployment, and inflation in the OECD, 1960–1989
Sources: OECD, *Historical Statistics*; OECD, *Economic Outlook*

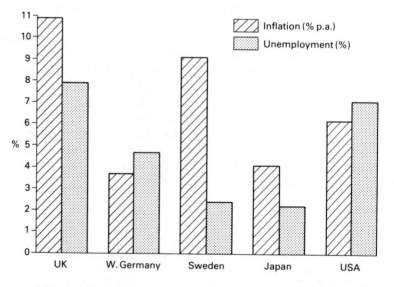

Fig. I2 Cross-country experience of inflation and unemployment, 1973–1988
Sources: OECD, *Historical Statistics*; OECD, *Economic Outlook*

highlights the very different experience of unemployment and inflation of five OECD economies: the UK, West Germany, Sweden, Japan, and the USA. For example, within Europe, the difference between average unemployment in the UK, Sweden, and West Germany is striking. Similarly, average inflation has differed between almost 11% in the UK and less than 4% in West Germany.

The great boost to inflation occurred at the end of the 1960s/beginning of the 1970s. There was much talk in the USA of the inflationary financing of the Vietnam War, in Europe of wage explosions and rising trade union militancy. Rising inflation undermined the viability of the Bretton Woods system of fixed exchange rates which had operated since the war. Macroeconomic analysis had to be adapted to a different exchange rate regime. Performance was dented further by the occurrence of the first oil price shock in 1973. It was subsequent to this shock to the supply side of the economy that the major economies experienced the first synchronized deep recession in the postwar era and the associated emergence of mass unemployment. By 1975 there were 15 million people out of work in the major industrialized economies as compared with only 8 million two years earlier. Not only did growth plummet and unemployment soar, but inflation gathered pace (Fig. I1).

In the face of this turbulence, economists looked more searchingly at their macroeconomic models. An objective of this book is to reflect some of the important outcomes of that reassessment. The focus is on the analysis of inflation, unemployment, and, in the open economy, international competitiveness (the real exchange rate). The key dynamic issue of the slowdown in productivity growth (see e.g. Maddison 1987) is not treated here because it has not yet been the subject of a thorough theoretical reappraisal; certainly the move to restrictive demand policies has, via sluggish investment, played some role.

The Analysis of Inflation and Unemployment

During the Golden Age of the 1950s and 1960s, there was a reasonable degree of consensus among macroeconomists as to how the economy worked. At the heart of the consensus was the Keynesian model of aggregate demand, and much of the attention of researchers was directed towards clarifying theoretically and empirically the determinants of aggregate demand: consumption, investment, money supply, money demand. Rather little attention was paid to the supply side of the economy. Keynes himself had worked with perfect competition in the *product market*, but emphasized market imperfections in the *labour market* which prevented the money wage from falling freely when the supply of labour exceeded the demand. The simple tool with which the bulk of mainstream macroeconomists tended to think—the *IS/LM model*—was based on fixed prices and money wages. To this was added, in an *ad hoc* way, the famous *Phillips curve* relation between the rate of increase of money wages or prices (inflation) and the rate of unemployment. The Phillips curve was an empirical relationship which showed that, at lower rates of unemployment, wage inflation was higher. This composite model, which lacked a well developed account of the supply side of the economy, was known, especially in the USA, as the *neoclassical synthesis*. This is a misleading name, since today we think of it as Keynesian; we compromise by referring to it as the *Keynesian–neoclassical synthesis*.

In Part I of the book, we follow through the evolution of the theory of employment and inflation beginning with a schematic *classical model* against which Keynes's *General Theory* was directed. The classical approach to macroeconomics consisted of a simple model in which the real side of the economy—output, employment—could be analysed separately from the nominal side—prices, inflation. The real side is modelled using perfectly competitive markets so that the level of aggregate output and employment is fixed by the clearing of the labour market and the technical conditions of production. The price level in the economy is pinned down by the supply of money, and, by extension, the rate of inflation is equal to the growth rate of the money supply. Keynes attacked the classical theory of employment, arguing that the economy could get stuck at a position away from full employment and pointing to the active role of government in counteracting such a situation.

We then sketch the consensus model of the 1950s and 1960s (the Keynesian–neoclassical synthesis). As noted earlier, this consisted of a Keynesian model of aggregate demand to determine employment (*IS/LM*) supplemented by a Phillips curve to show the rate of inflation. The consensus was shattered as the existing model was unable to deal adequately with the economic turbulence from the end of the 1960s. For example, the empirical adequacy of the Phillips curve was undermined by the events of the day as inflation continued to rise although unemployment had stopped falling. Research efforts then split in three main directions.

First, there was a resurgence of a classical approach to the theory of employment and inflation. This began with Friedman's treatment of *accelerating* inflation (Friedman 1968). Friedman sought to reassert the need to use a market-clearing microeconomic basis for macroeconomics by defining the *natural rate of unemployment* as the rate fixed by the clearing of the labour market. Any deviation of unemployment from the natural rate was presented as arising from informational failures in the labour market. With all participants fully informed of market possibilities, the economy would always be at the natural rate with constant inflation. Friedman's policy message was clear: government intervention to reduce unemployment below the natural rate would result in accelerating inflation. Ever higher wage inflation relative to pre-existing price inflation would be required in order to persuade workers that the real wage was higher than it was and thereby to elicit a higher supply of labour than would be forthcoming if the actual real wage were known. The consequence would be increasing rates of price inflation.

A yet stronger classical approach followed Friedman's analysis with the appearance in the late 1970s of the *New Classical Macroeconomics*. The principle result of the new school was that, apart from the occurrence of unpredictable shocks to the economy, unemployment would be at the natural rate continuously. Even a short-run trade-off between unemployment and inflation was not possible.

The second line of new research took its lead from the work of Keynes. The re-emergence of mass unemployment gave renewed momentum to economists working on the reinterpretation of Keynes's theory of employment. Economists such as Clower, Leijonhufvud, and Malinvaud sought to clarify and make more rigorous the microeconomic basis for the existence of persistent unemployment. Malinvaud focused on an issue with which policy-makers were particularly concerned, the relationship between real wages and unemployment, and identified two types of *involuntary unemployment* (a situation in which workers are prepared to accept work at the going real wage). In a situation of *classical unemployment*, a higher real wage leads to higher unemployment, but in a situation of *Keynesian unemployment*, a higher real wage reduces unemployment.

The third direction of research can best be understood as a response to unsatisfactory aspects of the first two and constitutes the subject matter of Part II, much of Part III, and Part IV of the book. It emerged—mainly in Europe—from the attempts of applied economists to explain the rise in unemployment in the 1970s and early 1980s. They were dissatisfied with the absence of an explanation of the process of inflation from the 'Keynes reappraisal' approach. Yet they were sympathetic to the notion that much of the unemployment was involuntary. Friedman's model of inflation with its expectations-augmented Phillips curves was an attractive one, yet the insistence of Friedman, and even more of the New Classical economists, on a *market-clearing* microeconomic basis for the theory did not appear to fit easily with the policy problem at hand—the persistence of high rates of unemployment.

Thus, the third wave of research moved to base the analysis of unemployment and inflation on the behaviour of labour and product markets under conditions of imperfect competition. The *imperfect competition model* that was developed (sometimes referred to as the *NAIRU (non-accelerating inflation rate of unemployment)* model) combines Keynesian features with the existence of an equilibrium rate of unemployment. It is beginning to be referred to as the 'New Keynesian' approach.[1] With imperfectly competitive labour and product markets, the *equilibrium rate of unemployment* will not be a market-clearing rate. It is simply the

---

[1] 'New Keynesian' should not be confused with other approaches, referred to as 'neo-Keynesian', 'post-Keynesian', or 'new Cambridge'.

rate of unemployment at which inflation is constant. The idea is that, in an
economy in which both workers and firms have market power (there is not
perfect competition with atomistic price- and wage-taking agents), each
group will attempt to get hold of a particular share of the economy's
product. It is easiest to think of the competing claims of workers and firms
for a share of output per head. Suppose that the competing claims are
inconsistent, i.e. that the claim of workers to real wages and of firms to real
profits sum to more than is available in output per head. Then each side
will attempt to secure its claim by using its market power—workers will
secure higher money wages and firms will put their prices up. The result is
rising inflation.

But what determines the rate of unemployment at which the competing
claims are consistent? All sorts of institutional, historical, and technical
factors come into play to affect the relative bargaining power of the groups.
For example, the extent to which the work-force is unionized obviously
affects its market power. A major influence on wage-bargaining power is
the state of the labour market, a ready measure of which is the rate of
unemployment; when unemployment rises, wage-bargaining power declines because the costs to workers of using their market power to gain
wage increases rise. With high unemployment, the prospects for workers to
get another job, either during the course of any industrial dispute over pay
or if the dispute threatens the viability of their employer, are poor.

Figure I3 illustrates the basic imperfect competition model. The real
wage is measured on the vertical axis and employment along the horizontal
one. The statistically measured labour force is shown as LF on the
employment axis, with the result that the amount of unemployment can be
measured explicitly as the difference between employment and the labour

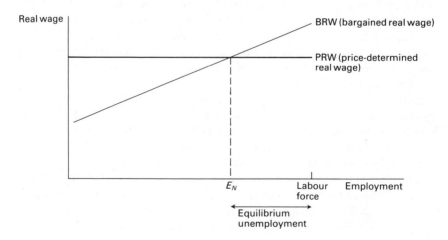

Fig. I3 The basic imperfect competition model

force. We can show easily how the imperfect competition model generates an equilibrium rate of unemployment at which inflation is constant. The claim by workers for a real wage is shown by the line labelled BRW. BRW stands for the 'bargained real wage'; it is the real wage that unions seek through their wage negotiations. As employment rises and unemployment falls, the bargained real wage increases; the BRW in Fig. I3 is upward-sloping, reflecting the increase in the bargaining power of labour as unemployment falls. The claim of firms for real profits is shown by the PRW line. PRW stands for 'price-determined real wage'. This shows what is left in terms of real wages once firms in aggregate have taken their profits. The logic of the price-determined real wage is that imperfectly competitive firms use their market power to maximize profits by setting prices relative to costs of production; aggregated out over the whole economy, this divides output per worker into the real wage and real profit per worker. The PRW line in Fig. I3 is horizontal. It seems empirically to be the case that the price-determined real wage does not vary with the level of employment, and we look in some detail at a number of explanations for this. It is clear from the diagram that there is a single level of employment (rate of unemployment)[2] at which real wage and profit claims are consistent, i.e. where the BRW and the PRW intersect. With employment higher than E_N, the equilibrium level of employment, the bargained real wage exceeds the price-determined real wage. There is conflict over the division of output per head and this conflict will be reflected in rising inflation as each group seeks to secure its real claim on output by raising money wages or prices.

This general approach has its roots in both Keynesian and neoclassical economics. As Rowthorn (1977) pointed out, it has origins as well with Marx. The earliest analysis of the role of unemployment in reducing the power of workers—of exerting a disciplinary effect—can be found in Marx's notion of the *reserve army of labour*. The surplus of unemployed workers served the function of holding down wages. More recently, it can be argued that in the 1930s, Kalecki's Marxist–Keynesian macroeconomic analysis anticipated the approach here (Sawyer 1982). The applied work on unemployment based on the imperfect competition model has been led by the Centre for Labour Economics at the London School of Economics (e.g. Layard and Nickell 1985; for a comprehensive treatment see Jackman *et al.* 1989). International studies along these lines were published in the *Economica* Supplement of 1986.

The effect on the equilibrium rate of unemployment (the NAIRU) of shifts in union bargaining power, of the implementation and collapse of incomes policies, of changes in taxation, and of terms-of-trade shocks such

---

[2] By assuming the labour force is constant, the level of unemployment implies a particular rate of unemployment.

as an oil price rise have been incorporated into the empirical applications of the imperfect competition model.

The model can be readily extended to the analysis of the open economy. In the open economy, the sustainability of a particular rate of unemployment depends not just on constant inflation but also on the maintenance of equilibrium in the balance of payments.

In the open economy, the equilibrium rate of unemployment in the above sense will no longer be unique but will rise as the real exchange rate depreciates (i.e. as competitiveness rises). The depreciation of the real exchange rate raises the claims of the overseas sector on domestic resources: the real cost of imports rises. This requires a fall in the real wage to render consistent the claims on output per head from real wages, real profits and real import costs, and can be brought about only by a rise in unemployment. There is another competing-claims equilibrium at the higher rate of unemployment. But the sustainability of the equilibrium rate of unemployment in the long term requires that the combination of the real exchange rate and the unemployment rate be consistent with external balance. In general, this is as true for fixed as for floating exchange rate regimes.

We develop a simple reinterpretation of the famous Salter–Swan diagram in which the internal balance schedule is interpreted as showing combinations of competitiveness (the real exchange rate) and the level of unemployment at which competing claims are satisfied. Together with the external balance relationship between the real exchange rate and the level of unemployment, the *long-run sustainable unemployment rate* is determined. When combined with an aggregate demand schedule, the diagram can be used to show what happens to actual unemployment in response to a range of policy measures.

We further develop this model for the case of two countries together. In a world dominated by discussion of the European Monetary System and common currencies, analysis of policy coordination between countries is of growing importance. We develop a diagrammatic apparatus which takes account both of a straightforward Keynesian analysis of aggregate demand interrelations between economies, and also of the interrelations that arise via inflation.

The Structure of the Book

Parts II, III, and IV of the book concentrate on the presentation of the imperfect competition model. The models of Part I provide a systematic introduction to the analysis of the twin issues of unemployment and inflation. The role of the competitive microeconomic foundations of these models is highlighted, and motivation is provided for moving to the development of a model based on imperfect competition. At key points throughout the book, perfect competition is used as a benchmark with which the results under imperfect competition are compared. The third function of Part I is to enable the presentation of a number of the basic building blocks required in the imperfect competition model. For example, the Keynesian aggregate demand analysis and its distillation into the *IS/LM* diagram are used throughout. Friedman's expectations-augmented Phillips curves are transplanted from his model with competitive product and labour markets into the imperfect competition model. The *Rational Expectations Hypothesis*—first introduced as a foundation stone of the New Classical macroeconomics—is applied later to the imperfect competition model.

Part II opens with a discussion of wage- and price-setting under imperfect competition. The working of the macroeconomic model built on this foundation and sketched above is presented in some detail. The rest of Part II deals with policy analysis in the imperfect competition macro model. The use of policy measures to shift the equilibrium rate of unemployment focuses on fiscal supply-side policies and on incomes policies. Here, the role of the government as a third claimant on the economy's output per head is clarified. Including the government in the model means that output per head must be split three ways, into real wages, real profits, and real tax receipts. If the government raises its rates of taxation, then this reduces the output per head available to the private sector. Higher taxation will have the effect of raising the equilibrium rate of unemployment since higher unemployment is required to dampen union wage claims and render all three claims consistent. The use of incomes policies to reduce the equilibrium rate of unemployment by lowering wage claims at each level of employment is examined.

Attention then turns to the effect of policy on actual employment, and the issue of the crowding-out effect of a fiscal expansion is addressed. To look at the dynamics of inflation, we analyse the effect on inflation of deviations of unemployment from the equilibrium rate. The case of a government switching from the pursuit of an *accommodating monetary policy* (where the money supply is allowed to rise in line with inflation) to a non-accommodating policy (such as the use of a growth rate rule for the money supply) is examined in some detail.

In the final chapter in Part II, the opportunity is taken to look in more depth at a number of policy issues which relate to the role of wage bargaining in macroeconomics. The question of the appropriate hypothesis to use for modelling inflation expectations is addressed—what are the consequences of using adaptive or rational expectations, and how does the choice of hypothesis relate to the structure of wage-bargaining? The second topic pursued in greater depth is that of incomes policy, an issue that can be analysed very naturally in the setting of a model of imperfect competition. The difficulties that lie in the way of the successful implementation and maintenance of an incomes policy are outlined. The last part of the chapter shows in a simple way how dynamic considerations can be introduced; in particular, we look at the ramifications for the economy of a slowdown in productivity growth.

Part III on the open economy begins with a review of the standard extensions of aggregate demand analysis to take account of trade and international flows of capital. The supply side is then brought in with the introduction of imported materials as an additional claimant on output per head—additional to the claims of real wages, profits, and taxation. We show how to modify the pricing rule for the open economy and introduce the central concept of international competitiveness. If the government tries to keep unemployment too low, upward pressure on wages and prices will ensue. This will damage the international competitiveness of the economy and lead to a deterioration of the current account of the balance of payments.

Under floating exchange rates, much attention has been given to the famous Mundell–Fleming results regarding the relative effectiveness of fiscal and monetary policies in changing levels of output and employment: that fiscal policy is totally ineffective and monetary policy very effective when exchange rates are flexible. However, these results are reversed when there is 'real wage resistance', i.e. when workers seek recompense in higher money wages for any erosion of their real wage through exchange rate depreciation. Clearly, this is an issue of considerable importance to policy-makers when considering the appropriate policy mix. Real wage resistance is a property of the open economy imperfect competition model and permits a clear discussion of this issue. The contributions of Sachs and Dornbusch are reflected in the analysis.

Considerable attention is also given to the question of how exchange rate expectations are formed and why they matter. In addition, we discuss how to analyse the impact of a raw materials price shock and also examine the issue of policy interdependence.

The fourth part of the book begins with a chapter that represents both an introduction to Part IV and a conclusion to the previous three parts. The aim is to present a series of 'stylized facts' which appear to characterize the operation of modern industrialized economies and to see how the three different strands in modern macroeconomic research can account for these 'facts'. Six stylized facts are discussed:

1   Real wages show no strong cyclical pattern, but if anything there is a tendency for a pro-cyclical pattern; i.e., an upswing is associated with a rise in real wages.
2   A large proportion of unemployment in the 1980s is involuntary and cannot be explained either in terms of mistaken expectations about the

rate of inflation or monetary growth, or in terms of search activity.

3 Firms generally would like to produce more if the real wage remained constant—they are constrained in their output by the level of aggregate demand.

4 Changes in nominal aggregate demand provoke changes in quantity, i.e. of output and employment, and only subsequently changes in prices and wages.

5 Shifts in unemployment arising from changes in aggregate demand appear persistent, with the result that approximately constant inflation is observed at many different rates of unemployment.

6 There is a range of unemployment rates across countries in the 1980s which appears to be related to the type of wage-bargaining institutions.

It is argued that the Malinvaud–Keynesian research initiative (the fixed-price model) is quite consistent with the first four of the facts, to the extent that the economy tends to be in the regime known as 'Keynesian unemployment'. However, the model is unsatisfactory in that the assumption of perfectly competitive labour and product markets lies uneasily with the assumption of fixed prices and wages and provides no explanation for the prevalence of 'Keynesian unemployment'. By contrast, the New Classical approach provides an entirely coherent set of micro-foundations but is hard put to account for the stylized facts.

We see that the imperfect competition model appears to provide a useful approach to accounting for the 'facts'. The remainder of Part IV addresses two sorts of questions raised by the confrontation of the model with the stylized facts: first, the issue of the microfoundations for the imperfect competition model, and second, the extensions to the model that are required if facts 5 and 6 are to be accounted for.

Chapters 17 and 18 have been included to provide readers with an adequate back-up in the microeconomic foundations for the imperfectly competitive behaviour that is assumed in Parts II and III. Chapter 17 examines the theoretical bases of wage formation of the type captured in the bargained real wage curve. The monopoly union model, models of bargaining and models in which employers set the wage above the market-clearing level (the so-called *efficiency wage*) are presented. The section on efficiency wages looks at various explanations for employers in *non-union* firms unilaterally setting wages above market-clearing levels. The concept of efficiency wages helps to make the imperfect competition analysis relevant for industrialized economies in which unions play little part in wage-setting.

Using the micro analysis, we look at the relationship between wage-setting institutions and employment outcomes and attempt to address the sixth stylized fact. The role of the degree of centralization of wage-bargaining in affecting unemployment is discussed.

This is followed by a chapter on pricing behaviour. In the bulk of the book we assume a very simple pricing rule of normal cost pricing. (Firms set prices as a mark-up on unit costs at a standard level of capacity utilization.) In Part IV, we show that the pricing behaviour predicted by normal cost pricing can be thought of either as arising from the application of a rule of thumb in an uncertain world, or as the outcome of profit-maximizing behaviour under imperfect competition (i.e. marginal cost pricing) under circumstances in which the elasticity of demand moves pro-cyclically and hence the mark-up varies in a counter-cyclical way. We look at reasons why this may be the case.

The third and final topic addressed in Part IV is that of the apparent persistence or *hysteresis* of the unemployment rate. This is a subject born of the experience of the 1980s, when economists began investigating the link between the impact of changes in actual unemployment and the equilibrium rate of unemployment. Attempts were made to explain the apparent failure of inflation to fall continuously when the unemployment rate was pushed up as the result of a decline in aggregate demand, and therefore for the absence of strong forces pushing unemployment back to the equilibrium rate. One approach has identified the role of high unemployment in creating a pool of long-term unemployed. It has been argued that high unemployment results in the long-term unemployed becoming demoralized and deskilled and less able to exert downward pressure on wage-bargaining. The result is that the equilibrium rate of unemployment rises. The topic provides a symmetry to the book by reintroducing the question of the importance of Keynesian economic problems. If hysteresis is important, then the Keynesian emphasis on changes in aggregate demand in determining unemployment feeds through to affect the equilibrium rate of unemployment.

Economic Institutions and Macroeconomic Models

The increasing attention of researchers to the diversity of economic performance within the group of OECD economies in the past decade and a half has inevitably sharpened interest in the appropriate modelling of institutions even at the level of a macroeconomic model. The situation in the bulk of the industrialized economies outside the USA where unions play a significant role in wage-setting provides the institutional basis for the concentration in this book on imperfectly competitive labour markets. Table I1 indicates the proportion of the labour force which is unionized in a number of OECD economies; in many cases these figures greatly underestimate the importance of collective bargaining agreements, since non-unionized workers are frequently covered by the collective agreement. Similarly, the choice of imperfect competition in product markets reflects

Table I1 Union density in OECD countries

% of non-agricultural wage and salaried employees belonging to unions, 1984/5

Sweden	95	Italy	45	Japan	29
Austria	61	W. Germany	42	France	28
Australia	57	Canada	37	USA	18
UK	52				

Source: Freeman (1988: 66, Table 1)

the importance of the manufacturing and services sectors in the major industrialized economies. In manufacturing and in many services, price-setting behaviour is a more accurate 'stylized fact' than is the extreme case of perfect competition. The importance for these economies of manufac-tured goods in their trade flow, along with the virtually universal recognition that goods do not sell at uniform prices in different national markets, makes the imperfect competition model applicable to the open economy as well.

For an adequate analysis of the US economy, it may be necessary to have a model that incorporates both imperfectly competitive and perfectly competitive sectors of the economy. If they have to opt for a single sector, the bulk of US economists choose to assume perfect competition. With only one in five US workers unionized, it is more difficult to justify the use of imperfect competition in the labour market—although some recent research in the USA suggests that even in ununionized firms employers will set the wage above the minimum necessary to elicit the desired number of hours of work (efficiency wages). We show in Part IV that the behaviour of employers in this way makes the imperfect competition model directly applicable. Nevertheless, an element of non-US bias remains in the adoption of a thoroughgoing imperfect competition approach. The extensive treatment of the open economy also reflects more closely the needs of analysts of Western Europe, Japan, and the smaller economies of Australia, New Zealand, and Canada. While the stylized facts outlined above appear to characterize the USA (e.g. Blanchard and Fischer 1989; Ball *et al.* 1988; Greenwald and Stiglitz 1988), the appropriateness of imperfect competition as the microeconomic foundation for a satisfactory macro explanation is more contentious for the USA than it is for the other major economies.

A Theory in a State of Flux

The general approach to modelling unemployment and inflation as described in Parts II, III, and IV of this book has not settled into a standardized accepted set of equations. It is in a state of flux, with vigorous debate on, for example, hysteresis, the operation of bargaining in labour markets, the open economy, and so on. What we try to do in this book is to boil these new developments down into a series of simple, related models. We do not capture all the different positions adopted. The aim is to make this important area accessible to as wide an audience as possible. At a more advanced level, some of the analysis presented in Parts II and IV can be found in the recent text by Blanchard and Fischer (1989).

PART 1

The Background: Macroeconomics with Competitive Microfoundations

1

The Classical Model of Employment and Inflation: Market-Clearing and the Quantity Theory of Money

In the years immediately before the ideas of Keynes's *General Theory* captured the imagination of economists and policy-makers, the classical[1] model was the basis for answering macroeconomic questions.[2] The classical model (also known as the Quantity Theory model) rests on the microeconomic foundation of perfectly competitive markets for labour, goods, and bonds. All markets are competitive and are also assumed to clear very quickly. Built on this base, the classical model has three characteristics, which will be explained in detail in the following pages:

C1 Employment and output are determined in the labour market by the demand for labour (marginal product of labour) and the supply of labour.

C2 The Quantity Theory of Money establishes the connection between the money supply and the price level. The price level varies to ensure that real aggregate demand, a function of the real money supply, is brought into line with the supply of output determined in the labour market.

C3 Aggregate savings and investment are equated at full employment by a flexible interest rate.

Each of these features has implications for macroeconomic policy. From C1, it follows that there is *no lasting involuntary unemployment*. Any temporary involuntary unemployment would disappear as real wages declined. From C2, increases in the money supply lead simply to price rises. Monetary policy has no real effects. This is the property known as the

[1] The term 'classical' can be misleading. Its use in macroeconomics and its adoption by the school of 'New Classical Macroeconomics' should be clearly distinguished from its traditional use in the history of economic thought to denote the economics of Smith, Ricardo, and Marx.

[2] Keynes used Pigou's *The Theory of Unemployment* (1933) as the representative refined 'classical theory' of the determination of employment against which to set his ideas. The classical model that we present is not supposed to reflect perfectly a specific historical school of thought. For a detailed textbook presentation see Ackley (1978: pt. II).

neutrality of money. From C3, increases in government expenditure reduce private investment by an equal amount, there is *complete crowding-out*, and there are no multiplier effects.

We will examine each of these results in turn.

1.1   The Classical Model

1.1.1   The Competitive Labour Market

Demand for Labour and Supply of Output by Competitive Firms

The levels of employment and output are the (related) major short-run decisions faced by a firm operating in perfectly competitive labour and product markets. The short run is the decision-making horizon for which the firm's capital stock is assumed constant. In order to maximize profits, the firm will hire extra labour until the marginal product of labour equals the real wage. For each firm, the real wage is given; labour can be hired at a given money wage and the price level for output is exogenous to

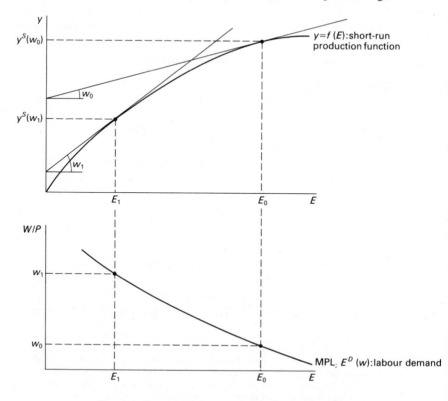

Fig. 1.1 Demand for labour: perfect competition

the firm. The marginal product of labour depends on the firm's capital stock. Given its plant and equipment, additional inputs of labour will result in a specific increment of output: the marginal product of labour.

Figure 1.1 illustrates the employment decision. The top panel shows the short-run production function $y = f(E)$, where y is output and E is employment. Output is a function of, i.e. depends on, the number of workers employed. (Note that, where variables can be measured in either real or nominal terms, lower-case letters denote real values and upper-case letters, nominal values. Hence y is real output and income and Y is nominal or current price output and income.) The slope of this function, $dy/dE = f'(E)$, is the marginal product of labour (MPL). The firm will choose the level of employment according to the exogenous real wage, represented in the diagram by the slope of the tangent to the production function.[3] Each worker is employed only if the marginal product is greater than or equal to the real wage received. As the real wage rises from w_0 to w_1, profit maximization requires that the marginal product of labour rises from $MPL_0 (= w_0)$ to $MPL_1 (= w_1)$, where w is the real wage. Labour demanded will be reduced from E_0 to E_1. The lower panel of Fig. 1.1 shows the demand for labour (marginal product of labour) curve explicitly as a function of the real wage.

The employment condition can be expressed in several equivalent ways:

- *Marginal product of labour equals the real wage*: as above, if MPL $> W/P$, expand output and employment until they are equal, where W is the nominal wage and P, the price level.
- *Marginal revenue product of labour equals the nominal wage*: if $P \cdot MPL > W$, expand employment and output until they are equal; i.e., if the value (to the firm) of the marginal product of labour ($P \cdot MPL$) exceeds the cost to the firm of that extra unit of labour (the money wage), then it is worthwhile increasing employment until this margin is eliminated.
- *Price equals marginal cost*: produce where marginal cost equals the market price in order to maximize profits; i.e., $P = MC = W/MPL$. The firm equates the benefit of producing an extra unit of output (P) to the cost, i.e. the extra wages incurred through the production of the extra output. This is equal to $(W \Delta E)/\Delta y = W/MPL$, since $MPL = \Delta y/\Delta E = 1/(\Delta E/\Delta y)$ where Δx refers to the change in the value of the variable x.

---

[3] A useful way of seeing why this maximizes profits, just using the production function diagram, is as follows. Total real profits, $\pi = y - wE$; so if $w = w_0$, $y = \pi + w_0 E$. π is thus the constant term of any straight line in the top panel of Fig. 1.1, with a slope of w_0. To maximize profits, the firm will choose y and E on the highest possible such line. The combination (y, E) has to be on (or within) the production function, so the combination of y and E that enables the firm to be on the highest line is where the line just touches (is tangential to) the production function.

In short, the employment demand of firms is a function of the real wage:

$$E^D = E^D(w)$$

[marginal product of labour condition]

where $E^D(w)$ means 'a function of' the variables(s) inside the bracket, and output supplied is a function of employment demanded:

$$y^S = y^S(E^D).$$

[short-run production function]

Supply of Labour and Demand for Consumer Goods by Households

Households are faced with the decision of allocating their time between work, which generates income and hence enables the purchase of consumer goods and/or the accumulation of wealth via savings, and leisure. The decision as to how to maximize utility is purely a matter of individual taste. The indifference curves in the top panel of Fig. 1.2 illustrate the household's willingness to sacrifice leisure for consumer goods and savings. The rewards in terms of consumer goods and savings that are available from one unit of labour are reflected in the prevailing real wage. A linear budget constraint is drawn showing the possible levels of income from employment that a worker can obtain. Utility is maximized where the budget constraint is parallel to the highest indifference curve.

A higher hourly real wage, w_1, induces two responses from the household. On the one hand, since leisure has become more costly, less will be demanded and hence more hours will be worked (substitution effect, from α to β in the top panel of Fig. 1.2). On the other hand, a higher wage will permit the same amount of consumption from fewer hours of work and therefore will tend to lower hours of work since in general more leisure is demanded as income rises (income effect from β to γ in the top panel of Fig. 1.2). In the classical theory (and in macroeconomics in general) it is assumed that the former effect dominates. By plotting the points α and γ from the top panel of Fig. 1.2 into real wage–employment space in the lower panel, the upwards-sloping supply of labour curve is produced. Employment is measured in terms of hours.

From the households' leisure–goods choices, the aggregate labour supply function is derived:

$$E^S = E^S(w).$$

[labour supply]

A by-product of this decision is the aggregate demand for consumer goods, the consumption function:

$$c^D = c^D(w),$$

[consumption function]

where c^D is the demand for consumption goods in real terms. From the perspective of economics after Keynes, this aggregate consumption

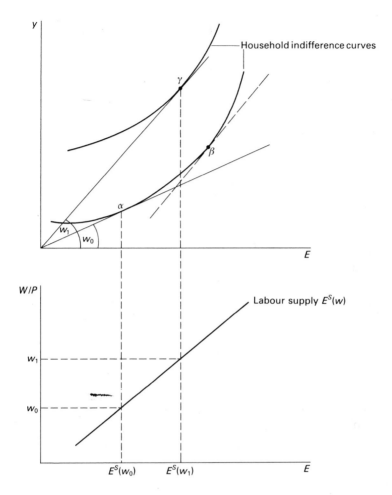

Fig. 1.2 Supply of labour

Income and substitution effects on labour supply in response to real wage changes

function is odd because it assumes that anybody prepared to work in order to buy consumer goods faces no obstacle. Consumption demand mirrors the *supply* of labour decision, rather than reflecting the demand for labour. Because the level of employment is endogenous in the sense that households choose how much labour to supply, only the price (i.e. the real wage) and not the quantity of labour (E) and hence income ($wE = y$) is to be found in the consumption function.

Equilibrium in the Labour Market: $E^D = E^S = \bar{E}$

Both the demand and the supply of labour depend on the real wage. In the

classical model, the labour market clears, establishing the equilibrium
(market-clearing) real wage and the equilibrium level of employment
$(\bar{w}, \bar{E})$. (*Note*: $\bar{x}$ denotes the equilibrium value of the variable x.)

Thus $E^D(\bar{w}) = E^S(\bar{w}) = \bar{E}$. Via the short-run production function, this
equilibrium level of employment fixes the equilibrium level of output:

$$y^S(\bar{E}) = \bar{y}.$$

With consumption demand a function solely of the real wage, aggregate
consumption at equilibrium is fixed by the equilibrium real wage:

$$\bar{c} = c^D(\bar{w}).$$

Figure 1.3 shows the equilibrium value of the real wage, employment,
and output—*all* are determined in the labour market. Any temporary
displacement of the labour market from equilibrium is quickly eliminated

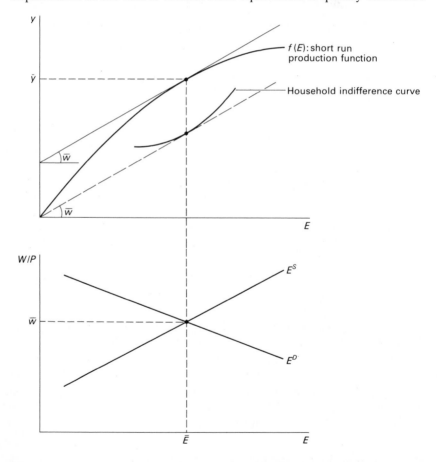

Fig. 1.3 Equilibrium in the labour market: equilibrium values of the real wage,
employment, and output

through the movement of the real wage. The real wage will rise when the demand for labour exceeds the supply and vice versa. In the case of excess supply of labour ($E^S > E^D$), real wages will fall. This will simultaneously raise the demand and reduce the supply of labour, re-establishing the unique equilibrium at $\bar{E}$.

An economy with a perfectly competitive labour market which clears very rapidly has no involuntary unemployment. The economy is on the supply of labour curve, which means that all those wishing to work at the going real wage are able to do so. Any unemployment is therefore voluntary; in other words, it reflects the *choice* of leisure over goods (obtainable through work).

1.1.2 The Product and Money Markets; Savings and Investment

In the classical model, the Quantity Theory of Money holds: real money balances are demanded in proportion to real income. We can express this as

$$M^D/P = (1/v)y,$$

where M^D is the nominal demand for money balances and v is the velocity of circulation. By assumption in the Quantity Theory, the velocity of circulation is constant: one unit of money finances a fixed number of units of output. Equilibrium in the money market requires that the demand and supply of money are equal, and in the classical world it is assumed that the money supply is exogenous (equal to $\bar{M}$):

$$M^D = M^S = \bar{M}. \quad \text{[money market equilibrium]}$$

This implies that the monetary authorities are able to fix the supply at the desired level, $\bar{M}$. Since labour-market-clearing sets equilibrium output for the economy at $\bar{y}$, we have

$$y^D = y^S = \bar{y}. \quad \text{[product market equilibrium]}$$

Hence, with v, $\bar{M}$, and $\bar{y}$ all fixed exogenously, the Quantity Theory equation amounts to a theory of the determination of the price level, P. It is therefore possible to rewrite the Quantity Theory of Money to identify the determinants of the price level:

$$P = v(\bar{M}/\bar{y}).$$

To summarize, we have $\bar{y}$ fixed in the labour market. Given $\bar{y}$, the demand for money is $M^D/P = (1/v)\bar{y}$. Any increase in money supply in excess of money demand is used to buy goods. To the extent that y^D exceeds $\bar{y}$, prices rise. Therefore prices rise until the real value of the money supply is brought into line with the demand for real money balances at the level of output determined in the labour market, $\bar{y}$; P rises until $\bar{M}/P = M^D/P = (1/v)\bar{y}$.

A characteristic result of the classical model noted above is that increases in the money supply lead simply to higher prices. From the price level equation above (with v, $\bar{M}$, and $\bar{y}$ exogenous), it follows that in equilibrium a 10% increase in the money supply leads to a 10% increase in prices. A 10% rise in the money supply produces inflation by initially raising aggregate demand above the fixed level of supply, $\bar{y}$, as the result of the higher level of cash balances. By pushing aggregate demand above supply, prices are boosted. Indeed, prices will rise until the discrepancy has been eliminated. This requires a rise in prices of 10%. In this model, the price level changes immediately to bring real aggregate demand, y^D, into line with $\bar{y}$.

The role played by the interest rate in the classical model is that of bringing savings and investment into equality at full employment. The full employment level of savings available to the bond market, $\bar{s}$, is the difference between real income at full employment ($\bar{y}$) and real consumption ($c^D(\bar{w})$):

$$\bar{s} = \bar{y} - c^D(\bar{w}).$$

Note that aggregate savings is unaffected by any change in aggregate demand—only equilibrium output and the equilibrium real wage matter.

Investment is a negative function of the interest rate:

$$i^D = i(r),$$

where i is real investment, r is the interest rate, and $di/dr < 0$. In the classical view, investment demand is negatively related and is very sensitive to changes in the rate of interest. The interest rate is thought of as the opportunity cost of borrowing in order to finance investment. By reducing the cost of borrowing, a lower interest rate would raise investment and vice versa.

The interest rate is presumed to respond very rapidly to any excess of investment over savings and vice versa. Investment in excess of savings reflects an excess supply of bonds and would call forth a fall in bond prices and a higher interest rate.[4] Conversely, suppose that investment falls

---

[4] A bond is a debt instrument used by a firm or the government when it wishes to borrow money. The bond entails the payment of interest and the repayment of the principal according to a specific timetable. The simplest type of bond is the consol or perpetuity, which has no date of maturity; i.e., it carries the obligation to pay interest for ever. There is a market in which bonds are traded. In other words, having lent money to a firm or government in exchange for a bond, an individual is able to resell that bond on the secondary bond market. A bond traditionally pays fixed amounts of money in interest on specific dates. This fixed amount (the coupon) is indicated on the bond. Consider a consol with a face value of £100, which pays £5 per annum. This provides an interest return to the holder of 5%. Now suppose that the interest rate in the economy rises to 8%. No one will buy our bond for £100 because it provides a return of only 5%. What would someone be prepared to pay? The market value of the bond, MV, is equal to the coupon (C) divided by the current interest rate (r_t). In our example, $MV = C/r_t = 5/0.08 = £62.50$. A higher interest rate reduces the market value of the bond.

because firms become more pessimistic about their future sales (i.e., there is a shift in the function $i^D = i(r)$). In the classical model, this leads to a fall in the interest rate until $i^D = \bar{s}$ again. As with the labour market, the bond market is assumed to adjust very quickly to any disequilibrium. This means that a temporary fall in investment has no effect on aggregate demand, output, or employment.

There is no multiplier process in the classical model: a fall in investment does not create a multiple contraction of income and output. Any temporary decline in investment demand has no effect on consumption via a decline in the income accruing to those engaged in the production of investment goods because consumption is dependent on the real wage and not on current income.

Since both the level of output and that of consumption are fixed by their full employment values, any increase in government spending has the effect of reducing private investment by exactly the same amount. Complete *crowding-out* occurs through the working of the bond market. The fixed level of savings represents the demand for bonds (see Fig. 1.4). The supply of bonds comprises first the demand for loans by firms (equal to the supply of bonds by firms) for investment purposes, which depends inversely on the interest rate $(i^D = i(r))$. The second component of the supply of bonds comes from the government when it seeks to finance expenditure in excess of its tax revenue by borrowing from the public. Any increase in the supply of bonds by the government to finance extra spending will *ceteris paribus* depress the bond price, raise the interest rate (in Fig. 1.4 from r_0 to r_1), and reduce private investment. Total output remains unchanged; only its composition is altered.

In presenting the simple classical model, the implications for aggregate demand of the Quantity Theory of Money and of savings and investment have been considered separately. Implicitly, it has been assumed that, out

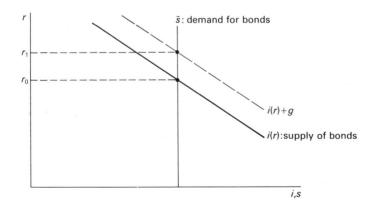

Fig. 1.4 The bond market: an increase in bond-financed government spending

of equilibrium, the interest rate adjusts faster than the price level so that investment is always equal to its full employment level. The more sophisticated presentation of the classical model[5] shows clearly why an assumption such as this is necessary.

1.2   Summarizing the Classical Model using Aggregate Demand and Supply

A useful way of summarizing the properties of the classical model, and one that facilitates comparisons with other models, in particular with Keynes's model, is provided by the aggregate supply/aggregate demand (AS/AD) diagram. This is constructed in a quadrant with the price level on the vertical axis and the level of output on the horizontal. The classical aggregate supply curve is simply a vertical line at $\bar{y}$, since changes in the price level shift neither the labour demand nor the labour supply curves and hence cannot affect the level of output (Fig. 1.5). A fall in the price level would raise the real wage above its market-clearing level, creating excess supply in the labour market. The excess supply of labour would generate a reduction in money wages, pushing the real wage back to its equilibrium level.

The aggregate demand curve is the set of P, y combinations at which there is macroeconomic equilibrium. In the classical model, real income is equal to $\bar{y}$; a high price level (P_H) means that real cash balances are below real cash balances demanded at $\bar{y}$, with the result that the demand for output is below $\bar{y}$ (i.e. $y^D < \bar{y}$).[6] This produces a point on the aggregate

---

[5] A more precise way of writing the classical model is to state aggregate demand as the sum of investment demand, consumption demand, and a component dependent on excess money balances:

$$y^D = i^D(r) + c^D(\bar{w}) + \mu(\bar{M}/P - \bar{y}/v),$$

where μ is a positive constant. The rest of the model is:

$$\dot{P} = \alpha(y^D - \bar{y})$$

$$\bar{y} = \bar{s} + c^D(\bar{w})$$

$$\dot{r} = \beta(i^D(r) - \bar{s}),$$

where $\dot{x}$ refers to the proportionate change in the variable x and α and β are positive constants.

Thus, by substituting the expression for y^D into that for $\dot{P}$ and substituting for c^D, we get

$$\dot{P} = \alpha[(i^D(r) - \bar{s}) + \mu(\bar{M}/P - \bar{y}/v)].$$

Hence, although there is no problem in equilibrium, in disequilibrium any excess of investment over savings will push up both prices and the interest rate. One way around this is to assume that the interest rate adjusts faster than the price level.

[6] In terms of the model in n. 5, where

$$y^D = i^D(r) + c^D(\bar{w}) + \mu(\bar{M}/P_H - \bar{y}/v),$$

the shortfall of $\bar{M}/P_H$ below $\bar{y}/v$ has the effect of reducing aggregate demand y^D below $\bar{y}$.

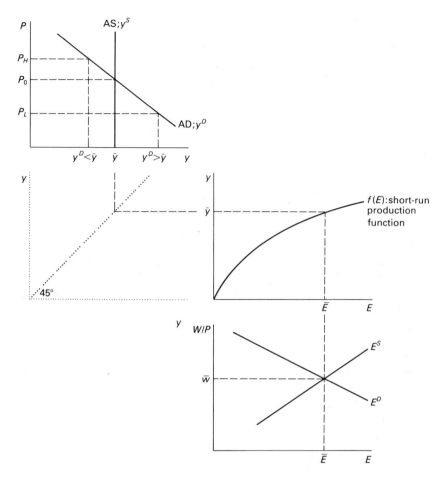

Fig. 1.5 Aggregate supply and aggregate demand in the classical model

demand curve to the north-west of $(P_0, \bar{y})$ (Fig. 1.5). Conversely, a low price level, P_L, implies that real money balances are above the level demanded with income of $\bar{y}$. Hence $y^D > \bar{y}$, and a point on the aggregate demand curve to the south-east of $(P_0, \bar{y})$ is fixed. Any increase in the money supply will shift the aggregate demand curve to the right, since a higher price level will be required to reduce the real value of money balances to the level demanded at each output level.

Aggregate supply conditions uniquely fix the level of output. The implications of changes in monetary and fiscal policy are therefore limited. Changes in the money supply, as noted above, shift the aggregate demand curve and produce a change in the price level in the same direction. Output remains unchanged. Any rise in government spending leads to an immediate rise in the interest rate and a consequent fall in investment, with the result that the aggregate demand curve remains unchanged. Only the composition of output is altered; neither its level nor prices are affected.

1.3   Conclusions and Policy Implications

On the basis of a set of rapidly clearing markets, the classical model provides a complete macroeconomic system. The model neatly separates the real and monetary spheres: all real variables are determined by the clearing of the labour market; the price level is fixed by the nominal money supply. The price level changes only in response to changes in the money supply or to changes in the velocity of circulation if payment habits change. Output and employment change only in response to changes in technology (shifts in the demand for labour curve) or to changes in household tastes or in the population of working age (shifts in the supply of labour curve).

Governments can alter only the price level and the composition of output. Implicitly, the government in the classical model is an agent that controls the supply of money to ensure price stability, provides public goods, and maintains an environment of rapidly clearing, perfectly competitive markets. With such perfect markets, the expectations of all agents—firms and households—are fulfilled. There is no involuntary unemployment or unsold goods. The only macroeconomic malfunction—inflation—would arise from irresponsible behaviour on the part of the monetary authorities.

2

Keynes's Model of Employment

In the 1930s macroeconomic malfunction took the form of mass unemployment. Economists imbued with the classical model were ill-equipped to provide a diagnosis. The prevailing economic conditions provided the backdrop to Keynes's model. In line with the classics, Keynes upheld the assumption of perfect competition. But unlike them, he assumed that the labour market does not clear quickly. In particular, he argued that money wages are inflexible in a downward direction. Moreover, even if money wages were to fall, Keynes argued that the labour market might still fail to clear. This raised the possibility of persistent involuntary unemployment.

Keynes's model has a set of characteristic features:

K1 With a fixed money wage, employment and output are determined by aggregate demand in the product market.

K2 The rate of interest (r) equilibrates the real demand and supply of money; it does *not* bring investment into line with full employment savings.

K3 A fall in investment reduces aggregate demand and therefore output and employment. This effect is magnified by the multiplier since consumption demand depends on income (the wage and employment). A fall in investment reduces incomes; in turn, consumption demand declines further, reducing demand, output, and employment. It is the level of output (not the interest rate) that changes to bring planned saving into line with planned investment.

The policy implications of Keynes's model differ sharply from those of the classics. From K1, it follows that there can be involuntary unemployment in equilibrium. Full employment is not the only equilibrium. From K2, an increase in the money supply can have real effects; if it changes the interest rate then it may affect investment and therefore aggregate demand, output, and employment. From K3 and K1, it follows that fiscal policy can affect the level of aggregate demand and therefore can alter the level of employment. Crowding-out is of no or little importance.[1]

---

[1] For an excellent retrospective discussion of the *General Theory* and the theoretical developments represented by it, see Patinkin (1987).

2.1   Keynes's Model of Employment: *IS/LM* Analysis and Aggregate Demand and Supply

In the classical model, the level of output and employment is fixed by conditions in the labour market, i.e. by the supply side of the economy. The exact opposite would be the case if output were solely a function of aggregate demand, i.e. if additional demand were to bring forth additional output at constant prices. This is the case modelled in the textbook *IS/LM* analysis. Keynes's model is a little more complicated than the *IS/LM* model, since he assumed a perfectly competitive supply side of the economy, in which it would be necessary for prices to change in order to bring the supply of output into line with the demand. In Keynes's basic model with a fixed money wage, just as in *IS/LM*, aggregate demand fixes the level of output and employment; but unlike *IS/LM*, prices change in order to bring supply into line with demand. This second step is unnecessary in *IS/LM* because it is assumed that the supply side is perfectly elastic at the existing price level, with the result that changes in demand are mirrored in output changes without any alteration in price.

In setting out Keynes's model, we follow a two-step procedure beginning with the analysis of aggregate demand. This step is clearest if the price level as well as the money wage is assumed constant—in other words, if the *IS/LM* model is used. We then move on to the second step, which is to bring in Keynes's analysis of aggregate supply. In the second step we see how, with a fixed money wage, the price level changes to bring aggregate supply into line with aggregate demand. Throughout this chapter, some familiarity with *IS/LM* is assumed. However, the model is set out fully with further mathematical and diagrammatic details supplied in the Appendix. By running through the model, it is possible to highlight points of specific importance for the analysis of employment and the comparison with other models.

2.1.1   Output and Employment Determination in *IS/LM*: the Role of Aggregate Demand

In Keynes's model, it is the level of aggregate demand for goods and services in the economy that fixes the level of output and employment. Hence it is to the goods and money markets that we first turn. The *IS/LM* framework provides a convenient tool for characterizing the equilibrium level of real aggregate demand for output and the equilibrium interest rate, i.e. the situation in which real planned expenditure equals output and money supply equals money demand. The *IS/LM* model is constructed in interest rate–output space, with the interest rate on the vertical axis and the level of output on the horizontal. The *IS* curve shows the combinations of interest rate and output level at which there is equilibrium in the goods market. Equilibrium in the goods market means that the demand for output, i.e. planned expenditure in real terms, is equal to the supply of output: $y^D = y^S$. The *LM* curve shows the combinations of interest rate and output level at which there is equilibrium in the money market, i.e. at which the money supply is equal to money demanded: $M^S = M^D$. It is useful to run through the derivation of both the *IS* and the *LM*, since a clear presentation of the aggregate demand side is essential for the full analysis, including that of the supply side, which constitutes Keynes's model. In the discussion of aggregate demand in the *IS/LM* model, it will be assumed that the price level and money wages are constant. The economy is presumed to be operating where there is excess capacity in the form of both capital and labour, so that any increase in demand will elicit additional output at an unchanged price and any additional demand for labour will be met at an unchanged wage. Keynes's model of the supply side is considered below.

Derivation of IS

Aggregate demand refers to the planned real expenditure in the economy as a whole. To the extent that aggregate demand exceeds real output, there will be unsatisfied demand for goods which will result in the unplanned rundown of stocks. It is assumed that planned demand for consumption and fixed investment is satisfied, with the result that any excess of demand over output leads to an involuntary fall in stocks. Such unplanned stock changes provide information to producers to increase their level of output. Output rises until it is equal to planned expenditure:

$$y^D = y. \qquad \text{[goods market equilibrium]}$$

Aggregate demand comprises planned expenditure on consumption and investment by the private sector and planned government spending. Suppose that there is a rise in consumption. Purchases of consumer goods rise by more than had been expected, with the result that stocks of consumer goods fall, leaving total investment (which includes stocks) in excess of planned investment (planned fixed investment plus planned stock changes). Hence planned expenditure can be written as

$$y^D = c + i^P(r, A) + g, \qquad \text{[planned expenditure]}$$

where c is consumption, i^P is planned investment, and g is government spending, all in real terms. The consumption function is

$$c = \bar{c} + c_y(y - t),$$

where $\bar{c}$ is a constant and a proportion c_y of current disposable income is consumed: $0 < c_y < 1$. t is the real *total* tax revenue, and if we take a linear tax function, then

$$t = t_y y, \qquad \text{[tax function]}$$

where $0 < t_y < 1$. Thus the consumption function is

$$c = \bar{c} + c_y(1 - t_y)y. \qquad \text{[consumption function]}$$

Keynes's consumption function differs from the classical consumption function in an important respect. For Keynes, consumption depends on *current* income and hence on the employment status of the household, whereas in the classical view it is the full employment real wage that fixes consumption.

Planned investment is

$$i^P = i^P(\overset{-}{r}, \overset{+}{A}),$$

and by assuming a linear form, we have

$$i^P = A - i_r r, \qquad \text{[investment function]}$$

where planned investment is negatively related to the interest rate and positively related to expected future profitability, the determinants of which are proxied by the term A. (Plus and minus signs above the arguments of functions indicate the sign of the partial derivative.) Keynes laid much stress on expectational or confidence factors in determining investment behaviour, emphasizing that shifts of the investment function arising from changes in A (Keynes's 'animal spirits') could be of greater significance than movements along the investment function in response to interest rate changes.

The *IS* curve is defined by the goods market equilibrium condition. The planned expenditure equation is substituted into the goods market equilibrium condition to define an equilibrium locus of combinations of the interest rate and output:

$$y = \frac{\bar{c} + A + g}{1 - c_y(1 - t_y)} - \frac{i_r}{1 - c_y(1 - t_y)} r. \qquad \text{[IS curve]}$$

An intuitive explanation of the *IS* is presented in Fig. 2.1 (where government spending and taxation are omitted to unclutter the diagram). From the *IS* equation we see that, at any interest rate, the equilibrium level of output is equal to the sum of autonomous consumption, government spending, and the level of investment associated with the specific interest rate, all multiplied by the multiplier $(1/[1 - c_y(1 - t_y)])$. Thus at a high interest rate, planned investment will be low, which will dampen planned expenditure—hence, for equilibrium, the level of output must be low. In Fig. 2.1, at r_H, planned investment $(i_0 = A - i_r r_H)$ and autonomous consumption are shown. Multiplying $i_0 + \bar{c}$ by the multiplier gives output equal to planned expenditure, y_0, on the *IS* curve. Similarly, at a low interest rate, planned expenditure will be high owing to high planned investment. Goods market equilibrium dictates a correspondingly high output level. Hence the *IS* curve is negatively sloped in the figure.

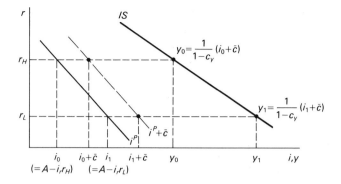

Fig. 2.1 Deriving the *IS* curve

Using the *IS* equation and the diagram, we can separate the determinants of the slope and position of the *IS* into three groups.

1 Any change in the size of multiplier will change the slope of the *IS*. For example, a rise in the propensity to consume will increase the multiplier, rotating the *IS* anti-clockwise and making it flatter.

2 Any change in the interest sensitivity of investment will lead to a consequential change in the slope of the *IS*: a less interest-elastic investment function will be reflected in a steeper *IS* curve.

3 Any change in autonomous consumption or in government expenditure ($\bar{c}$, g) will cause the *IS* to shift by the change in autonomous spending times the multiplier. A change in the variable A in the investment function shifts *IS* by $(\partial i/\partial A)\Delta A$ times the multiplier.

To make statements 1–3 precise, the simple mathematics and geometry of the *IS* curve using linear consumption, investment, and tax functions are presented in the Appendix to this chapter.

Policy can be used to manipulate the *IS* through channels 1 and 3. For example, if income tax is proportional, i.e. if $t = t_y y$, a lower tax rate increases the size of the multiplier and, as in 1 above, swings the *IS* to the right, making it flatter. Any change in government spending will shift the *IS* in the manner described in 3 above. For example, a rise in government spending will lead to a decline in stocks of goods in the economy, which will prompt a higher level of production. The *IS* shifts in parallel fashion to the right.

A central feature of Keynes's model is the way in which quantities adjust through the multiplier process to take the economy to a *stable* equilibrium away from full employment. A fall in planned investment from a value of i_0 to i_1 leads, as we have seen, to a multiple contraction of output and employment until the level of income has fallen to the extent required to make planned saving equal to the lower level of investment. Initially, income falls by the fall in investment, Δi. As the result of the fall in income, consumption declines by $\Delta c = c_y \Delta i$. This fall in consumption in turn reduces income, and in the next round consumption falls once more: $\Delta c = c_y(c_y \Delta i) = c_y^2 \Delta i$. To calculate the total drop in income, we sum the series:

$$\Delta y = \Delta i + c_y \Delta i + c_y^2 \Delta i + c_y^3 \Delta i + \ldots$$
$$= \Delta i/(1 - c_y).$$

Omitting taxation and government spending for simplicity, at the new equilibrium planned investment is equal to planned saving; since at the new equilibrium $y = y^D$, this implies that $y = \bar{c} + c_y y + i_1$. Subtracting consumption from each side gives

$$\bar{s} + s_y y = i_1$$

planned saving = planned investment,

where $s_y = 1 - c_y$, i.e. the marginal propensity to save, and $\bar{s} = -\bar{c}$ is dissaving at $y = 0$.

Another way of focusing on quantity adjustment to a new goods market equilibrium is to characterize positions off the *IS* curve in the *IS/LM* diagram (Fig. 2.2). At point x with output y_1, to the left of the *IS* curve, there is excess demand in the goods market because at the interest rate r_1, planned expenditure is equal to y_1^D. With aggregate demand in excess of output, stocks will fall and output will rise until $y = y^D$ on the *IS*. The converse situation prevails at point z with output y_2, to the right of *IS*.

Derivation of LM

To fix the rate of interest and level of output, it is necessary to bring in the money market and define the *LM* curve. For Keynes, the classical view

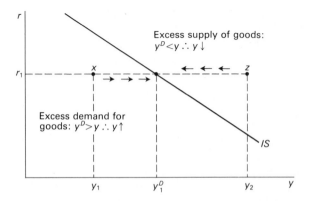

Fig. 2.2 Adjustment to goods market equilibrium

that real money balances are demanded in proportion to real income was inadequate. He proposed two further motives for holding money, the speculative and precautionary motives, in addition to the demand for money to finance transactions. Most important for Keynes was the speculative motive. He argued that money is a financial asset and as such is a substitute for the other asset that he included in his model, the long-term bond. One special feature of money as compared with bonds is that its capital value is safe. Bonds, on the other hand, pay interest to the holder and their capital value varies inversely with the interest rate. They are risky.

The availability of more than one financial asset provides individuals with the opportunity to speculate: if an individual believes that the current interest rate is above the level she considers normal, then she will expect the interest rate to fall to normal in due course.[2] Under these circumstances, the individual will choose to hold financial assets over and above the money required for transactions (and precautionary) purposes in the form of bonds. She will expect to reap a capital gain on the bonds as the interest rate falls to normal. Conversely, at an interest rate sufficiently below 'normal', she will hold financial assets in the form of money to avoid taking a capital loss when the interest rate regains its normal level.[3] Keynes presumed that the subjective assessment of the 'normal' interest rate would vary across the population, producing a smooth inverse relationship between the interest rate and the aggregate demand for speculative money balances (see Fig. 2.3).

A more general rationale for the negative dependence of the demand for money on the interest rate was developed by Tobin (1958). Instead of assuming, as had Keynes, that each individual is certain about what he or she expects the future rate of interest on bonds to be, Tobin focused on the implications of investor uncertainty. In the simplest version of Tobin's model, *risk-averse*[4] individuals allocate their portfolio between a riskless asset which pays no interest (money) and a risky one with a positive expected return (bonds). The individual's utility depends positively on the

---

[2] Note for future reference that this is an example of *regressive expectations*. When expectations are formed in a regressive way, agents assume that the future value of a variable will be a particular value that it has had in the past.

[3] For example, suppose that the normal rate of interest is believed to be 4% by one agent. The bond is issued at a face value of £100, and pays £5 per annum. If the market interest rate is 4%, the market value of the bond will be £x, where $0.04x = 5$; i.e., $x = 5/0.04 = £125$. If the interest rate is 2%, then $x = 5/0.02 = £250$. Suppose the current interest rate is 2% and the agent believes it will rise to its normal level of 4%. If she holds £250 worth of bonds, then she receives 2% in interest, i.e. £5, but will expect to lose (£250 − £125) = £125. With an interest rate of 2%, this agent will hold no bonds.

[4] Someone is risk-averse if, when offered a fair bet, would refuse it; i.e., if offered the choice between receiving £50 with certainty or the chance of £100 (or zero!) on the outcome of the toss of a fair coin, the individual would always take the certain £50. In other words, the individual prefers a *certain* value of £50 to an uncertain return with an *expected* value of £50.

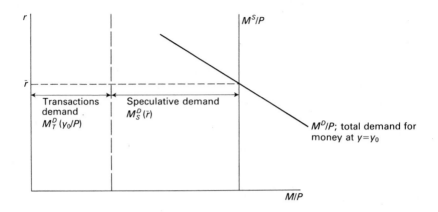

Fig. 2.3 The demand for money: speculative and transactions demand at income level y_0

return from holding the asset and negatively on the risk associated with holding it. To maximize utility, the individual will hold a mixture of the two assets, trading off the benefits of a higher expected return against the associated risk according to his own preferences. A higher interest rate would lead the individual to substitute bonds for money as the higher expected return would offset the additional risk incurred. Thus Tobin derived an inverse relationship between the demand for money and the interest rate. This is often denoted the *asset demand for money*.

Figure 2.4 can be used to illustrate Tobin's theory. The vertical axis represents the expected return from the portfolio and the horizontal axis, the risk associated with the portfolio. The investor is uncertain about the capital gain or loss, G, associated with investing £1 in bonds. He has a probability distribution for G which has a mean of zero. The return on the portfolio depends on the interest rate on bonds, on G, and on the proportion A_2 of the portfolio that is held in bonds ($A_1 + A_2 = 1$, where A_1 is the proportion held in cash and A_2 the proportion held in bonds):

$$R = A_2(r + G).$$

The expected return on the portfolio is

$$E(R) = \mu_R = A_2 r.$$

Tobin measured the risk of the portfolio by the standard deviation of the return on the portfolio, σ_R. A portfolio is risky when there is a high probability of large deviations (i.e. capital gains and losses) from the expected return, μ_R. The risk of the portfolio, σ_R, depends on the proportion of the portfolio in bonds and on the standard deviation of the capital gains, σ_G:

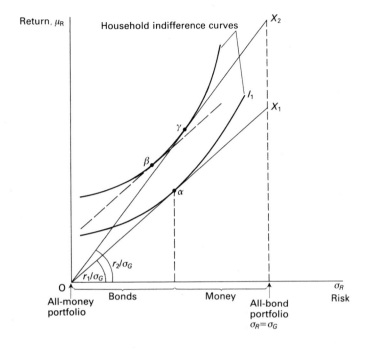

Fig. 2.4 Tobin's model of portfolio selection

$$\sigma_R = A_2 \sigma_G.$$

Thus, in Fig. 2.4 it is possible to represent the opportunity locus facing the investor as a straight line showing the cost in terms of greater risk associated with attaining a higher expected return. The opportunity locus is $\mu_R = (r/\sigma_G)\sigma_R$ and has a slope equal to the interest rate divided by σ_G. An all-money portfolio is represented by the origin since the expected return and risk are both zero. An all-bond portfolio ($A_2 = 1$) will occur when the risk on the portfolio is equal to σ_G. Figure 2.4 shows the opportunity locus associated with an interest rate of r_1 as OX_1.

In the same diagram the indifference curves of individuals are drawn. These will be positively sloped since risk-averse individuals will be indifferent between some combination of low mean and variance and high mean and variance. In the diagram the indifference curves are concave upwards: as the riskiness of the portfolio increases, the individual requires a higher and higher increase in the return to take on additional risk. With the interest rate at r_1 and indifference curve I_1, the portfolio represented by point α is chosen. A higher interest rate swivels OX_1 to OX_2: the familiar income and substitution effects come into play. The income effect is the move $\alpha \rightarrow \beta$ and the substitution effect is the move $\beta \rightarrow \gamma$. While the income effect may lead to a reduction in the proportion of the portfolio held in bonds (as in Fig. 2.4), the substitution effect increases bond holdings since the return associated with a given variance has increased. It is normally assumed that the substitution effect outweighs the income effect to ensure an inverse relationship between the interest rate and the demand for money.

Subsequent analysis is made simpler if we assume that the demand for money is in real terms and if we use a linear function. The two components of the demand for money function are:

1   transactions demand:
$$\frac{M_T^D}{P} = L_T(\overset{+}{y}) = \frac{1}{v_T}y$$

2   speculative or asset demand:
$$\frac{M_A^D}{P} = L_A(\overset{-}{r}) = \bar{m} - m_r r,$$

with $\bar{m}$, v_T, and m_r positive constants. The constant, v_T, is the velocity of transactions balances. Thus, the demand-for-money function can be summarized:

$$\frac{M^D}{P} = L(\overset{+}{y}, \overset{-}{r}) = \bar{m} - \bar{m}_r r + \frac{1}{v_T}y, \qquad \text{[demand for money]}$$

with the demand for real money balances positively related to real income and negatively related to the interest rate. The transactions motive dictates the dependence of the demand for money on the level of output, y: a higher real income level implies the need for more money for the higher desired level of transactions. The speculative or asset motive provides for the negative dependence of the demand for money on the interest rate.

Money market equilibrium requires that the demand and supply of money are equal:

$$\frac{M^D}{P} = \frac{M^S}{P}, \qquad \text{[money market equilibrium]}$$

where

$$\frac{M^D}{P} = L(y, r) = \bar{m} - m_r r + \frac{1}{v_T}y; \qquad \text{[demand for money]}$$

$$\frac{M^S}{P} = \frac{\bar{M}^S}{P}; \qquad \text{[supply of money]}$$

i.e.,

$$r = \frac{\bar{m} - \bar{M}^S/P}{m_r} + \frac{1}{v_T m_r}y. \qquad \text{[LM equation]}$$

We will maintain the assumption that the money supply is fixed

exogenously by the monetary authorities.[5] The locus of money supply
equal to money demand equilibria—the *LM* curve in the $r-y$ diagram—
will be upward-sloping (see Fig. 2.5). This reflects the fact that the
restoration of equilibrium in the money market requires that changes in the
level of income are associated with changes in the interest rate in the same
direction. At low income levels, the transactions demand for money is low
(see Fig. 2.5 top left panel). For the demand for money balances to equal
the given supply, asset (speculative) demand must be high. A low interest
rate will ensure this, since the proportion of the population believing the
interest rate to be below its 'normal' level will be small. Expected capital
losses on bond holdings will create a high speculative demand for money

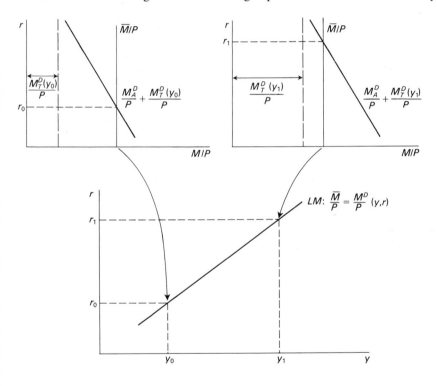

Fig. 2.5 The upward-sloping *LM*

[5] This is a very strong assumption and is the subject of intense debate in the field of
monetary economics. By assuming exogeneity of the money supply, the responses of the
private financial sector to official monetary policy are ignored. Important early discussions of
the possibility that profit-seeking behaviour on the part of banks and non-bank financial
institutions can operate to offset attempts by the monetary authorities to alter monetary
conditions are to be found in the UK *Radcliffe Report* (1957) and in Gurley and Shaw (1960).
For a clear discussion of the possible endogeneity of the money supply, readers are referred to
Chick (1977). An adequate discussion of these complex issues lies beyond the scope of this
book.

balances. In terms of Tobin's approach, asset demand for money will be high when the interest rate is low, since the returns from bond-holding relative to the risks involved are low. The converse argument associates a high income level with a high interest rate (see Fig. 2.5 top right panel).

From the derivation of the *LM* curve, there are four ways in which the position and or the slope of the *LM* can be affected.

1 *A change in the transactions velocity of circulation* The transactions velocity of circulation, v_T, is the constant, reflecting the proportional relationship between income and the demand for transactions balances. It is the number of units of income that one unit of transactions balances can finance. Any rise in the transactions velocity as the result of financial innovation (e.g. introduction of credit cards, development of non-bank financial institutions) will rotate the *LM* to the right (clockwise), making it flatter.

2 *A change in the interest sensitivity of the asset or speculative demand for money* A more interest-sensitive demand for money, reflecting the fact that small changes in the interest rate will have large effects on the portfolio mix between money and bonds, will produce a flatter *LM* curve.

3 *A change in the money supply* An increase in the money supply will shift the *LM* curve to the right, since at any interest rate, with a given asset demand for money, a higher money supply will require higher transactions balances to bring money demand into line with the higher supply. A higher output level will generate the higher transactions demand.

4 *A change in the price level* For a given interest rate, with a higher price level, the available transactions balances (unchanged) can only finance a lower amount of output. The *LM* shifts to the left.

The simple mathematics and geometry of the *LM* curve required to make statements 1–4 precise are presented in the Appendix to this chapter.

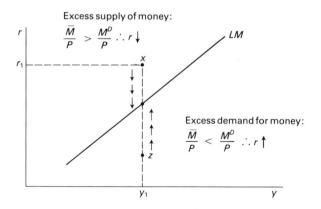

Fig. 2.6 Adjustment to money market equilibrium

At a point such as x above the LM in Fig. 2.6, the interest rate r_1 is too high for money market equilibrium at an output level of y_1. There is excess supply of money (excess demand for bonds) at this interest rate, with the result that, as the excess money balances are channelled into the bond market, the bond price is bid up and the interest rate reduced. The converse situation of excess demand for money is true of a point such as z below the LM curve.

The IS/LM Model

By combining the goods and money markets, the equilibrium level of output and the interest rate are fixed. The IS and LM equations are as follows:

$$y = \frac{\bar{c} + A + g}{1 - c_y(1 - t_y)} - \frac{i_r}{1 - c_y(1 - t_y)} r \qquad [IS \text{ curve}]$$

$$r = \frac{\bar{m} - \bar{M}^S/P}{m_r} + \frac{1}{v_T m_r} y. \qquad [LM \text{ curve}]$$

Given values for the exogenous variables, the values for the two unknowns, r and y, can be deduced which solve the IS and LM equations simultaneously.

To summarize the IS/LM model, it is useful to conduct comparative-static exercises, i.e. to disturb the IS/LM equilibrium by changing one of the exogenous variables. In order to discuss the adjustment path of the economy in the face of such a disturbance, it is necessary to say something about the speed of adjustment in each market. The most plausible simple assumption to make is that money market disequilibria are cleared very rapidly as compared with disequilibria in the goods market. In diagrammatic terms, this means that the economy returns to the LM curve rapidly—the adjustment occurring through changes in the interest rate. Goods market adjustment takes place more slowly since it involves adjustments to production and employment.

In the first example (Fig. 2.7(a)), government spending rises from g_0 to g_1. The new IS is IS_1 to the right of the original one. In the first instance, the rise in government spending produces excess demand for goods and results in unplanned inventory decumulation. Output and employment rise, and the economy moves from A to B. The rise in real income associated with higher output boosts the transactions demand for money, with the result that there is excess demand for money balances at B. Bonds are sold, causing the bond price to fall and the interest rate to rise ($B \rightarrow C$). The rise in the interest rate dampens the excess demand for goods by reducing investment demand; nevertheless, at C there remains excess demand owing to increased consumption demand associated with

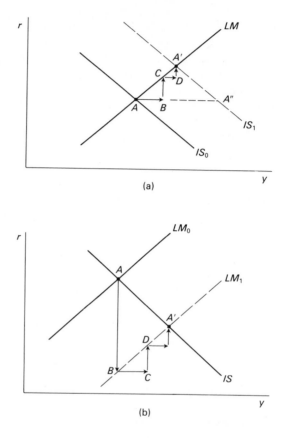

(a)

(b)

Fig. 2.7 Comparative statics in the *IS/LM* model (a) Fiscal policy: rise in government spending (b) Monetary policy: rise in money supply

the multiplier effects of the rise in government spending. Output and employment rise further $(C \to D)$. The adjustment process continues until the new equilibrium at A' is attained. The full multiplier expansion of output $(A \to A'')$ does not occur because of the rise in the interest rate and consequential fall in interest-sensitive spending associated with a fiscal expansion undertaken in the presence of a fixed money supply.

In the second example (Fig. 2.7(b)), the government increases the money supply through the use of open market operations—it enters the money market purchasing bonds in exchange for newly printed money. The *LM* curve shifts to the right to LM_1. The immediate effect of the government's action is to create excess supply of money; the implied excess demand for bonds raises bond prices and lowers the interest rate. The economy moves from A to B, immediately attaining the new money market equilibrium along LM_1. The fall in the interest rate creates excess demand in the goods market by stimulating investment. Higher investment demand pushes up output and employment; raising output from B to C. At C, there is once again money market disequilibrium as excess demand for money accompanies the rise in output. The interest rate rises $(C \rightarrow D)$. Adjustment of output and the interest rate will continue until the new equilibrium at A' is reached.

2.1.2 Aggregate Demand and Aggregate Supply in Keynes's Model

Aggregate Demand

To facilitate comparison with the classical model, the information characterizing goods and money market equilibria can be transferred from the IS/LM diagram to form the aggregate demand curve in the (P, y) quadrant. The position of the LM curve is dependent on the price level, since as noted above in statement 4 a change in the price level, by altering the real value of money balances, will affect money market equilibrium. In Fig. 2.8, the economy is initially characterized by IS_0 and LM_0 with the price level at P_0. At a lower price level, P_1, the value of real money

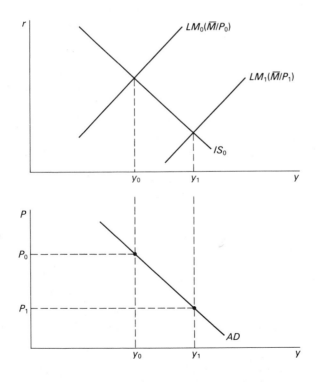

Fig. 2.8 Derivation of the aggregate demand (AD) curve

balances rises and therefore a higher level of real income is required at each interest rate to soak up the additional money balances and maintain money market equilibrium. Hence the LM associated with P_1 lies to the right of LM_0.

In the lower panel of Fig. 2.8, the locus of goods and money market equilibria are traced out in (P, y) space to form the aggregate demand curve: the initial price level P_0 is associated with a relatively low level of output, while the low price level P_1 is associated with a high level of output. The reason is clear: a lower price level raises the real value of money balances, thereby creating an excess supply of money in the hands of the public. As a consequence, the demand for bonds rises, the bond price rises, the interest rate falls, and investment and hence aggregate demand are raised. The negative slope of the aggregate demand curve resulting from the effect of changes in the price level on the demand for money, and via the interest rate to investment, is known as the *Keynes effect*.

Aggregate Supply

For the classics, employment was always at the market-clearing level, with the result that aggregate supply was fully described by a vertical line at the full employment level of output. By contrast, Keynes was concerned to demonstrate the existence of equilibrium output levels away from that associated with full employment. The analysis of goods market equilibrium that forms the basis of the IS curve is designed to refer to the situation when the economy is not always at full employment. Away from full employment, output in the economy is determined by planned expenditure, *not* by the amount that could be supplied in a fully employed economy. Because of the possibility of equilibria at less than full employment, it is necessary in representing Keynes's model to examine the supply curve to the left of full employment.

In a perfectly competitive product market, the marginal product of labour curve $(E^D(w))$ shows the level of employment that will be chosen at each real wage. The aggregate supply curve shows how much output will be supplied at each price level for any given money wage. It is possible to translate the information contained in the marginal product curve into an aggregate supply curve, if we hold the money wage constant. With the money wage equal to W_0, a price level of P_0 implies a real wage equal to $w_0 = W_0/P_0$ (see Fig. 2.9). This corresponds to employment E_0, and via the short-run production function, to an output level of y_0. The first point on the aggregate supply curve for W_0, $(AS(W_0))$, is at (P_0, y_0). A higher price level (P_1), with the same money wage, implies a lower real wage and higher employment and output (y_1)—and gives a second point on the $AS(W_0)$ curve.

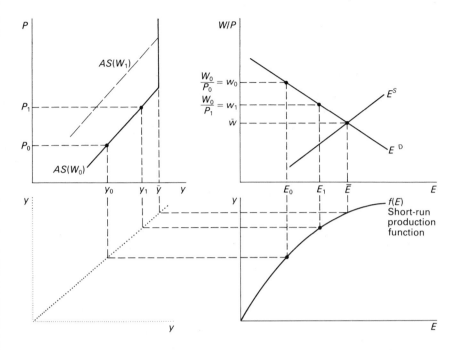

Fig. 2.9 Derivation of Keynes's aggregate supply curve

If the money wage in the economy is higher than W_0, there will be a new aggregate supply curve, higher than the original one. With a higher money wage, higher prices will be required to bring forth any given output level, since marginal costs have risen. The new aggregate supply curve can be derived in Fig. 2.9 using exactly the same procedure as used to derive the first one. The general conclusion is that the aggregate supply curve (which can also be thought of as the economy's marginal cost curve) will be shifted up by increases in the money wage.

At full employment, i.e. where the demand for labour (marginal product) and supply of labour curves cross, the aggregate supply curve becomes vertical, since this is the maximum output that can be produced. Keynes's analysis of aggregate supply at full employment is identical with that of the classics. His claim to provide a more general theory was based on the ability to include situations both at *and below* full employment.

Aggregate Demand and Aggregate Supply

By combining the aggregate demand and aggregate supply curves, it is possible to present Keynes's model in a way that makes it particularly easy to compare with the classical model. Figure 2.10 shows the full employment equilibrium in an economy with a money wage equal to W_0 and with

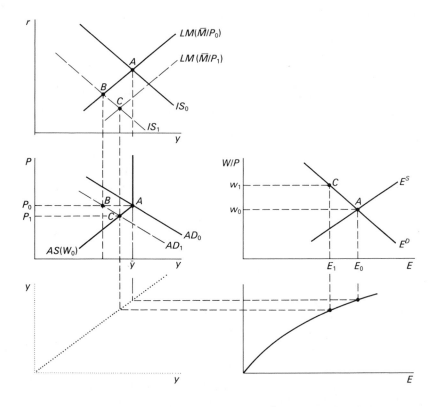

Fig. 2.10 Keynes's model in an aggregate supply/aggregate demand diagram

aggregate demand, AD_0. To depict Keynes's underemployment equilibrium, we assume an exogenous decline in investment from i_0 to i_1 as the
result of a dampening of entrepreneurs' 'animal spirits'. The IS shifts to the
left, to IS_1, which produces a leftward shift in the aggregate demand curve
from AD_0 to AD_1. In the very short run output demanded falls, as shown
by the move from A to B. The fall in demand for output creates unsold
stocks of goods, and in time prices will fall to clear the stocks—assuming a
competitive product market. The fall in prices from P_0 has two effects:
(1) it boosts demand a little via the Keynes effect (the LM shifts to
$LM(\bar{M}/P_1)$, pushing the economy along AD_1 to C, and (2) it raises the
real wage from w_0 to w_1. The economy moves up the marginal product
curve in the labour market diagram from A to C and employment and
output contract to the new lower level demanded. Given the assumption of
a fixed money wage, the economy will remain at C. The change in
aggregate demand drives the level of output and employment—supply
adjusts to demand.

2.2 Keynes Versus the Classics

The simplified versions of Keynes's model and that of the classics are summarized in the diagrams in Fig. 2.11. The contrast which strikes the eye immediately is that between the aggregate supply curves in the two cases: the classical aggregate supply curve is vertical at the full employment output level, whereas Keynes's aggregate supply curve is upward-sloping in the region up to full employment. This difference reflects contrasting views of the labour market. In the classical model, at the labour-market-clearing output level, $\bar{y}$, a rise in prices reduces the real wage, which would make it profitable for firms to raise employment. However, extra labour will not be forthcoming at a lower real wage and indeed, some workers will leave employment. A situation of excess demand for labour characterizes the labour market, and money wages are bid up until the original real wage, $\bar{w}$, is reached once more. The classical model assumes that the adjustment of money wages to any rise in prices occurs immediately with the result that the AS curve is vertical at $\bar{y}$.

In Keynes's model, as we have seen, the belief that involuntary unemployment could exist, meant that, from a situation of say, y_1, with the real wage above $\bar{w}$, a rise in the price level would, by reducing real wages, prompt an increase in output and employment. This produces the upward-sloping part of the aggregate supply curve for the money wage W_0. Eventually, if the price level keeps rising to P_0, the real wage will be reduced to $\bar{w}$, consistent with full employment. All of the involuntary unemployment will than have disappeared and the classical analysis will prevail. This produces the vertical section of the aggregate supply curve.

Referring to Fig. 2.11, let us compare the models under the following

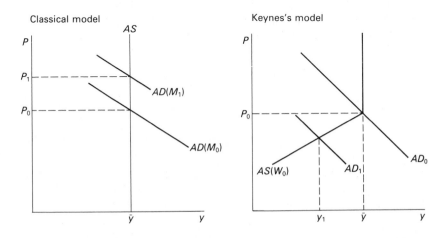

Fig. 2.11 Comparison between Keynes and the classics

circumstances: first let us consider the implications of an exogenous decline in investment; second, let us look at the use of fiscal policy; and finally, let us consider the use of monetary policy.

Exogenous fall in investment   In the classical model, an exogenous fall in investment produces an immediate fall in the interest rate sufficient to ensure that investment resumes its full employment level, equal to full employment savings, $\bar{s}$, the level of which in turn is a function only of the full employment real wage. There is no shift in the aggregate demand curve. The economy remains at P_0, $\bar{y}$.

In Keynes's model (as discussed above in relation to Fig. 2.10), lower investment shifts the aggregate demand curve to the left (e.g. from AD_0 to AD_1). Prices fall to clear the stocks of unsold goods, and this pushes up the real wage and reduces employment and output to y_1. Because of the fall in output and incomes, savings fall into line with the new lower level of planned investment. The economy is characterized by involuntary unemployment.

Fiscal policy   In the classical model, any rise in government spending will have the effect of pushing up the interest rate until investment has been reduced by exactly the amount of the rise in government expenditure. The AD curve will remain unchanged. There will be no further ramifications.

In Keynes's model, beginning with involuntary unemployment at output y_1, a rise in government spending will shift the aggregate demand curve to the right (e.g. back to AD_0 in Fig. 2.11). Prices will be pushed up by the additional demand for output, and this will lower the real wage, making it profitable for firms to raise employment and increase output to meet the additional demand. With the appropriate fiscal boost, the economy moves to full employment at P_0, $\bar{y}$.

Monetary policy   In the classical model, a rise in the money supply from M_0 to M_1 shifts the aggregate demand curve to the right and the price level rises sufficiently to bring the demand for output back into line with the supply, $y^s = \bar{y}$. The rise in prices lowers the real wage, boosting the demand for labour. Since there is no additional labour forthcoming at a lower real wage, there is excess demand in the labour market and money wages are bid up until the real wage is back at the full employment level, $\bar{w}$. In sum, prices and money wages rise by exactly the amount of the increase in the money supply, leaving all real magnitudes in the model unchanged.

From a situation of involuntary unemployment at y_1 in Keynes's model, let us consider the impact of an expansion in the money supply. The government increases the money supply by engaging in open market operations to purchase bonds from the general public. The excess demand for bonds raises the bond price and pushes the interest rate down. A lower interest rate boosts investment demand and sets the multiplier process of income expansion in train. In Fig. 2.11, the aggregate demand curve shifts to the right (e.g. back to AD_0). The associated rise in prices lowers the real wage and makes profitable the additional employment. A sufficient monetary expansion will return the economy to full employment. We will return below to problems that Keynes foresaw with the use of monetary policy in situations of involuntary unemployment.

The comparison between the classical and Keynes models serves to highlight three fundamental differences in the conception of the macro economy.

1   *Where are output and employment determined?*   In the classical model, employment and output are set in the labour market at the intersection of the marginal product of labour (demand for labour) and the supply of labour curves. In Keynes's model, it is the level of aggregate demand that fixes output and employment. In the classical model, aggregate demand adjusts to supply through changes in the price level. In Keynes's model, changes in the price level cause the supply of output to adjust to aggregate demand through altering the real wage and hence the profitability of marginal employment. The money wage is assumed constant.

2   *Investment and full employment*   In the classical model, it is the flexible interest rate that ensures that investment is equal to the given full employment level of savings. In Keynes's model, investment is a function of the interest rate and of expectations of future profitability ('animal spirits'). Savings are not fixed at a unique full employment level, but rather, depend on the level of actual employment. If investment falls, planned savings are brought into equality with the lower level of investment through the reduction in employment and income.

3   *The multiplier*   In the classical model, consumption is not a function of the level of employment. It depends only on the real wage. Hence there is no multiplier effect of changes in investment on output.

2.3   Keynes's Model and Falling Money Wages

A central component in the above presentation of Keynes's model of involuntary unemployment is the failure of money wages to fall. This market imperfection led, in the context of a fall in autonomous demand, to the real wage rising and the consequent fall in employment and output to the level of output demanded. We can summarize the argument as follows:

$\downarrow i \rightarrow \downarrow y^D \rightarrow \downarrow P,$ which, with fixed $W, \rightarrow \uparrow w \rightarrow \downarrow E \ \& \ \downarrow y^s.$

In the classical model, a fall in investment would not affect output because of the rapid adjustment of the interest rate. However, even if it did, the effect would be transitory: prices would fall to clear the goods market and money wages would decline to clear the excess supply in the labour market. The full employment real wage would be rapidly re-established and equilibrium restored.

Did Keynes's analysis of involuntary unemployment stand or fall on the existence of a fixed money wage? In his view it did not: 'a willingness on the part of labour to accept lower money-wages is not necessarily a remedy for unemployment' (Keynes 1936: 18). In other words, even if the problems involved in securing a fall in money wages were overcome, Keynes felt that full employment would not always prevail. In his view, there were additional obstacles to the self-righting properties of the economy. He focused on two issues in particular: the possibility of the existence of a *liquidity trap*, and the possible insensitivity of investment to the interest rate.

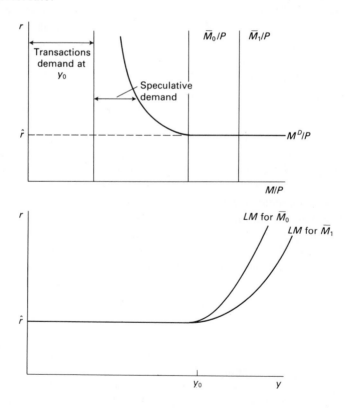

Fig. 2.12 The liquidity trap and the horizontal *LM*

2.3.1 The Liquidity Trap Argument

The term 'liquidity trap' was used by Keynes to refer to the special case where the speculative demand for money is perfectly elastic at the interest rate $\hat{r}$ (see Fig. 2.12). In other words, although individuals have different views as to the normal interest rate, in the liquidity trap the actual interest rate is so low that everyone believes it will *rise* to its normal level. If the government seeks to increase the supply of money (from M_0 to M_1), it will purchase bonds from the public using newly printed money. Because of the liquidity trap, remaining bond-holders will be prepared to sell bonds to the authorities at the existing price. Since higher bond prices are not required to elicit sales of bonds by the public, as is the case outside the liquidity trap, the interest rate does not fall. The additional money that has entered the economy is willingly held as money balances. If there is a liquidity trap at $\hat{r}$, then the *LM* curve will be horizontal (for income levels below y_0).

The existence of a liquidity trap means that the aggregate demand curve is vertical at y_0 because changes in the price level which alter the real money supply have no effect on output. A lower price level raises the real money supply and shifts the *LM* to the right. However, at the liquidity trap these additional real money balances are willingly held and there is no portfolio shift to bring about a change in the rate of interest and hence to stimulate investment (Fig. 2.13). More precisely, at any interest rate, there is in the economy a set of individuals who hold money only for speculative purposes and another set who hold only bonds. Of course, members of both sets hold money for transactions purposes. Let us consider the response of the bond-holders to a fall in the price level. The lower price level raises the value of transactions balances above the desired level. What happens to these additional balances? In normal circumstances the bond-holders will purchase additional bonds, since believing that the interest rate is above normal, they will want to hold their speculative assets in the form of bonds, to take advantage of the expected capital gain. However, at the liquidity trap, even the bond-holders are pessimistic about the prospects of a fall in the interest rate below $\hat{r}$ and will hold on to their extra money balances.

Using exactly the same logic, the aggregate demand curve will not *shift* in the face of a change in the money supply. Note that if the price level rises above P_H (Fig. 2.13), the leftward shift of *LM* will lead to a rise in the interest rate and a fall in output. Thus for $P > P_H$, the aggregate demand curve is downward-sloping.

2.3.2 The Interest-insensitive Investment Argument

If investment is completely insensitive to the rate of interest, the *IS* curve will be vertical (see Fig. 2.14). A vertical *IS* translates into a vertical

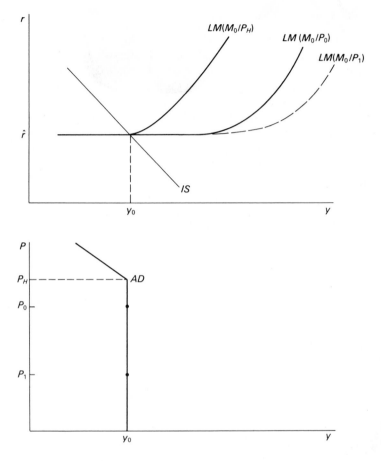

Fig. 2.13 The liquidity trap and the vertical AD curve

aggregate demand curve; a fall in the price level which increases the real money supply and brings with it a fall in the interest rate will have no consequential effect on investment.

2.3.3 Keynes's Model with Flexible Money Wages

Before looking at how the existence of either a liquidity trap or interest-insensitive investment can prevent the return to full employment, let us see how Keynes's model will operate when money wages are flexible. In Fig. 2.15 the economy is initially at full employment (point A). Investment falls, reducing the level of aggregate demand. Employment falls as lower prices push up the real wage. There is involuntary unemployment at E_1 (point B). At B, there is excess supply in the labour

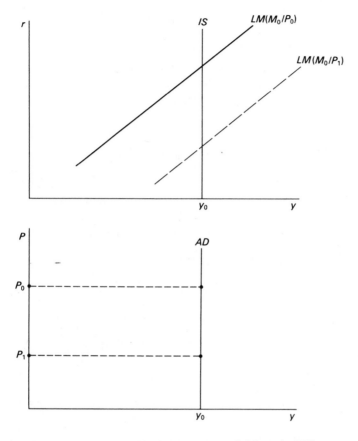

Fig. 2.14 Interest-insensitive investment and the vertical AD curve

market; i.e., there are people willing to work at the existing real wage for whom jobs are not available. *If* the money wage is flexible downwards, then the situation of excess supply in the labour market will produce a fall in money wages. If money wages fall sufficiently to bring the real wage back down to its full employment level, output and employment will expand back to $\bar{E}$, $\bar{y}$. Looking at Fig. 2.15, the aggregate supply curve shifts down (to $AS(W_1)$) with the fall in money wages, and the economy moves along the aggregate demand curve (AD_1) back to full employment (point C). Extra demand to make up for the original fall in investment is created by the drop in the price level, which boosts the real money supply, shifting the LM to the right (to $LM(\bar{M}/P_2)$). The interest rate falls and investment rises. The economy is back at full employment with a lower interest rate, a lower price level, and lower money wages.

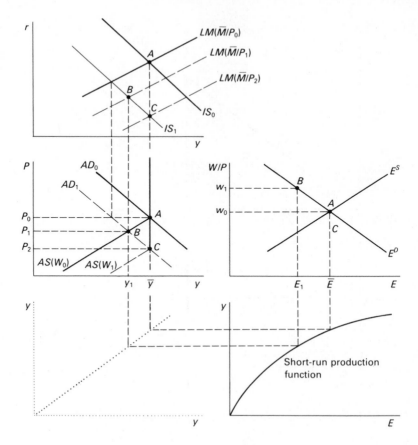

Fig. 2.15 Keynes's model: flexible money wages
$w_1 = W_0/P_1$; $w_0 = W_0/P_0 = W_1/P_2$.

Case (i): Liquidity Trap

The existence of a liquidity trap creates a break in the equilibrating process described above because there is no mechanism to make good the shortfall of aggregate demand created by the initial fall in investment. In Fig. 2.16, the economy is at A with full employment. As the result of the decline in investment, the aggregate demand curve shifts to AD_1 and prices fall to P_1 to clear the goods market. Suppose that money wages fall sufficiently (from W_0 to W_1) to re-establish the full employment real wage, $\bar{w} = W_1/P_1$. Employment back up to full employment is profitable and the supply of output returns to $y^s = \bar{y}$ as the economy moves up the new aggregate supply curve $AS(W_1)$. But output supply exceeds demand $(\bar{y} > y^D)$, which pushes prices down again (to P_2). The real wage rises to w_1. In the case above, it was the fall in prices that increased the real money

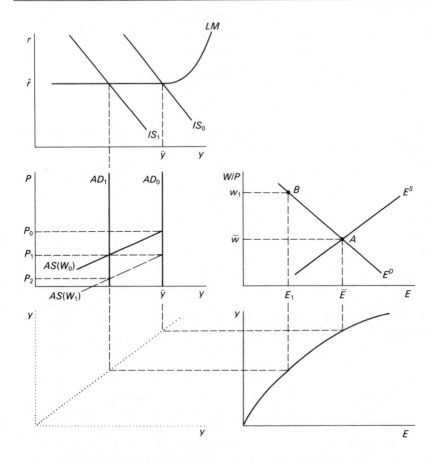

Fig. 2.16 Keynes's model: flexible money wages and the liquidity trap
$$w_1 = W_1/P_2 = W_0/P_1; \; \bar{w} = W_1/P_1 = W_0/P_0.$$

supply, lowered the interest rate, and boosted investment. With a liquidity trap, this mechanism is blocked. A vertical AD curve means that the economy will remain stuck at point B.

Case (ii): Interest-Insensitive Investment

As noted earlier, if investment is not responsive to changes in the rate of interest, the aggregate demand curve will again be vertical; even if changes in the price level lead to changes in the interest rate (i.e. if there is no liquidity trap), this has no effect on investment and hence none on output.

2.3.4 The Role of the Marginal Propensity to Save

The common feature of both the above cases is that mechanisms in the economy that in principle could reverse an exogenous fall in aggregate demand may fail to operate. These failures are reinforced by a further problem. Following the fall in autonomous investment from i_0 and i_1 (owing to a greater pessimism on the part of entrepreneurs as to expected future returns from investment), aggregate demand is

$$y^D = \bar{c} + c_y y + i_1,$$

where, either because of a constant interest rate associated with a liquidity trap or because investment is insensitive to the interest rate, investment remains fixed at the new lower level, i_1. With downward flexibility of money wages, employment rises. The increase in consumption demand associated with the rise in employment is $c_y \Delta y$. The total rise in aggregate demand is therefore $c_y \Delta y$, which is less than the increase in output, Δy, because of the key assumption made by Keynes that the marginal propensity to consume is less than one. With supply exceeding demand, there will once more be unsold goods. Prices, output, and employment fall. The real wage once again lies above its full employment level. Looking at the problem in this way helps to highlight the importance of Keynes's assumption that the marginal propensity to consume is less than one. In other words, Keynes believed that increased supply and the incomes that accompany it do not generate an equal increase in demand.

A particularly sharp way of seeing this point is to take a hint from the Polish economist Kalecki's analysis.[6] Kalecki made the simple assumption that all wage income is spent on consumption and that all profit income is saved: there is no saving out of wages and no consumption out of profits. Investment is assumed to be exogenous; it does not depend on the interest rate, which means that changes in the price level cannot affect investment. On this assumption, it is easy to show profit and wage income and investment and consumption demand in the labour market diagram (Fig. 2.17). Take full employment: on Kalecki's assumptions, the area under the real wage will equal consumption demand, and the area under the marginal product curve above the real wage will equal profits.[7] At full employment equilibrium, real income = consumption + investment = real wage bill + total real profits. Since the wage bill is equal to consumption, real investment must be equal to the amount of total real profits (top panel of Fig. 2.17).

[6] In 1935 (the year before the publication of Keynes's *General Theory*), the Polish economist Michal Kalecki published an article in a Polish journal entitled 'The Mechanism of the Business Upswing', which provides a vivid description of why cutting money wages would not provide a way out of the mass unemployment symptomatic of depression (Kalecki 1971a).

[7] Looking at the first unit of employment along the horizontal axis, the marginal product of labour curve shows output produced by that unit of labour. The wage component is w. Thus the remainder—the difference between the MPL and w—is the amount of profit associated with the employment of the first unit of labour. Similarly, each subsequent unit of employment is associated with an amount of profit. Total profits at E are equal to the sum of the profits associated with the employment of each unit of labour up to E and hence equal the area under the MPL curve above the wage line.

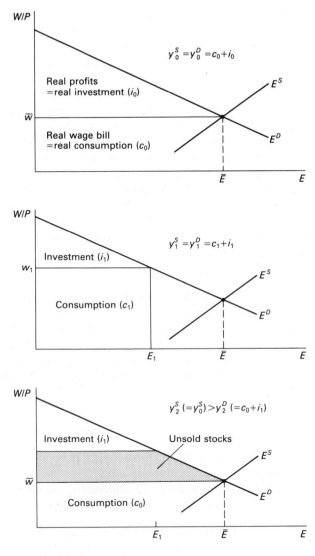

Fig. 2.17 Kalecki on demand-deficient unemployment

An equilibrium at less than full employment will be characterized by a situation such as that shown in the middle panel of Fig. 2.17. The lower level of exogenous investment is shown by the reduced size of the investment triangle. Now suppose that the money wage falls, lowering the real wage to its full employment level. The result is shown in the bottom panel: although the wage bill and hence consumption have increased with the rise in employment, investment demand remains unchanged—by

assumption. Hence at full employment there are once more unsold stocks
of goods, as shown clearly in the diagram. It is the fact that entrepreneurs
do not adjust their demand for investment goods automatically into line
with supply that produces a situation in which demand is inadequate to
sustain full employment. Falling prices will push the real wage up again,
and the economy will return to the situation depicted in the middle panel.
In Kalecki's words, 'The accumulating stocks will sound the alarm for a
new price reduction of goods which do not find any outlet. . . . On balance
only a price reduction will have occurred, offsetting the advantage of the
cost reduction to the entrepreneurs since unemployment going hand in
hand with under-utilization of equipment will reappear' (1971a: 27).

The link between Keynes and Kalecki lies with the assumption that the
marginal propensity to consume in each model is less than one. In
Kalecki's presentation, since consumption equals the wage bill, the
marginal propensity to consume is equal to the change in the wage bill
associated with a change in income: in real terms,

$$dc/dy = d(wE)/dy.$$

The intuition behind the result that Kalecki's marginal propensity to
consume is less than one is that a profit-maximizing firm will raise the level
of output only if marginal profits are positive. For marginal profits to be
positive, the real wage bill cannot rise by the full extent of the rise in real
output. The wage bill rises by less than output, and hence if as Kalecki
assumes all wages are consumed, the marginal propensity to consume is
below one.[8]

2.3.5 Summary

Hence, with flexible money wages and the marginal propensity to consume
less than one, either a liquidity trap or interest-insensitive investment
would suffice to hold the economy in an underemployment equilibrium.
Perhaps more accurately, the situation envisaged by Keynes was one in

---

[8] To show that $d(wE)/dy$ is less than one, we note that, since

$$y = \pi + wE,$$

$$dy = d\pi + d(wE),$$

where π is total real profits. Dividing both sides by dy gives

$$1 = d\pi/dy + d(wE)/dy.$$

With profit maximization, a rise in output can occur only if w falls, and the fall in w must
imply that profits rise ($d\pi/dy > 0$)—otherwise the increase in output would not have been
undertaken. Hence, since $d\pi/dy > 0$ and

$$1 = d\pi/dy + d(wE)/dy,$$

we have the result that

$$d(wE)/dy < 1; \text{i.e., } dc/dy < 1.$$

which money wages and the interest rate would be falling very slowly. Unemployment would persist for long periods of time. (We return in Chapter 5 to the question of whether the comparative-static *IS/LM* framework adequately captures the central thrust of Keynes's argument with the classics.)

Keynes believed that his theory of demand-deficient involuntary unemployment did not rest on rigid nominal wages. Nevertheless, he felt that, as regards practical policy analysis and prescription, it was a sensible assumption. He stated that 'the money-wage level as a whole should be maintained as stable as possible, at any rate in the short period' (1936: 270). Keynes believed that declining wages (and prices) were not conducive to the restoration of prosperity because, by creating uncertainty about how far the decline might go, they could result in firms' delaying their employment (and investment) decisions.

Given that for Keynes a fall in real wages was a necessary condition for a return to full employment, he argued that a simpler and safer way of achieving this than by attempting to reduce money wages was to raise aggregate demand and hence prices. There was another reason for his preference for the latter of the two ways of cutting real wages. Keynes felt that a policy of encouraging cuts in money wages introduced an additional complicating element into the inherently difficult issue of real-wage cuts. The extra complication was wage relativities. Whereas money-wage cuts could give the impression that one's wage relative to others in similar jobs was being cut, an across-the-board price rise would not be subject to such a misinterpretation.

2.4   The Real-Balance Effect: the Classical Rejoinder to Keynes

By developing a macroeconomic system in which persistent involuntary unemployment can occur, Keynes had thrown down a challenge to proponents of the classical model. The problem for the classics was to provide a mechanism through which aggregate demand would be restored to the full employment level without the need for government intervention. In order to be a general rebuttal of Keynes's model, the mechanism would have to be effective even if there were a liquidity trap or if investment were unresponsive to the interest rate.

The classical response was to call attention to the so-called *real balance effect* (also known as the *Pigou effect*): if consumer expenditure is a function of the real money supply, then excess supply in the goods market (caused for example by a drop in investment as a consequence of increased pessimism), which is reflected in falling prices to clear the unsold goods, will raise the value of cash holdings and boost consumer spending. Thus, even if the classics moved on to Keynes's ground by accepting the possibility of a liquidity trap or interest-insensitive investment, they were able to re-establish the full employment property of a self-equilibrating private economy.

In the extreme Keynesian case of a vertical aggregate demand curve arising from either a liquidity trap or interest-insensitive investment, the economy can get stuck at an underemployment equilibrium. The introduction of a real balance effect on consumption recreates a downward-sloping aggregate demand curve because a fall in the price level directly moves the *IS* to the right; lower investment demand, leading to lower prices, raises consumption demand. (We will go through this in more detail below.) Employment and output would return to their equilibrium market-clearing values. The classics saw their mechanism as logically irrefutable, since any shortfall of aggregate demand from full employment output would lower prices; a sufficient lowering of prices would generate the consumption demand to fill the gap—otherwise prices would simply keep falling.

Let us work through the operation of the real balance effect more carefully. The inclusion of wealth in the consumption function is quite consistent with the classical view. Households are viewed as maximizing utility over their lifetime subject to a lifetime budget constraint. This is a way of summing up *life-cycle* and *permanent income* theories of consumption.[9] For each household, their total wealth in real terms (i.e. the lifetime budget constraint) is equal to the sum of the net present value of their labour income, income from profits, real money balances, and credits less debts. For the economy as a whole, credits and debts cancel out. Thus, real wealth is equal to the net present value of current and future disposable income and real money balances. For short-run analysis, future values of income are taken as given. This gives the result that current consumption expenditure, based on utility maximization over the lifetime of the household, is a function of current income and real money balances:

$$c = c(\overset{+}{y}, M \overset{+}{/} P).$$

For simplicity, we will assume a linear consumption function:

$$c = \bar{c} + c_y y + c_m(M/P),$$

where $\bar{c}$, c_y, and c_m are positive constants, $0 < c_y < 1; 0 < c_m < 1$. Any rise in wealth will, by reducing the need to save to provide the desired future consumption stream, produce an increase in current consumption. When the price level changes, the real value of nominal money balances changes and hence wealth changes.

---

[9] The intertemporal utility-maximizing approach to consumption was developed independently by M. Friedman (1957) as the permanent income hypothesis and by Modigliani and Brumberg (1954) as the life-cycle hypothesis.

With consumption a function of M/P, the IS will be shifted by any change in M/P. For IS or goods market equilibrium,

$$y = y^D.$$

Now,

$$y^D = \bar{c} + c_y(1 - t_y)y + c_m(M/P) + A - i_r r + g;$$

therefore in equilibrium,

$$y = \frac{\bar{c} + c_m (M/P) + A + g}{1 - c_y(1 - t_y)} - \frac{i_r}{1 - c_y(1 - t_y)} r. \qquad [IS \text{ curve}]$$

Any fall in the price level will shift the IS curve to the right, since at each interest rate there will be a higher level of output demanded, and therefore for equilibrium level of output, y, must be higher.

In the two panels of Fig. 2.18, the re-emergence of a downward-sloping aggregate demand curve in both of Keynes's special cases—the liquidity trap and interest-insensitive investment—is illustrated. In the liquidity trap case, case (a), although a change in the price level has no effect on the LM, it shifts the IS because of the real balance effect. In case (b), whereas a

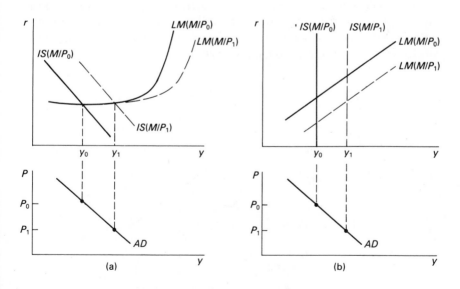

Fig. 2.18 The Pigou effect
(a) Liquidity trap and the Pigou effect
(b) Interest-inelastic investment and the Pigou effect

shift in the *LM* arising from a lower price level had no effect on output in the case of a vertical *IS* (interest-inelastic investment), with wealth effects in the consumption function, the *IS* itself shifts to the right in the face of a fall in the price level.

The core of the classical response to Keynes is that, with consumption a function of the real money supply, in a situation in which the supply of output exceeds the demand, prices continue to fall until consumption demand has risen sufficiently to bring y^D into line with the level of supply determined by labour-market-clearing. In Fig. 2.19, it is possible to follow the argument proposed. Suppose the economy is initially at full employment at point A. The classics go on to Keynes's ground by assuming that there is an exogenous fall in investment from i_0 to i_1 and that investment remains at the lower level of i_1 throughout. Subsequent to the drop in investment demand, prices fall because of excess supply of goods. With lower prices, employment and output fall because of the rise in real wages. The economy moves from A to B. The classics argue that money wages fall to reflect the excess supply in the labour market. Thus, employment and output rise back to their full employment levels. Meanwhile the problem of the excess supply of goods remains. The response of the classics was to say that any excess supply of output would create further falls in prices, and that this would boost consumption demand through the real balance (Pigou) effect until aggregate demand was equal to full employment output. In the aggregate demand diagram (Fig. 2.19), the economy moves down the aggregate demand curve associated with i_1 from B to C. In the new equilibrium at full employment, the economy is characterized by a different mix of output—investment is lower and consumption is higher—and by a lower price level and money wage.

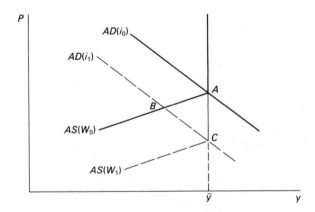

Fig. 2.19 Self-equilibration of the economy through the Pigou effect

2.5   Interim Conclusions on Keynes's Model

Keynes provided economic policy-makers with a powerful alternative to the classical model. He showed how a turn to pessimism on the part of private entrepreneurs, resulting in reduced investment spending, would plunge the economy into a period of involuntary unemployment. The unemployment would disappear if the government increased its expenditure programmes by the amount required to take aggregate demand up to its full employment level. Higher government demand would raise the price level and, given a fixed money wage, would reduce the real wage, rendering profitable the required capacity. Output would rise to equal aggregate demand at the full employment level. Keynes agreed with the classics that real wages had to fall to restore full employment; his great departure was to propose reasons for their failure to fall in the absence of government intervention. Expansionary fiscal policy was able to secure a fall in the real wage by raising the general price level.

Keynes believed that for institutional reasons excess supply in the labour market would not tend to drive down money wages. Nevertheless, his theory did not rest on a rigid money wage as we have seen in Section 2.3—even if money wages decline, this would not necessarily bring about the required fall in *real* wages because of the persistent deficiency of demand. In Keynes's model, entrepreneurial pessimism would not be offset automatically by a decline in the interest rate as the classical model held. Since the higher employment induced by the initial fall in real wages would only boost consumption demand by some proportion of the rise in real income, a demand gap would remain. In Keynes's model, demand below the full employment level keeps the real wage above the full employment level.

Keynes's model provided a theoretical basis for a new role for government economic intervention. The private sector could not be viewed as inherently self-stabilizing. The government can ensure full employment through its ability to offset changes in aggregate demand emanating from the private sector.

The initial response from the supporters of the classical macroeconomic model to Keynes's demonstration of the possibility of persistent involuntary unemployment was to propose a mechanism through which aggregate demand would be restored to full employment even if there were no response at all of investment to lower prices. The Pigou (real balance) effect states that consumption depends on the real value of money balances. The relevance of this form of consumption function is that, since a positive gap between output supplied and aggregate demand will imply falling prices (assuming a perfectly competitive product market), a sufficient fall in the price level will always be forthcoming to bring aggregate demand up to the full employment level by raising consumption.

If the Pigou effect is valid, this rejoinder appears to narrow further Keynes's claim to have provided a general theory. In the light of the Pigou effect, Keynes's model appears to have shrunk to the special case of rigid money wages; i.e., the culprit is an imperfectly functioning labour market which prevents downward pressure on money wages from emerging in response to excess supply. Of course, Keynes had sought to provide a truly general account of the absence of self-equilibrating forces keeping the economy at full employment.

For the first twenty to twenty-five years of the post-war period, a consensus view of macroeconomics was built up. The Keynesian theory of income determination was firmly rooted at the heart of the mainstream paradigm. The paradigm came to be knowm, particularly in the USA, by the rather confusing name of the *neoclassical synthesis*. To minimize confusion, we will refer to it as the *Keynesian-neoclassical synthesis*. During the 1950s and 1960s research efforts were directed towards elaborating the determinants of aggregate demand: consumption, investment, money supply, and money demand functions. It was agreed that the *IS* was negatively sloped and the *LM* was positively sloped. Work on the consumption function, for example, was especially successful. Research on the life-cycle theory produced the consensus view that intertemporal optimization by the household is modified by the existence of imperfections in financial markets and by the existence of liquidity constraints which prevent the desired smoothing of the consumption stream over the lifetime. Keynes's simple absolute income theory of consumption was thus modified, but the key result of a marginal propensity to consume out of current income of less than one, and hence the existence of the multiplier, was confirmed.

While the theoretical possibility of the Pigou effect is acknowledged in the Keynesian-neoclassical synthesis, it was felt to have little practical significance. Prices and wages were held to adjust only slowly to the prevailing market conditions and could not be relied on to ensure continuous full employment. In terms of economic policy, the conclusion of the mainstream remained true to Keynes: because of sluggish adjustment of prices and wages, intervention by the government is necessary and desirable to prevent excessive fluctuations in employment and output. Econometric models built on this basis were successful in forecasting developments and were used for detailed policy formulation.

The great challenge to the Keynesian-neoclassical synthesis and its Keynesian core came in the 1970s and 1980s. But it began with the empirical failure of the dominant model to explain and predict the rising inflation in the USA in the late 1960s. It is to the issue of inflation and the inadequacies of the Keynesian theory in respect to the analysis of inflation that we now turn.

Appendix: Simple Mathematics and Geometry of *IS/LM*

A2.1 The *IS* Curve

Assume that the consumption, investment, and tax functions are linear:

$$c = \bar{c} + c_y(y - t)$$

$$t = t_y y; \qquad \text{[tax function]}$$

and therefore

$$c = \bar{c} + c_y(y - t_y y)$$
$$= \bar{c} + c_y(1 - t_y)y. \qquad \text{[consumption function]}$$

The investment function is

$$i = i(r, A)$$
$$= A - i_r r. \qquad \text{[investment function]}$$

In goods market equilibrium,

$$y = y^D$$
$$= c + i + g$$
$$= \bar{c} + c_y(1 - t_y)y + A - i_r r + g.$$

Solving for y gives

$$y = \frac{\bar{c} + A + g}{1 - c_y(1 - t_y)} - \frac{i_r}{1 - c_y(1 - t_y)} r. \qquad \text{[IS curve]}$$

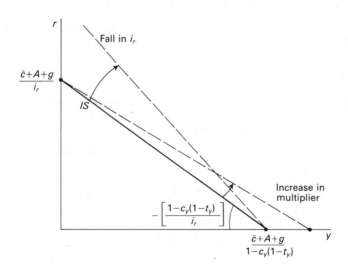

Fig. 2.20 The *IS* curve

Construct the *IS* curve in $r-y$ space by first setting $r = 0$ to get the intercept of the *IS* curve on the y-axis (Fig. 2.20); when $r = 0$,

$$y = \frac{\bar{c} + A + g}{1 - c_y(1 - t_y)};$$

similarly for the intercept of the *IS* curve on the r-axis; when $y = 0$,

$$r = \frac{\bar{c} + A + g}{i_r}.$$

Using the linear functions and Fig. 2.20, it is easy to make statements 1, 2, and 3 on p. 33 precise.

Change in the Size of the Multiplier

An increase in the multiplier has no effect on $(\bar{c} + A + g)/i_r$ since $y = 0$, with the result that the r-intercept is unaffected. A rise in the multiplier simply shifts $(\bar{c} + A + g)/[1 - c_y(1 - t_y)]$ to the right along the horizontal axis. The *IS* rotates counter-clockwise, as shown in Fig. 2.20.

Change in the Interest Sensitivity of Investment

A reduction in the interest sensitivity of investment has no effect on $(\bar{c} + A + g)/[1 - c_y(1 - t_y)]$ because $r = 0$. Thus the y-intercept is unaffected. A fall in i_r simply shifts $(\bar{c} + A + g)/i_r$ up the vertical axis. The *IS* rotates clockwise, as shown in Fig. 2.20.

Change in the Components of Autonomous Spending

An increase in $\bar{c}$, A, or g produces a parallel outward shift of the *IS* curve since the slope of *IS* is unchanged (not shown).

A2.2   The *LM* Curve

Assume that the demand-for-money function is linear and write it in real terms:

$$M^D/P = \bar{m} - m_r r + \frac{1}{v_T} y.$$

[demand-for-money function]

The supply of money is a constant:

$$M^S/P = \bar{M}^S/P.$$ [supply-of-money function]

Money market equilibrium requires that

$$M^D/P = M^S/P$$

and hence

$$\bar{m} - m_r r + \frac{1}{v_T} y = \bar{M}^S/P.$$

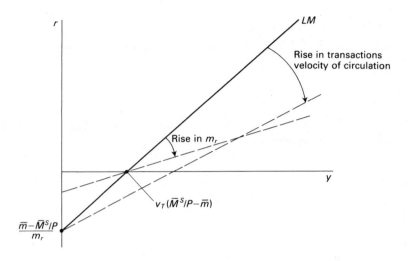

Fig. 2.21 The *LM* curve

Solving for r gives

$$r = \frac{\bar{m} - \bar{M}^S/P}{m_r} + \frac{1}{v_T m_r} y. \qquad [LM \text{ curve}]$$

Construct the *LM* curve in $r-y$ space by first setting $r = 0$ to get the intercept of the *LM* curve on the y-axis (Fig. 2.21); when $r = 0$,

$$y = v_T(\bar{M}^S/P - \bar{m});$$

similarly for the intercept of the *LM* curve on the r-axis; when $y = 0$,

$$r = \frac{\bar{m} - \bar{M}^S/P}{m_r}.$$

It is straightforward to make precise the statements on p. 40 as to the implications for the *LM* of parameter changes.

Change in the Transactions Velocity of Circulation

A rise in the transactions velocity of circulation v_T as the result for example of financial innovation means that the intercept of the *LM* with the vertical axis is unchanged while the intersection with the horizontal axis moves to the right. Thus the *LM* rotates clockwise, becoming flatter, as shown in Fig. 2.21.

Change in the Interest Sensitivity of the Demand for Money

A rise in m_r, the interest sensitivity of the demand for money, has no effect on the intercept of the *LM* with the y-axis. It shifts the intercept with the vertical axis upward. Thus the *LM* rotates in a clockwise direction about the horizontal intercept, becoming flatter (Fig. 2.21).

Change in the Money Supply

A rise in the money supply shifts the *LM* rightwards with no change in the slope. The size of the shift will be $v_T(\Delta M^S/P)$ (not shown).

Change in the Price Level

A rise in the price level shifts the *LM* leftwards with no change in the slope. The size of the shift will be $v_T(M^S/\Delta P)$ (not shown).

3

Inflation and Unemployment: Friedman's Model

3.1 The Keynesian/Phillips Model of Inflation and the Keynesian– Neoclassical Synthesis

The economic environment that provided the context for Keynes's *General Theory* was one of unemployment, falling prices, and depression. For economists schooled in the Keynesian tradition but working in the 1950s and 1960s, unemployment was receding as a policy problem and inflation was emerging. Did they have anything to say about wages and prices? There was little in the *General Theory* about the determinants of movements in money wages; it simply relied on perfect competition as the model of price determination. Keynesians in the post-war years viewed this as unsatisfactory, for two reasons. On the pricing side, a competitive theory of pricing suggests that the real wage should move counter-cylically; i.e., the real wage should fall during a boom. Yet there appeared to be little evidence of this. Secondly, an account of inflation was required. The response of post-war Keynesians engaged in macroeconometric modelling and policy formation was *ad hoc*. On the one hand, they adopted the empirical finding that lower levels of unemployment are associated with higher rates of change of money wages (the so-called *Phillips curve*) as an explanation of wage inflation. On the other hand, they adopted *mark-up pricing*[1] so that price inflation is equal to wage inflation.

The model of inflation grafted on to the mainstream macroeconomic model of the 1960s (the Keynesian–neoclassical synthesis) was the relationship between the level of unemployment and the growth rate of money wages discovered by Phillips using UK data for the period 1861–1957 (Phillips 1958). A linear version of the Phillips curve can be written as

---

[1] Mark-up pricing is discussed in detail in Parts II and IV. It means that, as a first approximation, $P = (1 + \mu) W/LP$ where μ is a percentage mark-up covering profits, overheads, etc., and LP is labour productivity. What is relevant here is the implication that, for constant productivity, $P = W$.

$$\dot{W} = \alpha\,(\bar{U} - U),\qquad\text{[Phillips curve]}$$

where $\bar{U}$ is the rate of unemployment at labour market equilibrium and α is a positive constant. Wage inflation will be higher, the tighter is the labour market. With the labour market in equilibrium, wage inflation is zero. Figure 3.1 illustrates the Phillips curve relation.

Let us put the Phillips curve together with the Keynesian model of aggregate demand to present a stylized version of the paradigm macroeconomic model of the 1960s: the Keynesian–neoclassical synthesis. As noted in the characterization of the synthesis at the end of the previous chapter, the model comprised a Keynesian system of output and employment determination captured by the IS/LM model with downward-sloping IS and upward-sloping LM. This was combined with the view that money wages and prices are sluggish in the short run. Keynes's analysis of aggregate supply with perfect competition in the product market was put to one side. Lying behind the use of sticky prices was an implicit assumption of an oligopolistic product market, but this idea was not developed in any detail. It was simply *assumed* that in practice product market imperfections mean that a change in aggregate demand results in a change in output supplied by firms rather than a change in price (as would be the case with perfect competition). Furthermore, it was *assumed* that prices change in line with changes in money wages—this is the *ad hoc* assumption of mark-up pricing referred to earlier.

The Keynesian–neoclassical synthesis can be summarized as follows:

$$y = y^D\,(g, t_y, M^S/P)\qquad\text{[IS/LM equilibrium]}$$

$$\dot{W} = \alpha(\bar{U} - U)\qquad\qquad\text{[Phillips curve]}$$

$$\dot{P} = \dot{W}.\qquad\qquad\qquad\text{[mark-up pricing]}$$

The model is completed with the definition of $\bar{U}$ as the rate of unemployment associated with labour market equilibrium. In this model the labour market does not determine the level of output and employment

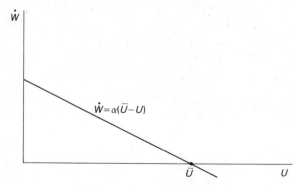

Fig. 3.1 The Phillips curve

(this is fixed by aggregate demand); its role is to determine the rate of wage inflation. Inflation is zero only at the labour market equilibrium level of output. However, the economy can remain at a higher level of output at the cost of higher inflation.

The operation of the Keynesian–neoclassical synthesis is depicted in Fig. 3.2. The model can be presented more easily if the Phillips curve is drawn 'backwards':[2] since employment in the production function and labour market quadrants runs from left to right, changes in unemployment

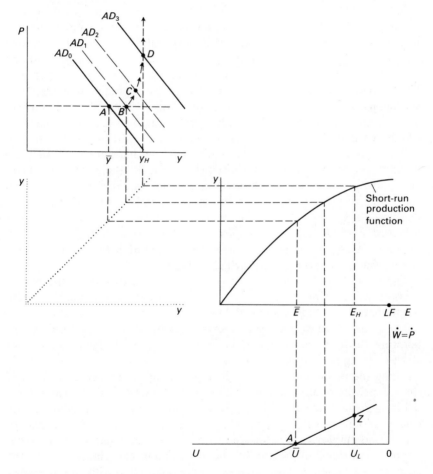

Fig. 3.2 The Keynesian–neoclassical synthesis model: a sustained demand expansion and the Phillips curve

[2] This convention is used throughout the book. Technically, U in the diagrams measures the number of those unemployed as opposed to the rate of unemployment. We still, however, continue to refer to U as the rate of unemployment. So long as the labour force is constant, the difference is one of scale alone.

associated with changes in employment can be shown automatically if the unemployment scale runs from right to left. The zero point on the unemployment axis coincides with the statistical definition of the labour force, LF, shown on the employment axis.

Let us assume that the economy begins in labour market equilibrium with inflation equal to zero: at point A in the diagram. The government then introduces a *sustained* expansion of aggregate demand by undertaking to raise the money supply by a fixed rate each period. The aggregate demand curve in Fig. 3.2 therefore shifts outward each period, from AD_0 to AD_1 to AD_2, etc. In the short run, with sticky wages and prices, output expands beyond the full employment level and the economy moves from A to B. But the Phillips curve tells us that an output level of B associated with unemployment below $\bar{U}$ will produce rising money wages and, via mark-up pricing, rising prices. Rising prices will, for a given aggregate demand curve, lead to a fall in output. With the aggregate demand curve shifting rightward each period, rising prices will dampen the rise in output. The economy moves from B to C. Eventually, according to the model, the economy will end up at point D shown in the aggregate demand quadrant, with output above the level associated with labour market equilibrium and unemployment below $\bar{U}$. In subsequent periods, the economy moves vertically upward from D with prices and money wages rising at a constant rate equal to the growth rate of the money supply. In the Phillips curve diagram, the economy is at Z. In the new equilibrium, the government has achieved a reduction in unemployment at the cost of higher constant inflation. Along the path to the new equilibrium at Z the economy faces rising inflation, but once Z is reached, inflation remains constant.

The choice by the government of a slower growth rate of the money supply than in the previous example would result in a new equilibrium with output between $\bar{y}$ and y_H and with lower inflation than associated with y_H.

The policy implications of the Keynesian–neoclassical synthesis incorporating the Phillips model of inflation are twofold. First, because of short-run wage and price stickiness, the government has a role to play in ensuring the maintenance of low unemployment in the face of *downward* shifts in private sector demand. Although the Phillips curve indicates that a fall in aggregate demand (owing for example to a fall in investment) will lead eventually to falling prices, the government can avoid the loss of output and employment associated with this slow adjustment by intervening to boost demand. Secondly, the government can choose to run the economy with unemployment below the rate associated with labour market equilibrium by accepting a positive but finite rate of inflation.

This composite model appeared to be working satisfactorily in empirical terms until the second half of the 1960s, when inflation in the USA went on rising after unemployment had stopped falling. According to the Phillips curve, rising inflation is associated with *falling* unemployment. The predictive shortcomings of the Keynesian/Phillips model of inflation in turn led to closer theoretical scrutiny. On closer inspection, the model appeared to incorporate behaviour that was clearly irrational. Figure 3.3 highlights the source of the problem. The Keynesian–neoclassical synthesis model suggests that the government can achieve an equilibrium for the economy at point Z with unemployment of U_L and positive inflation. If we look at the panel beneath the Phillips curve diagram, the labour market is depicted. Unemployment of U_L implies that employment is higher than is consistent with labour market equilibrium. For firms to be supplying the amount of output associated with the high employment of E_H, the real wage must be w_L. For workers to supply the amount of labour E_H, the real wage must be at a high level, w_H. Clearly, there is an inconsistency here. The inconsistency can be explained by irrational behaviour on the part of workers: if workers suffer from *money illusion*, then they may mistake the money wage inflation that characterizes point Z for higher real wages. In other words, the labour market would be characterized by the combination of w_L and E_H—an 'equilibrium' in which the real wage lies beneath the labour supply curve. But why should workers continue to behave in this way once they had realized their mistake?

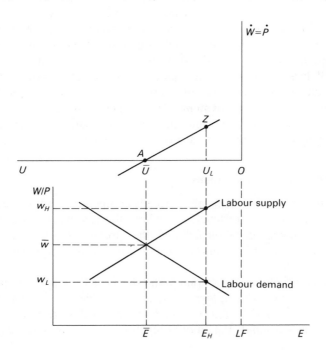

Fig. 3.3 The Keynesian–neoclassical synthesis, the Phillips curve, and the labour market

The empirical failure of the Keynesian/Phillips model of inflation in the late 1960s, combined with a growing sensitivity to its theoretical shortcomings, created fertile ground for the reception of Milton Friedman's model of inflation.

3.2 Friedman's Model of Inflation

In his presidential address to the American Economics Association in 1967,[3] Milton Friedman laid out a simple macroeconomic model which re-established the traditional classical results but at the same time was able to explain the empirical observation of an inverse relationship between inflation and unemployment. Friedman was able to explain both the increase in inflation as unemployment fell through the mid-1960s—which the classical model could not—and the rise in inflation after unemployment stopped falling in the late 1960s—which the Keynesian–neoclassical synthesis model could not. Friedman's highly influential presentation established itself as a standard in the economics profession. He skilfully captured the mainstream by proposing that, while markets clear in the long run where classical results obtain, they do not necessarily clear at full employment in the short run because of a lack of perfect information on the part of all agents. Using the idea of imperfect information, he was able to provide a coherent microeconomic foundation for the empirical finding of Phillips and to show why the relationship broke down at the end of the 1960s. A lack of information, rather than the irrationality of money illusion, creates the possibility of temporary deviations from the long-run equilibrium of full employment. The combination of classical results holding in the long run and short-run fluctuations of output and employment will be referred to as Friedman's model.

3.2.1 Friedman's Assumptions

Friedman assumes that firms are perfectly competitive and produce at the profit-maximizing output level, i.e. where the real wage is equal to the marginal product of labour. Since the product market is perfectly competitive, each firm assumes it can sell as much as it wants to at the going price.

Secondly, Friedman argues that in the short run the economy can be at a position with lower unemployment than is possible to sustain in the long run. In such a situation (e.g. in Fig. 3.4 with a real wage of w_0), workers will none the less supply the amount of labour that firms demand (i.e. E_0).

---

[3] Published as 'The Role of Monetary Policy' in the *American Economic Review* (1968). For a fuller account of Friedman's model, see Friedman (1974).

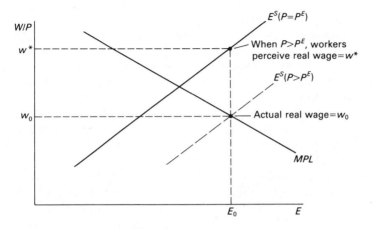

Fig. 3.4 Friedman's labour market diagram

They do so because they believe that the real wage is actually w^*. As will be explained in detail below, Friedman proposed that workers could be temporarily mistaken about the actual real wage in circumstances where the price level is changing. Since the consumption bundle of workers is made up of a whole multitude of items, a correct assessment of the real wage in terms of the price index of consumption is likely to be far more difficult than is the calculation by firms of the real cost of labour to them, i.e. in terms of the price of the firm's own output. Hence for Friedman, firms are always—in the short run as well as the long run—on the marginal product of labour curve. Workers are on their labour supply curve, but the supply curve will shift when workers make their labour supply decision based on incorrect information, i.e. when they have mistaken expectations about the price level.

3.2.2 Friedman's Results

Before setting out the operation of Friedman's model in full, it is useful to have a summary of the results:

F1 Markets clear in the long run with expectations fulfilled, but not necessarily in the short run. This means that in the long run, output and employment are determined in the labour market as in the classical model. In the short run, the economy can be shifted away from the long-run market-clearing output and employment level because changes in aggregate demand create forecasting errors and, as a result, shift the labour supply curve.

F2 The market-clearing (i.e. long-run) rate of unemployment is called the *natural rate of unemployment* (NRU). At the NRU, there is no involuntary unemployment. This rate of unemployment may be higher than is compatible with the usual idea of full employment, but the unemployment is entirely voluntary since it reflects the choice by individuals to engage in search activities.

F3 The rate of inflation is stable at the NRU. Only at this rate of unemployment is inflation anticipated correctly. If unemployment is below the NRU, then inflation will be increasing and vice versa. There is a vertical *long-run Phillips curve* at the NRU which implies that no long-run trade-off between unemployment and inflation is possible.

F4 Long-run policy implications: the Quantity Theory of Money holds in the long run so that an increase in the money supply leads only to higher prices; money is therefore neutral in the long run; there is 100% crowding-out of private expenditure by government spending.

F5 Short-run policy implications: both monetary and fiscal policy have real effects, but monetary policy is much more powerful than fiscal policy.

3.3 The Natural Rate of Unemployment

3.3.1 Inflation and Unemployment

The working of Friedman's model is most clearly understood from an example. Assume that the economy is in full equilibrium with unemployment at the natural rate and that the government wants to try to reduce unemployment further. For Friedman, the natural rate of unemployment was a level of 5% or 6% even in the early 1970s. The government uses its policy instruments to keep the level of real aggregate demand (y^D) higher than the level of output associated with labour-market-clearing (y_N) (top panel of Fig. 3.5). Turning to the middle panel of Fig. 3.5 (the labour market), it is clear that, for workers to supply the E_1 amount of labour required to produce output equal to y^D, they will require a real wage of w^*. On the other hand, firms will demand E_1 workers only if the real wage is w_1. How can this apparent contradiction be resolved? The existence of demand for output in excess of supply produces rising prices. The rise in prices takes the price level above its expected level. For firms who are aware of the rise in prices, it means a fall in the real wage to w_1 and higher demand for labour. But because of their inability to observe the actual price index for consumption goods, workers are assumed to base their labour supply decision on the *expected* real wage, where they use prices from previous periods to form their expectation of prices this period. In other words, labour supply is $E^S = E^S(w^E)$, rather than $E^S = E^S(w)$,

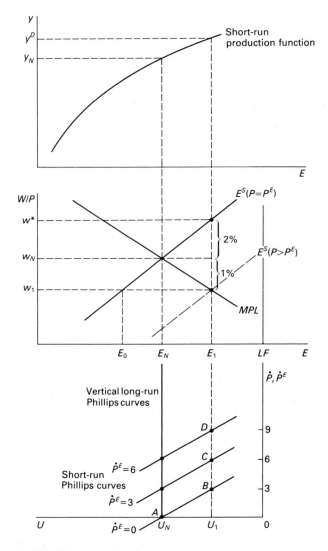

Fig. 3.5 Friedman's model: the natural rate of unemployment

because of the inability of workers to observe the price level. (x^E denotes the value of the variable x which the relevant agents expect to prevail for the current period.) The expected real wage is $w^E = W/P^E$, which can be written as

$$w^E = W/P^E = (W/P)(P/P^E).$$

Hence the labour supply equation is

$$E^S = E^S(W/P^E) = E^S[(W/P)(P/P^E)],$$

and any change in P/P^E shifts the labour supply curve.

Figure 3.5 shows the case where the actual price level exceeds the expected price. If $P > P^E$, then the labour supply curve will shift to the right because it is the workers' belief (based on their expectations) that the real wage is higher than it actually is. Therefore more labour will be supplied at the actual real wage level. For example, with the real wage w_1, when price expectations conform with the facts *ex post* (i.e. when $P = P^E$), the labour supply curve is $E^S(P = P^E)$ and labour supply will be E_0. If however prices are above the expected price level on which the labour supply decision is taken (i.e. if $P > P^E$), then the labour supply curve is $E^S(P > P^E)$ and labour supply will be E_1.

Returning to our example, with the government pushing aggregate demand above full employment supply, because demand exceeds the initial output level of y_N, prices rise. They continue to rise until supply, y^S, has risen to the level of output demanded, y^D. The rising price level has the effect of pushing down the real wage from w_N to w_1 (Fig. 3.5). In our example, let us assume that the real wage has fallen by 1% from w_N to w_1; i.e.,

$$\dot{w} = \dot{W} - \dot{P} = -1\%.$$

Hence, the rate of price inflation, $\dot{P}$, is $\dot{P} = 1\% + \dot{W}$.

But how much will money wages rise? Here we can pinpoint the source of the divergence between the real wage that workers expect to receive at E_1 and the real wage that firms are willing to pay. For workers to supply the amount E_1 of labour, the *expected* real wage must *rise* by 2% from w_N to w^*, and this means that the money wage must rise by 2% more than the expected rate of price inflation, $\dot{P}^E$:

$$\dot{W} = 2\% + \dot{P}^E.$$

For simplicity, it is best to start with a situation of zero inflation:

$$\dot{P}_{-1} = \dot{W}_{-1} = \dot{P}^E = 0,$$

where x_{-1} denotes the value of the variable x in the previous period. Friedman assumed that workers form their expectations of inflation by looking at past experience, revising their expectations as inflation changes. The simplest example of such a process of *adaptive expectations* is that inflation this period is expected to be at the level it turned out to be last period. This reflects rapid adaptation of expectations to past events. Let us make this assumption:[4]

$$\dot{P}^E = \dot{P}_{-1}. \quad \text{[adaptive inflation expectations]}$$

Putting together the lines of the story to date, we have

$$\dot{P}_0 = 1\% + \dot{W}_0$$
$$= 1\% + (2\% + \dot{P}^E)$$
$$= 1\% + (2\% + 0)$$
$$= 3\%$$

and

$$\dot{W}_0 = 2\%.$$

In other words, workers, by incorrectly believing that inflation will be zero as it was last period, interpret the rise in money wages of 2% as a rise in real wages of the same amount and are therefore willing to supply the amount E_1 of labour. The fact that prices actually rise by 1% *more* than do money wages means that the real wage is 1% lower than it was originally, and therefore it is profitable for firms who have access to correct information to increase their employment.

Employment has been raised by the government through its policy measures but the consequence has been a rise in the rate of inflation, since only through an *unanticipated* rise in the price level can the illusion be created that the real wage has risen, when in fact it has fallen.

3.3.2 The Phillips Curves: Short-Run and Long-Run

The path of inflation associated with the government's policy can be shown explicitly in the Phillips curve diagram: this is the third panel of Fig. 3.5. Just as in the earlier presentation of the original Phillips curve, unemployment is measured from right to left with unemployment rising as we move leftwards. The statistically measured labour force is fixed at LF in the middle panel, so we can identify this level of employment with unemployment of zero in the bottom panel. Higher unemployment to the left in the bottom panel matches lower employment in the panel above. On the vertical axis of the bottom panel, price and wage inflation are measured.

We can see the usefulness of the Phillips curve diagram in the present example. Initially, the economy is at E_N with a real wage of w_N. The corresponding unemployment rate is U_N. We have assumed a starting point of zero inflation. The increase in aggregate demand raises employment to E_1, reducing unemployment to U_1. The fall in unemployment was possible because of the rise in money wages which led workers to believe that the real wage had risen. In this example, prices rose by 3%. Hence unemployment of U_1 is associated with inflation of 3%. We can now draw in the *short-run Phillips curve* associated with zero expected inflation by

Table 3.1 The inflationary process: an example

Period	E	$\dot{P}^E$	$\dot{W}$	$\dot{P}$	w	Real wage gap for workers to make up[a]
−1	E_0	0	0	0	w_N	0
0	E_1	0	2	3	w_1	+2
1	E_1	3	6	6	w_1	+3
2	E_1	6	9	9	w_1	+3
3	E_1	9	12	12	w_1	+3
⋮	⋮	⋮	⋮	⋮	⋮	⋮

[a]The difference between the actual real wage at the given level of employment and the real wage at which that amount of labour will be supplied.

joining points A and B. (The construction of the short-run Phillips curves is explained in more detail in the box below.)

In the following period, period 1, expected inflation will have changed from zero to 3% (see Table 3.1). For workers to continue to supply labour at the level of E_1, money wages will have to rise by expected inflation of 3% plus 3% to take the real wage from the actual level in period zero of w_1 up to w^*. Hence money wages must rise by $\dot{W}_1 = 6\%$. If output is to remain at y^D, prices must also rise by 6% so as to maintain the real wage at its existing level of w_1 (see Table 3.1). For period 1, a second short-run Phillips curve is relevant. Each time the expected rate of inflation changes, the short-run Phillips curve shifts. Note in Figure 3.5 that each short-run Phillips curve is labelled by the expected rate of inflation. This is the reason the curves are know as *expectations-augmented Phillips curves*.

In period 2,

$$\dot{W}_2 = \dot{P}_2^E + \text{real wage gap for workers to make up}$$

$$= 6\% + 3\%$$

$$= 9\% = \dot{P}_2.$$

Period after period, as long as the government keeps demand at y^D, employment will remain above E_N but inflation will be higher each year.

Construction of Short-Run Expectations-Augmented Phillips Curves

To define a short-run Phillips curve it is necessary to specify the expected rate of inflation. We begin with expected inflation of zero:

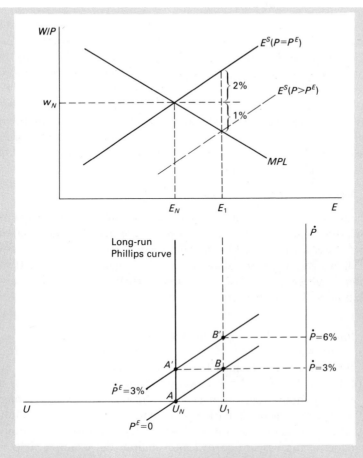

Fig. 3.6 The construction of short-run Phillips curves

$\dot{P}^E = 0$. With employment at the natural rate, E_N, the real wage is w_N and money wages and prices will remain unchanged. A is the first point on the expectations-augmented Phillips curve for $\dot{P}^E = 0$ in Fig. 3.6. To shift the economy to the higher employment level of E_1, money wages must rise by 2%, which with expected inflation of zero is sufficient to take the expected real wage for workers up to w^* and induce a supply of labour equal to E_1. But businesses will increase employment to E_1 only if the real wage has fallen by 1%. Therefore there is price inflation of 3%, the real wage falls by 1%, and firms hire labour equal to the amount E_1. Price inflation of 3% at unemployment U_1 defines point B on the short-run Phillips curve for expected inflation of zero. By joining up points A and B, the first short-run Phillips curve is constructed.

To derive a second short-run Phillips curve, assume expected inflation of 3%. The economy will remain at the natural rate of unemployment, U_N, if money wages and prices both rise by the expected rate of inflation, i.e. if $\dot{W} = \dot{P} = 3\%$. The real wage remains at w_N. This defines point A' on a second short-run Phillips curve. For a lower unemployment rate of U_1 to be achieved, the government must boost aggregate demand sufficiently to secure the supply and demand for labour equal to E_1. For the supply of labour to equal E_1, wage inflation will have to be 3% above expected inflation to take the expected real wage up from w_1 to w^*:

$$\dot{W} = \dot{P}^E + 3\% = 6\%.$$

For the demand for labour to equal E_1, price inflation will also have to be at 6% so as to reduce the real wage to w_1. The second point on the $\dot{P}^E = 3\%$ short-run Phillips curve will therefore be at $\dot{P} = 6\%$, U_1 shown by B' on the diagram. In the same way, the short-run Phillips curves associated with any particular expected rate of inflation can be constructed.

Friedman's point F3 is now clear. Only at $U = U_N$ will inflation remain constant. As we have seen, with lower unemployment of $U = U_1$, the inflation rate continues to rise. In an exactly analogous way, with higher unemployment than U_N, the inflation rate continues to fall. On the other hand, if the economy remains at $U = U_N$, then inflation will be constant, since the expectations of all market participants are consistent and fulfilled at this unemployment rate and real wage. Labour supply decisions are being made on the basis of correct information. For example, if $U = U_N$ and $\dot{P} = 6\%$, money wage inflation and price inflation will continue at a rate of 6%. The real wage will remain unchanged at $w = w_N$.

In summary, the expectations-augmented Phillips curve can be written as

$$\dot{P} = \dot{P}^E + \alpha(U_N - U).$$
[short-run (expectations-augmented) Phillips curve]

With adaptive expectations, we have $\dot{P}^E = \dot{P}_{-1}$, and therefore $\dot{P} = \dot{P}_{-1} + \alpha(U_N - U)$. Only when unemployment is equal to U_N is inflation equal to its expected rate, or in other words is constant; i.e., $\dot{P} = \dot{P}_{-1}$ only when $U = U_N$.

Friedman called the unique unemployment rate U_N, where inflation is constant, the natural rate of unemployment. He defined the natural rate of unemployment as the rate corresponding to labour-market-clearing, $E^D = E^S$, with expectations fulfilled. He used the term 'natural' because:

1   he wished to separate real forces from monetary ones;

2   he wished to emphasize that the NRU depended on technology as
    embodied in the marginal product of labour curve and on tastes,
    embodied in the labour supply curve;[5]
3   he wished to convey that the government had to accept the natural rate
    of unemployment or else face ever-increasing inflation.

In Friedman's model, there is no long-run trade-off between unemployment and inflation as was characteristic of the Keynesian/Phillips model.
In that model, there was a single Phillips curve indicating the ability of the
government to choose a lower rate of unemployment than was consistent
with labour market equilibrium at the cost of a higher *but constant* rate of
inflation. By contrast, in Friedman's model the trade-off is available only
in the short run and is illustrated by the short-run Phillips curves. As the
expected rate of inflation changes from period to period, the short-run
Phillips curves shift. The absence of a long-run trade-off in Friedman's
model is represented by the fact that the *long-run Phillips Curve* is vertical
at $U = U_N$. The long-run Phillips curve shows the set of points in the
inflation–unemployment quadrant that are consistent with stable inflation.
Another way of saying that the long-run Phillips curve is vertical is: 'if you
want stable inflation, then you must accept unemployment at the natural
rate.' The vertical long-run Phillips curve is shown in Figs. 3.5 and 3.6. In
Fig. 3.6, the long-run Phillips curve is derived by joining points A and A'
at which inflation is equal to expected inflation.

3.3.3   The Natural Rate of Unemployment and 'Full' Employment

At the natural rate of unemployment, employment is equal to the labour
supply at the current real wage (which equals the expected real wage). In
other words, there is no involuntary unemployment at U_N. Yet the
econometric estimates which sought to identify the rate of unemployment
at which inflation was constant suggested that the natural rate was higher
than had been considered a full employment level of unemployment.
Friedman met this objection by explaining that some part of the natural
level of unemployment will be made up of a revolving pool of people who
have chosen not to work in order to search for better jobs more efficiently.
Note that it is assumed in the model of *search unemployment* that, in order
to engage in search, it is necessary to give up one's current job. This
assumption implies that a central cost of search is the earnings forgone.
    The theory of search unemployment was developed by Phelps (1970).
He sought to provide an account of why, in a world in which there is no

---

[5] Although Friedman pointed out that 'legal minimum wage laws . . . and the strength of
labor unions all make the natural rate of unemployment higher than it would otherwise be'
(Friedman 1968: 9), this is inconsistent with his analysis which assumes that wages and prices
are determined in the market place. However, without reference to unions, Friedman's
analysis would have had much less resonance in the analysis of inflation in the late 1960s.

auction room co-ordination of supplies with demands,[6] there will always be
a pool of *voluntarily* unemployed individuals. Once the idea of an
auctioneer setting wages is abandoned, it must be presumed that the
individual firms set them, and the higher the wage a particular firm sets,
the faster it will attract labour. Given the resulting dispersion of wage
offers, workers will spend time looking, before accepting a job. In Phelps's
words, 'The expectation of a dispersion of wage rates by suppliers of labor
causes positive unemployment to be normal' (1970: 132).

Such *search unemployment* will be higher:

- the less good is information about vacancies—information will tend to
  be worse, the more variety there is in a technical sense among workers
  and jobs;
- the higher is the unemployment benefit–earnings ratio.

The unemployment benefit–earnings ratio is called the *replacement ratio*.
A higher replacement ratio lowers the cost of search activity and therefore
shifts the labour supply curve to the left. The reason the labour supply
curve shifts left is that fewer people than before are immediately prepared
to work at each real wage. Because of the increased attractiveness of
search, more have given up their jobs and entered the pool of searchers.
Hence the gap widens between the labour supply curve, which measures
those people immediately prepared to accept a job at each wage, and the

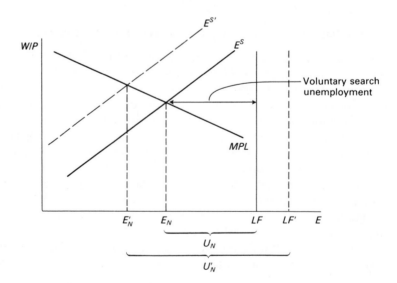

Fig. 3.7 The effect of a higher replacement ratio on the natural rate of
unemployment

[6] The neoclassical concept of the 'Walrasian auctioneer' is discussed in some detail in ch. 5.

labour force, the total number in the economy seeking work. A lower cost of search may also increase participation in the labour force, shifting LF to the right (to LF' in Fig. 3.7). This raises the natural rate of unemployment from U_N to U'_N.

The search model provides a variant on Friedman's account of workers' misperception when higher than expected inflation associated with a rise in aggregate demand pushes unemployment below the natural rate. The Phelps version stresses the heterogeneity of workers and jobs, and the costs of obtaining information. When demand rises, firms will seek additional workers and will offer higher wages. Workers perceive these as more attractive wages relative to those from competing firms, and the rate of job acceptances rises, pushing unemployment down. Once the *general* nature of the wage increases becomes clear to workers, some will be dissatisfied with their recent job acceptance and will quit and return to search for a better offer. The fall in unemployment is temporary and is sustained only by the illusion of an increase in the number of more attractive job offers.

3.4   Money in Friedman's Model

3.4.1   Long-Run Market-Clearing with Fulfilled Expectations

The labour market is cleared in the long run (with fulfilled expectations) in Friedman's model through changes in the real quantity of money. Figure 3.8 helps illustrate how this works. Let y_N be the level of output corresponding to U_N, the natural rate of unemployment. We can call y_N the natural rate of output. A vertical line is drawn in the IS/LM quadrant

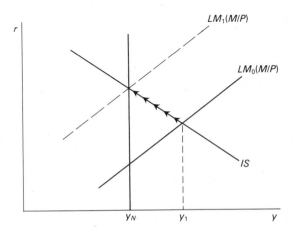

Fig. 3.8 Long-run market-clearing: the role of the real money supply

at the natural rate of output. Now suppose that the *IS* and *LM* curves intersect to the right of y_N. This implies that aggregate demand for output exceeds the natural rate of output. Recalling the analysis of Section 3.2, the maintenance of such a level of output and employment implies inflation in excess of that anticipated. Above y_N inflation will be increasing, and below y_N inflation will be falling. Suppose for example that the economy is at y_1 in Fig. 3.8. The *LM* curve depends on the real money supply. If the nominal money supply and inflation are initially constant at y_N, then at y_1 inflation will be rising. Hence M/P will be falling: real money balances are declining. This means that the *LM* is moving to the left, raising the interest rate and lowering output. Output falls because of the fall in investment. The *LM* will continue to shift leftward until LM_1 intersects y_N.[7]

Changes in the real money supply associated with increasing inflation when unemployment is below the natural rate ensure that eventually the economy is at $y = y_N$, $E = E_N$, and $U = U_N$. Of course, at higher unemployment than U_N the converse process is presumed to occur: falling inflation raises the real value of the money supply and, through the Keynes effect, lowers the interest rate and raises investment, ensuring a return to the natural rate.

What did Friedman mean by his dramatic statement that 'inflation is always and everywhere a monetary phenomenon'? He meant that in his model the government can maintain inflation only by suitably increasing the money supply. The mechanism for ensuring long-run market-clearing at the natural rate highlights the implicit assumption about monetary policy in the analysis of ever-increasing inflation in Section 3.2 above. For the economy to follow the path $B \rightarrow C \rightarrow D \rightarrow$ etc. in Fig. 3.5, the government must allow the money supply to grow in line with inflation. Otherwise, M/P will be falling and shifting employment and output back towards the natural rate.

3.4.2 Friedman's Version of the Quantity Theory of Money

In Friedman's reformulation of the classical model, the Quantity Theory results (and hence the neutrality of money) hold in the long run but not in the short run; i.e., an increase in the growth rate of the money supply will have a temporary real effect of raising output and employment; but eventually the economy will return to the original real position although with a higher rate of inflation. Conversely, a reduction in monetary growth would reduce employment and output in the short run, but eventually the economy would be back at the natural rate with lower inflation.

[7] This is exactly true only if the government adjusts the growth rate of the money supply to equal the rate of inflation arrived at at y_N. If the growth rate of the money supply is held constant, then the economy will in the first instance overshoot the natural rate, with output falling below y_N. Eventually the economy will come to rest at the natural rate, with inflation equal to the growth rate of the money supply.

To illustrate the processes at work, assume that the initial situation is one of equilibrium at the natural rate with the growth of the money supply equal to inflation (and expected inflation). Thus, $\dot{M} = \dot{P} = \dot{P}^E = 6\%$ and the economy is at point A in Fig. 3.9. To summarize,

$$y = y_N, \qquad E = E_N, \qquad \text{and } U = U_N;$$
$$\dot{M} = \dot{P} = \dot{P}^E = 6\%.$$

Now, suppose that the government introduces an expansionary monetary policy by permanently raising the growth rate of the money supply from 6% to 10%. The purpose may be to reduce unemployment.

Step 1   With $\dot{M}_1 = 10\%$ and inflation still at 6%, the real money supply will have risen and the LM shifts to the right to LM_1. Output rises to y_1 and unemployment falls to U_1 (see Fig. 3.9).

Step 2   Inflation rises above 6% and the economy is at a point such as B.

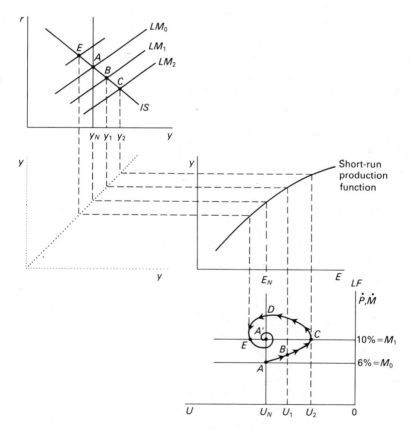

Fig. 3.9 The short-run and long-run effects of monetary policy

As long as inflation remains below 10%, the real money supply will continue rising and shifting the *LM* to the right. Unemployment will go on falling.

Step 3 This process continues until point *C* is reached. Once inflation equals the growth rate of the money supply (10%), the real money supply will cease rising.

Step 4 However, the story does not stop at *C*. Since unemployment is below U_N, inflation will continue to rise. With $\dot{P} > \dot{M}$, the real money supply begins to decline, shifting the *LM* back to the left. As the *LM* moves from LM_2 to LM_1 to LM_0, unemployment rises towards the natural rate. During this phase (from *C* to *D* in the Phillips curve diagram) *both* inflation and unemployment are rising: inflation is rising because unemployment is still below U_N; unemployment is rising because aggregate demand is falling, owing to the falling real money supply.

Step 5 Once the economy is at *D*, inflation will cease to rise since $U = U_N$. However, because inflation has risen above the growth rate of the money supply, the real money supply will continue to fall: the economy will overshoot U_N, suffering a period of unemployment *above* the natural rate (from *D* to *E*).

Eventually, the economy comes to rest at *A'*, with inflation equal to 10%, i.e. equal to the growth rate of the money supply. Unemployment and output are at the natural rate. In Friedman's model, expansionary monetary policy leads to a short-run decline in unemployment. In the long run, there is no improvement in output and unemployment and the economy is faced with a higher rate of inflation.

3.5 Fiscal Policy in Friedman's Model

3.5.1 100% Crowding-Out in the Long Run

In Friedman's model, fiscal policy can (like monetary policy) be used to raise output and employment in the short run, but not in the long run. (We will see below that Friedman thought there were also limitations to the efficacy of fiscal policy even in the short run). In the long run, an increase in government expenditure will simply crowd-out an equivalent amount of private spending.

In Fig. 3.10, the economy is initially at the natural rate at point *A*. The government adopts an expansionary fiscal policy which shifts the *IS* to the right from IS_0 to IS_1. At point *B*, inflation will rise faster than the fixed rate of growth of the money supply with the consequence that the real money supply will fall, moving the *LM* curve to the left until it reaches LM_1.

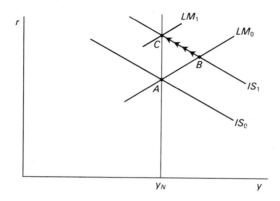

Fig. 3.10 Fiscal policy: 100% crowding-out in the long run

Ultimately, the economy will be at point C, i.e. with the same output level as at the outset. There will have been a period of higher output but this will be short-lived. Given a fixed monetary stance, the increase in government spending is financed by borrowing from the public. This has the effect of raising the supply of bonds, which depresses their price and puts up the interest rate. The higher interest rate dampens investment demand and leaves output at C with a higher component of government expenditure and lower private investment than was the case at A. Since output and consumption at A and C are identical, the increase in government spending must be exactly matched by a fall in investment brought about by the rise in the interest rate.[8]

3.5.2   Tax Changes and the Natural Rate

Friedman highlighted the role of changes in both direct and indirect tax rates in altering the natural rate of unemployment. The argument mirrors the microeconomic discussion of the effect of tax changes in the goods–leisure choice. Higher income tax will reduce hours of work for a given pre-tax wage (assuming that leisure is a normal good and that as before the substitution effect outweighs the income effect). In Fig. 3.11, the labour supply curve shifts left to E_S'. The natural rate of employment falls to E_N'. At the new natural rate, the real gross wage paid by employers (the real product wage, RPW) is shown by the intersection of the new labour supply curve and the labour demand curve. The real post-tax wage which is being received by workers (the real consumption wage, RCW) is shown by the original labour supply curve at E_N'. This is the real take-home

---

[8] If there is a real balance effect on consumption, then a rise in government spending crowds-out a mixture of investment and consumption.

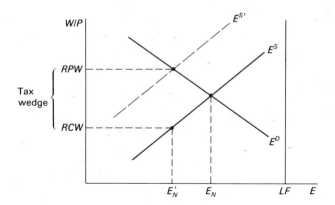

Fig. 3.11 Tax changes and the natural rate

wage required to elicit the supply of E'_N amount of labour. The difference between the two (RPW − RCW) is the real tax revenue per worker and is known as the *tax wedge*. The tax wedge between the real consumption wage and the real product wage is shown in Fig. 3.11.

A rise in indirect taxes will induce an identical response, with the natural rate of unemployment rising. The labour demand curve will shift downward since the value of the marginal product of labour is reduced by the imposition of the tax. The natural rate of unemployment rises as before to U'_N.

3.6 Macroeconomic Policy and the Permanent Income Hypothesis

3.6.1 Tax Policy

In Friedman's model, the use of tax policies to fine-tune the economy will be ineffective. President Johnson used a temporary tax surcharge in 1968 to fine-tune the economy in a downward direction, and it was indeed ineffective in reducing consumption expenditure. What was Friedman's explanation? In his view, the origin of the particularly weak effect of a temporary tax policy such as a surcharge lies with the way consumption decisions are made. Friedman argued that consumption expenditure depends not on actual income but on 'permanent' income: this was the Permanent Income Hypothesis (PIH). By permanent income, he meant the income the individual expected to earn on average over his lifetime. As noted earlier, the PIH highlights the role of wealth in the consumption function since the individual's decision problem was thought of in terms of allocating lifetime wealth over the annual stream of consumption. Using permanent rather than current income as the basis for their consumption decision was, in Friedman's view, the rational way for individuals to behave. It implied borrowing or saving as actual income fell below or exceeded permanent income.

The PIH implies that a cut (or increase) in taxes will have no effect on consumer spending *unless* it is thought to be permanent. The shifts in the labour supply curve and the change in the natural rate discussed above assume that the tax changes are viewed as permanent. A sharp contrast with the Johnson tax surcharge is provided by the Reagan tax cuts of 1982 which were widely publicized as permanent.

3.6.2 Monetary Policy

Friedman's analysis of consumption behaviour summarized in the permanent income hypothesis produced a consumption function with the real money supply as an argument. The real money supply entered via the real balance (Pigou or wealth) effect. In Friedman's view, a rise in real cash balances, by increasing wealth, would lead to the purchase of additional consumer goods. He also believed that higher M/P would lower the interest rate through the effect of additional purchases of bonds. This would raise investment (the standard Keynes effect) *and* raise consumption. The latter path was seen by Friedman to reflect rational consumer behaviour, whereby a lower interest rate would lead current consumption to be substituted for future consumption.

Thus, in the Friedmanite world, monetary policy is particularly potent in the short run since it operates on demand through three channels:

(1) increased $M/P \rightarrow$ lower $r \rightarrow$ increased i [Keynes effect]
(2) increased $M/P \rightarrow$ increased c [Pigou effect]
(3) increased $M/P \rightarrow$ lower $r \rightarrow$ increased c
                              [intertemporal substitution effect].

The belief that there were many substitutes for money—such as consumption goods—underlined Friedman's criticism of Keynes's liquidity trap. Friedman argued that investor nervousness about possible capital losses on long-term bonds would not lead to a portfolio switch from bonds to money. Rather, lower long-term bond holdings would result in higher consumption or the purchase of Treasury bills or short-term bonds. Friedman argued that in any realistic model there are more than two assets (money and long-term bonds), and that therefore the liquidity trap was simply a theoretical curiosity.

3.7 Conclusions

The first major challenge to the post-war paradigm model of macroeconomics took place at the end of the 1960s. The Keynesian–neoclassical synthesis with its Keynesian system of output and employment determination supplemented with the Keynesian/Phillips model of inflation proved to be inadequate as an empirical model. In the light of the heightened critical scrutiny, theoretical inconsistencies in the model were thrown into relief. Friedman sought to shift the mainstream of analysis back towards the classical tradition by creating a model rooted in neoclassical microeconomics which could encompass both the empirical successes and failures of the Keynesian–neoclassical synthesis. He identified informational problems as preventing labour-market-clearing at the unique natural rate of unemployment.

In Friedman's model, there is a long run where classical results hold and a short run where deviations from the natural rate can occur. This separation enabled Friedman to develop his central argument that, while governments were certainly able to choose a low rate of unemployment for the economy, the consequence would be *ever-increasing inflation* if the chosen rate lay below the natural rate of unemployment. Only with inflation rising and therefore at a higher level than that anticipated by households making their labour supply decision, is it possible to maintain employment above the natural rate of employment.

Friedman's argument was simple: households base their labour supply decision on the expected real wage, for which they have to rely on outdated price information. If the estimate of the current real wage is based on last period's rate of inflation, then rising inflation creates a misperception on the part of workers and leads to the supply of more labour than would have been chosen had the actual *ex post* real wage been known. Given the assumption of adaptive expectations, unemployment below the natural rate requires that this illusion be recreated each year and hence implies rising inflation.

By using the Permanent Income Hypothesis to incorporate the real-balance effect into the analysis, Friedman downplayed the potential for lasting Keynesian problems of unemployment above the natural rate. Any shortfall in demand, although causing a temporary decline in output, would not be magnified through lower consumption because the PIH much reduces the size of the multiplier. In principle, consumers are not rationed by lower employment because it is assumed that they can sustain their 'permanent' consumption level by borrowing or by running down their savings. Furthermore, falling inflation at unemployment above the natural rate will boost demand again through the three channels outlined in Section 3.6: the Keynes effect, the Pigou effect, and intertemporal substitution.

The policy implications of Friedman's model are clear. In the long run, the economy is at the natural rate of unemployment with the rate of inflation equal to the growth rate of the money supply. The Quantity Theory stands in the long run: a higher money supply leads to proportionately higher prices. In the long run, the real effect of higher government spending is fully offset by the crowding-out of an equivalent amount of private spending. Output is at the natural rate with the extra government spending simply displacing an equal amount of private spending. In the short run, deviations from the natural rate are possible. Short-run monetary policy is effective in raising output and employment but would be reflected in rising inflation. Even in the short run, attempts to use fiscal policy in the form of tax cuts to achieve lower unemployment are futile if they are viewed as temporary.

Friedman drew the conclusion from his analysis that the role of monetary policy was primarily to 'prevent money itself from being a major source of economic disturbance' (Friedman 1968: 12). Hence monetary policy should publicly adopt a steady growth rate of a monetary aggregate, and this, he argued, would make a major contribution to the avoidance of either inflation or disinflation of prices.

4

The New Classical Macroeconomics

Economic developments in the 1970s provided a major jolt to the confidence of working macroeconomists. The large industrialized economies began to suffer from 'stagflation'—the combination of rising unemployment, rising inflation, and slow growth. Having adjusted their intellectual and econometric apparatuses to incorporate the expectations-augmented Phillips curve, the occurrence of the first oil shock in 1973 forced attention once again on to the supply side. As noted in Chapters 2 and 3, the elaboration of the post-war consensus model (the Keynesian–neoclassical synthesis) had paid scant attention to supply-side features. The absence of an adequate supply side to the model was reflected in the confusion that surrounded the question of the appropriate policy response to the oil crisis. The basic policy instinct of those imbued with the 1950s and 1960s paradigm was that governments should intervene to help stabilize the real economy. This clashed with the Friedmanite diagnosis that attempts to maintain employment in the face of a rise in the natural rate of unemployment would simply exacerbate the problem of rising inflation.

The apparent incompleteness of the paradigm model and the new emphasis on the supply side helped to create fertile ground for the radical reassessment of macroeconomics which emerged in the mid-1970s. The origins of the *New Classical Macroeconomics* lay in dissatisfaction with the failure of the orthodoxy to incorporate fully the rational optimizing behaviour of individual economic agents. The paradigm-breakers sought to create a new macroeconomics based on the comprehensive adoption of market-clearing microeconomics. In so doing, they produced macroeconomic results that echoed those of the pre-Keynesian tradition of the classical model.

The second characteristic feature of the new model took as its point of departure dissatisfaction with Friedman's account of the reasons for short-run deviations of the economy from its natural rate. The new classicals sought to create a model in which classical results hold continuously (except for random disturbances). The uncompromising emphasis on the rational behaviour of optimizing agents meant that

Friedman's use of *adaptive expectations* to explain the persistence of informational errors by workers in their labour supply decisions was unacceptable. The proponents of the new model highlighted the fact that only by assuming that agents make systematic mistakes about expected prices can a short-run trade-off between inflation and unemployment be created. Systematic errors were seen as inconsistent with rational behaviour. The new classicals therefore replaced adaptive expectations with the radical hypothesis of *rational expectations*. Under rational expections, there are no systematic errors in making price forecasts.

The policy implications of the New Classical model are clear and unequivocal. There is no role for the government in securing the operation of the economy at the natural rate, since, apart from random disturbances, the economy is continuously in equilibrium at the unique natural rate. Furthermore, any systematic attempt by the government to reduce unemployment below the natural rate will be totally unsuccessful. The combination of rational expectations with a thoroughgoing market-clearing micro substructure means that agents know (or at least behave as if they know) that there is a single real equilibrium in the economy. In response to an announced expansion of demand by the government, they will simply adjust prices and wages upward immediately, leaving the economy at the natural rate of unemployment with a higher price level.

The New Classical Macroeconomics (NCM) makes the following assumptions:

1 All economic agents are rational optimizers who base their decisions only on real factors.
2 Markets clear more or less continuously. If they did not clear, then there would always be profitable transactions which were not being carried out. For example, the unemployed could raise their utility by undercutting the wage that employers were currently paying.
3 Prices are correctly anticipated because of *rational expectations*, and hence there are no systematic errors in making price forecasts. Thus, apart from random disturbances, there are no transactions taking place at the wrong prices.

From these assumptions, the NCM model derives the three standard classical results. What makes the model new as well as classical is that the results hold continuously (Hoover 1988: 14).

N1 Output and employment are determined in the labour market. There is a unique natural rate of unemployment.
N2 Anticipated changes in the growth of the money supply lead directly to inflation; they have no real effects.
N3 There is 100% crowding-out of fiscal policy.

We will examine how the twin foundations of rapidly clearing markets and rational expectations combine to provide such powerful results in the sections below.[1] It must be emphasized here that the Rational Expectations Hypothesis (REH) can be separated from the other pillar of the NCM. Combined with different (non-classical) microeconomic foundations, the REH produces non-classical results.[2]

4.1 Rational Expectations and the New Classical Propositions: an Introduction

A crude definition of the New Classical model is Friedman's model plus rational expectations. It was Friedman's assumption of adaptive expectations that permitted inflation to deviate from expected inflation and hence allowed the labour supply curve to shift, producing cleared markets away from the natural rate. The introduction of the Rational Expectations Hypothesis was essential to restore the full-blown classical macroeconomic outcomes. As applied in the NCM, the REH requires us to assume that:

1 everyone knows the structural equations characterizing the economy;
2 everyone believes that all markets are cleared; and
3 everyone knows that everyone knows assumptions 1 and 2. This is the so-called *common knowledge* assumption.

Given these assumptions, there is a unique level of employment that clears the labour market, and hence there is a unique natural rate of unemployment. Via the short-run production function, this level of employment implies a unique output level (given the capital stock). This establishes the result N1 above. For aggregate demand to be equal to the labour-market-determined natural output level, the real money supply must be fixed (given government expenditure and tax rates). Accordingly, any increase in the nominal money supply will be immediately reflected in the corresponding increase in prices to keep the real money supply constant (result N2 above). Finally, there is 100% crowding-out of private expenditure by government spending because the output level is fixed at the level corresponding to the natural level of employment (result N3 above).

Under rational expectations, forecasting next period's price level (or inflation rate) is straightforward as long as assumptions 1–3 above hold. The price level expected to obtain next period is simply next period's expected money supply divided by the unique real value of the money supply, $\bar{m}$, required to ensure that demand is equal to the natural rate of output:

[1] For a more detailed examination of the origins, methods, and results of the New Classical Macroeconomics, readers are referred to Hoover (1988). The book is accessible yet rigorous, conveying the detail of the New Classical arguments, their power, and their shortcomings without unnecessary mathematics.

[2] Begg (1982) explains this point clearly and at length.

$$P^E_{t+1} = M^E_{t+1}/\bar{m},$$

where M^E_{t+1} is the expected value of the money supply in period $t + 1$ and $\bar{m}$ is the value of M/P necessary to ensure that real aggregate demand is equal to the natural level of output.

The value of the money wage, W^E_{t+1}, that will clear the labour market can be forecast in a similar way:

$$W^E_{t+1} = \bar{w} \, P^E_{t+1},$$

where $\bar{w}$ is the market-clearing real wage.

These are the 'rational' expectations of the money wage and the price level; they are rational because they assume that everyone is making the fullest use of all available information. They take such a simple form because of the New Classical assumption of market-clearing with complete information, which fixes $\bar{m}$ and $\bar{w}$ uniquely.

In turn, to assume that markets clear is, according to the New Classical model, a consequence of rational behaviour. The link between rationality and market-clearing drawn by the new classicals is based on the observation that if markets are not cleared then there are profitable transactions available that are not being exploited. Given the first NCM assumption—that all agents know the structural equations of the economy—the persistence of unexploited profitable opportunities is irrational.[3]

Given the formation of price and wage expectations as outlined above, an *anticipated* increase in monetary growth (i.e. a policy change of which agents are aware) will lead simply to a jump in the rate of price and wage inflation to keep the real money supply and real wage constant. The *LM* curve remains fixed, the real wage remains at $\bar{w}$, and unemployment remains at the natural rate (Fig. 4.1). Since $\dot{P} = \dot{P}^E$, the labour supply curve remains fixed. The only changes observed would be higher inflation (wage and price) and a higher nominal interest rate, since the nominal interest rate is equal to the real interest rate plus expected inflation:

$$r_N = r_R + \dot{P}^E.$$

Note that in the Phillips curve diagram—the bottom panel of Fig. 4.1—the short-run Phillips curves are irrelevant. There is no trade-off even in the short run between inflation and unemployment. The economy jumps directly from A to C on the announcement of the rise in money supply growth.

[3] However, the logical connection between unexploited profitable opportunities and uncleared markets disappears once imperfect competition is introduced. As we will discuss in more detail in pts. II and IV, with imperfect competition in product and labour markets, the economy will generally be off the labour supply and marginal product of labour curves, with no incentive for further transactions to occur. In other words, the market-clearing assumption could be a logical deduction by agents only in an economy that is and is known to be perfectly competitive.

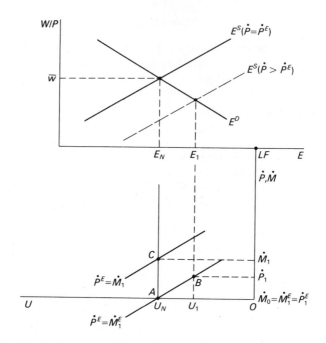

Fig. 4.1 Anticipated and unanticipated monetary expansion in the New Classical model

If there are many different product and labour markets with prices P_{1t}, P_{2t}, P_{3t}, ..., P_{nt}, and money wages W_{1t}, W_{2t}, ..., W_{mt}, then as long as individuals have no reason to believe that the separate market demand and supply schedules have shifted relative to one another because, for example, of changes in preferences or technology, they will assume constant relative prices and therefore will assume that

$\dot{P}_{it} = \dot{M}_t^E$ for all product markets i, from 1 to n;

$\dot{W}_{jt} = \dot{M}_t^E$ for all labour markets j, from 1 to m.

In other words, all prices and money wages will be expected to grow at the expected growth rate of the money supply.

If the assumed monetary growth rate, $\dot{M}^E$, is correct, then the real wage is correctly anticipated and employment is at the natural (market-clearing) level:

$$E^S = E^D = E_N;$$

unemployment is at the natural rate. Inflation is equal to the growth rate of the money supply because all markets are instantaneously cleared.

Let us examine the effect of an *unanticipated* monetary expansion. In this case, a rise in the rate of monetary growth from $\dot{M}_0$ to $\dot{M}_1$ occurs without the knowledge of private economic agents. In each *individual* product market, prices rise faster than the rate at which producers believe that general prices are going to rise. Producers interpret the rise in the price of their own commodity as an increase in its relative demand; hence they increase supply. This leads to a general rise in wages as the overall demand for labour rises: the response is an increase in labour supply. Thus the additional nominal demand pushes prices up faster than expected, with the result that the labour supply curve shifts to the right (top panel of Fig. 4.1). As shown in the Phillips quadrant, inflation in excess of its expected level leads to a movement of the economy up the expectations-augmented Phillips curve (fixed by the *expected* growth rate of the money supply, $\dot{M}_1^E$) from A to B. A rise in output above the natural rate and fall in unemployment below the natural rate has occurred. However, as soon as agents realize that monetary growth has risen to $\dot{M}_1$, inflationary expectations will be adjusted immediately and the economy will move to point C. This example highlights the impossibility of the government *systematically* attempting to achieve a lower than 'natural' rate of unemployment. If agents expect the government to attempt to achieve lower unemployment, then they will immediately adjust their inflation expectations, offsetting the real effects of the policy before they have occurred.

The stark conclusion of the NCM is the result called *policy neutrality* or *policy invariance*: systematic government policy cannot alter the level of output or employment. Sargent and Wallace, leading proponents of the New Classical model, state:

In this system [NCM], there is no sense in which the authority has the option to conduct countercyclical policy. To exploit the Phillips Curves it must somehow trick the public. But by virtue of the assumption that expectations are rational, there is no feedback rule that the authority can employ and expect to be able systematically to fool the public. This means that the authority cannot expect to exploit the Phillips Curve equation even for one period. Thus combining the natural rate hypothesis with the assumption that expectations are rational transforms the former from a curiosity with perhaps remote policy implications into an hypothesis with immediate and drastic implications about the feasibility of pursuing countercyclical policy. (Sargent and Wallace 1976: 177–8)

Although policies to alter the level of output and employment are ruled out by the NCM, the authorities are able to effect nominal changes, such as reducing the rate of inflation. Suppose that the economy is at the natural rate and a reduction in inflation from 10% to 5% is desired. All that is necessary in a New Classical world is for the government to announce that it is reducing the rate of monetary growth from 10% to 5%. However, if the authorities are *mistaken* in believing that expectations are rational, *or* if their stated intention of holding to a lower monetary growth rate is not believed in the private sector, then the consequences are serious. A sudden announced tightening of monetary policy (reduction of the growth rate of the money supply) will, in the absence of rational expectations or of the credibility of the policy, lead to a fall in output as the real money supply declines. The policy announcement has no effect on inflation expectations and they are therefore not revised. This means that inflation is less than expected and the labour supply curve shifts to the left (Fig. 4.2). By pushing unemployment above the natural rate, inflation will decline—the economy will move from A to B in Fig. 4.2. However, while the rate of inflation continues to exceed the growth rate of the money supply, output and employment will continue to fall. Eventually, unemployment will have risen sufficiently to have reduced inflation to the growth rate of the money supply. The economy will begin to move back to higher employment. (Refer back to Section 3.4 for the step-by-step adjustment process under adaptive expectations.) In the end, the economy will find its way back to the natural rate with expected inflation equal to the new lower growth rate of the money supply and will be characterized by lower inflation (point Z in Fig. 4.2).

Instead of the swift costless drop in inflation as the consequence of

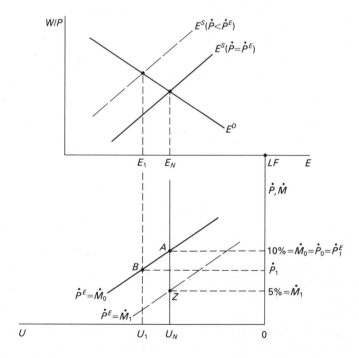

Fig. 4.2 Unemployment above the natural rate as the result of a lack of credibility of announced reduction in money supply growth

publicly adopting lower monetary growth (i.e. the instantaneous move from A to Z in Fig. 4.2), which was envisaged on the mistaken assumption of rational expectations and credibility, there is a lengthy period of unemployment in excess of the natural rate.

4.2   Tools of the New Classical Macroeconomics

4.2.1   The Rational Expectations Hypothesis

The Rational Expectations Hypothesis has a number of attractive features which are highlighted by a comparison between it and adaptive expectations. In Chapter 3 (Friedman's model), it was assumed that the expectations held by workers about how prices will develop over the year ahead were formed entirely on the basis of past experience of inflation (adaptive expectations). Indeed, we used a particularly simple example of adaptive expectations, where inflation this year is expected to be exactly what it turned out to be last year. In other words, there is complete adaptation to what happened in the previous year. More generally, the Adaptive Expectations Hypothesis states that expected inflation this period is equal to last period's expected rate of inflation plus a correction term to take account of the amount by which last period's forecast was proved wrong by the actual path of inflation:

$$\dot{P}^E_t = \underset{\substack{\text{previous}\\\text{forecast}}}{\dot{P}^E_{t-1}} + \underset{\substack{\text{correction}\\\text{term}}}{\Gamma(\dot{P}_{t-1} - \dot{P}^E_{t-1})}, \qquad 0 < \Gamma \le 1.$$

The closer is the correction coefficient, Γ, to zero, the less account is taken of the error that occurred in last period's forecasting exercise. With a coefficient Γ equal to one, the full extent of the forecast error is taken into account:

$$\dot{P}^E_t = \dot{P}^E_{t-1} + \Gamma(\dot{P}_{t-1} - \dot{P}^E_{t-1})$$
$$= \dot{P}^E_{t-1} + 1(\dot{P}_{t-1} - \dot{P}^E_{t-1})$$
$$= \dot{P}_{t-1}.$$

Although under the Adaptive Expectations Hypothesis agents are responding to their mistakes, they are doing so in an entirely mechanical and 'unintelligent' way. It may have struck readers as odd in the example of Friedman's inflationary process (Table 3.1, Fig. 3.9) that in each period, when workers expect that the money wage rise they accept will provide them with the real wage w^* at which they will supply a level of employment above the natural rate, they are disappointed. Yet in spite of repeated disappointment, they persevere with the same procedure for forming their expectations of inflation, and repeat the mistake each period. It may be presumed that eventually workers will attempt to develop an improved rule for forming their inflationary expectations. Perhaps they will get the idea that every time demand in the economy rises because of an increase in monetary growth (signalled by the appearance of an increase in new jobs available), although money wages go up faster than before, prices also rise faster, cancelling out any apparent real wage gain. In other words, they will formulate a new rule for calculating expected inflation, for example that expected inflation depends on expected monetary growth.

Of course, in making macroeconomic forecasts of inflation from macroeconometric models, economists do not proceed by applying an adaptive expectations rule. Rather, they plug into their model of the economy values for the initial conditions and for exogenous variables such as government policy instruments. One of the *outputs* from the model is the predicted rate of inflation. The idea of rational expectations is that all agents proceed at least implicitly in a similar way: they make the best use they can of all the available information about the structure of the economy and the policy measures of the government in order to form their expectations of inflation. Thus, rational expectations avoids two of the chief objections to the Adaptive Expectations Hypothesis: (1) the irrationality of making systematic errors, and (2) the complete reliance on partial information (i.e. only past information) as the basis for making forecasts.

Whereas adaptive expectations makes use of very partial information by private sector agents, rational expectations goes to the opposite extreme of assuming that all available information is used efficiently. The idea of rational expectations was spelled out by Muth in 1961: 'Expectations tend to be distributed for the same information set about the prediction of the theory' (1961: 316–17). This means that the agent's subjective forecast of the variable in question, say, the price level P^E, is equal to the 'objective' mathematical expectation of P conditional on the available information. The information set is assumed to include the structure of the economic model, the values of the exogenous variables (e.g. government policy settings), and the past values of the endogenous variables. The theory states:

$$P_t^E = E(P_t \mid \Omega_{t-1}),$$

where P_t^E is the value of P that the agents expect to prevail in period t, and $E(P_t \mid \Omega_{t-1})$ is the mathematical expectation of P conditional on the information available at the time the forecast was made, i.e. Ω_{t-1}. Another way of stating this application of rational expectations is that the subjective expectation of P, P_t^E, differs from the outturn, P_t, by only a random error ε_t, which has a mean of zero:

$$P_t^E = P_t + \varepsilon_t.$$

The error is random, which means that it is not correlated with the information set available at time $t - 1$ when the forecast was made.

A crucial plank of the REH is that the information set Ω_{t-1} is available to all agents in the economy. Private-sector agents and the government are presumed to have access to the *same* information.

4.2.2 The Phillips Curve and the Lucas Supply Equation

According to the New Classical model, if monetary growth is correctly forecast, unemployment will always be at the natural rate. More generally, real variables change only if there are changes in underlying parameters (e.g. a population change which shifts the labour supply schedule). The theory appears not to have room for the fluctuations in unemployment and other real variables (e.g. output) that are observed. How can the NCM explain the observation of an inverse relationship between unemployment and inflation (i.e. the Phillips curve)? One answer provided by the New Classical economist Lucas is that the observed relationship arises from confusion by economic agents between changes in the general price level, i.e. inflation, and changes in relative prices (Lucas 1972). Whereas changes in relative prices signal a *real* change in the economy (e.g. reflecting changing tastes) and call forth output and employment adjustments as between industries, inflation is a purely nominal phenomenon to which agents make no real response.

An example illustrates how the confusion between inflation and relative price changes can create real changes. Suppose that a money supply increase of 7% is expected. All agents therefore expect prices to rise by 7%. However, they observe prices in individual markets rising by more than 7%. How are they to respond? How are they to interpret the unexpected price rises? Individual agents seeing prices in their particular market(s) rising by more than the expected increase will assume that

- either they have made a mistake in expecting monetary growth of 7%, i.e. $\dot{M}^E = 7\%$ was wrong;
- or demand in *their* market has risen (e.g. owing to a change in tastes), causing an increase in *relative* prices;
- or both.

If the second or third alternative holds, then firms will raise their output.

Lucas argues that the extent to which output and employment increase in response to an unanticipated rise in inflation depends on the variability of inflation in the past. If inflation has been highly variable in the past, then firms will interpret the unexpected rise in prices as a general rise in inflation. They will therefore make little if any adjustment to output and employment. On the other hand, if inflation has been pretty constant, the unexpected rise in prices will be interpreted as a *relative* price effect, and output and employment will be raised.

The relationship between the interpretation of unexpected changes in inflation and the past experience of inflation generates predictions consistent with the observations that are labelled short-run Phillips curves. Of course, the government cannot exploit this relationship because it rests on the inability of private-sector agents to disentangle absolute from relative price changes. Higher price rises associated with any systematic attempt to raise activity by increasing the money supply would be identified immediately as a rise in inflation, not a relative price effect. There would be no response from the economy in terms of output and employment.[4]

This analysis has been formalized in Lucas's famous *surprise supply equation*:

$$U = U_N - \tau(1 - \theta)(\dot{P} - \dot{P}^E) + \varepsilon,$$

where τ is the supply response to a change in relative prices, θ is the variability of inflation, and ε is a random error with a zero mean. As θ, the variability of inflation, increases towards one, the short-run Phillips curve becomes vertical. This reflects the argument above that higher variability of inflation means that an observed deviation of inflation from its expected level will be interpreted as a purely nominal phenomenon. If $\theta = 0$, i.e. if inflation has been constant in the past, then a discrepancy between inflation and expected inflation will be interpreted as a relative price effect and unemployment will deviate from its natural rate.

The Lucas supply equation says that, with fully anticipated inflation, unemployment will be at the natural rate except for a random error. The equation can equally well be written in terms of output:

$$y = y_N + \tau(1 - \theta)(\dot{P} - \dot{P}^E) + \varepsilon.$$

Only a surprise in inflation will produce a deviation of output from the natural level, y_N. Thus it is only if actual monetary growth differs from expected that output and employment can deviate from the unique supply-determined natural rate. The crucial point of the NCM is that, although rational agents care only about real values, i.e. relative prices, they exist in an environment in which it is hard to distinguish relative from general price movements. The rationality of the agents means that only the unanticipated or 'surprise' components of aggregate demand variables affect output and employment. This is the result introduced earlier as policy invariance or policy neutrality.

---

[4] For a clear, more formal discussion of this so-called 'signal extraction' problem, see Hoover (1988: 31–5).

4.3   How Do We Assess the Rational Expectations Hypothesis?

The general principle of rational expectations is of the highest importance in economics, indeed in the analysis of any decision-making situation. It states that agents will use all the relevant information at their disposal in making decisions rationally, and, in so doing, will assume that everyone else is doing the same. Agents assume that there is so-called 'common knowledge' that everyone uses rational expectations. Game theory is based on these assumptions.

There are, moreover, many situations where such an analysis is appropriate. For instance, we all share the belief that drivers drive on the left-hand side of the road in the UK and on the right-hand side on the Continent. Given that such beliefs are common knowledge, it pays us to behave in the same way ourselves, so that the beliefs are rational. It is an example of rational expectations behaviour.

On the other hand, it is less plausible to suppose that the economy as a whole behaves in such a way. First, there is no agreement, even among economists, on the correct model of a macroeconomy. We all know the consequences for accidents of drivers not driving on the accepted side of the road. But most people have no conception of how, in terms of a model, inflation is affected by an increase in the money supply. Secondly, even if there is a true model of the economy, rational expectations gives no account of how most people are going to learn about it, let alone how strong proponents of alternative models are going to learn the truth.

Thus the Rational Expectations Hypothesis is something of a tease for economists, when applied to the macroeconomy. Reliance on adaptive expectations (or other simple rules for forming expectations) will always be unsatisfactory; but in the foreseeable future it is difficult to see what it can be replaced with. Economists need to be sensitive to the inadequacies of adaptive expectations, but responsible enough not to yield to the temptations of advising governments on the basis of a distorted view of reality, as some of the rational expectations theorists have done.

5

The Keynesian Counter-Attack: Fixed-Price Models

While the experience of rapid inflation in the 1970s provided a real-world impetus for New Classical attempts to create a new paradigm model of macroeconomics, the emergence and persistence of levels of unemployment way above those typical of the 1950s and 1960s reinvigorated the Keynesians. The beginnings of the reassessment of Keynes's theory of employment are to be found in the mid-1960s with the work of Clower (1965) and Leijonhufvud (1967, 1968). They sought to provide a more rigorous microeconomic foundation for Keynes's claim that the economy can remain for long periods of time away from full market-clearing equilibrium. This led to the development of the idea of so-called *non-Walrasian equilibria* and was based on a rejection of the use of standard neoclassical market-clearing (Walrasian) microeconomics as the microfoundation for macroeconomics. The clash between the approach of the reinterpreters of Keynes and that of the new classicals is evident.

In the 1970s the non-Walrasian reinterpretation of Keynes was taken further by the work of Malinvaud (1977), whose objective was to analyse different types of unemployment. He took the opposite microeconomic benchmark from the new classicals; instead of assuming rapidly clearing markets, he assumed that money wages and prices are fixed. He relied on the theoretical developments made by the reinterpreters of Keynes to provide coherent arguments for the existence of temporary equilibria away from full market-clearing. Malinvaud's central question was to look at the characteristics of such temporary equilibria and in particular to identify the circumstances under which a rise in real wages would raise or lower unemployment. He defined a situation in which higher real wages would raise unemployment as *classical unemployment*, and a situation in which higher real wages would reduce unemployment, as *Keynesian unemployment*.

5.1 The Background to the Reinterpretation of Keynes's Theory of Employment: Walras's Law

The stimulus for the attempt to construct coherent microeconomic foundations for Keynes's theory was an attack coming from the neoclassical general equilibrium school. This line of attack was less *ad hoc* and more fundamental than the real-balance effect discussed in Chapter 2. It sought to provide a general proof of the impossibility of persistent involuntary unemployment in an economy with perfectly competitive markets by accounting simultaneously for the state of all markets. The argument can be seen most clearly using a simple world in which there are only two markets—for goods and for labour.[1] For each individual household, the amount of consumption goods it demands depends on the value of the labour it plans to *supply*. We will work in nominal terms:

$$Pc^D = WE^S; \tag{5.1}$$

Value of planned consumption = Value of planned sales of labour.

For each firm, the value of its planned sales must equal the value of its planned purchases, i.e. of investment goods and of labour. In nominal terms,

$$Py^S = Pi^D + WE^D; \tag{5.2}$$

Value of planned sales = Value of planned purchases of
(investment goods + labour).

We can express these statements in the form of a principle:

P1 For each agent in the economy, intended purchases are equal to intended sales. Hence no agent in the economy can spend more than they expect to earn through their sales respectively of labour and goods.

Walras's Law is based on this principle and on a second one:

P2 Each agent can buy or sell as much as they wish (of labour and goods) at the going market prices.

On the basis of the two principles, Walras's Law states that, if one market is in excess supply (e.g. the labour market), then this will be balanced by excess demand in the other market (goods). If we subtract (5.2) from (5.1) and rearrange, we get

$$P(c^D + i^D - y^S) = W(E^S - E^D) \tag{5.3}$$

Value of excess demand = Value of excess supply
for goods   of labour.

[1] We have deliberately taken the simplest case, omitting problems caused by explicit analysis of profits and asset-holding to make the argument clear.

Now, prices are assumed to rise in the face of excess demand in the goods
market, and money wages to rise in the face of excess demand in the labour
market:

$$\dot{P} = \mu_G(c^D + i^D - y^S)$$
[excess demand in goods market]

$$\dot{W} = \mu_L(E^D - E^S)$$
[excess demand in labour market]

where μ_G and μ_L are positive constants.

Thus from (5.3), where excess demand in the goods market must be
equal to excess supply in the labour market, we can see that if prices are
rising in the goods market then money wages are falling in the labour
market (and vice versa). (In other words, sign $\dot{P}$ = −sign $\dot{W}$, where sign $\dot{x}$
denotes the sign of the variable $\dot{x}$.)

From Walras's Law, any excess supply in the labour market is matched
by excess demand in the goods market and this implies rising prices and
falling money wages. Why should this be so, and why is it important?

The reason why excess supply in the labour market has a counterpart in
the form of excess demand in the goods market is that excess supply in the
labour market implies that output is below the equilibrium level. Hence
there is too little output relative to the demand for goods based on the
desired supply of labour. Therefore there is excess demand for goods. The
converse situation of excess demand in the labour market would mean that
output was *above* the equilibrium level, thereby creating excess supply in
the goods market. Under Walras's Law, excess demand in one market is
matched by excess supply in another: the sum of excess demands is zero.
The significance of this result is that, as we will see below, the existence of
disequilibria of this kind produces price and wage movements that will
have the effect of clearing both markets.

But what is the macroeconomic content of Walras's Law? If money
wages respond to excess supply in the labour market by falling and to
excess demand by rising, and if, likewise, excess supply in the product
market produces falling prices and excess demand, rising prices, then we
can see the implications of a situation where there is both excess supply of
labour and excess demand for goods. Money wages will be falling and
prices rising: the combination implies a falling real wage.

Figure 5.1 illustrates the neoclassical application of Walras's Law. The
upper panel of the diagram shows the short-run production function
described in Fig. 1.1. The household indifference curves and the budget
constraint are shown. As always, the slope of the budget constraint is the
real wage. However, both the indifference curves and the budget
constraint are drawn relative to the vertical intercept i^D, rather than
relative to the origin (as was the case with Fig. 1.2). The reason for this is

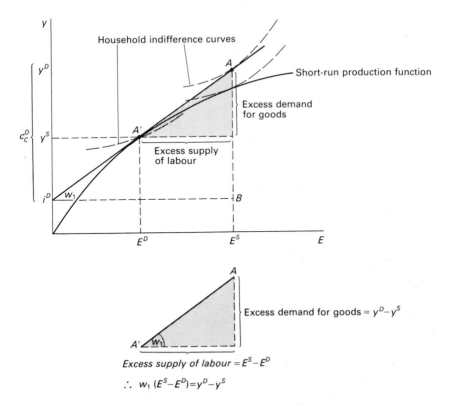

Fig. 5.1 Walras's Law applied to the macroeconomy

that, with the simple consumption function

$$c^D = wE^S,$$

aggregate demand will equal the sum of the constant amount of investment, i^D, and consumption demand, wE^S, which is the vertical distance AB in the upper panel of the figure. Under the principles on which Walras's Law is based, households make their consumption decisions on the basis of the *desired* level of employment E^S. Point A is therefore fixed by the tangency of the household indifference curve to the budget constraint with no reference to the *actual* level of employment. Thus, with the wage w_1, aggregate demand is equal to y^D.

Turning from the aggregate demand for output to aggregate supply requires us to find where the real wage, w_1, is equal to the marginal product of labour. This fixes point A' and aggregate supply is equal to y^S. Clearly, with the real wage equal to w_1, $y^D > y^S$: there is excess demand for goods.

In the labour market, labour supply is determined by the same utility-maximizing decision that fixed the amount of consumption demand—i.e. by the tangency of the budget constraint and the household indifference curve (point A). Labour supply is E^S. The demand for labour by firms is the other side of their output decision: labour demand is fixed at point A' and is E^D. Since the real wage lies above the level of the marginal product of labour at E^S, the demand for labour falls short of the supply: there is excess supply of labour.

As the lower panel of Fig. 5.1 makes clear, the excess demand in the goods market exactly matches the real value of the excess supply in the labour market. This produces the combination of a falling money wage and a rising price level. The falling real wage returns the economy to equilibrium at full employment.

The failure of a private economy to generate the fall in real wages required to restore equilibrium at full employment was the centrepiece of Keynes's analysis. If Walras's Law holds, then the proof that real wages fall when there is excess supply of labour would be a body blow to Keynes, since for him falling real wages was a sufficient as well as a necessary condition for ensuring full employment. Keynes's argument was that real wages cannot be reduced to the full employment level because the persistence of *inadequate* demand for goods means that prices are *falling*. The neoclassical argument based on Walras's Law contradicts this by its claim that an excess supply of labour (unemployment) is accompanied by an excess demand for goods (rising prices) because consumption demand arises from planned labour supply (at full employment) and not from the lower level of actual employment.

While the Pigou (real balance) effect gave the classics one line of attack against Keynes's *General Theory*, the application of Walras's Law appeared to provide a more theoretically satisfying one. The reformulation in terms of Walras's Law began with rigorous microeconomic foundations of utility and profit maximization under competitive conditions. It sought to show that on the basis of optimizing behaviour any temporary misalignment of relative prices—say, a real wage that was too high to produce full employment—would disappear because money wages would fall in response to the excess supply of labour and goods prices would rise in response to the accompanying excess supply of goods. The assumption that the demand for consumption goods was based on desired supplies of labour meant that Keynes's problem of the multiplier contraction of demand, and with it the danger that prices would *fall* and prevent the real wage from declining, was eliminated.

Thus, while the simple classical response to Keynes was directed towards showing the *beneficial* effects of *falling* prices (the Pigou effect), the more fundamental, sophisticated neoclassical argument rests on the presumption that prices *rise* when there is unemployment.

5.2 Keynes's Model as the General Case: Clower's Dual-Decision Hypothesis

The problem for Keynes's model posed by Walras's Law provided the starting point for a fruitful reformulation of the Keynesian insight. Clower stated the issue bluntly: 'either Walras law is incompatible with Keynesian economics, or Keynes had nothing fundamentally new to add to orthodox economic theory' (Clower 1965: 110). He settled on the former position, arguing that the rejection of Walras's Law is central to Keynes's model and that 'standard Keynesian macroeconomics' as it had developed in the 1950s and 1960s failed to recognize this.

Before looking at Clower's general argument, it is helpful to give a direct comparison between the neoclassical and Keynesian interpretations of a less than full employment situation as suggested by Clower. Clower's point is that Walras's Law does not explode Keynes's model because Keynes implicitly argued that Walras's Law was invalid. It does not hold because demand and supply functions, in Keynes's view, depended on *actual* transactions rather than *desired* ones. For example, consumption demand was a function of actual income and employment, not of desired employment. In other words, for Keynes, excess supply of labour is not associated with excess demand for goods; in his eyes, it was precisely the failure of individuals to secure employment that constrained or rationed their consumption demand.

We can use the diagram presented in Fig. 5.1 to highlight the difference between a world where Walras's Law holds and one where it does not. The diagram is reproduced in Fig. 5.2. In Keynes's interpretation (denoted by

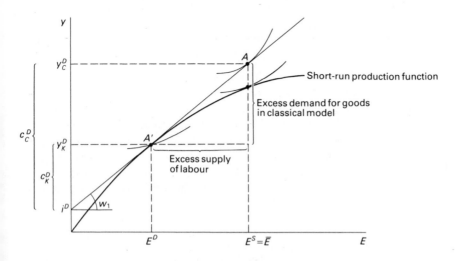

Fig. 5.2 Walras's Law: Keynes versus the classics

the subscript, K), there is excess supply of labour (the amount $E^S - E^D$), and aggregate demand is equal to output at y^S since $y^S = y^D = c_K^D + i^D$, where c_K^D is consumption demand: $c_K^D = w_1 E^D$. The fundamental point is that, since households can get employment only if firms demand it, their income will be equal to $w_1 E^D$; so the highest indifference curve they can get to is at A' in Fig. 5.2. The economy is fully characterized by point A'. There is no excess demand for goods since consumption demand is limited by employment at E^D. In short, for Keynes, there is only one market in disequilibrium: there is excess supply of labour at A'. The economy is stuck at A'.[2] For the Classics, there are two markets in disequilibrium: excess supply of labour and excess demand for goods. In the classical case, the simultaneous pressure for falling wages and rising prices reduces the real wage and the economy moves directly back to full market-clearing equilibrium.

Clower argued that underlying Keynes's model was a more general theory of economic behaviour than that which lay behind the Walrasian equilibrium model. The more general model was the one that took account of transactions occurring away from full equilibrium, with the consequence that supply and demand functions contain incomes—i.e. prices *and* quantities, rather than simply prices as in the neoclassical (Walrasian) model. From this viewpoint, the possibility of transactions occurring at equilibrium was a special case of the more general model.

Clower formulated the 'dual-decision hypothesis' as an alternative behavioural rule to the principles lying behind Walras's Law above (P1 and P2). The essence of the dual decision hypothesis states the following.

P3   Each household makes its expenditure decision when it knows how much income it will have, i.e. once the level of employment is known.

P4   Each firm decides how much labour to employ when it knows the level of its sales, i.e. once it knows how much income it will have.

More precisely, the dual-decision hypothesis consisted of a two-stage decision-making process. In the first stage, agents calculate their demands and supplies for goods and labour at current market prices. These 'Walrasian' demands and supplies are labelled by Clower as 'notional' since, in a world where trades take place at non-equilibrium prices, the Walrasian demands and supplies may not be realizable. The second stage is where what Clower calls 'effective' demands and supplies are worked out. In this stage the agents maximize the relevant utility or profit function subject not only to their budget constraint but also to the 'quantity

---

[2] Of course, Keynes acknowledged that there was excess supply of labour at A' and hence that money wages might be falling; but, as we have seen, he also argued that this would not necessarily increase y^D; so the economy would remain at A', albeit perhaps with falling wages and prices.

constraint', i.e. how much labour they can sell; how many goods they can sell. From Clower's perspective, behaviour in the Walrasian market-clearing model is therefore a special case of the dual-decision hypothesis. The special case where notional demands are indeed effective is valid only in conditions of full employment.

Clower saw this hypothesis as providing a sound microeconomic foundation for Keynes's *General Theory*—a theory centred on the operation of the economy away from full market-clearing equilibrium. The characteristic position of the economy away from full equilibrium in the tradition of Keynes has led to the theory being labelled 'disequilibrium economics'. It is perhaps more accurate to refer to the economics of 'non-Walrasian equilibria'. Clower argued that neoclassical macroeconomics based on Walras's Law applied to full equilibrium only. He summarized the achievement of this full equilibrium as follows. Assume a real wage w_0. Agents formulate spending and earning plans based on this: The results in terms of demand and supplies of goods and labour are fed into a central 'market authority', which we can think of as a large computer named the Invisible Hand (IH). The IH calculates excess demands and supplies and applies the adjustment rules: raise prices/wages if there is excess demand; do the reverse if there is excess supply to eliminate the disequilibria. Once the new equilibrium prices have been calculated, IH announces them and trading takes place.

Walras's metaphor for the process through which the equilibrium set of prices is found was an auction. He suggested thinking of the process as follows. The auctioneer calls out prices for commodities and labour. Agents calculate the net excess demand (defined as demand minus supply; negative excess demand indicates the presence of excess supply) at this price and communicate them to the auctioneer. The auctioneer aggregates excess demands for every commodity and proceeds by trying new prices, raising the price for commodities in excess demand and lowering the price for those in excess supply. The process of groping towards the set of full equilibrium prices is labelled *tâtonnement*. Only with the process complete could goods and labour change hands.

The *tâtonnement* process is the fundamental weak link in the Walrasian generalization of the classical model. There is no explanation of how equilibrium prices are set apart from the expository device of the auctioneer. Even less plausible is the requirement that no trades take place before the full market-clearing set of prices has been found. In reality, transactions occur continuously. No explanation is provided for the *assumption* that price adjustment is instantaneous.

Clower's interpretation of Keynes's claim to provide a general theory—many would say the correct interpretation—is as follows. Keynes fundamentally and simply denied that there was a mechanism for bringing about the instantaneous readjustment of prices to equilibrium. He did not claim that such a mechanism was logically impossible. He said that in industrialized economies it did not exist. His theory was *general* in the sense that it was a theory of industrialized economies as they operated.

Replacing Walras's Law by permitting trading to occur at non-equilibrium prices and introducing the dual-decision hypothesis creates a microeconomic foundation for the multiplier. It provides a demonstration that, even if the real wage remains at the full employment level, a fall in exogenous demand (e.g. investment) triggers a multiple contraction of employment and output. A diagrammatic example helps to show this.

In Fig. 5.3, the economy is initially at A_0 with the full employment level of investment i_0 and the full employment wage, w_0. Firms are maximizing profits by producing at A_0, with w_0 equal to the marginal product of labour. Investment declines to i_1. Lower demand for investment goods leaves firms quantity-constrained—they cannot sell as much as they want to at the going price and wage combination. Hence the fall in the demand for firms' products between positions A_0 and A_1 causes them to reduce their hiring (from E_0 to E_1). The labour hiring decision depends not only on prices (the real wage) but on the demand for their output. Households find themselves constrained in their labour supply decision by the demand for labour. The drop in jobs available to E_1 pulls down consumption demand, which lowers the effective demand for goods even further. The economy is at A_2. The cumulative contraction continues to A_Z, where investment (i_1) plus consumption ($c_Z = w_0 E_Z$) is equal to output. This process of adjustment is equivalent to that of the multiplier.

The implications of admitting the possibility of transactions occurring at non-Walrasian equilibrium prices was pursued by Axel Leijonhufvud. He

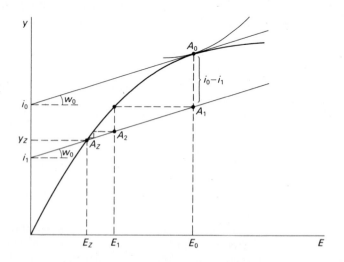

Fig. 5.3 The multiplier and the dual-decision hypothesis

sought to rehabilitate Keynes's emphasis on transactions taking place through time and to highlight the opportunities created by this for the intervention of disequilibrating processes, of which the multiplier is the most famous example.

5.3   Leijonhufvud's Defence of Keynes

In his reinterpretation of Keynes, Leijonhufvud argues that the essential message of Keynes about the divergence of the economic system from the classical model was obscured by its representation in a comparative-static model such as *IS/LM* or aggregate supply/aggregate demand. By pressing Keynes's model into such a mould, the argument between Keynes and the Classics was reduced to a dispute over the determinants of the consumption, investment, and demand-for-money functions.

This methodology produced the textbook result that persistent Keynesian unemployment required either (1) rigid money wages or (2) a rigid interest rate (an absolute liquidity trap) or (3) rigid investment (entirely interest-insensitive). A real balance effect on consumption rendered the latter cases invalid and left Keynesian unemployment dependent on rigid money wages.

But Leijonhufvud's claim was that Keynes believed in *neither* (1), (2), nor (3); to get Keynes's results, '[i]t is sufficient only to give up the equally strong assumption of instantaneous price adjustments' (Leijonhufvud 1967: 402). He took Keynes's purpose to be to examine the implications for the behaviour of economic agents of imperfect and costly information in a world where the future is uncertain. Keynes believed that, in the face of a lack of information about future sales, employment opportunities, and returns on investment, agents would look to past experience for guidance. This would mean that money wages, the price level, the interest rate, and investment would be at least somewhat sticky. Such price stickiness would lead to transactions occurring at the wrong prices and the possibility of lasting unemployment.

Suppose a wave of pessimism produced a fall in autonomous investment. Workers' expectations about job opportunities and the wage they would expect to receive would (even in the absence of trade unions) prevent money wages and prices from falling immediately by the extent necessary to generate effects in financial markets sufficient to offset the fall in investment. Workers will have a notion of the wage they will accept—a so-called *reservation wage*—which will depend on past experiences and on observations of the current wage for a similar job. Only as the process of searching for a job continues will the reservation wage be adjusted. The absence of an auctioneer to set the market wage means that the gathering of information about jobs and wages takes time and is costly.

In a similar fashion, the past pattern of interest rates would influence agents' views of possible future interest rates, and because of this would limit the extent to which the current interest rate would fall. Finally, entrepreneurial expectations as to the profitability of future investment were thought by Keynes to be dominated by expectations of sales, which in turn depended on current sales. Current sales were not presumed by firms always to be at the full employment level.

This approach suggests that any disturbance to aggregate demand in the economic system (such as a change in investment) would have only a small effect on money wages and therefore on marginal costs and the price level. The consequently small rise in the real money supply would have only a limited effect in lowering interest rates because expectations about the 'normal' interest rate are rooted in past experience: too few investors may believe that a further fall in interest rates is likely for them to switch from money into bonds. A small fall in the interest rate may have little effect on fixed investment—entrepreneurs' expectations may be dominated by the wave of pessimism which initially reduced investment and by the low level of their current sales relative to normal output.

Leijonhufvud's central point was that the equilibrating processes emphasized by the neoclassicals have to take place through time and not instantaneously, as in the classical model. This means not only that the re-equilibration process will be slow but, more importantly, that the time taken creates the possibility of disequilibrium processes intervening. The simplest example of this is the multiplier. This is an adjustment process taking the economy further away from equilibrium. It operates when the economy is shifted away from full employment and households adjust their consumption decisions to their employment status. The downward adjustment of consumption would worsen the sales of firms and result in a further cut-back in employment (refer back to Fig. 5.3). In Leijonhufvud's words, '[t]he multiplier feedbacks mean that the system tends to respond to parametric disturbances in a "deviation-amplifying" manner—behaviour which cannot be analyzed with the pre-Keynesian apparatus' (Leijonhufvud 1967: 409).

A second example of a disequilibrium process concerns financial markets. A period of recession brought on by a decline in autonomous investment may have the effect of raising liquidity preference and consequently raising interest rates because of the greater uncertainty about returns to financial assets. In other words, pessimism about investment in real assets (the cause of the fall in investment) may spill over into increased nervousness about returns to financial investment (the cause of increased liquidity preference). Thus, lower autonomous investment may be associated with a *higher* interest rate: precisely the opposite reaction to that required for neoclassical re-equilibration.

A final example is the situation where consumers hold off from purchases of goods because of uncertainty about how far prices will fall. The real balance (Pigou) effect requires the opposite reaction: a fall in the price level immediately stimulates consumption.

5.4 Keynesian and Classical Unemployment: Fixed-Price Quantity-Constrained Models

In the 1970s, Clower's and Leijonhufvud's 'non-Walrasian' reinterpretation of Keynes was taken a step further by Malinvaud. Malinvaud argued that Keynes was basically interested in 'temporary equilibria' such as A_Z in Fig. 5.3 which are arrived at while W and P remain fixed. While it is not clear that Keynes would have agreed, the temporary equilibrium method has produced useful insights. The method is based on the empirical premise that wages and prices move slowly, and focuses on the behaviour of quantities outside full equilibrium by assuming rigid wages and prices. The fixed-price method takes issue with the implausibility of the neoclassical Invisible Hand. The sharpest contrast with the Invisible Hand mechanism, in which prices are adjusted to excess demands and supplies to produce the equilibrium set of prices before any transactions occur, is to assume that transactions occur at non-equilibrium prices and that those prices remain fixed.

Malinvaud was involved in the French national planning bureaucracy in the 1950s and 1960s and was accustomed to models in which prices were set on a mark-up basis and where unions dominated the labour markets—i.e. where neither prices nor wages moved rapidly in response to changes in demand. This promoted an interest in the question of the implications for the economy of a change in the real wage (W/P), assuming an arbitrary starting level for the money wage, W, and the price level, P. Debates between the government and trade unions in those years frequently focused on the relationship between the two aspects of an increase in real wages: the possible negative effect on employment of higher costs on the one hand, and the possible positive effects of higher demand on the other. The importance of analysing unemployment was sharpened in the 1970s by the reappearance of mass unemployment in Europe for the first time since the war.

Thus, starting from the background of a Keynesian economist—but with dissatisfaction at the intellectual foundations of 1950s and 1960s Keynesianism and with an interest in the policy issues of the time—Malinvaud introduced a new question into the macroeconomic theory debate. Instead of dwelling on the finer details of the existence of non-Walrasian equilibria, he looked specifically at the question of whether a rise in the real wage would raise or lower employment. It could lift employment by releasing the sales constraint in the goods market if higher real wages raised consumer demand; on the other hand, real wages are a cost to producers, and an increase could lead employers to reduce their demand for labour. Using the fixed-price method, Malinvaud showed that both results are possible depending on the characteristics of the initial temporary equilibrium. The policy implications of this rather abstract analysis are striking: under some circumstances, labelled by Malinvaud as *Keynesian unemployment*, higher real wages will reduce unemployment; under different conditions, called *classical unemployment*, higher real wages will raise unemployment. If policy can affect real wages, then by Malinvaud's reasoning it is very important for policy-makers to be able to distinguish a situation of Keynesian from one of classical unemployment.

5.4.1 Malinvaud on Classical and Keynesian Unemployment

Malinvaud takes the money wage (W), the price level (P), and the nominal money supply (M) as fixed. Although in the fixed-price tradition a component of autonomous demand is not usually included, we will use it in the simple presentation here; it permits the development of the argument in a way that can be more easily compared with the preceding analysis, without losing the insights that are most important for present purposes. It is then possible to examine the effects on employment of changes in W, P, M, and A, nominal autonomous demand. Two rules characterize non-clearing market behaviour:

1 Do not buy before you know how much you can sell.[3] This is Clower's dual-decision hypothesis.

- For *households*, this implies that $c^D = wE^D$: demand for consumer goods depends on current employment. This is a Keynesian consumption function and contrasts with the classical view that $c^D = wE^S(w)$, i.e. that consumer demand depends on desired labour supply at the current real wage. In the classical model, the real wage is the only argument of the consumption function.
- For *firms*, this implies that $E^D = E(y)$. Employment demand depends on current output supplied. The classical equivalent is $E^D = E[y^S(w)]$; i.e., demand for labour depends on desired output supply at the current real wage. The two definitions will coincide at the Walrasian equilibrium.

2 The short side of the market determines quantities. If transactions do not take place at a price where demand is equal to supply, it is necessary to specify the quantities actually traded. The short-side rationing rule establishes this. Although it sounds technical, the assumption captures the

[3] In Malinvaud's full model there is a regime known as 'repressed inflation', where it is possible for consumer goods to be rationed. In this case, the rule is: Do not sell before you know what you can buy.

rather obvious point that agents cannot be forced to engage in transactions that they do not want to make. In the labour market, the rule is $E = \min[E^D, E^S]$.

Actual employment is the minimum quantity of employment demanded or supplied. For example, if $E^S > E^D$, i.e. if there is excess of supply of labour, then the rule states that actual employment will equal labour demand. Firms cannot be obliged to employ more people than is profitable at the current wage. In the product market,

$$y = \min[y^S, y^D].$$

Firms will produce whichever is lower of the level of output it is profitable to supply at the going real wage (y^S) and the level of output demanded at the going price.

Given these rules, we want to see what the level of employment will be when W, P, and A (autonomous demand) are not at their equilibrium values. To begin with, assume that $W = W_0$, $P = P_0$, and $A = A_0$, i.e. that all values are equilibrium ones. If A then falls to A_1, the path of adjustment to the new 'temporary equilibrium' can be traced once a time lag is introduced into the system:

$$y_t^D = c_t^D + a_t,$$

where $c_t^D = w_0 E_{t-1}$ and a is real autonomous demand ($a = A/P$). Consumption demand is a function of last period's income, indicated by the subscript $t - 1$ on employment.

The economy is initially at full employment equilibrium at point B (the same point is depicted in both panels of Fig. 5.4). At B the following statements hold:

$$y_0^D = c_0^D + a_0$$
$$c_0^D = w_0 E_0^D$$
$$E_0^D = E(y^S(w_0))$$
$$\therefore E = E^D = E^S$$

and

$$y = y^D = y^S.$$

Consider a fall in real autonomous demand from a_0 to a_1. Output demand is

$$y_1^D = c_1^D + a_1 = w_0 E_0 + a_1.$$

Since this output (see Fig. 5.4) lies beneath y_0^D and therefore below $y^S(w_0)$, there is excess supply of output and, according to rule (2), output is constrained to the level demanded;

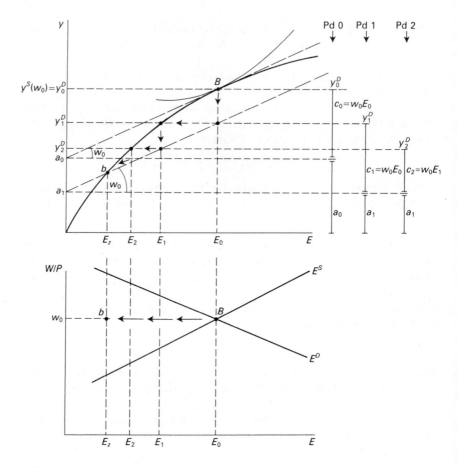

Fig. 5.4 Quantity adjustment to a temporary equilibrium with employment, E_z

$$\therefore \; y_1 = y_1^D.$$

Since $y_1^D < y^S(w_0)$, employment demand will be constrained as well:

$$E_1^D = E(y_1),$$

which is less than $E(y^S(w_0))$. Hence employment is determined by the demand for output:

$$E_1 = E_1^D = E(y_1).$$

The demand side is the shorter side of the market and dictates the level of employment. In the *next* period (period 2) consumption demand falls, since

$$c_2^D = w_0 E_1$$

and

$$y_2^D = w_0 E_1 + a_1.$$

With the assumption of fixed prices, and using the two rules of the fixed-price method (the dual-decision hypothesis and the short-side rule), the movement of the economy from full employment equilibrium at B to a temporary equilibrium at b is traced (Fig. 5.4). The reason for the emergence of unemployment was the fall in autonomous demand. The initial effect was magnified because of the consequent reduction in workers' incomes and the effect of this on consumption. The equilibrium at b is called temporary because sooner or later prices will change. The equilibrium is different from the unemployment equilibrium in Keynes's model because the real wage remains fixed at w_0. In the lower panel of Fig. 5.4, this aspect of the temporary equilibrium is especially vivid. The *assumption* of fixed prices and wages produces the result that the economy lies off *both* the labour supply and demand curves. (For an individual firm under perfect competition, position b would never be observed; since the firm believes it can sell as much as it likes at the going price, it will expand output to point B. We return to this problematic aspect of the Malinvaud model below.)

Given that the economy is at b, Malinvaud's next question was what would happen if the real wage were to rise. One way of thinking about this question is to try to identify whether it is the level of real wages that is constraining employment below the full employment level. From point b, a rise in the real wage actually raises employment. The intuition is clear: higher real wages mean higher consumption demand, and as long as the real wage remains *below* the marginal product of labour (see Fig. 5.5), firms can profitably meet the extra demand.[4]

As illustrated in Fig. 5.5, a rising real wage produces falling unemployment until point d is reached—i.e. until the real wage has risen up to the level of the marginal product of labour, i.e. at w_2 (point d). Any *further* rise in the real wage will not produce a rise in employment since firms will not find it profitable to hire more labour ($w > MPL$).

The situation between points b and d where a higher real wage raises employment was called *Keynesian unemployment* by Malinvaud. Here firms are constrained by insufficient demand. They would like to produce more at the going real wage but cannot do so because they cannot sell the output. The product market is in excess *supply*. The labour market is also in excess supply—at the going real wage, workers would wish to supply more labour but are unable to because of inadequate demand for their services.

---

[4] In Malinvaud's discussion of classical and Keynesian unemployment, the possibility that a rise in the real wage could *reduce* aggregate demand by dampening investment is ignored. We return to the implications of the dependence of investment on profitability and hence on the real wage in pt. II below.

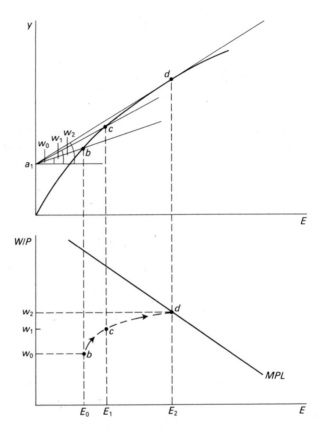

Fig. 5.5 Higher real wage leads to higher employment: Keynesian unemployment

If the real wage rises above w_2 to w_3, employment falls from E_2 to E_1 (see Fig. 5.6). Since firms cannot be forced to employ more labour than is profitable, employment is set at the level where the marginal product of labour is equal to w_3. At this level of employment and real wage, total demand for output is equal to

$$y^D = w_3 E_1 + a_1$$

(position e' in Fig. 5.6). This exceeds the supply, $y^S(w_3)$ (point e in the figure). Hence, the goods market is characterized by excess demand, while excess supply continues to prevail in the labour market. Such a combination, where employment can be raised only by a fall in the real wage, was called *classical unemployment* by Malinvaud.

Depending on the level of the real wage, a given level of employment can have the character of Keynesian or classical unemployment. Take the employment level E_1 in Fig. 5.7, for example. At $w = w_3$, the unemploy-

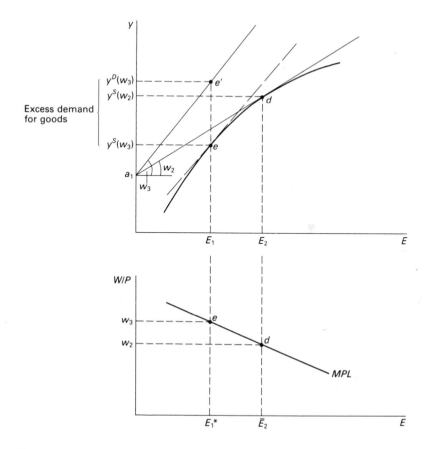

Fig. 5.6 Higher real wage leads to lower employment: classical unemployment

ment is classical and the economy is at point e in the lower panel. In the upper panel, the excess demand in the goods market is represented by the difference between e and e'; a lower real wage would raise employment. With $w = w_1$, the unemployment is Keynesian and the economy is at point c; a higher real wage would raise employment.

Although classical and Keynesian unemployment have the different characteristics discussed above, both are forms of *involuntary unemployment*. Involuntary unemployment is defined as a state in which there are individuals prepared to work at the current real wage but who are unable to find jobs. The economy is at a position that is off the supply curve of labour to the left. Figure 5.8 illustrates the involuntary unemployment associated with a situation of classical unemployment (top panel) and Keynesian unemployment (bottom panel). In Chapter 3 above, the nature of *voluntary unemployment* and in particular the phenomenon of *search unemployment* was discussed.

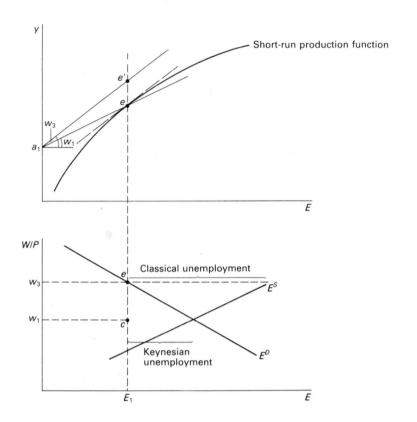

Fig. 5.7 Keynesian unemployment at $w = w_1$; classical unemployment at
$$w = w_3$$

5.4.2 Unemployment, Real Wages, and Aggregate Demand: Malinvaud and Keynes

With a given level of autonomous demand, the temporary equilibria of Keynesian and classical unemployment trace out the shape of an arrowhead in the labour market diagram. This is shown in Fig. 5.9. Focusing on the bottom panel, with real autonomous demand, $a = a_1$, the lower part of the arrowhead shows the possible Keynesian unemployment equilibria: all lie below the MPL curve. (Points b and d were derived in Fig. 5.5.) The upper part of the arrowhead shows classical unemployment. (Points d and e were derived in Fig. 5.6.) For clarity, the top panel of Fig. 5.9 illustrates only the shift of point d to d' associated with a higher level of autonomous demand. With higher autonomous demand of $a = a_2$, aggregate supply equals aggregate demand at a lower real wage w_2 (using the equation $y^S(w) = y^D(= wE + a)$). Using the same procedure as in

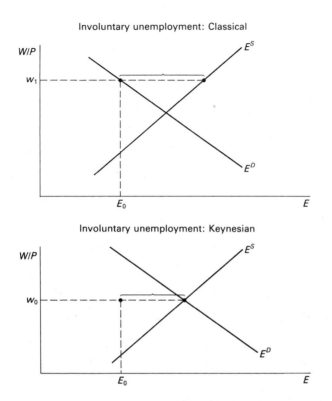

Fig. 5.8 Involuntary unemployment: classical and Keynesian

Fig. 5.5 and 5.6, the full arrowhead $b'd'e'$ associated with higher demand can be derived.

This presentation is useful when considering the effectiveness of aggregate demand measures. With the economy initially placed along bd, a boost in autonomous demand by the government will raise the level of employment. Assuming that prices and wages are fixed, the economy moves horizontally to a point on a new arrowhead appropriate to a higher level of demand. With $w = w_2$, the economy would shift to point d'. At d', Keynesian unemployment has been eliminated. Full employment has not been achieved: to eliminate the remaining unemployment, the economy must shift on to another arrowhead with its point at f. Higher autonomous demand is required, along with a fall in the real wage.

Keynes's insight about the effect on unemployment of lowering real wages is reflected here. His model concerned points such as d and d'—i.e. points on the boundary between classical and Keynesian unemployment. He sought to demonstrate that, to shift from d' to full employment at f,

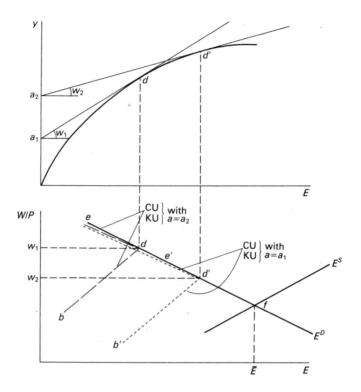

Fig. 5.9 Keynesian and classical unemployment (KU and CU): the effect of a change in autonomous demand

both a fall in real wages and a rise in autonomous demand was essential: his argument with the classics was that endogenous mechanisms could not be relied on to generate the necessary extra demand. By allowing for arbitrary wages and prices to prevail in temporary equilibria, Malinvaud provided a result even stronger than that of Keynes: with autonomous demand at a_2 and the economy at d', lower real wages unaccompanied by any change in autonomous demand would produce *higher* unemployment as the economy moved along $d'b'$. By assuming that prices adjust quickly to clear unsold goods from the product market, Keynes's model was restricted to points along the marginal product of labour curve.

*5.4.3 Malinvaud's Diagram

Malinvaud's own diagram illustrating Keynesian and classical unemployment assumes that aggregate demand is a function of the real money supply. As we have seen earlier, this could operate through the channel of the so-called Keynes effect where a higher real money supply reduces the

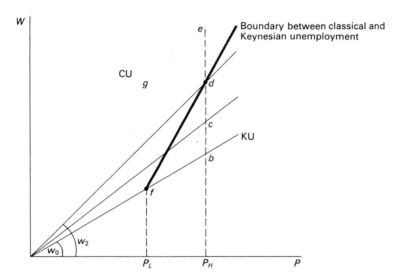

Fig. 5.10 Malinvaud's diagram to show Keynesian and classical unemployment

interest rate and boosts investment (assuming the absence of both a liquidity trap and interest-insensitive investment). The so-called Pigou effect through which consumption is a function of real money balances would provide an alternative route.

Figure 5.10 presents a simplified version of the Malinvaud diagram which is constructed in $W-P$ space. With W and P on the axes, the real wage is constant along a ray from the origin. Assume that the initial real wage is w_0 and that, with a given nominal money supply M, a price level of P_L (low) will generate sufficient real aggregate demand, $y^D = wE + a(M/P)$, to secure full employment at f. Real autonomous demand is written explicitly as a function of the real money supply M/P. Along the ray w_0, there is a point b which maps point b from Fig. 5.5 into $W-P$ space. Aggregate demand at b is below that required for full employment, and hence a higher price level, P_H, is required to reduce the value of autonomous demand. Point d corresponding to its namesake in Fig. 5.5 lies vertically above b; the real wage is higher (w_2), but the price level and hence (for Malinvaud) the level of autonomous demand is the same.

By altering the real wage and the price level (which changes the level of autonomous demand), it is possible to trace the set of combinations of the money wage and the price level required to keep the economy on the marginal product of labour curve. This line fd divides the diagram into areas of classical and Keynesian unemployment. Points like b and c to the right of the line denote Keynesian unemployment; points like e (corresponding to point e in Fig. 5.6) above the line denote classical unemployment.

What additional insights are provided by the presentation of Keynesian and classical unemployment in this way? The choice of the money wage and the price level for the axes provides a vivid depiction of the different equilibria associated with arbitrary combinations of these. The aspect most at odds with Keynes's own analysis is the choice of the price level as the proxy for the level of autonomous demand (Trevithick 1978). This means that, from an arbitrary initial position in the region of Keynesian unemployment, a sufficient fall in the price level will eliminate the Keynesian unemployment. The economy will then be on the border between Keynesian and classical unemployment. If the price level is an argument in the aggregate demand function, then a downward flexible money wage is a sufficient condition for the achievement of full employment.

The problem as Keynes saw it was whether there were endogenous forces in the economy which would cause it to move *along* the boundary in the direction of full employment at f. Malinvaud's model takes us no further in the analysis of that problem: the diagram simply illustrates the limitations of a policy either of cutting money wages or of raising aggregate demand (cutting prices).

1 A reduction in the money wage with no change in the price level (and therefore in autonomous demand) moves the economy from a point on the borderline (such as d in Fig. 5.10) where there is unemployment into the region of Keynesian unemployment (in Fig. 5.10, from a point such as d to c or b) as the result of the reduction in consumption demand.

2 A reduction in the price level at a given money wage takes the economy from the borderline (d) into classical unemployment (g) because the real wage rises above the marginal product of labour.

Malinvaud's diagram is less well suited to show the effect of changes in fiscal and monetary policy. A higher level of government spending would require a higher price level than P_L to reduce autonomous demand so as to offset the higher government spending and leave the level of aggregate demand unchanged. The real wage associated with full employment is unchanged and therefore full employment will be represented by a point f' further to the right along the $w = w_0$ ray (see Fig. 5.11). Indeed, the boundary between Keynesian and classical unemployment will shift to the right, with the implication that higher government spending means a fall in the amount of Keynesian unemployment for a given real wage. The same conclusion follows for a rise in the money supply from M_0 to M_1.

The fixed-price method highlights the implications of the economy getting stuck at the wrong $W-P$ combination. The dual-decision hypothesis provides a rationale, based on individual decision-making, for transactions occurring at the wrong prices. If the economy is initially at full

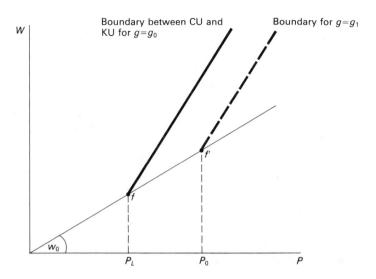

Fig. 5.11 Malinvaud's diagram: a rise in government spending

employment, and is subject to a downward movement of investment, the fixed-price model adopts Clower's dual-decision hypothesis to explain why the multiplier process of quantity contraction will occur, leaving the economy at a temporary equilibrium below that implied by the initial fall in investment. But by simply assuming rigid money wages and a rigid price level, the model provides no explanation for what sustains the temporary equilibrium. Presumably prices and wages will change eventually. The model assumes perfectly competitive firms, yet it is irrational for individual firms in a situation of Keynesian unemployment not to expand employment and output (since the real wage is below the marginal product of labour). In short, the fixed-price model does not address two central and interrelated questions:

1 How are prices and wages set?
2 Are quantity-constrained agents compatible with perfect competition?

We return to these questions in Parts II and IV below.

5.5 Conclusions

Perhaps perversely, the formalization of the market-clearing model by the neoclassical theorists, through the application of Walras's Law, provided new impetus to the supporters of the Keynesian tradition. The neoclassical reformulation showed the outcome of individual agents maximizing profits and utility based on their chosen supplies of output and labour at given prices combined with a *tâtonnement* process through which prices are adjusted in response to excess demands and supplies. The relevant insight of this approach was that an excess demand in the goods market would occur in conjunction with excess supply in the labour market. Such a combination would produce rising prices and falling money wages and, therefore, falling real wages. The mechanism of the Invisible Hand or a fictitious auctioneer was invoked as a metaphorical device to ensure that prices and wages were adjusted to eliminate excess demand and supply *before* any transactions occurred. The fact that demand for consumption goods was based on desired supplies of labour meant that Keynes's problem of the multiplier contraction of demand, and with it the danger that prices would fall and prevent the real wage from declining, was eliminated.

In the absence of an invisible hand, transactions can take place at the wrong prices. Leijonhufvud highlighted the fact that the time taken for transactions to be completed creates the possibility of disequilibrium phenomena occurring. When agents make their expenditure decisions on the basis of current income rather than desired income (i.e. employment for households, sales for firms), a multiplier contraction of output and employment can occur. Individuals and firms will be constrained at least to some extent by their current incomes whenever they do not have access to a perfect capital market. In other words, only when it is possible to borrow against expected future earnings to permit a smooth expenditure stream is the purchase of consumer goods by households and of labour by firms independent of current employment.

Looked at in this light, it is the neoclassical model that begins to have the appearance of a very special case. In the rehabilitation of Keynes, Clower, Leijonhufvud, Malinvaud, and others have sought to highlight the strength of the assumptions about behaviour and institutions that are necessary to support the classical macroeconomic system.

Leijonhufvud's reinterpretation of Keynes emphasized the stickiness of prices, wages, the interest rate, and investment and created a plausible framework within which to place the fixed-price models. Malinvaud simply assumes that such stickiness exists and then examines the characteristics of the temporary equilibria away from full employment. The fixed-price models attempt to specify more precisely the microeconomic behaviour (in the form, for example, of rationing) that characterizes arbitrary wage–price combinations. This has led to the demarcation of Keynesian from classical unemployment. Keynesian unemployment is a situation where a higher real wage would raise employment by releasing the sales constraint on firms (raising aggregate demand). In classical unemployment, a higher real wage would reduce employment since some marginal employment would become unprofitable.

The reinterpretation of Keynes through the dual-decision hypothesis, Leijonhufvud's arguments about the role of time and the effect of an uncertain future and costly information in bringing to prominence the role of expectations, and the development of the fixed-price method enlivened the debate from the Keynesian side about how the macroeconomy works. But the project of creating a macroeconomic model that would stand on rigorous microeconomic foundations and provide an alternative to the new classical one was incomplete—especially in regard to modelling wage, price, and interest rate dynamics. In addition, the expectations formation process used by Keynes required more rigorous examination. Finally, the question of whether the assumption of perfectly competitive labour and product markets was the appropriate microeconomic basis for a macro model had scarcely been addressed.

While Malinvaud's analysis answered many questions, it failed to explain how wages and prices were determined and why perfectly competitive agents were quantity-constrained. In the past decade research in the non-classical tradition has been directed towards using the microeconomic foundations of *imperfectly competitive markets* as the basis for a coherent analysis of inflation and unemployment. In Part II, we present a simple macroeconomic model based on imperfectly competitive product and labour markets which can be used for the analysis of unemployment and inflation, and of policy alternatives. The model is a simple version of models that are now frequently used in the contemporary analysis of unemployment and inflation. Such models are often (especially in Europe) referred to as NAIRU models. In Part III the model is extended to deal with the open economy and the central issue of international competitiveness. The open economy model is a simplified version based explicitly on imperfectly competitive markets of what is sometimes known as the Mundell–Fleming–Dornbusch model. Finally, in Part IV the issue of the explicit microeconomic foundations for the imperfect competition model from the theory of imperfect competition is addressed. Although the classical tradition culminating in the New Classical Macroeconomics of Chapter 4 is not discussed at length again, reference is made to its results as a benchmark with which the results under imperfect competition are compared. In particular, in Chapter 16, the stylized facts of macroeconomic behaviour are presented. The consistency of each of the three new research initiatives in macroeconomics—New Classical, fixed-price, and imperfect competition—with the stylized facts is examined.

PART II

Imperfect Competition Macroeconomics in the Closed Economy

6

The Basic Imperfect Competition Model

To make sense of current economic policy debates, it is necessary to have a model in which problems of inflation and unemployment can both be analysed. In the Introduction, we set out the bare bones of a simple imperfect competition model[1] which lies behind much applied work on the question of unemployment in open and closed economies. It was noted there that the assumption of imperfectly competitive labour and product markets is perhaps more appropriate to the non-US industrialized economies. In this part of the book, we build up and put to work an imperfect competition model tailored to the requirements of analysing these economies.

One of the benefits of working with imperfect competition is that it is possible to discuss explicitly how wages and prices are set. Wages are set either through collective bargaining negotiations or as the result of employer strategies, and prices are set by imperfectly competitive firms. In this part of the book we assume that wages are set through bargains between unions and employers; in Part IV, we show how similar results emerge from employer behaviour in the absence of unions.[2] By contrast, under perfect competition, equilibrium wages and prices emerge from the market; workers, employers, and firms do not make pricing decisions, they are price- and wage-takers. Price- and wage-setting is put to one side entirely in the fixed-price/-wage models discussed in Chapter 5 above.

The microeconomic foundations of collective bargaining in a contemporary industrialized economy and of price-setting in an economy dominated by large firms are set out in detail in Part IV. Here, we draw on those results to construct a simple model with which macroeconomic behaviour can be analysed. Large chunks of the analytical apparatus reviewed in Part

---

[1] This approach to macroeconomics has become common in the last decade, especially in Europe. One of the earliest models with similar features to the one we will present is Rowthorn (1977). Perhaps the best known presentation of an imperfectly competitive macro model is Layard and Nickell (1985). In turn, they acknowledge their intellectual debt to Blanchard, whose work was published in Blanchard (1986). See also Sawyer (1982) for a similar model presented as part of the Kaleckian tradition. Layard and Nickell have played the leading role in the empirical application of the imperfect competition model.

[2] The latter case in known as *efficiency wages* (see ch. 17 below).

I will be used here—for example the *IS/LM* framework for analysing aggregate demand, and the concepts of adaptive and rational expectations. The introduction of imperfect competition modifies the working of the labour market diagram and provides a different rationalization for the expectations-augmented Phillips curves.

In the imperfect competition model, the level of unemployment depends on the level of aggregate demand in the economy. The reason is straightforward: since imperfectly competitive firms produce where the marginal product of labour exceeds the real wage, it will be profitable for them to increase output in response to an increase in demand in the product market, if the real wage remains constant. However, although this means that the government can choose the rate of unemployment by adjusting the level of aggregate demand, it may nevertheless face the consequence of rising inflation.

One of the starkest contrasts between the imperfect competition model and Friedman's model of inflation (Chapter 3) is that the imperfect competition model provides a quite different rationalization for the genesis of inflation. For Friedman, the crucial mechanism is that an injection of money (nominal demand) creates misperceptions on the part of workers, who therefore supply more labour than they would have done had they been correctly informed. By contrast, inflation in the imperfect competition model can be thought of as arising from the existence of inconsistent claims on the economy's real income. At a given level of labour productivity (i.e. output per worker), firms through their pricing decisions claim a certain amount of output as profits per worker. Workers also lay claim to part of output per head—the real wage—by bargaining a money wage relative to the expected price level. If these claims sum to more than is available, i.e. the level of output per worker, then inflation rises as each party seeks to secure its claim through price- or wage-setting. Each side uses its market power to raise prices or money wages in an attempt to realize its claim.

In general, there is a unique rate of unemployment at which the competing claims are reconciled and inflation is constant. This is the *competing claims equilibrium rate of unemployment* or the *non-accelerating inflation rate of unemployment*, the NAIRU. For brevity, the term *equilibrium rate of unemployment* or NAIRU will be used.[3] As noted in the Introduction, a simple way to think about this concept is to suppose that the amount of the output per head that is left for real wages after

---

[3] We discuss in detail in sect. 6.3 below the difference between the equilibrium rate of unemployment (NAIRU) and the natural rate of unemployment. To minimize confusion, the term equilibrium rate of unemployment (NAIRU) is used in this book *only* in the imperfect competition model; natural rate of unemployment is used *only* to refer to the rate of unemployment fixed by the clearing of perfectly competitive markets with complete information.

profits have been subtracted is constant as the level of employment rises. On the other hand, union real wage claims rise with rising employment. If at a given level of employment these two real wages are not equal, e.g. if the real-wage and real-profit claims sum to more than output per worker, then higher unemployment is needed to dampen union bargaining power. This will reduce union real wage claims into line with the output per head available once profits have been deducted. Only at this higher rate of unemployment, i.e. at the equilibrium rate or NAIRU, will inflation be constant.

Money plays a role in the imperfect competition model since rising inflation at rates of unemployment below the equilibrium rate of unemployment will require an accommodating rise in the money supply for real aggregate demand and hence employment to remain constant.

Before developing the imperfect competition model, it is useful to have a summary of the results.

A1   There is a unique equilibrium rate of unemployment at which inflation is constant (the NAIRU). At this rate of unemployment, the expected real wage that unions can negotiate is equal to the real wage that results from firms setting prices so as to achieve a specific mark-up of price over costs.

A2   The equilibrium rate of unemployment is not a market-clearing rate. In general, there is involuntary unemployment at the NAIRU in the sense that there are workers prepared to work at the existing real wage who cannot get jobs.

A3   Levels of actual employment and output are determined by aggregate demand in the product market. If the level of aggregate demand produces a rate of unemployment below the equilibrium rate of unemployment, then inflation will be rising. If unemployment is above the equilibrium rate, inflation will be falling. To sustain a rate of unemployment below the NAIRU, the government must accommodate the rising inflation through an expansion in the money supply.

6.1   Wage- and Price-Setting under Imperfect Competition: the Equilibrium Rate of Unemployment

6.1.1   Wage-Setting as the Outcome of Collective Bargaining

Money wages are set in a variety of ways, and a number of these are examined in detail in Part IV. Here we will make the simple assumption that wages are set through collective bargaining negotiations between unions and employers, industry by industry. Unions, on behalf of their members, are concerned with the *real* wage. This means that wage negotiations take place on the basis of *expectations* about the price level that will prevail over the period of the wage contract. The consumer price level will depend on the outcomes of all wage bargains and cannot be known with certainty at the time of wage negotiations. Given the expected price level, the level of the bargained real wage will depend on a multitude of factors. However, a key determinant is the state of the labour market, and in particular the rate of unemployment.

We noted in the Introduction Marx's analysis of the role of the so-called reserve army of labour (the unemployed) in the functioning of the capitalist economy. He argued that unemployment was functional for capitalism because it exerted discipline over the workers. In times of high unemployment workers would be prepared to work for less, and in Marx's view to work harder, than at a time when alternative jobs were readily available. He argues that the reserve army plays a role in demoralizing the working-class movement and undermining its organizational strength. The higher is unemployment, the lower is the bargaining power of workers:

Taking them as a whole, the general movements of wages are exclusively regulated by the expansion and contraction of the industrial reserve army, and this in turn corresponds to the periodic alternations of the industrial cycle.(Marx 1976, i; 790)

Unions will be able to negotiate a higher expected real wage when unemployment is low since a tight labour market will provide the unions with a credible threat of strike action if their claims are not agreed to. If, in the typical case, a tight labour market coincides with a buoyant product market, then employers will be more willing to concede higher wage increases than to risk the loss of production through industrial action at a time when order books are full and stocks are low. Conversely, high unemployment will weaken union bargaining strength. Since other household members are more likely to be out of work, the loss of income associated with strike action will be more damaging. With high unemployment, there will be little chance of gaining temporary work during a strike. In addition, the possibility that industrial action could threaten the viability of the employer, and the higher probability of unemployment if the present job is lost, act to dampen union wage claims. From the employer's point of view, the balance between the costs of a strike and of a given increase in wages shifts as unemployment rises, raising resistance to wage claims. More formal arguments, based on union behaviour and also on the wage decisions of employers in the absence of unions (so-called efficiency wage models) for the inverse relationship between the bargained real wage and unemployment, are provided in Chapter 17.

We can formalize the relationship between the state of the labour market and wage bargaining as follows:

$$w^B = b(\bar{U}), \quad \text{[bargained real wage (BRW)]}$$

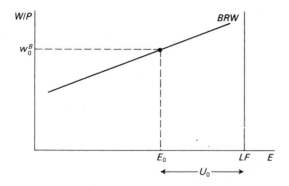

Fig. 6.1 The bargained real wage curve (BRW)

where $db/dU < 0$ and unemployment is equal to the labour force (LF) minus the level of employment (E). Figure 6.1 shows the bargained real wage curve (BRW); as employment rises, the bargained real wage rises. The labour force is assumed to be independent of the real wage and is shown by a vertical line at the level of employment, $E = LF$. At a level of unemployment U_0, the bargained real wage is w_0^B. In terms of money wages, the wage-setting equation is

$$W = P^E b(U). \qquad \text{[wage equation]}$$

A higher expected price level, P^E, will result in proportionately higher money wages since the union's objective is the real wage, w^B.

Table 6.1 provides an indication of the responsiveness of real wages to unemployment in a number of industrialized economies—this reflects the slope of the bargained real-wage curve. The data show the estimated effect of a 1% rise in the unemployment rate in reducing the real wage. From

Table 6.1 Unemployment and real wages in the wage equation

Estimated effect of 1% point rise in unemployment rate in reducing the real wage (%)

Italy	0.7	Belgium	1.6	Austria	3.7
Denmark	0.9	France	1.9	Switzerland	4.6
USA	0.9	W. Germany	2.1	Sweden	4.6
UK	1.1	Netherlands	2.8	Norway	7.5
				Japan	14.7

Source: Alogoskoufis and Manning (1988: 443, Table 5).

Table 6.1, it appears that the slope of the bargained real-wage curve differs widely across economies. We return to examine possible explanations for and implications of these variations in Part IV (Section 17.3).

6.1.2 Price-setting under Imperfect Competition

When firms in aggregate set prices in relation to their costs, a real wage is implied. The objective here is to identify how changes in employment affect the level of the real wage implied by the price that is set. We are interested to see how price-setting fixes the *price-determined real wage*.

Before moving to imperfect competition, it is worth highlighting what the 'price-determined real wage' looks like under perfect competition since this is a very familiar case. In perfect competition profit maximization means that price is equal to marginal cost, and by definition, marginal cost is equal to the money wage divided by the marginal product of labour. We have therefore the familiar result that profit maximization under perfect competition requires the (price-determined) real wage to be equal to the marginal product of labour. Since the marginal product of labour falls as employment rises, the real wage falls with employment. In perfect competition, the 'price-determined real wage' curve in the real wage–employment diagram is just the marginal product of labour curve.

We now develop the imperfectly competitive analogue to the perfectly competitive case. It is important to stress at the outset that there is no general agreement as to how prices are set under imperfect competition. However, in spite of the continuing disputes over the correct theory, there is broad agreement about what the price-determined real wage curve looks like in reality. In other words, there are several different explanations for the same set of empirical observations. Since we are concerned here with the price-determined real wage curve itself and its part in a macroeconomic model, rather than with the ins and outs of the theory of price-setting under imperfect competition, it is the consistency of the empirical findings that matters most. There is general agreement that under imperfect competition prices do not respond much to changes in demand (for the UK, see Coutts *et al.* 1978; for the USA, Tobin 1972a; Bils 1987). This means that the price-determined real wage curve is fairly flat. We use a flat price-determined real wage curve throughout the book.[4]

Let us turn briefly to the various explanations for this; a more detailed analysis is provided in Chapter 18 below. Taking the lead from the analysis of perfect competition, let us first consider the standard theory of imperfect competition: monopoly. Here, profit maximization dictates that

---

[4] It is shown in pt. IV that a downward-sloping price-determined real wage curve would make no essential difference to the macroeconomic analysis. However, it is less consistent with the 'stylized facts' of macroeconomic behaviour—see ch. 16.

marginal revenue be set equal to marginal cost and produces the familiar formula for the monopolist's price:[5]

$$P = \frac{1}{1 - 1/\varepsilon} MC$$

$$= \frac{1}{1 - 1/\varepsilon} \frac{W}{MPL},$$

where ε is (the absolute value of) the elasticity of demand, and MC is marginal cost which is equal to W/MPL with MPL denoting the marginal product of labour. The term $1/(1 - 1/\varepsilon)$ shows the amount by which marginal cost is *marked up* to form the price. A lower elasticity of demand means a higher mark-up. It is clear from this expression that, if the elasticity of demand is constant, then, just as under perfect competition, the price-determined real wage will slope in the same way as the marginal product of labour curve:

$$W/P = (1 - 1/\varepsilon)MPL.$$

However, under imperfect competition this need not be so, and indeed the empirical evidence suggests that the elasticity of demand is not constant. Rather, it seems that the mark-up falls as employment and output rise, reflecting the fact that the elasticity of demand rises with employment. Figure 6.2 illustrates the declining mark-up on marginal cost as employment rises and the associated flat price-determined real wage curve.

One argument that has been put forward to account for the pro-cyclical elasticity of demand (i.e. that elasticity rises with a rise in output) is based on the fact that customers develop a loyalty to a particular firm. In a boom

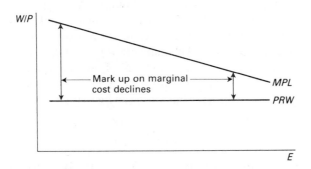

Fig. 6.2 The price-determined real wage curve (PRW)
Price set as a mark-up on marginal cost; mark-up declines as employment rises

---

[5] For full derivation of this formula see ch. 18 below. Here, note that profits $= Py - WE$; $P = P(y)$ from the demand curve and $y = y(E)$ from the short-run production function. Maximizing $P(y(E))y(E) - WE$ with respect to E implies $dP/dy(dy/dE)(y) + P(dy/dE) = W$ or $P = (1 - 1/\varepsilon)^{-1}(W/MPL)$ where $\varepsilon = |(dy/dP)(P/y)|$ and $MPL = dy/dE$.

firms face a rise in potential new customers, so it may be rational for them to invest in gaining the loyalty of these new customers by lowering their prices (Bils 1987, 1989). In other words, the mark-up is reduced as the level of output (and employment) rises.

A quite different explanation for the failure of prices to respond to changes in demand, and hence for the existence of a flat price-determined real wage curve, was accepted virtually universally in the 1970s. This is the view that prices are set by imperfectly competitive firms as a fixed mark-up over normal unit labour costs. It is known as *normal cost pricing*. What are normal unit labour costs? Normal unit labour costs are wage costs per unit output $(= WE/y = W/LP)$, where LP is labour productivity (y/E) at a normal level of capacity utilization. Alternatively, the idea is that under imperfect competition firms may use excess capacity as a way of deterring the entry of other firms into the industry. This means that marginal costs will be fairly flat at average output levels. For simplicity of exposition, we choose the latter interpretation and assume that labour productivity is constant and there is a constant mark-up. Both the normal cost pricing hypothesis and the imperfect competition theory with pro-cyclical elasticity of demand predict that the price-determined real wage curve is flat. Because of the simplicity of its use in a macroeconomic setting, we use normal cost pricing as the price-setting rule.

The simplest form of the normal cost or mark-up pricing rule is

$$P = (1 + \mu)(W/LP); \tag{6.1}$$

i.e., the price is set by marking up normal unit labour costs (W/LP) by a percentage, μ. The mark-up μ and labour productivity LP are assumed invariant to changes in employment and output. The size of the mark-up will depend inversely on the elasticity of demand and directly on the concentration of industry and the extent of collusion or co-ordination between firms in the industry. The mark-up will also depend on the ease of entry into the industry. In the development of the macro model, it is more convenient to express the mark-up in a different way. If we let $m = \mu/(1 + \mu)$, then the pricing equation can be written as

$$P = \frac{1}{1 - m} \frac{W}{LP}. \tag{6.1'}$$

(We will refer to the mark-up as m from this point on.) If $m = 0.2$, $W = £100$, and $LP = 5$, then the price will be set at $P = £25$. The usefulness of expressing pricing behaviour in the form of (6.1') is clear when we look explicitly at the claims on labour productivity implicit in the pricing decision. We can rearrange (6.1') as follows:

$$P = mP + W/LP$$
Price = Profit per unit + cost per unit $(=$ average cost).

Dividing each side by P and rearranging gives

$$LP = mLP + W/P;$$

i.e.,

Output per head = Real profits per head + real wages per head.

In other words, given the mark-up m, the level of labour productivity, and the money wage, the price set by firms implies a specific value of the real wage. This is the price-determined real wage:

$$w^P = W/P = LP(1 - m).$$
[price-determined real wage (PRW)]

Using the numerical example above, the price-determined real wage is equal to $100/25 = 4$. Output per head is divided between real profits of 1 per head and real wages of 4. The price-determined real wage (PRW) is shown in Fig. 6.3.

6.1.3 The Equilibrium Rate of Unemployment: Combining Wage- and Price-setting

Since workers seek a real wage through their negotiations with employers and firms seek a real profit per worker through their setting of prices, it is not surprising that these claims may be inconsistent. By 'inconsistent', we mean that the real wage and real profit per worker add up to more than the available output per worker. As Fig. 6.4 shows, the bargained real wage and the price-determined real wage are equal only at a single level of employment, E_N. This level of employment fixes the equilibrium rate of unemployment, U_N.

If unemployment is any lower than this (at U_L, for example), the

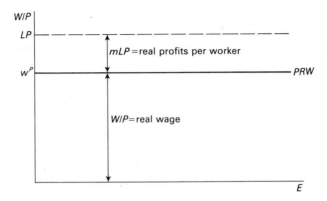

Fig. 6.3 The price-determined real wage curve (PRW)

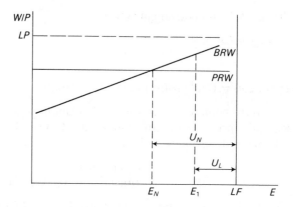

Fig. 6.4 The labour market diagram with imperfect competition

bargained real wage exceeds the price-determined real wage. In other words, the lower unemployment boosts the bargaining power of workers and raises the proportion of output per head that they claim. Since firms are not prepared to lower their claim to profits to accommodate the greater demands of workers, an impasse arises. There are just two ways in which the inconsistency between the two sets of claims can be resolved without leading to accelerating inflation. On the one hand, unemployment can be pushed up to the equilibrium rate again. The rise in unemployment has the effect of weakening the position of labour and reducing the bargained real wage to the level of the price-determined real wage.

The only other alternative is for the equilibrium rate of unemployment itself to be shifted to a lower rate of unemployment such as U_L. How can this be achieved? A glance at Fig. 6.4 suggests that the only way to alter the equilibrium rate is to shift either the bargained real wage curve (BRW) or the price-determined real wage curve (PRW). In order to achieve a lower equilibrium rate of unemployment, it would be necessary to lower the BRW or raise the PRW. Figure 6.5 shows how a downward shift in the BRW or an upward shift in the PRW produces an equilibrium rate of unemployment at lower unemployment. In the upper panel of the figure the BRW shifts downwards so that $w^B = w^P$ at U_L. This is the new equilibrium rate of unemployment, U'_N. In the lower panel, the same result is achieved by an upward shift of the PRW from PRW to PRW'.

In Chapter 7, we discuss in some detail policies that are available to shift the equilibrium rate of unemployment. For example, the government could lower the BRW by reducing the rate of income tax. Lower income taxation would have this effect because workers would require their employers to pay them a lower wage and yet would expect to receive the same *take-home* pay. The basic point here is that when the government is included in the analysis output per head must be split three ways: real

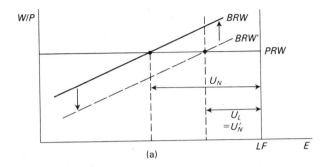

(a)

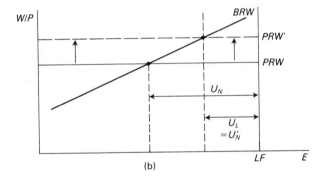

(b)

Fig. 6.5 The achievement of a new equilibrium rate of unemployment at lower
unemployment
(a) Downward shift in BRW to BRW' (b) Upward shift in PRW to PRW'

wages, real profits, and real tax revenue. A reduction in the government's
claim through lower taxation means that it is possible for the two
private-sector claims to be met at lower unemployment. Thus, if the
government cuts taxation, there is a lower equilibrium rate of unemployment.

As a second example, the government may be able to shift the BRW
curve downwards by negotiating an incomes policy with the unions. In the
context of an incomes policy, the unions may agree to exercise restraint in
wage negotiations and lower their claim to output per head at each level of
employment. This shifts the BRW curve down and enables the economy to
operate at a lower equilibrium rate of unemployment. Of course, one
reason why the unions may agree to exercise bargaining restraint in the
context of an incomes policy is in return for the government agreeing to
maintain the rate of unemployment at the new equilibrium level.

If the bargained real wage and price-determined real wage are equal at
the current rate of unemployment, then that will be the equilibrium rate of

unemployment; inflation will be constant. If the bargained real wage and price-determined real wage are not equal, inflation will be rising or falling. We now explain why inflation behaves in these ways.

6.2   Inflation in the Imperfect Competition Model

Our first task in this section is to show why inflation is constant at the equilibrium rate of unemployment. In other words, it is necessary to demonstrate the connection between stable inflation and the existence of a competing-claims equilibrium, where the claim of workers for real wages and of firms for profits, sum to output per head. Once the existence of stable inflation at the equilibrium rate of unemployment is established, we turn to the explanation of rising inflation when unemployment is lower than the equilibrium rate and falling inflation when unemployment is higher than the equilibrium rate. Both long- and short-run Phillips curves are derived. Later in the section, the role that money plays in the process of inflation is introduced. For the economy to remain at the equilibrium rate, the real money supply must be constant; i.e., at the equilibrium, the rate of inflation must be equal to the fixed growth rate of the money supply: $\dot{P} = \dot{M} = $ constant at $U = U_N$.

6.2.1   Wage Inflation, Price Inflation, and the Phillips Curves

The intuition behind the existence of constant inflation at the equilibrium rate of unemployment is straightforward. At the equilibrium rate, the real wage claimed by workers is equal to the price-determined real wage arising from firms' pricing decisions (the BRW intersects the PRW). Let us suppose that inflation in the economy is 6%. Workers enter their wage negotiations with the ability to secure an expected real wage equal to the bargained real wage. To keep the real wage constant (and therefore equal to the bargained real wage), they require a money wage rise that will make up for the expected rise in prices in the year to come. Suppose they expect prices to rise by 6% (just as they have done in the past). A money wage rise of 6% will therefore be negotiated. Now, firms must set their prices so as to secure their profit margin. With money wages set to rise by 6%, firms must raise prices 6% in order to keep their profit margin unchanged. Thus, prices rise by 6% and the price-determined real wage remains unchanged. We observe that price and wage inflation remains unchanged at 6%. With price and wage inflation equal to 6%, the bargained real wage remains equal to the price-determined real wage at the equilibrium rate of unemployment. When there is consistency between competing claims of workers and firms (i.e. at the equilibrium rate of unemployment), the expectations of all parties are fully satisfied. Workers achieve their bargained real wage and firms achieve their desired profit margin, and prices and wages rise exactly as expected by each party.

When unemployment is below the equilibrium rate, and hence the competing claims on output per head are inconsistent, inflation rises. Let us take a simple example as before. Suppose that unemployment is at U_L, a rate below the equilibrium rate, that the existing real wage is equal to the price-determined real wage, w^P, and that workers expect inflation to be 6% in the coming year. With unemployment of U_L, the bargained real wage lies above the price-determined real wage and unions will therefore seek to negotiate a money wage rise that will take the real wage up to w^B, the bargained real wage. Since they expect inflation to be 6%, a money wage rise *higher* than 6% will be negotiated so as to secure w^B. With money wages set to rise by *more than 6%*, firms will have to increase prices by more than 6% if they are to achieve their desired profit margin. Thus, we observe wage and price inflation of more than 6%. Unemployment lower than the equilibrium rate is associated with rising inflation. In this case, we can see that the expectations of all parties are not satisfied. With price inflation higher than 6%, i.e. higher than expected by the unions when they negotiated their money wage rise, the real wage outturn will be less then the bargained real wage.

By taking a rate of unemployment higher than the equilibrium, exactly the same reasoning gives the result that inflation is falling and that the expectations of all the parties are not fulfilled. It is only at the competing-claims equilibrium rate of unemployment that the claims on output per head of all parties can be met exactly. At a higher rate of unemployment, union bargaining power is weakened and the bargained real wage lies beneath the price-determined real wage. In other words, the claims of the two parties fail to exhaust the output per head that is available. In such a situation, when they expect inflation of 6%, unions are able only to negotiate a money wage increase below this. With their costs rising by less than 6%, firms raise their prices by less than 6% and keep their profit margins unchanged. Thus inflation falls—it turns out to be less than the expected rate of 6%, with the result that unions achieve a real wage above the bargained real wage. Expectations are not fulfilled.

To summarize, at any rate of unemployment lower than the equilibrium rate it is impossible for the claims of all parties to be met, and their attempts to do so by pushing up nominal wages and prices produce rising inflation. At unemployment above the equilibrium rate, the sum of real wage and real profit claims is less than output per head and this results in lower inflation than had been expected; wage and price inflation fall. To make the discussion of inflation more precise, we derive explicit expressions for wage and price inflation.

We begin by deriving an expression for wage inflation from our wage-setting equation. From the wage bargaining equation, it is possible to derive an expression for wage inflation:

$$\dot{W} = \dot{P}^E + (w^B - w_{-1})/w_{-1}, \qquad \text{[wage inflation]}$$

where the subscript -1 denotes the previous period. The wage inflation equation says that money wages will rise by the expected increase in price inflation (this will keep the real wage constant) plus the amount required to take the real wage from its value last period (w_{-1}) to the value of the bargained real wage (w^B). If for example unemployment is such that w^B is 4.2 and the pre-existing real wage (w_{-1}) is 4, then money wages will rise by the expected rate of inflation $(\dot{P}^E)$ plus $(4.2 - 4)/4 = 5\%$ to take the real wage up to the right level (i.e. up to w^B).

Derivation of Wage Inflation Equation

We define the expected rise in the real wage to take it from its level in the preceding period, w_{-1}, to the level of the bargained real wage, w^B as the *gap*. Thus, we have

$$\text{Gap} \equiv \% \text{ change in expected real wage}$$

$$= \dot{W} - \dot{P}^E$$

$$= (w^B - w_{-1})/w_{-1}.$$

Therefore, we have

$$\dot{W} - \dot{P}^E = (w^B - w_{-1})/w_{-1},$$

which implies

$$\dot{W} = \dot{P}^E + (w^B - w_{-1})/w_{-1}.$$

To complete the description of wage inflation, the question of inflation expectations must be addressed. For the moment we assume that expected inflation at the start of period t, $\dot{P}_t^E$, is equal to actual price inflation the previous period, $\dot{P}_{t-1}$. As discussed in Chapter 3 above, this is the simplest form of *adaptive expectations*:

$$\dot{P}_t^E = \dot{P}_{t-1}. \qquad \text{[price inflation expectations]}$$

Turning to price inflation, we can derive the expression directly from equation (6.1'):

$$\dot{P} = \dot{W} - \dot{LP}, \qquad \text{[price inflation]}$$

on the assumption that the mark-up m is constant. Hence price inflation is equal to the rate of increase of unit costs, which in turn is equal to wage inflation less the growth of labour productivity.

Derivation of Price Inflation Equation

Since $P = 1/(1 - m)(W/LP)$, the change in P,

$$\Delta P = \frac{1}{1 - m} \Delta\left(\frac{W}{LP}\right).$$

Dividing through by the expression for the price level gives

$$\frac{\Delta P}{P} = \frac{\Delta(W/LP)}{W/LP}.$$

We can write $\Delta(W/LP)$ in full as (approximately)

$$\Delta\left(\frac{W}{LP}\right) = \frac{LP\Delta W - W\Delta LP}{(LP)^2}.$$

Substitution back into the $\Delta P/P$ expression gives

$$\frac{\Delta P}{P} = \frac{LP(\Delta W) - W(\Delta LP)}{(LP)^2} \frac{LP}{W}$$

$$= \frac{\Delta W}{W} - \frac{\Delta LP}{LP}.$$

Alternatively, we can use logs to derive the expression for inflation. Taking logarithms of the price equation,

$$\ln P = \ln(1/1 - m) + \ln W - \ln LP.$$

Differentiating with respect to time gives

$$d\ln P/dt = d\ln W/dt - d\ln LP/dt,$$

and therefore

$$\dot{P} = \dot{W} - \dot{LP}.$$

By using the rules of wage- and price-setting behaviour developed above, we can show that only when unemployment is at the equilibrium rate, U_N, will inflation be constant. Before doing this, we must clarify what the actual real wage will be. At a level of employment other than E_N where $w^B = w^P$, is the actual real wage equal to the bargained real wage or the price-determined real wage, or does it lie somewhere in between? The answer depends on the timing of wage- and price-setting decisions. A simple assumption is that at the start of the year wage negotiations take place, and money wages are set on the basis of the rate of inflation expected to prevail over the coming year. Immediately afterwards, firms set their prices. This assumption implies that the real wage is always equal to w^P. For example, suppose, as in Fig. 6.6, that employment is at E_1 and

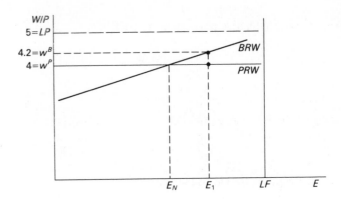

Fig. 6.6 Inconsistent claims on output per head at employment E_1

the unions negotiate wage increases to secure $w^B(E_1) = 4.2$. Setting prices immediately after this, firms will raise prices sufficiently to ensure their desired profit margin; this will push the real wage back down to 4, i.e. to w^P. In other words, this timing assumption means that the pre-existing real wage w_{-1} is always equal to w^P and that $(w^B - w_{-1})/w_{-1}$ is the percentage gap between the BRW and the PRW.

Figure 6.6 helps illustrate why there will be rising inflation at an employment level E_1 above E_N. At E_1, unions are claiming a real wage of 4.2 and firms, profits per worker of 1. The total of the claims on output per worker is therefore equal to $4.2 + 1 = 5.2$; this exceeds the 5 units of output per worker that are available. The union secures a money-wage increase to take the expected real wage up to 4.2—but firms respond by raising prices so as to reduce the real wage to 4. The process is repeated in subsequent periods.

Derivation of the Unique Equilibrium Rate of Unemployment

The unique equilibrium rate of unemployment can be derived directly from the behavioural equations above:

$$\dot{W} = \dot{P}^E + (w^B - w_{-1})/w_{-1};$$

$$\dot{P} = \dot{W} - \dot{LP},$$

and assume for simplicity that $\dot{LP} = 0$:

$$\dot{P}^E = \dot{P}_{-1}.$$

We also need to use the timing assumption for wage- and price-setting:

$$w_{-1} = w^P.$$

By substituting the wage inflation equation into the price inflation equation, we have

$$\dot{P} = \dot{P}_{-1} + (w^B - w^P)/w^P.$$

At an equilibrium rate of unemployment, inflation is constant so that

$$\dot{P} = \dot{P}_{-1}.$$

Hence at a NAIRU,

$$0 = (w^B - w^P)/w^P.$$

Since the bargaining function $w^B = b(U)$ is a monotonic inverse function of the rate of unemployment (i.e., it slopes upward in the wage–employment diagram) and w^P is constant, there is a unique rate of unemployment, U_N, at which $w^B = w^P$. This is the equilibrium rate of unemployment. If we use a simple linear function for the bargained real wage, we can arrive at an explicit expression for the NAIRU: if $w^B = b(U) = \bar{b} - b_u U$, then for competing claims equilibrium we require that $w^B = w^P$; i.e.,

$$\bar{b} - b_u U = w^P$$

$$= LP(1 - m),$$

and therefore

$$U_N = [\bar{b} - (1 - m)LP]/b_u.$$

Using the labour market diagram and the wage- and price-setting rules, we can illustrate the following results and at the same time derive the short- and long-run Phillips curves which will be used throughout the analysis of policy:

1 With $U = U_N$, $w^B = w^P$ and there is constant inflation.

2 With $U < U_N$, $w^B > w^P$ and there is rising inflation.

3 With $U > U_N$, $w^B < w^P$ and there is falling inflation.

In Fig. 6.7, the Phillips curve diagram has been drawn beneath the labour market diagram in exactly the same way as was done for Friedman's model in Chapter 3: employment equal to the labour force defines zero unemployment in the Phillips curve diagram. Unemployment rises from right to left.

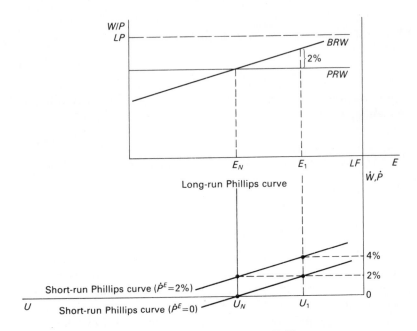

Fig. 6.7 Deriving long- and short-run Phillips curves

The *long-run Phillips curve* is defined as the locus of rates of unemployment and inflation at which inflation is constant. Only at an unemployment rate of U_N is inflation constant, since this is the only point at which the bargained real wage is equal to the price-determined real wage. With $w^B = w^P$, there is no discrepancy between the pre-existing wage and the expected real wage that unions are able to secure through money-wage negotiations. Hence $\dot{W} = \dot{P}^E + 0 = \dot{P}_{-1} = \dot{P}$; i.e., inflation remains constant at last period's level. The long-run Phillips curve is vertical at the equilibrium rate of unemployment, U_N, and is shown in Fig. 6.7.

The *short-run Phillips curve* shows the rate of price inflation associated with each rate of unemployment, given the expected rate of price inflation. To plot the short-run Phillips curves so as to be able to follow the path of wage and price inflation, we need the following equations derived above:

$$\dot{W} = \dot{P}^E + (w^B - w_{-1})/w_{-1} \qquad \text{[wage inflation]}$$

$$\dot{P} = \dot{W} - \dot{L}P \qquad \text{[price inflation]}$$

$$\dot{P}_t^E = \dot{P}_{t-1} \qquad \text{[price inflation expectations]}$$

and we assume that $\dot{L}P$ is zero.

To define a short-run Phillips curve, it is necessary to specify the expected rate of inflation. Let us assume that $\dot{P}^E = 0$. If $U = U_N$, then wage inflation will be

$$\dot{W} = 0 + [b(U_N) - w_{-1}]/w_{-1}$$
$$= 0 + 0 = 0,$$

since the bargained real wage at U_N is equal to the price-determined real wage which is last period's real wage. From the price inflation equation, we know that prices will be raised in line with wages to maintain profit margins; hence price inflation will also be zero. The first point on the short-run Phillips curve for $\dot{P}^E = 0$ is at $(0, U_N)$. To locate a second point on this short-run Phillips curve, take unemployment of U_1. Lower unemployment here raises union bargaining power and pushes w^B above w^P. If we suppose that this gap is 2%, then money wages will rise by

$$\dot{W} = 0 + 2 = 2\%,$$

so as to take the real wage up to $w^B(U_1)$. Immediately, prices will be raised in line with the increase in costs, $\dot{P} = \dot{W} = 2\%$, and we have another point on the $\dot{P}^E = 0$ short-run Phillips curve.

In exactly the same way, short-run Phillips curves for different rates of expected inflation can be constructed (see Fig. 6.7). For example, if inflation is expected to be 2%, then actual price and wage inflation at U_N will be 2%; at U_1, $\dot{W} = \dot{P}^E + 2\% = 4\%$; etc.

Table 6.2 provides simple numerical examples of the cases of constant, rising, and falling inflation, depending on whether unemployment is equal to, less than, or greater than U_N. Only in the constant inflation case (1)

Table 6.2 Inflation and the equilibrium rate of unemployment

Period	$\dot{P}^E$	'Gap' = $(w^B - w_{-1})/w_{-1}$	$\dot{W}$	$\dot{P}$	U
0	6	0	6	6	U_N
Case (1) Constant inflation: $U = U_N$					
1	6	0	6	6	U_N
2	6	0	6	6	U_N
⋮	⋮	⋮	⋮	⋮	⋮
Case (2) Rising inflation: $U = U_1$					
1	6	2	8	8	U_1
2	8	2	10	10	U_1
⋮	⋮	⋮	⋮	⋮	⋮
Case (3) Falling inflation: $U = U_2$					
1	6	−2	4	4	U_2
2	4	−2	2	2	U_2
⋮	⋮	⋮	⋮	⋮	⋮

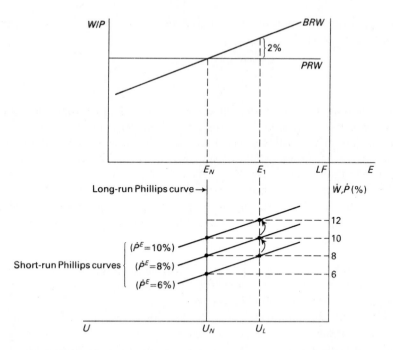

Fig. 6.8 Rising inflation: unemployment below the equilibrium rate

does the economy remain on a single short-run Phillips curve. For example, in case (2) (Fig. 6.8), the economy will move in each period from one short-run Phillips curve to a higher one associated with the new higher expected rate of inflation. In case (3) (Fig. 6.9), with unemployment above the equilibrium rate, inflation falls each period since w^B lies below the actual real wage.

6.2.2 Inflation and Money

How does money fit into this model of inflation? There is a clear formal similarity between the unique equilibrium rate of unemployment (NAIRU) and the unique natural rate of unemployment of Friedman's model. The short-run Phillips curves indexed by expected inflation and the vertical long-run Phillips curve testify to this. However, in Friedman's model rising inflation at a level of unemployment below the natural rate was generated by an increase in the money supply, which created misperceptions on the part of workers ($P > P^E$) and caused the labour supply schedule to shift to the right. Monetary expansion was the driving force behind rising inflation. In the imperfect competition model, up to this point money has scarcely been mentioned; rising inflation appears at lower unemployment rates because a fall in unemployment shifts the balance of

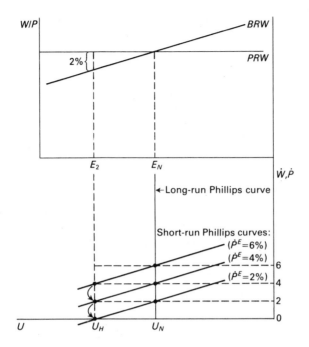

Fig. 6.9 Falling inflation: unemployment above the equilibrium rate

bargaining power from employers to unions. When the bargained real wage exceeds the price-determined real wage, bargained money-wage increases rise relative to expected inflation. Nevertheless, money cannot be neglected in the imperfect competition model. The reason is clear once we consider more carefully the implications of inflation for the real money supply and hence for the level of aggregate demand and employment. Recall that any change in the real money supply shifts the LM curve and *ceteris paribus* means a change in aggregate demand and in the level of employment.

Consider the situation depicted in Fig. 6.10. In the initial situation unemployment is at the equilibrium rate and inflation is 4%; the implicit assumption is that the nominal money supply is rising at 4% p.a. as well, so as to keep M/P unchanged and aggregate demand fixed. A fiscal boost then shifts the IS to IS_1, raising output and employment. With expected inflation at 4%, the opening up of a 2% gap between the current real wage and the bargained real wage pushes inflation up to 6%. With inflation now at 6%, the pursuit of an *unchanged* monetary growth rule would imply a *decline* in the real money supply. Hence the LM would shift to the left and employment would fall. For the economy to remain at E_1, with lower unemployment than the NAIRU, the authorities must allow the money

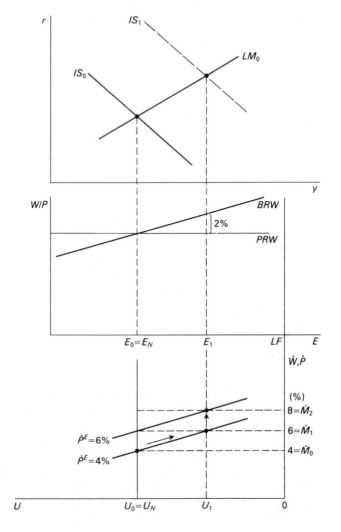

Fig. 6.10 Unemployment below the equilibrium rate: rising inflation with accommodating monetary policy to keep *LM* fixed at LM_0

supply to rise at the new higher rate of 6%. The following period, with inflation rising to 8%, a further rise in monetary growth will be required (see Fig. 6.10). The policy of allowing the money supply to rise with the rise in inflation and hence to leave the level of real aggregate demand, output, and employment unchanged is known as an *accommodating monetary policy*. For the real money supply, M/P, to remain constant, any growth in P must be matched by an equal growth in M; i.e., $\dot{M} = \dot{P}$. We discuss accommodating and non-accommodating monetary policies in more detail in Chapter 7.

In our example, the episode of increasing inflation was sparked off by a fiscal expansion which brought about the shift in bargaining power. However, what was required to sustain the inflationary episode was an accommodating monetary policy. As we show in Chapter 7, if the government fails to accommodate the rising inflation by allowing the money supply to increase in line with prices, the economy will experience falling aggregate demand and employment. Eventually, the economy will return to the equilibrium rate of unemployment, with inflation equal to the growth rate of the money supply. Any combination of fiscal and monetary policy or a shift in private-sector demand can change the level of employment, shifting it away from E_N, and initiate upward (or, in the case of employment below E_N, downward) pressure on inflation; an accommodating monetary policy is required to sustain the inflationary (or disinflationary) process.

6.3 Comparing the Equilibrium Rate of Unemployment (NAIRU) with the Natural Rate of Unemployment

This is a useful point at which to present a direct comparison between the imperfect competition model, with its unique equilibrium rate of unemployment or NAIRU, and Friedman's model, with its unique natural rate of unemployment. As has been stressed, the fundamental difference between the models relates to their microfoundations. In Fig. 6.11 the imperfect competition model is shown in part (a) and Friedman's model in part (b). In comparing the two, the first point to note is that we can draw the labour supply curve on the imperfect competition diagram; it will lie below the bargained real-wage curve. Similarly, a marginal product of labour curve can be superimposed on the imperfect competition diagram. This illustrates that the constant inflation rate of unemployment arising from the competitive behaviour of atomistic agents in labour and product markets would be different from that arising from the imperfectly competitive behaviour represented by the BRW and PRW curves.

Under imperfect competition, the market power of unions enables them to achieve a higher bargained real wage than the real wage at which the individual workers would be prepared to take a job. Similarly, the market power of the imperfectly competitive firms enables them to *mark up* their marginal cost when setting the price. By contrast, for the perfectly competitive firm, price equals marginal cost; there are no supernormal profits under perfect competition.

If we turn to a comparison between the mechanisms through which inflation is generated in each case, the initiating factor in the imperfect

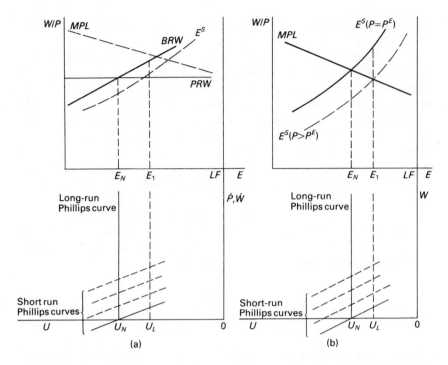

Fig. 6.11 Comparison between the imperfect competition model and Friedman's model
(a) Imperfect competition model (U_N = equilibrium rate of unemployment (NAIRU))
(b) Friedman's model (U_N = natural rate of unemployment)

competition model is a change in the level of aggregate demand which shifts employment away from U_N (Fig. 6.11(a)). Any change in employment creates a change in the relative bargaining power of the parties; a higher level of employment enables workers to secure a higher money-wage rise in the expectation of taking their real wage up to the level indicated by the *BRW*. Mark-up pricing implies that prices rise in line with wages and the economy moves along the short-run Phillips curve associated with the initial expected rate of inflation. Since inflation has risen, the authorities will have to raise the money supply if they wish to maintain real aggregate demand and keep employment at E_1. In the next period, with higher expected inflation, money wages rise by expected inflation plus the amount necessary to secure the expected real wage at E_1. The economy moves up to another short run Phillips curve.

In the Friedman model, the initiating factor in a bout of rising inflation is a monetary impulse. A rise in the money supply pushes up prices and raises the demand for goods. However, it is the fact that the *unexpected rise in prices* creates misperceptions on the part of workers which enables the supply of labour to rise and the additional output demanded to be produced. Workers believe that real wages have risen and increase their supply of labour: the economy moves up the short-run Phillips curve (Fig. 6.11(b)). For more labour than E_N to be supplied again in the following period, given the incorporation of inflationary expectations by the workers, the government must create a new and larger monetary 'surprise' in the following period in order that prices again rise by more than expected.

In both the imperfect competition model and Friedman's model, there is a unique unemployment rate at which inflation is constant and equal to the growth rate of the money supply, and this defines a vertical long-run Phillips curve. The crucial difference between the models is the labour and product market behaviour.

6.4 Employment in the Imperfect Competition Model

In the imperfect competition model, output, y, is fixed by the *demand for output*. The level of output in the economy depends on the level of aggregate demand in the IS/LM diagram, and this, via the short-run production function, determines the level of employment. Given the assumption that labour productivity is constant, there is a very simple relationship between the level of output and the level of employment in the economy: $LP = y/E$, which means that $E = y/LP$. For convenience, let us write the level of employment associated with the level of output demanded as

$$E = E(y^D) = y^D/LP;$$
$$\text{[employment equation (EAD)]}$$

i.e., the demand-determined level of employment is denoted in the labour market diagram by the EAD (Employment determined by Aggregate Demand) function. (The EAD simply maps the IS/LM intersection into the labour market diagram). In Fig. 6.12, IS_0 and LM_0 determine the level of output and employment[6]—the EAD is EAD_0, a vertical line in the labour market diagram. With a more expansionary fiscal stance, the IS

---

[6] Although in the partial equilibrium microeconomic analysis of imperfect competition, both the real wage and aggregate demand are determinants of employment, at the aggregate level, the real wage drops out. The micro argument is simply that a rise in money wages in one firm leads to a rise in its price and hence to a fall in the demand for the output of the firm and in its employment. Because the money wage has gone up and by assumption (partial equilibrium) the general price level has remained constant, a higher real wage (measured in terms of the general price level) is associated with lower employment. In aggregate, a money wage rise raises *all* prices, and it is not meaningful to talk of an *exogenous* rise in real wages having an effect on employment. Thus, the only determinant of aggregate employment in the short run is the level of real aggregate demand. This issue is discussed in more detail in pt. IV.

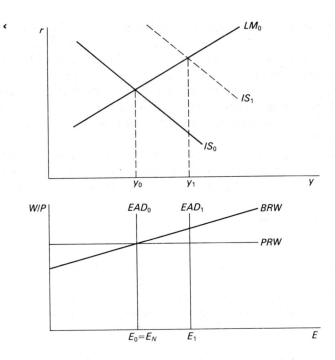

Fig. 6.12 Output and employment determination in the imperfect competition model

becomes IS_1, with the result that the EAD shifts to EAD_1 in the labour market diagram. At this level of employment, inflation will be rising. Of course, as discussed earlier, for the LM to remain fixed at LM_0 the government must allow the money supply to rise with inflation. If it does not accommodate the rising inflation, the real money supply (M/P) will fall, shifting the LM to the left. As the LM shifts, the level of output declines. Thus the EAD shifts leftward. For the EAD to remain fixed, $\dot{M}$ must equal $\dot{P}$.

Only at the equilibrium level of employment is a *constant* monetary growth rate consistent with an unchanging level of employment. Another way of stating this is to say that the *long-run equilibrium* output level for the economy, in the sense that inflation is constant, is fixed by the intersection of the bargained real-wage and price-determined real-wage curves. We return in Part IV to the possibility known as *hysteresis*, in which the level of actual unemployment affects the equilibrium rate of unemployment. If this is true, then the equilibrium level of output is not independent of the recent history of actual unemployment, and hence aggregate demand, in the economy.

*6.4.1   Keynesian and Classical Unemployment in the Imperfect Competition Model

Keynesian Unemployment in the Short Run

It is sometimes argued (especially by trade unions) that employment will rise in response to higher real wages. In other words, the unemployment is characterized as Keynesian (cf. Chapter 5 above). For such a claim to be true, aggregate demand has to vary positively with the real wage and, secondly, employment must be demand-constrained. Let us investigate more closely. Aggregate demand will vary positively with the real wage if the propensity to consume out of wage income is greater than the propensity to consume out of profit income. A higher real wage and lower profits would then imply higher consumption demand. In the standard consumption function, income from profits and from wages is treated identically.

To this point, we have assumed that the EAD curve is vertical, i.e. that employment required to meet aggregate demand is independent of the real wage. Now we will show that the EAD may have a positive slope: there may be a positive *demand-side* relationship between the real wage and employment. If we assume that all wages are consumed (i.e. that there are no savings out of wages) and that all profits are saved, then we have a very simple consumption function in which consumption is dependent on real wages. In this case,

$$y^D = wE + i(r)$$

and with constant labour productivity,

$$y^D = w(y/LP) + i(r).$$

In goods market equilibrium, $y = y^D$, which implies that

$$y = \frac{1}{1 - w/LP} i(r) \qquad \text{[\emph{IS} equation]}$$

As illustrated in Fig. 6.13, there is a different *IS* for each level of the real wage. For a given interest rate, a higher real wage means a higher average propensity to consume and therefore a larger multiplier. A higher level of output is therefore required for goods market equilibrium. In the lower panel of Fig. 6.13, a positively sloped EAD curve is traced out.

With a positively sloped EAD, suppose the economy is initially at point *A* in Fig. 6.14. If the bargained real wage curve shifts up as a result, for example, of increased union militancy, the economy will move to *B*. Employment will rise as the result of the higher aggregate demand associated with the higher real wage level. For actual real wages to rise and influence demand, we must assume that prices are not set *immediately* after wages (see box on timing of wage- and price-setting). Although the

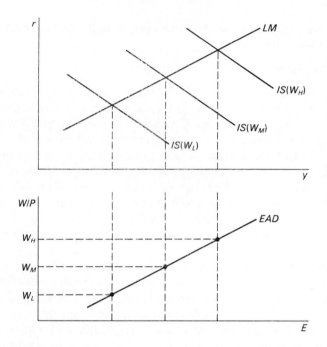

Fig. 6.13 Aggregate demand varies positively with the real wage

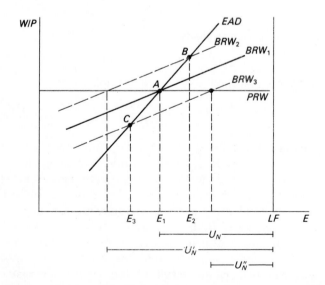

Fig. 6.14 Shifts in BRW when there is a positively sloped EAD

Note: For the economy to move from *A* to *B* following the shift in the BRW to BRW$_2$, the
real wage must be equal to w^B; i.e., prices are not set immediately after wages

positive association between employment and the real wage suggested at the outset of this discussion has been demonstrated, it is essential to see that, at a point such as B, the economy is characterized by rising inflation. Unemployment has been reduced by the rise in aggregate demand owing to the rise in real wages, but it is below the equilibrium rate of unemployment; the NAIRU associated with BRW_2 is U'_N shown on the diagram.

Similarly, if the BRW shifts downwards as the result of an incomes policy or legislative changes, then employment will fall as the economy moves to point C. In this case, unemployment is above the equilibrium rate and the economy will experience falling inflation.

Timing of Wage- and Price-Setting

The standard assumption in the imperfect competition model is that prices are set immediately after wage increases have been negotiated. As we have seen above, this timing assumption means that the actual real wage is always equal to the price-determined real wage. An immediate pricing response to cost increases ensures that the target profit margin is always achieved. If, for example, unemployment is below the equilibrium rate with the bargained real wage in excess of the price-determined real wage ($w^B > w^P$), then, although wages will rise by expected inflation plus the increase required to take the real wage to w^B, the immediate marking up of prices means that the real wage is reduced to w^P. Fig. 6.15(a) illustrates how this timing assumption produces a constant real wage equal to w^P in a situation in which w^B exceeds w^P (see Fig. 6.15 overleaf).

In practice, however, prices do not rise immediately to preserve profitability. There are time lags between wage- and price-setting and vice versa. To the extent that price changes lag behind wage changes, the actual real wage will diverge from the level of the price-determined real wage. A simple assumption which highlights this case is the exact reverse of the one above: wages rise at the start of the period and prices rise at the end (see Fig. 6.15(b)). In this case, the real wage is always equal to the BRW.

Consumption may well vary with changes in the real wage because of the differential in propensities to consume from wage and profit income. But investment, too, may be sensitive to changes in the real wage. In the investment function introduced earlier, $i = i(r, A)$, A represents expectations of profitability. One determinant of expected profitability may be the current rate of profit defined as Π/K where Π refers to total profits in nominal terms and K is the replacement value of the capital stock. In

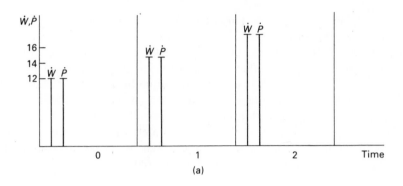

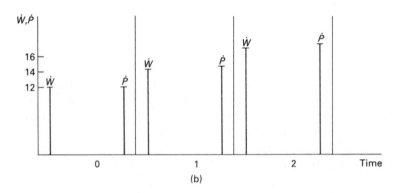

Fig. 6.15 The timing of wage and price rises: implications for the real wage
(a) Prices rise immediately after wages rise: $w = w^P$
(b) Wages rise at start of period; prices at the end: $w = w^B$
Assumptions: $\dot{P}^E = \dot{P}_{-1} = 10\%$; w^B exceeds w^P by 2%

the short run, K can be considered fixed. By definition, the profit rate is equal to the profit share multiplied by the output–capital ratio: $\Pi/K = (\Pi/Y)(Y/K)$. Unless the output–capital ratio changes very sharply, changes in the profit share mirror changes in the profit rate. With constant labour productivity, a rise in the real wage means a fall in the profit share:

$$\text{Profit share} = \Pi/Y = (Y - WE)/Y,$$

and dividing through numerator and denominator by the price level, P, gives

$$\Pi/Y = (y - wE)/y$$
$$= 1 - w/LP.$$

In these circumstances, higher real wages will dampen investment. The slope of the EAD will depend on whether the positive effect of real wages on consumption outweighs their negative effect on investment.[7]

Having noted the routes through which aggregate demand can depend on the real wage, the neutral assumption of a vertical (real-wage-independent) EAD will be made for the remainder of this part of the book.

Classical Unemployment in the Short Run

There are no clear reasons to expect the occurrence of classical unemployment in a *closed* economy with imperfect competition. If it happened that real wages were pushed temporarily above the marginal product of labour (for example, because of a marked upward shift in the bargained real wage curve), so that some output and hence employment was rendered unprofitable, it would be expected that firms would raise their prices. If customer loyalties are important in such markets and produce a reluctance to raise the price, then the firm should supply the demand at a loss and therefore maintain employment in order to retain loyalties. We will see in Part III that a much more plausible scenario for the occurrence of classical unemployment exists in an open economy where firms are constrained from raising prices by the behaviour of their overseas competitors (Section 11.6 below).

A standard argument which we have not touched on is that a higher real wage will alter the optimal capital–labour ratio for the firm and for the economy as a whole. While not wishing to minimize the importance of this effect, it is a longer-run question and can be set to one side in our analysis of the short and medium run.

6.5 Summary

The key feature of the imperfect competition model is that, given the structural characteristics of the economy which determine the position of the bargaining function and the price-determined real wage function, the government faces a trade-off between unemployment and rising inflation if it seeks to reduce unemployment below the equilibrium rate. Only by the use of policy tools that operate on the BRW and PRW curves directly, and hence *shift* the equilibrium rate of unemployment, can the government secure a lower unemployment rate consistent with stable inflation.

---

[7] A more complicated investment function than $i = i(r, A)$ would include relative factor prices to take account of the role of an increase in the capital stock (i.e. investment) in altering the technique of production—the capital–labour ratio. The real wage would appear as a determinant of the desired capital stock, with a rise in the real wage relative to the cost of capital provoking a shift towards a more capital-intensive technique. Hence a positive relationship between the change in the real wage and the level of investment is a possibility.

One of the means available to the government for shifting the equilibrium rate of unemployment is the supply-side effects of changes in taxes. By altering the wedge between the real consumption wage and the real product wage, the government is able to alter the rate of employment at which the claims of unions and firms are consistent. In other words, the government's share of real income claimed through the tax system is a choice variable, the macroeconomic implications of which can be examined readily in the imperfect competition model (see Chapter 7). The ability of the government to improve the level of productivity in the economy through expenditure on training is a further means by which the equilibrium rate of unemployment can be lowered.

To the extent that an incomes policy can affect the level of the expected real wage that unions are able to negotiate at each rate of unemployment, it provides an additional instrument which is available for the purpose of shifting the equilibrium rate of unemployment (Chapter 7).

The imperfect competition model permits the analysis of the impact of changes in demand on output, employment, and inflation. The presentation of the imperfect competition model earlier in this chapter indicates that, if the government pursues a non-accommodating monetary policy, i.e., if the money supply is not permitted to increase in line with inflation, then aggregate demand and hence output and employment will be constant only when inflation is equal to the growth rate of the money supply and unemployment is at the equilibrium rate. An accommodating monetary policy enables the economy to remain at an unemployment level away from the equilibrium rate but with the consequence of falling (if $U > U_N$) or rising (if $U < U_N$) inflation.

The imperfect competition model displays both similarities and contrasts with Friedman's model. The similarity rests on the existence of a rate of unemployment at which inflation is constant—there is a vertical long-run Phillips curve in each model. However, Friedman's natural rate of unemployment is a market-clearing rate (assuming that agents are fully informed of price movements), while the NAIRU is the rate of unemployment at which the competing claims of labour and firms in the economy are consistent. Central to the equilibrium rate of unemployment is the notion of market power and the role of unemployment in moderating that power. By contrast, the natural rate of unemployment emerges from the atomistic behaviour of individual workers and firms.

7

Economic Policy and the Imperfect Competition Model

The imperfect competition model is characterized by a unique rate of unemployment at which inflation is constant. In such a model, it is natural to look initially at the policies available to government to reduce the equilibrium rate of unemployment. What types of economic policy can shift the equilibrium rate of unemployment? Clearly, policies that shift the bargained real wage curve (BRW) or the price-determined real wage curve (PRW) can be adopted if a sustainable reduction in unemployment is to be achieved. A shift in either the BRW or the PRW results in a shift in the long-run Phillips curve to the new equilibrium rate of unemployment. Supply-side fiscal measures provide the means for the achievement of lower unemployment without the consequence of rising inflation. For example, on the tax side, measures taken by the government to reduce its share of output per head enable the competing claims of the private sector to be reconciled at lower unemployment. It has also been suggested that government expenditure programmes on industrial training are able to reduce the equilibrium rate of unemployment by raising productivity. In the final part of the discussion of fiscal measures, we address the question of whether changes in unemployment benefit have an effect on the BRW or PRW and hence on the equilibrium rate of unemployment. In Friedman's natural rate model discussed in Chapter 3, changes in unemployment benefit were shown to affect the natural rate of unemployment by altering the trade-off between search activities and employment. Is there a similar effect on the equilibrium rate of unemployment?

In addition to fiscal measures, the obvious tool for reducing the equilibrium rate of unemployment is to implement an incomes policy. The use of negotiation to lower the unions' bargained real wage as well as that of government-imposed incomes policies such as the 'tax-based incomes policy' is examined.

The second issue in policy analysis is how policy affects actual employment. Suppose that the economy has suffered a negative demand shock with the result that actual unemployment has risen above the equilibrium rate. Although, as we have seen in Chapter 6, there will be downward pressure on inflation when unemployment is above the NAIRU, the arguments developed in Chapter 5 suggest that re-equilibrating forces taking the economy back to the equilibrium rate may be very weak. As a second example, if the government has succeeded in lowering the equilibrium rate of unemployment, can it use fiscal policy in the way envisaged by Keynes to boost the level of aggregate demand and enable the economy to move speedily to the NAIRU? The answer requires an examination of the so-called crowding-out debate with its analysis of both the flow and stock effects of fiscal measures on demand.

The final section of the chapter focuses on inflation, and in particular on the use of a monetary growth rule as a policy instrument to achieve constant inflation. The question at issue is how the economy reacts to the adoption of a monetary target. In the initial situation the government pursues a policy of keeping unemployment below the equilibrium rate at the expense of rising inflation by allowing the money supply to rise in line with inflation. The government then switches to a policy of not accommodating the rising inflation—it adopts a growth rate rule for the money supply. We trace the implications for inflation and unemployment. Since we are working with adaptive expectations, the announcement of a monetary growth rule will not produce an immediate jump of the economy to the new equilibrium. Rather, a lengthy process of adjustment of employment, inflation expectations, and inflation ensues. This provides an introduction to the fuller discussion of expectations in Chapter 8.

7.1 Policies to Shift the Equilibrium Rate of Unemployment: Supply-Side Fiscal Policy and Incomes Policy

The equilibrium rate of unemployment can be reduced by either a downward shift in the bargained real wage curve (BRW) or an upward shift in the price-determined real wage curve (PRW). In either case, compatibility between real wage claims of workers and real profit claims of firms occurs at a higher level of employment (Fig. 7.1). The equilibrium rate of unemployment falls from U_N to U'_N. The long-run Phillips curve shifts to the lower equilibrium rate of unemployment, and all of the short-run Phillips curves are now drawn with reference to the new long-run Phillips curve (Fig. 7.1). There are two reasons why the government may introduce policies that reduce the equilibrium rate of unemployment. On the one hand, they may wish to run the economy at a lower rate of unemployment while keeping inflation constant. Figure 7.2(a) illustrates the implementation of a policy of reducing the equilibrium rate of unemployment which enables inflation to be held constant at its pre-existing level of 5%. The economy moves from A to B in the Phillips curve diagram.

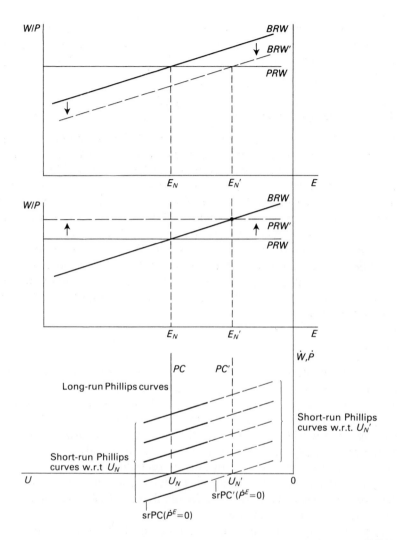

Fig. 7.1 Shifting the equilibrium rate of unemployment by shifting the BRW or PRW curves

Short-run Phillips curves associated with U_N are shown by a solid line; short-run Phillips curves associated with U_N' are shown by a broken line

On the other hand, the authorities may wish to use a policy of shifting the equilibrium rate of unemployment as a means of reducing inflation while holding unemployment constant. Figure 7.2(b) illustrates this case. Unemployment is kept at the original level of U_0. By lowering the equilibrium rate of unemployment to U_N', the economy now experiences falling inflation with unemployment of U_0. The relevant short-run Phillips curves are those drawn with reference to the new, lower, equilibrium rate of unemployment, U'_N, so that with expected inflation of 10%, inflation falls to 8%, then 6%, etc. The economy moves from A to B to C, etc., in Fig. 7.2(b).

7.1.1 Supply-Side Fiscal Policy

Two different types of supply-side fiscal effects will be considered: changes in taxation, and changes in government expenditure on training. Intuitively, it is clear that, if we think of output per head as being divided three ways between workers (wages), firms (profits), and the government (taxation), then changes in taxation implying a reduction in the government's claim will enable private-sector claims to be consistent at a higher level of employment. As to expenditure increases, if the government raises its expenditure on training, then this can be expected to lower the equilibrium rate of unemployment through two mechanisms: first, increased training will raise productivity and shift the PRW curve upwards; secondly, more training will raise the effective labour supply and therefore shift the BRW curve downwards.

Taxation

The basic rationale for using changes in taxation to shift the equilibrium rate of unemployment is that, by reducing the government's claim on output per head, the competing claims of the private sector can be reconciled at a lower rate of unemployment. The difference between the real wage that workers receive, i.e. the post-tax real consumption wage, and the real cost of labour to the firm, i.e. the gross real product wage, is often referred to as the *wedge*. Lower taxation reduces the wedge.

To proceed in greater detail with the analysis of wedge-reducing policies, it is necessary to specify more carefully the definition of wages and prices. Once taxes and social security contributions are included, care is required, since money wages paid and net prices received by firms will generally differ from wages received and prices paid by workers and consumers. As before, W is the market wage. Therefore the 'consumption' wage, i.e. what the worker has left from W after deductions, is the market wage less employees' social security contributions and income taxation. As before, P is the price at which goods sell in the market—this will include indirect taxation. The price received by the employer will be the market price less indirect taxation:

$$P \equiv \text{market price of goods,}$$

$$W \equiv \text{market price of labour.}$$

It is the market wage divided by the market price that is measured on the

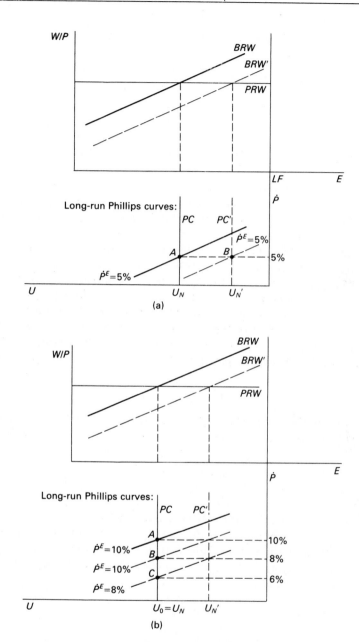

Fig. 7.2 Using policy to lower the equilibrium rate of unemployment:
(a) so as to be able to reduce unemployment and maintain constant inflation; (b) so
as to be able to reduce inflation

Short-run Phillips curves associated with U_N are shown by a solid line; short-run Phillips
curves associated with U_N' are shown by a broken line

vertical axis of the real wage–employment diagram. The real consumption wage is

$$RCW \equiv \frac{W(1 - t_y - s_{ee})}{P},$$

where t_y is the rate of income taxation and s_{ee} denotes the percentage rate of employee social security contributions.

The object of union bargaining is take-home pay in terms of consumption goods, i.e. the real consumption wage defined above. For any given W and P, any rise in income taxation or in employee social security contributions will reduce the real consumption wage. In order to maintain the real consumption wage in the face of higher direct taxation, unions will seek to negotiate a higher gross wage (W) from their employer: the BRW will shift upward.

We can make this intuitive argument more precise by asking how we draw the BRW in the labour market diagram once income tax and employee social security contributions are taken into account? We assume that the bargaining power of the union relates directly to the real consumption wage (RCW). Hence the bargained RCW will depend inversely on the level of unemployment, say $RCW^B = w^B(U)$. But in our diagram we want to show with the BRW the level of W/P which the union can bargain at each level of unemployment. Since

$$\frac{W}{P} = \frac{RCW}{1 - t_y - s_{ee}},$$

it follows that the bargained W/P at a given U will be the bargained RCW at that level of unemployment divided by $(1 - t_y - s_{ee})$. In other words,

$$BRW = \frac{RCW^B}{1 - t_y - s_{ee}} = \frac{w^B(U)}{1 - t_y - s_{ee}}.$$

[bargained real wage]

Thus, a rise in t_y or s_{ee} shifts the BRW curve upward.

Since firms are interested in their real profit margins, their concern is with offsetting the impact on their costs, i.e. on the real product wage, of changes in employers' social security contributions and in indirect taxation. The real product wage is

$$RPW = \frac{W(1 + s_{er})}{P(1 - t_i)},$$

where s_{er} denotes the percentage rate of employer social security contributions and t_i is the rate of indirect taxation. The real product wage shows the amount that firms have to pay out in wages in terms of the price of the product before indirect taxes are added. To maintain their profit margins, firms set the price (before indirect taxes are added) by marking up unit labour costs, including employer social security contributions:

$$P(1 - t_i) = (1 + \mu) \frac{W(1 + s_{er})}{LP}.$$

Therefore, by rearranging, we derive the price-determined real wage as

$$PRW = \frac{W}{P} = \frac{LP}{1 + \mu} \frac{1 - t_i}{1 + s_{er}}.$$

[price-determined real wage]

For the profit margin, μ, to remain unchanged in the face of a rise in indirect taxation or employers' social security contributions, there must be less output per head available for real wages: the price-determined real wage (W/P) falls.

To summarize, in order to reduce the equilibrium rate of unemployment, the government can lower the rates of direct taxation or employees' social security contributions, thereby lowering the BRW, or it can lower the rates of indirect taxation or employers' social security contributions, thereby raising the PRW.

Government Spending on Training

There are two channels through which increased government expenditure on industrial training lowers the equilibrium rate of unemployment. First, a more highly trained work-force will be characterized by higher productivity and this will shift the price-determined real wage upwards. Secondly, increased training will have the effect of lowering the bargained real wage curve. On the one hand, additional spending on training by the government makes it cheaper for employers to take on workers since they will not have to be trained. This will increase the pool of skilled labour available to the employer and thereby reduce union bargaining power. If businesses are constrained from expanding by a lack of skilled workers, then the existing skilled workers are able to raise the BRW. By widening this bottleneck, the government weakens the bargaining power of the skilled workers. It has also been argued that the duration of a spell of unemployment leads to the erosion of skills (Layard and Nickell 1986). If this is so, the effect of a growing proportion of long-term unemployed will be to raise the BRW.[1] A government (re)training programme can counteract this effect.

Can Changes in Unemployment Benefit Affect the Equilibrium Rate of Unemployment?

In Friedman's model with an atomistic labour market, changes in unemployment benefit have a direct effect on the natural rate of

---

[1] This issue is discussed in detail in ch. 19.

unemployment by shifting the labour supply curve (refer back to Fig. 3.7 in Chapter 3). Among those voluntarily unemployed are individuals searching for better jobs. A reduction in the unemployment benefit raises the costs of search, with the result that at any real wage the number prepared to accept employment is higher than previously: the labour supply curve shifts rightward. As Fig. 3.7 illustrates, the result of a lower unemployment benefit in the Friedman model is a lower natural rate of unemployment.

Is there a parallel relationship between the unemployment benefit and the equilibrium rate of unemployment in the imperfect competition model? The effect of changes in unemployment benefit on the equilibrium rate of unemployment can be thought of as operating on the BRW either via its effect on the labour supply curve or directly. The first channel derives from the idea that it is not the total stock of unemployed relative to the labour force that determines bargaining power, but rather that proportion which is involuntarily unemployed, i.e. those people prepared to take a job at the current real wage. The voluntarily unemployed are those engaged in search for a higher paid job.

Looking at Fig. 7.3, with a real wage of w_0 and employment of E_0, the mix between voluntary and involuntary unemployment is clear. If the labour supply curve shifts to the right (from E^S to $E^{S'}$ in Fig. 7.4) in response to a fall in unemployment benefit, then the number of voluntarily unemployed falls. At each level of employment, there is then a larger number of the involuntarily unemployed willing to take jobs at the real wage w_0. If this represents a slackening of the effective labour market then w^B at each level of employment would be lower; the BRW shifts downward to BRW' (see Fig. 7.4). If involuntary unemployment of $U = U_0^I$ (superscript I denotes involuntary unemployment) fixes the bargained real wage at a level of w_0 at E_0, then following the shift in the

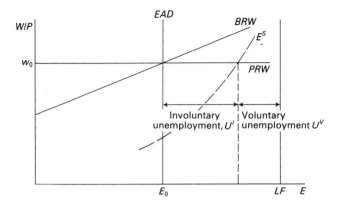

Fig. 7.3 The bargaining curve and the labour supply curve: voluntary and involuntary unemployment at $w = w_0$

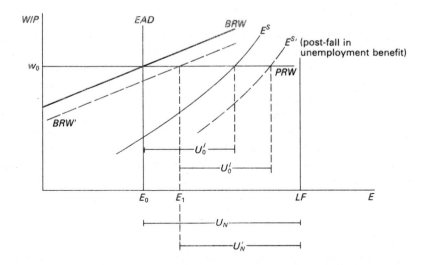

Fig. 7.4 Unemployment benefit and the equilibrium rate of unemployment

labour supply curve, a bargained real wage of w_0 will occur at an employment level of E_1. There will be a lower equilibrium rate of unemployment at U'_N. Whether or not such an effect exists, and if so how significant it is, remains an open question.

The second set of arguments go directly from the level of the unemployment benefit to the bargained real wage. If workers on strike are eligible for unemployment benefit, a lower benefit raises the cost of being on strike and this directly reduces union bargaining power. In addition, a fall in unemployment benefit raises the cost of job loss. Thus, to the extent that it is felt by union leaders or members that stronger bargaining increases the risk of unemployment, a cut in benefit will succeed in lowering the BRW curve.

A third argument is that the minimum real wage acceptable to union members is related to the level of unemployment benefit. The reason is that the level of the unemployment benefit sets a floor to the lowest rates of pay acceptable in the economy. A fall in unemployment benefit, by lowering the minimum real wage acceptable to workers, would have the effect of shifting the balance of bargaining power away from the unions. At each level of employment there would be a lower w^B; the BRW would shift downward.

The empirical significance of the effects of changes in unemployment benefit is hotly disputed.[2]

---

[2] See the survey of evidence presented in Fallon and Verry (1988: 266–74).

7.1.2 Incomes Policy

The idea of using an incomes policy to reduce the equilibrium rate of unemployment derives from the possibility of introducing measures that lower the bargained real wage curve. The most familiar form of an incomes policy directed towards this end is an agreement between unions and employers over wage restraint which may or may not involve the government. It does not have to be a formal agreement, and often does not carry the title of 'incomes policy'. Incomes policies have existed in Sweden and for a time in West Germany, but they have been informal and the term 'incomes policy' has not been used. We will suggest that a useful way to depict such a policy is that it results in the exercise of bargaining discretion by unions so that the bargained real wage curve lies below its maximum level.

The second, less familiar, type of incomes policy is one that is unilaterally imposed by a government to reduce the bargaining power of unions. Examples of such policies would be a tax-based incomes policy and the implementation of legislation against unions. In this case, the objective of the policy is not to produce bargaining discretion by unions but to lower the maximum bargained real wage itself. We will see that a tax-based incomes policy achieves this objective by altering the incentives facing *employers* when they are engaged in wage negotiations.

In the imperfect competition model, the gains from the ability of the government to negotiate an incomes policy are obvious; a downward shift of the bargained real wage curve has the effect of reducing the equilibrium rate of unemployment. We leave to Chapter 8 an investigation of the problems in securing union agreement to participate in an incomes policy. Suffice it to say here that it seems that the degree of centralization of union organization is an important determinant of the feasibility of such a policy.

Wage Restraint and Union Agreement

At each level of employment, union negotiators have a choice as to how hard they push wage negotiations. The limits to this choice are set at the upper end by employers and at the lower end by individual union members. The ceiling for bargaining intensity has been referred to as the *maximum bargained real wage* (MaxBRW) (Flanagan *et al.* 1982). The maximum bargained real wage is the expected real wage that unions can secure if they use their bargaining power to the full, i.e., if they use all the weapons at their disposal, including strikes. The MaxBRW will slope upward in the real wage–employment diagram. Changes in the environment in which the unions operate such as changes in industrial relations legislation will affect the weapons available to the unions and hence will shift the MaxBRW. Clearly, the bargaining militancy of the unions and the extent to which employees are organized will affect the position of the MaxBRW.

The position of the MaxBRW will also depend on the ability of firms to pay the wage and on their willingness to resist union demands. The employers will seek a minimum cost outcome by trading off the costs of a settlement against the costs of industrial action. The resistance of employers to union demands will also be related to the extent to which employers are organized. Employer resistance to wage claims may well be strengthened by employers acting in concert in wage negotiations, drawing on such weapons as strategic lock-outs[3] to offset unions' strike tactics.

The *floor* to the expected real wage actually negotiated by the unions is set by the *minimum acceptable real wage* function, MinARW. This is defined as the highest real wage which individual workers at local level will insist on, in the sense that they cannot be prevented by the union leadership from striking for it. Should the union leadership decide to operate along a BRW below the MinARW, we would expect to observe *unofficial* strike action as workers sought to negotiate higher wages at local level. The MinARW, though related to the concept of a minimum real wage target, should be interpreted more broadly than this. It can be considered as a many-sided constraint covering minimally acceptable conditions of work such as the intensity or speed of work, as well as wages, hours of work, holidays, etc. Should any or some combination of these constraints be violated, then the workers would insist on going on strike if this were necessary to rectify the shortfall in their minimum acceptable conditions of employment.[4]

In general, there will tend to be a gap between the minimum acceptable real wage and the maximum negotiable real wage at each level of employment. This gap defines the zone of bargaining discretion available to the unions between the constraints set by the employers on the one hand and by their members on the other (Fig. 7.5). Bargaining discretion exists because individual workers or small groups of workers would generally be unable to gain as favourable a settlement as could the union for the industry as a whole. Employers in a single firm would be unwilling to agree to wage increases that would require it to raise its prices relative to those of its competitors, since this would result in the loss of market share. On a broader front, however, such a wage increase might well be negotiable if the chance of firms losing out *vis-à-vis* their competitors in the same

---

[3] A strategic lock-out is a tactic adopted for example by employers in West Germany. Suppose the engineering industry union takes strike action in support of a wage claim. It will choose key plants to strike so as to maximize its effectiveness and minimize the cost of strike pay. The employers react by *locking out* workers at other plants, so as to raise the strike costs to the union.

[4] See Soskice (1978) for an explanation in these terms of the outbreak of wildcat (unofficial) strikes across Western Europe at the end of the 1960s.

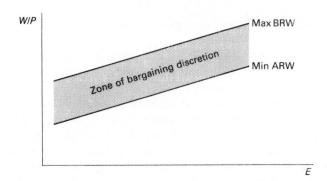

Fig. 7.5 The zone of bargaining discretion between the maximum bargained real wage (MaxBRW) and the minimum acceptable real wage (MinARW)

market were reduced. Such considerations serve to push the MaxBRW above the MinARW (see Fig. 7.5).

The bargaining curve along which negotiations actually take place, the BRW, generally lies between the MaxBRW and the MinARW. Its position depends on the decision by the union as to the degree of bargaining discretion to use. Should the union choose a level of bargaining intensity that pushes the BRW above the MaxBRW, then employers will refuse to grant the wage claim. Strikes will be won by employers and the BRW will be pushed back down to the maximum attainable level. The obvious question is, Why should unions exercise bargaining discretion? The observation that unions frequently operate at less than their maximum bargaining intensity can be accounted for by a number of factors. One rationale for such behaviour is union concern with the long-run future of the industry. The use of maximum bargaining intensity and the use of the associated weapons of industrial disruption might be thought likely to jeopardize investment plans in the industry. Another rationale is that unions may be concerned about the short-term employment consequences. We will argue later (Chapter 17), however, that this is not as common as might be thought.

Here we are concerned with the use of discretion by unions acting together to shift down the BRW and allow the equilibrium rate of unemployment to fall. The introduction of an incomes policy represents the formal or informal agreement by unions to reduce their bargaining intensity so that the BRW curve shifts downwards towards the MinARW curve. Agreement to an incomes policy may be based not simply on the quid pro quo of economic goods, such as increased government spending in exchange for bargaining restraint, but also on pay-offs of a more political nature. For example, the unions may secure an enhanced role in government economic policy-making, or changes in industrial relations legislation.

As noted above, negotiation of an incomes policy permits the government either to run the economy at lower unemployment while maintaining stable inflation or to reduce inflation while holding unemployment constant. If the incomes policy is used for the first objective and it breaks down, then rising inflation will occur unless the government reduces aggregate demand and allows unemployment to rise back to its original equilibrium rate. By contrast, if the policy is used to reduce inflation and it subsequently breaks down, then with the BRW returning to its initial level, the economy will have secured a fall in the rate of inflation; it can continue to operate at an unchanged rate of unemployment with inflation constant at the new lower rate. A permanent gain would have been secured for the economy even though the incomes policy was only temporary. Of course, it is essential for the government to *combine* the use of an inflation-reducing incomes policy with the appropriate monetary policy. Unless the growth rate of the money supply is reduced in line with the decline in wage and price inflation resulting from the incomes policy agreement, real aggregate demand will rise. This will push unemployment down and provoke higher wage claims.

We discuss in some detail the reasons why an incomes policy may tend to break down in Chapter 8. Finally, it is important to note that the *actual* real wage remains unchanged in the context of a downward shift in the BRW: it is only wage expectations that must be lowered. We will see however that this situation changes when we move to the open economy—in Chapter 11, we show that an incomes policy in an open economy requires a fall in the real wage.

Tax-based Incomes Policy (TIP)

The general idea of a tax-based incomes policy (see e.g., Wallich and Weintraub 1971; Jackman and Layard 1986) is to operate on the willingness of employers to concede wage claims. If we assume that unions are bargaining along the MaxBRW curve, i.e. if MaxBRW = BRW, then the policy aims to lower the MaxBRW. The policy consists of a tax levied on employers who pay money-wage increases in excess of a norm; i.e., there is a tax on $\dot{W} > \bar{W}$, where $\bar{W}$ is the norm for wage increases set by the government. The tax collected in this way is then returned to employers in total as a rebate per employee. If τ is the tax rate on wage increases in excess of the norm and s_i is the ith firm's share of total employment, the cost to the ith firm of exceeding the norm is

$$\tau(\dot{W}_i - \bar{W}) - s_i \Sigma_j \tau(\bar{W}_j - \dot{W}).$$

Thus, the total net tax facing the firm is $\tau(1 - s_i)\mathrm{d}\dot{W}_i$, where $\mathrm{d}\dot{W}_i$ is the amount by which the ith firm's wage rise exceeds the norm. But s_i, the ith firm's share of the total rebate, will be very small. As this tends to zero, the effective tax is $\tau d\dot{W}_i$. The higher is τ, the higher is the tax on excessive wage rises and the less willing employers will be to concede wage rises above the norm. The existence of the tax reduces the net costs to the employer from refusing to give in to strike threats from the unions in support of their wage claim. This shifts the balance of bargaining power in the employers' favour and lowers the MaxBRW curve along which bargaining is assumed to occur. Note that the price-determined real wage is unaffected because total wage costs in the economy are unchanged.

There are several problems associated with the imposition of a policy such as TIP.[5] In practice, union co-operation is required for such a policy to be successful and unions are very opposed to wages rising at different rates under any sort of incomes policy. Under a TIP, high-productivity firms will grant wage rises higher than the norm and pay the tax. This leads on to a second problem. It is likely that the tax rate τ will have to be very high to make it worth while for employers to take the risk of facing strike action by refusing wage rises above the norm. This will be particularly true to the extent that firms can pass the tax on in higher prices. Finally, TIPs face special problems in the public sector where the government is effectively paying the tax to itself. For the public sector, a TIP is therefore just like the imposition of a pay norm.

7.2   The Effect of Policy on Actual Employment: the Crowding-out Debate

In the first part of this chapter we have concentrated on the way in which changes in fiscal policy can be used to affect the equilibrium rate of unemployment. Throughout Section 7.1 it was assumed that the government could achieve whatever *actual* level of employment it wished through the use of aggregate demand policies. For example, it was implicit in the analysis of the use of supply-side fiscal measures, that, having chosen to lower the equilibrium rate of unemployment by reducing tax rates, the government would be able to take the level of actual employment up to the new NAIRU through the use of one of its aggregate demand tools—for example through an expansion of government spending. We now turn to the ability of the government to manipulate the level of aggregate demand. Can the government use deficit financing as a means of raising the level of activity in the economy? The main task of this section is to clarify the so-called crowding-out debate. Crowding-out refers to the effect on private expenditure of an expansion of government spending. The effects of a public-sector deficit on demand are best highlighted on the assumption that prices are constant. It is therefore possible to work with the *IS/LM*

---

[5] See e.g. Bosanquet (1983).

diagram alone. This permits a clarification of both the flow and the stock effects of a bond-financed deficit. In Section 7.3 the feedback from inflation to aggregate demand is directly addressed.

7.2.1 Crowding-out: Flow Effects

The usual definition of crowding-out is that it occurs whenever a rise in the public-sector deficit financed by bond sales results in a fall in the level of private spending. For ease of exposition, we will assume that the deficit arises from an increase in government spending. The above definition amounts to the assumption that the overall multiplier associated with the rise in government spending has a value of less than one: national income rises by an amount less than the value of the rise in government spending. For this to be true, private spending in the new situation must be lower than it was initially. However, we can show that an increase in government spending does not necessarily produce crowding-out as defined this way: private spending in total may not be reduced by the rise in government spending.

A bond-financed deficit has the effect of reducing private investment spending because it raises the interest rate. By raising income in the economy, higher government spending will boost the transactions demand for money, and with a fixed money supply, this will result in a rise in interest rates. Interest rates will rise because the higher transactions demand for money will lead individuals to sell bonds, thereby depressing the bond price. However, against this fall in private investment must be set the rise in private consumption induced by the incomes associated with the higher government spending.

The relative elasticities of the *IS* and *LM* curves determine whether or not the multiplier associated with a bond-financed deficit is less than one. The multiplier will be smaller, the lower is the elasticity of the demand for money with respect to the interest rate, since in the case of a very inelastic money demand function, the increase in money demand arising from higher income will have to produce a very large rise in the interest rate to reduce the asset demand for money. With respect to the *IS*, the multiplier will be lower, the more elastic is investment to the interest rate—since a given rise in the interest rate will produce a larger fall in investment.

It should also be noted that, with an investment function $i = i(r, A)$, where A represents the expectational factors in the investment decision, one component of A will be capacity utilization. The rise in capacity utilization will boost investment. The *IS* will be pushed outward. The capacity utilization effect will provide at least a partial offset to the standard 'crowding-out' of investment through higher interest rates (see Fig. 7.6). Increased government spending shifts *IS* from IS_0 to IS_1; the interest rate rises to r_1. However, the rise in output causes the investment

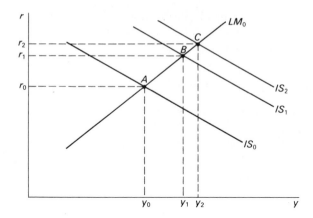

Fig. 7.6 Fiscal expansion: induced rise in investment

function and hence *IS* to shift further to the right. The economy is at *C*. Total investment at *C* can be higher or lower than it is at *A*.

Nevertheless, there may still be a tendency towards crowding-out even after account has been taken both of the fact that the government spending multiplier is not necessarily less than one and that investment is expected to react positively to higher government spending at each interest rate. To the extent that this is so, the government can offset the interest rate effects of a bond-financed deficit by adopting an appropriate monetary policy. The interest rate will remain constant as long as the government accommodates the rise in the demand for money induced by the bond-financed deficit by increasing the supply of money. If the government meets the additional demand for money by purchasing bonds at the existing price, bond prices will not fall and the interest rate will remain constant. By using monetary policy in conjunction with the fiscal expansion, the demand-dampening effect of higher interest rates is eliminated (Fig. 7.7).

For completeness, it is useful to examine the effects of a deficit that is financed by the creation of money, i.e. the case in which the government sells bonds to the central bank in exchange for newly printed money which the government then spends on its expansionary programme. The simple point to be made is that a money-financed deficit is not identical with a policy of the central bank accommodating the additional demand for money associated with a bond-financed deficit. In the second case, the central bank intervenes actively to ensure that sufficient additional money is available to keep the interest rate unchanged. By contrast, with a money-financed deficit, the central bank simply purchases bonds from the government equal in value to the deficit. Whether the interest rate is higher, lower, or unchanged depends on the relationship between the

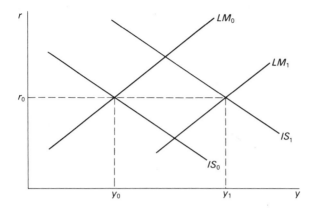

Fig. 7.7 Fiscal expansion: money supply expanded in line with additional demand for money, *r* remaining constant

change in the money supply and the demand for money associated with the deficit.

The Effect on the Interest Rate of a Money-financed Deficit

The interest rate will rise relative to its original level, r_0, if the increase in the demand for money associated with the rise in government spending exceeds the increase in the supply of money. To make the example very simple, we assume that the increase in the money supply is exactly equal to the nominal value of the additional government expenditure. (This assumption involves endowing the monetary authorities with powers of control over the creation of money that are quite unrealistic. However, the inclusion of a more complex monetary sector would not contradict the simple point that is being made.) The rise in the demand for money will depend first on the extra income generated by the rise in government spending, i.e. on the value of the multiplier, and secondly on the additional demand for money associated with the higher income.

The price level is assumed fixed, and for simplicity we assume that there is no change in taxation. The size of the deficit is simply equal to the rise in government spending, Δg. A money financed deficit implies that

$$\Delta g = \Delta(M^S/P).$$

Assuming r is initially constant, the additional money demanded as the result of the expansion induced by the rise in government spending depends on, first, the rise in output,

$$\Delta y = \frac{1}{1 - c_y \,(1 - t_y)} \,\Delta g,$$

and second, the rise in the demand for money associated with Δy:

$$\Delta \left(\frac{M^D}{P}\right) = \frac{1}{v_T} \,\Delta y,$$

where v_T is the 'transactions velocity' of circulation. (This assumes a simple linear demand for money function is

$$\frac{M^D}{P} = \frac{1}{v_T} \,y - br.)$$

Substituting Δy into the expression for the change in the demand for money gives

$$\Delta \left(\frac{M^D}{P}\right) = \frac{1}{v_T} \left(\frac{1}{1 - c_y \,(1 - t_y)}\right) \Delta g.$$

Thus, for the rise in the demand for money to exceed the rise in the supply, and hence for the interest rate to be higher subsequent to the money-financed deficit than it was before, requires that

$$\Delta \left(\frac{M^D}{P}\right) = \frac{1}{v_T} \left(\frac{1}{1 - c_y \,(1 - t_y)}\right) \Delta g > \Delta \left(\frac{M^S}{P}\right).$$

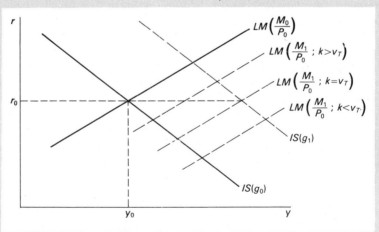

Fig. 7.8 The effect of a money-financed deficit on the interest rate
$r_1 \gtrless r_0$ as $k \gtrless v_T$, where k is the value of the multiplier, and v_T is the 'transactions velocity' of circulation

Since $\Delta(M^S/P) = \Delta g$, the condition for a rise in the interest rate is that the value of the multiplier, k, i.e. $1/\{1 - [c_y(1 - t_y)]\}$, exceeds the value of the transactions velocity of circulation, v_T. Figure 7.8 illustrates the possible outcomes of a money-financed deficit.

7.2.2 Crowding-out: Stock Effects

To this point, the possible effects on aggregate demand of the larger stock of bonds in the economy arising from a bond-financed deficit have been ignored. A sharper way of posing the question is to note that the existence of a government deficit as the consequence of an expansion in government spending implies that, as long as the deficit exists (and is not financed by money creation), there will be a continuing requirement to sell bonds to finance it. The stock of government bonds, i.e. the size of the national debt in the economy, will mount each year.

Showing that a bond-financed expansion in government spending implies the existence of a budget deficit (from a starting position of budget balance) is simply a matter of showing that the extra taxation generated by the expansion will be insufficient fully to finance the new government spending programme. Assuming for simplicity a proportional tax rate on income of t_y, there will be budget balance at the new equilibrium only if the change in taxation equals the change in government spending, i.e. if

$$\Delta t = \Delta g,$$

i.e. if $t_y \Delta y = \Delta g$, which implies that $\Delta y/\Delta g = 1/t_y$. There would have to be a multiplier with the value of $1/t_y$ for budget balance at the new equilibrium. But we know that the maximum value of the government spending multiplier (at a constant interest rate) is $1/\{1 - [c_y(1 - t_y)]\}$, which is less than $1/t_y$. There must therefore be a deficit at the new equilibrium.

For as long as the economy remains at the new level of output and maintains an unchanged monetary stance, the government will have to sell additional bonds to finance the deficit. Does this matter? It depends on whether government bonds are considered by private-sector agents to represent net wealth in the economy. It has been argued that bonds should not be considered as wealth (see box on whether bonds are net wealth). However, if this argument is not accepted,[6] then the consequences of a growing stock of government bonds associated with a deficit must be considered. Wealth is thought to affect behaviour in two ways. The

---

[6] For a clear discussion of objections, see Tobin (1980); also Buiter (1977, 1985) and B. M. Friedman (1978).

consumption function may have wealth as an argument—we have come across the inclusion of real money balances as a determinant of consumption in Part I (the so-called Pigou effect). More generally, theories of consumption with a life-cycle element contain wealth. An increase in wealth reduces the need to save out of current income to secure a steady consumption stream for retirement; consumption rises. The consumption function can be written as

$$c = c\,[(M \overset{+}{+} B)/P, \overset{+}{y}].$$

The 'wealth effect' in the consumption function means that a bond-financed expansion will shift the IS curve to the right.

Are Bonds Net Wealth?[7]

There is one line of thought which states that a growing stock of government bonds is of no economic consequence because bonds are not considered by agents to be net wealth. This argument has a pedigree stretching back to David Ricardo; it was revived in the 1970s by Robert Barro and is known as 'Ricardian Equivalence' (Barro 1974). Barro's argument is that government bonds do not represent net wealth in the economy as a whole to economic agents because they anticipate having to pay higher taxes in the future to enable the debt to be serviced. If true, this argument means that a bond-financed deficit is equivalent to a tax-financed one. However, the Barro argument can be criticized on the grounds that individuals are generally not indifferent to deferring their taxes and therefore do respond differently to a bond-financed deficit than to one financed through current taxation.

The second effect of bonds on behaviour operates through the demand-for-money function. This is the portfolio effect. The asset demand for money contains financial wealth as an argument. In the earlier discussion of the asset demand, attention was focused on the role of the interest rate in determining the proportionate allocation of a portfolio $(M + B)$ between money and bonds. At a given interest rate, higher wealth raises the demand for money and bonds in proportion to keep the portfolio balanced. Hence the overall demand for money (including transactions as well as asset demand) will depend positively on financial wealth:

$$M^D = L(\overset{+}{Y}, \overset{-}{r}, (M \overset{+}{+} B)).$$

---

[7] A very straightforward and accessible presentation of the issues involved can be found in Barro (1989).

The consequence of a bond-financed expansion in government spending will be to raise the proportion of bonds to money in the economy—since, by assumption, the money supply remains constant. This will lead to an increase in the demand for money. With a fixed money supply, higher demand for money produces a rise in the interest rate. Another way of seeing this consequence of a bond-financed expansion is to note that, starting in portfolio equilibrium, the government will be able to sell the extra bonds required to finance the increase in its spending only if it lowers bond prices. The interest rate will rise. In the IS/LM diagram, the 'wealth effect' of a bond-financed expansion is reflected in a leftward shift of the LM curve.

In Fig. 7.9, the initial situation of the economy is budget balance at y_0. A bond-financed expansion (raising g from g_0 to g_1) is then implemented with the money supply held constant: the IS shifts from IS_0 to IS_1 (from A to B). Once wealth effects are taken into account, there will be a further rightward shift of IS to IS_2, and a leftward shift of LM to LM_1. Note that, at the new IS/LM equilibrium at C, there is still a budget deficit. With government spending of g_1, output must be y_{BB} for budget balance. In Fig. 7.9 the new budget balance level of output will be at y_{BB}, where

$$y_{BB} - y_0 = (1/t_y)\Delta g.$$

While a budget deficit prevails, the wealth effects will continue to operate; i.e., there will be further rightward shifts of IS owing to the wealth effect

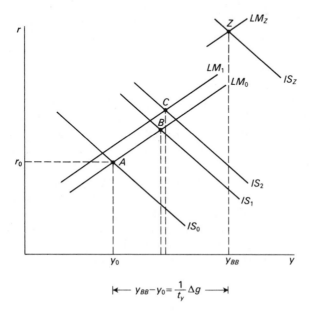

$$\longleftarrow \quad y_{BB} - y_0 = \frac{1}{t_y}\Delta g \quad \longrightarrow$$

Fig. 7.9 Crowding-out: wealth effects

on consumption and leftward shifts of the *LM* owing to the wealth effect on the demand for money. There are two possibilities (Blinder and Solow 1973):

1 *Instability* This occurs when the wealth effects push the level of output below its initial level. A budget deficit will continue to prevail since tax receipts will be reduced by the fall in income. The economy will experience downward instability.
2 *Stability* In this case, the negative wealth effect from the demand-for-money function does not fully offset the expansionary effects.

But as noted above, the only stable position for the economy will be when wealth is no longer changing, in other words when the budget is once again balanced: the new long-run equilibrium level of output is y_{BB}. It is clear from Fig. 7.9 that the maintenance of a fixed money supply implies that the interest rate will be much higher at the new equilibrium (point Z); the balance of private expenditure between investment and consumption would have shifted sharply towards consumption.

However, just as in the simple analysis of crowding-out, the effect on interest rates of the wealth effects of a government deficit can be offset by an adjustment of monetary policy. A policy of allowing the money supply to rise in line with increased demand for money will produce an equilibrium at y_{BB} with the interest rate unchanged at r_0.

7.3 The Effect on Inflation and Employment of the Adoption of a Monetary Growth Rule

In Chapter 6, it was shown how wage bargaining behaviour in conjunction with price-setting produces upward pressure on inflation when unemployment is lower than the equilibrium rate and downward pressure on inflation when unemployment is higher than the equilibrium rate. The economy can remain at levels of unemployment away from the NAIRU to the extent that any effect of changing inflation on aggregate demand, and hence on employment, is offset. The route through which changing inflation feeds back to affect the level of aggregate demand is via the real money supply and the Keynes and/or Pigou effects. In general, as we have seen in Part I, changes in the real money supply affect aggregate demand. Only when the rate of inflation is equal to the rate of growth of the money supply is the real money supply constant. The object of this section is to look more carefully than was possible in Chapter 6 at the dynamics of inflation and employment when the economy is away from the equilibrium rate of unemployment.

We begin with an economy experiencing rising inflation. The government holds unemployment below the equilibrium rate by allowing the growth of the money supply to adjust upward each year in response to the annual rise in inflation. Let us examine the implications of a simple switch of policy from one of accommodating inflation to a policy where the growth rate of the money supply is held fixed: in other words, where the government adopts a monetary growth rate rule. For the sake of clarity, we will ignore the difficulties that may well arise in the pursuit of such a rule. This requires us to assume that the money supply is exogenous and that the demand-for-money function does not shift about (for example owing to financial innovation).[8]

The implications of a switch to a monetary growth rule are shown clearly by using an illustrative example (Figs. 7.10 and 7.11, Table 7.1), where the path of inflation and unemployment in the periods subsequent to the policy switch are traced. The lengthy process of adjustment before the economy ends up at the equilibrium rate of unemployment with inflation equal to the growth rate of the money supply parallels the sluggish behaviour encountered in the analysis of Friedman's model. In period 0, unemployment is at U_0 below the equilibrium rate of unemployment and there is a 4% gap between the PRW and the BRW. Expected inflation is 8%. Wage- and price-setting occur and push inflation up to 12%. In period 1, with expected inflation of 12%, wage and price inflation rise to 16%. However, the government does not allow the money supply to rise by 16%; it keeps the growth rate of the money supply at 12% (the money supply growth rate target, $\dot{M}^T$) and holds it at this rate for future periods.

The first implication of the change of stance of monetary policy in period 1 is that the real money supply will have fallen—since the nominal money supply has grown more slowly than have prices. The LM shifts to the left

Table 7.1 Switch to non-accommodating monetary policy: numerical example

Period	$\dot{P}^E$	U	'Gap', i.e. $(w^B - w_{-1})/w_{-1}$	$\dot{W}$	$\dot{P}$	$\dot{M}$
0	8	U_0	4	12	12	12
1	12	U_0	4	16	16	12
2	16	U_1	2	18	18	12
3	18	U_2	0	18	18	12
4	18	U_3	−2	16	16	12
5	16	U_4	−4	12	12	12
6	12	U_4	−4	8	8	12
7	8	U_3	−2	6	6	12
⋮	⋮	⋮	⋮	⋮	⋮	⋮

[8] For a clear discussion of the difficulties faced by the authorities in attempting to control the money supply in the context of a sophisticated financial system, see Chick (1977), Goodhart (1975), Stevenson *et al.* (1988: ch. 5).

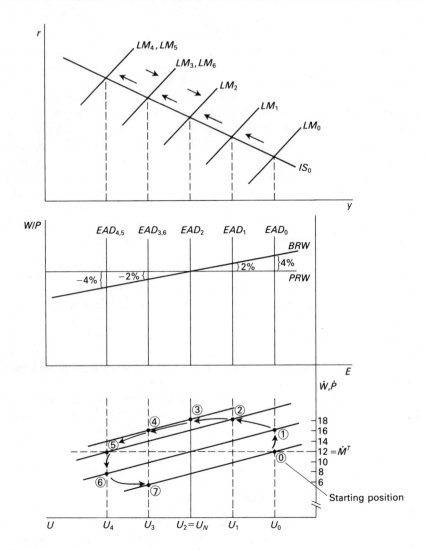

Fig. 7.10 Implications for inflation and unemployment of a switch from accommodating to non-accommodating monetary policy (i.e. adoption of a monetary growth rate rule)

from LM_0 to LM_1 (Fig. 7.10), pushing up the interest rate and reducing output and employment. In the lower panel of Fig. 7.10, the economy moves from the short-run Phillips curve ($\dot{P}^E = 12\%$) to the short-run Phillips curve ($\dot{P}^E = 16\%$). With higher unemployment, the gap between the BRW and the PRW has been narrowed to 2%, with the result that money wage increases in period 2 of $16 + 2 = 18\%$ are achieved (see Table

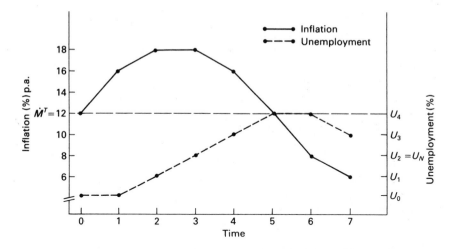

Fig. 7.11 The path over time of inflation and unemployment subsequent to the adoption of a monetary growth rate rule

7.1). Prices rise by 18%, but with monetary growth of only 12% an even more severe squeeze on output and employment follows, taking unemployment up to the NAIRU.

In period 3, with the discrepancy between the bargained real wage and the price-determined real wage eliminated, wages rise only by the amount of expected inflation: $\dot{W} = 18 + 0 = 18\%$. However, since inflation still lies above the monetary growth rate, a further depression in real economic activity is inevitable. The *LM* moves further to the left. Nevertheless, an important change in the economy takes place: with unemployment above the equilibrium rate of unemployment in period 4, money-wage inflation will be below expected inflation since unions are not in a sufficiently strong position to prevent a decline in their expected real wage: $\dot{W} = 18 + (-2) = 16\%$. Inflation has begun to fall.

In the next period, period 5, with unemployment still higher, relative union bargaining strength is weakened still further, opening up a larger negative gap between the BRW and the PRW. $\dot{W} = 16 + (-4) = 12\%$. Prices also rise by 12%, and for the first time since the rule was implemented there is no decline in the real money supply, since $\dot{M} = \dot{P} = 12\%$. In period 6 wage and price inflation will fall below 12%, with the consequence that unemployment will begin to fall.

The phases of adjustment can be summarized as follows.

● *Phase 1*: Rising unemployment and rising inflation. M/P falls, reducing output and employment since $\dot{M} < \dot{P}$. Inflation continues to rise while there is a positive gap between w^B and w^P. Even though the gap is shrinking, adaptive expectations mean that inflation will nevertheless continue to rise.

- *Phase II*: Rising unemployment and falling inflation. M/P continues to fall, but once unemployment is above the equilibrium rate of unemployment, inflation will begin to decline.
- *Phase III*: Falling unemployment and falling inflation. Only when inflation has fallen below $12\% = \dot{M}^T$ so that M/P is rising will unemployment begin to fall.
- *Phase IV*: Falling unemployment and rising inflation. Once unemployment falls below the equilibrium rate of unemployment, inflation will begin to rise once more, but while it remains below the growth rate of the money supply, unemployment will continue to fall. Table 7.2 highlights the salient features of each phase, and Fig.7.11 shows the time path of inflation and unemployment explicitly.

The numerical example is designed to highlight the lengthy and costly process of adjustment associated with the adoption of a money supply target. In the initial phase, after adoption of the policy, both inflation and unemployment rise. In the second phase, although inflation begins to fall, unemployment is pushed up higher than the equilibrium rate, with the associated cost of lost output. To make the discussion of the phases of adjustment as clear as possible, a simple numerical example was used. However, an *ad hoc* example is not a useful way to look at the issue of the long-run convergence properties of the model: does the rate of inflation eventually converge to $\dot{M}^T$ and unemployment to U_N? To look at the question of convergence, the accompanying box shows how to build an explicit model which converges in a straightforward way.

Just as in Friedman's model, if the economy experiences a negative demand shock which pushes unemployment above the NAIRU, there will be a considerable period of time before the economy returns to the equilibrium rate of unemployment. The loss of output and employment can be avoided by the intervention of the government to boost demand back to the level that produces unemployment equal to the NAIRU. In Chapter 8, the role of adaptive expectations in the out-of-equilibrium behaviour of the imperfect competition model is discussed.

Table 7.2 Switch to monetary growth target: adjustment phases

Phase	U cf. U_N	$\dot{P}$ cf. $\dot{M}^T$	implies	$\dot{P}$	$\dot{U}$
I	$U < U_N$	$\dot{P} > \dot{M}^T$	$\Rightarrow$	↑	↑
II	$U > U_N$	$\dot{P} > \dot{M}^T$	$\Rightarrow$	↓	↑
III	$U > U_N$	$\dot{P} < \dot{M}^T$	$\Rightarrow$	↓	↓
IV	$U < U_N$	$\dot{P} < \dot{M}^T$	$\Rightarrow$	↑	↓

*Convergence of the Economy to the Long-run Equilibrium where $\dot{P} = \dot{M}^T$ and $U = U_N$

A simple model in which convergence to the long-run equilibrium is relatively straightforward can be constructed in the following way. The long-run equilibrium is characterized by inflation equal to the target growth rate of the money supply and by unemployment at the equilibrium rate. We begin with the equations for price-setting, wage-setting, and inflation expectations:

$$\dot{P} = \dot{W} \qquad \qquad \text{[price-setting]}$$

$$\dot{W} = \dot{P}^E + \text{gap}, \qquad \text{[wage-setting]}$$

where as before 'gap' is defined as $\text{gap} \equiv (w^B - w_{-1})/w_{-1}$, i.e. as the percentage gap between the bargained real wage at the current level of unemployment and the pre-existing real wage;

$$\dot{P}^E = \dot{P}_{-1}.$$
$$\text{[adaptive inflation expectations]}$$

So

$$\dot{P} = \dot{P}_{-1} + \text{gap}. \qquad (7.1)$$

We assume that the gap is a linear function of the difference between U_N and U:

$$\text{gap} = \alpha(U_N - U);$$

i.e.,

$$\dot{P} - \dot{P}_{-1} = \alpha(U_N - U). \qquad (7.1')$$

From the IS/LM model, assume unemployment is determined by the logarithm of the current real money supply, $\ln m$:

$$U_N - U = \beta(\ln m - \ln \bar{m}), \qquad (7.1'')$$

where $\ln \bar{m}$ is the real money supply which sets $U = U_N$. So

$$\dot{P} - \dot{P}_{-1} = \alpha\beta(\ln m - \ln \bar{m}); \qquad (7.2)$$

by definition,

$$\ln m - \ln m_{-1} \equiv \dot{M} - \dot{P}. \qquad (7.3)$$

If $\dot{M}$ is fixed by the government at a constant target rate, $\dot{M}^T$, equations (7.2) and (7.3) are a pair of simultaneous equations in each period. That is, if the values of $\dot{P}_{-1}$ and $\ln m_{-1}$ are known, the values of $\dot{P}$ and $\ln m$ can be found by treating (7.2) and (7.3) as two simultaneous equations. Then, the next period, these values of $\dot{P}$ and ln m can be used to find the next period's values of $\dot{P}$ and ln m. And so on.

Alternatively, we can express (7.2) and (7.3) in terms of $\dot{P}$ and U. Subtracting the lagged equation of (7.1″) from the unlagged version gives

$$(U_N - U) - (U_N - U_{-1}) = \beta(\ln m - \ln \bar{m}) - \beta(\ln m_{-1} - \ln \bar{m})$$

or

$$U_{-1} - U = \beta(\ln m - \ln m_{-1}). \qquad (7.3')$$

And substituting (7.3′) into (7.3) gives, with $\dot{M} = \dot{M}^T$

$$U - U_{-1} = -\beta(\dot{M}^T - \dot{P}). \qquad (7.4)$$

Together with (7.1′),

$$\dot{P} - \dot{P}_{-1} = \alpha(U_N - U), \qquad (7.1')$$

we have two simultaneous equations in $\dot{P}$ and U. Given U_{-1} and $\dot{P}_{-1}$ — and also $\dot{M}^T$ — we can work out $\dot{P}$ and U. And this process can be repeated from period to period.

It is a useful exercise to start with some initial values of U_{-1} and $\dot{P}_{-1}$; choose values of α, β, U_N, and $\dot{M}^T$; and then set out the paths of U and $\dot{P}$ over time. We leave this to the reader.

A quicker way to see whether $\dot{P}$ and U converge eventually to $\dot{M}^T$ and U_N respectively is to concentrate the analysis just on $\dot{P}$ or just on U. For if either variable converges the other will; (7.1′) tells us that if $\dot{P} = \dot{P}_{-1}$, U must equal U_N and be constant; if U is constant, (7.4) tells us that $\dot{P} = \dot{M}^T$. So let us concentrate on the path of $\dot{P}$ over time. We can get rid of U in (7.1′) by first subtracting the lagged version of (7.1′) from the unlagged version:

$$(\dot{P} - \dot{P}_{-1}) - (\dot{P}_{-1} - \dot{P}_{-2}) = \alpha(U_N - U) - \alpha(U_N - U_{-1})$$

or

$$\dot{P} = 2\dot{P}_{-1} - \dot{P}_{-2} - \alpha(U - U_{-1}),$$

and then, by using (7.4) to eliminate $U - U_{-1}$,

$$\dot{P} = 2\dot{P}_{-1} - \dot{P}_{-2} + \alpha\beta(\dot{M}^T - \dot{P})$$

$$\dot{P}(1 + \alpha\beta) = 2\dot{P}_{-1} - \dot{P}_{-2} + \alpha\beta\dot{M}^T. \qquad (7.5)$$

The variable we are actually interested in — if we want to find out if $\dot{P}$ converges to $\dot{M}^T$ — is $(\dot{P} - \dot{M}^T)$. The reader can check that (7.5) can be rewritten as

$$(\dot{P} - \dot{M}^T)(1 + \alpha\beta) = 2(\dot{P}_{-1} - \dot{M}^T) - (\dot{P}_{-2} - \dot{M}^T). \quad (7.5')$$

Calling $\dot{P} - \dot{M}^T \equiv \dot{p}$,

$$\dot{p} = \frac{2}{1 + \alpha\beta}\dot{p}_{-1} - \frac{1}{1 + \alpha\beta}\dot{p}_{-2}. \quad (7.5'')$$

We are interested to see if $\dot{p}$ converges to zero. As an exercise, take initial values of $\dot{p}_{-1}$ and $\dot{p}_{-2}$; say both are 4%. Then choose different values of α and β, and see whether $\dot{p}$ converges to zero over time.

8

Wage Bargaining and Policy Analysis: Some Key Issues

In Chapter 7 the use of a variety of policy instruments was investigated so as to highlight the way in which policy affects the equilibrium rate of unemployment, actual employment, and inflation. In this chapter, several important issues raised in passing in Chapter 7 of particular relevance to the imperfect competition model are pursued in more depth. To begin with, we focus on the question of how to model expectations. We return to the comparison between adaptive and rational expectations which was introduced in Part I. Which hypothesis is the appropriate one to use? The relevance of the institutional structure of the economy (for example the extent of centralization of wage-bargaining institutions) to the choice of hypothesis is addressed.

The structure of wage-bargaining institutions is also relevant to the second part of the chapter which deals with problems in implementing an incomes policy. It is useful to think of the question of negotiating an incomes policy and the problem of defection in terms of the famous Prisoner's Dilemma game. The likelihood of collapse of an incomes policy because of the prisoner's dilemma can be related to the degree to which unions are centralized.

To conclude the discussion of the closed economy, we look at the implications for the working of the imperfect competition model of the inclusion of productivity growth. This introduces the idea that unions bargain for a specific *growth* of real wages.

8.1 Expectations Hypotheses

8.1.1 Adaptive and Rational Expectations Compared

In the concluding part of Chapter 7, we saw how the adjustment of the economy to the adoption of a new monetary policy—a money supply rule—in place of a policy of 'easy money' in order to stabilize inflation proved long and costly. The underlying reason for the lengthy adjustment to the new equilibrium with lower inflation lies with the way in which expectations were assumed to be formed. With adaptive expectations, the fact that the government has altered its monetary policy has no *direct* effect on expectations. Private-sector behaviour is entirely backward-looking, with the result that, after the adoption of the monetary growth rate rule, wage- and price-setting occur exactly as before; it is only when output and employment fall as the result of the decline in the real money supply that wage and price inflation are affected (refer back to Fig. 7.10 and Tables 7.1 and 7.2). Once actual inflation begins to fall, expected inflation in subsequent periods declines.

Let us turn to the alternative Rational Expectations Hypothesis (REH) introduced in Chapter 4, which provides for a direct link from government policy choices, such as the adoption of a monetary growth rate rule, to expectations of inflation. We will see that, first, applying the hypothesis to the imperfect competition model brings about a dramatic change in policy effectiveness; under REH, the only feasible rate of unemployment is the equilibrium rate of unemployment. Secondly, any announced change in money supply growth will cause inflation to change immediately to equal the new money supply growth rate. For example, Fig. 8.1 shows the jump from point A to point B on account of the announced increase in the growth rate of the money supply. There is no rise in output and employment. There is an exact parallel between the application of REH to the imperfect competition model and its application to Friedman's model. A way of dramatizing the implications of moving from an assumption of adaptive expectations to one of rational expectations is to consider a piecemeal shift of bargaining units from the use of the former to the use of the latter process. As pointed out in Chapter 4, a plausible reason for agents to shift from the use of adaptive to rational expectations is their dissatisfaction with the use of a rule that persistently misforecasts inflation.

Suppose that there are 100 industries in the economy, each with a separate union and employers' association. Negotiations about wage increases occur in each industry at the beginning of each period, and for convenience each industry is assumed to have equal weight in final output. To simplify the analysis, it will be assumed that we are operating in a world of certainty: there are no random shocks to the economy.

Initially, we assume that, in just one of the 100 industries, union and employers' association negotiators purchase this book and are convinced of the accuracy of the imperfect competition model of the economy presented. What difference will this knowledge in one industry make to inflationary expectations in subsequent wage negotiations, and to the average rate of inflation in the economy? Secondly, will it be in the interests of the single industry to undertake price- and wage-setting using rational expectations (RE), given the prevalence of adaptive expectations elsewhere?

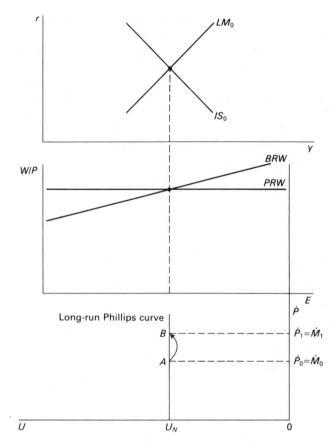

Fig. 8.1 Rational expectations: announced increase in monetary growth from $\dot{M}_0$ to $\dot{M}_1$; no real effects

There are 99 industries in which behaviour proceeds as before, on the basis of adaptive expectations. In these industries, expected inflation will be equal to last period's inflation, $\dot{P}^E = \dot{P}_{-1}$. In the single RE industry, negotiators know that theirs is the only industry to know about rational expectations. To make their forecast about next period's inflation, the negotiators must work through the model of wage- and price-setting. They will use all of the available information about both government policy and price and wage behaviour throughout the 100-industry economy.

Let us assume that the current state of the economy is characterized by an unemployment rate U_0 below the equilibrium rate of unemployment, with the consequence that inflation is rising continuously; the government pursues an accommodating monetary policy. The sensible assumption for the negotiators in the RE industry to make in the absence of any announced policy change is that the government will continue to play an accommodating role on the monetary side, maintaining unemployment at the target rate, U_0, by allowing the money supply to increase in line with whatever is the increase in the price level.

Given a rate of inflation in period $t - 1$ of 5%, and assuming that there is a gap of 2% between the bargained real wage and the price-determined real wage at U_0, the RE negotiators will reason as follows. Inflation in the coming period (period t), and hence their rational expectation of inflation in period t, will be a weighted average of inflation in the 99 industries still pursuing a policy of adaptive expectations and inflation in the single RE industry:

$$\dot{P}_t^E = \dot{P}_t = 0.99(\dot{P}_t^{AE}) + 0.01(\dot{P}_t^{RE}). \tag{8.1}$$

Knowledge of price-setting behaviour enables the RE negotiators to deduce that

$$\dot{P}_t^{AE} = \dot{W}_t^{AE} \text{ and } \dot{P}_t^{RE} = \dot{W}_t^{RE}$$

so that

$$\dot{P}_t^E = \dot{P}_t = 0.99(\dot{W}_t^{AE}) + 0.01(\dot{W}_t^{RE}). \tag{8.2}$$

With the knowledge that, in the adaptive expectations industries, expected inflation is equal to last period's inflation, it is clear that money-wage increases in that sector in period t will be

$$\dot{W}_t^{AE} = \dot{P}_{t-1} + [w^B(U_0) - w_{-1}]/w_{-1}$$
$$= 5 + 2$$
$$= 7\%. \tag{8.3}$$

Now, wage increases in the RE industry will be equal to the expected rate of inflation in the economy as a whole, $\dot{P}_t^E$ plus 2% to close the gap between the bargained real wage and the actual real wage:

$$\dot{W}_t^{RE} = \dot{P}_t^E + [w^B(U_0) - w_{-1}]/w_{-1}$$
$$= \dot{P}_t^E + 2. \tag{8.4}$$

By substituting (8.3) and (8.4) back into (8.2), the RE negotiators can solve for the actual rate of inflation in period t and thus for the rate they expect to prevail:

$$\dot{P}_t^E = \dot{P}_t = 0.99(\dot{W}_t^{AE}) + 0.01(\dot{W}_t^{RE})$$
$$= (0.99)(7) + (0.01)(\dot{P}_t^E + 2).$$

By collecting the terms in $\dot{P}_t^E$ on the left-hand side,

$$\dot{P}_t^E(1 - 0.01) = (0.99)(7) + (0.01)(2),$$

and therefore,

$$\dot{P}_t^E = 7 + (0.01/0.99)(2) = 7.0202\% = \dot{P}_t.$$

The economy-wide rate of inflation in period t turns out to be slightly higher at just over 7% than the 7% it would have been had price expectations throughout the economy been formed on the former basis of adaptive expectations. While in the 99 adaptive expectations (AE) industries prices rose by 7%, they rose by rather more than this in the RE industry. From (8.1),

$$\dot{P}_t = 0.99(\dot{P}_t^{AE}) + 0.01(\dot{P}_t^{RE}),$$

$$\dot{P}_t^{RE} = [7.0202 - (0.99)(7)]/0.01 = 9.0202\%.$$

An alternative way of seeing that inflation must have been at this rate in the RE industry is to note that, from (8.4), wages (and hence prices) in that industry must have risen by 2% more than expected inflation in the economy as a whole. This is necessary to ensure that the real wage in the RE industry is equal to w^B.

From the perspective of the unions, the crucial difference between the RE industry and the rest is that in the RE industry, by *correctly* calculating the rate of inflation for the coming period, the union actually secures the bargained real wage w^B at the prevailing rate of unemployment. By working through the model, the negotiators secured a money wage increase of 9.0202%, and with average inflation of only 7.0202%, this implies a real wage gain of the full 2% to close the gap between the BRW and the PRW in the RE industry. (Of course, employers in the RE sector maintain their profit margins unchanged, since they raise prices by the full extent of wage increases in that sector. To the extent that there is substitutability between the output of the different sectors, the RE employers will suffer output losses since, with price increases out of line with the AE sectors, there will be some switching of demand. We ignore this effect.) All other unions in the economy gained money wage increases of only 7%, and with prices overall rising by slightly more than this, they suffered the double blow of not only failing to achieve the expected rise in the real wage but actually being forced to accept a slight real wage reduction.

Such a result may induce broader acceptance of the use of the rational expectations formation process among wage negotiators. It is illuminating to consider the implications of 50% of industries moving from adaptive to rational expectations for their inflation forecasts. Using the same starting conditions as before, (8.2) becomes

$$\dot{P}_t^E = \dot{P}_t = 0.5\dot{W}_t^{AE} + 0.5\dot{W}_t^{RE} \tag{8.2'}$$

$$= (0.5)(7) + (0.5)(\dot{P}^E + 2).$$

Therefore $\dot{P}_t = 9\%$. This inflation rate compares with the 7% when all industries were using adaptive expectations and 7.0202% when only a single industry had switched to rational expectations. Just as the previous case, those industries using rational expectations achieved the bargained real wage, since $\dot{W}_t^{RE} = 11\%$ and $\dot{P}_t = 9\%$, while those still persisting with adaptive expectations experienced a substantial real wage cut as money wages increased much more slowly than did prices in the economy as a whole: $\dot{W}_t^{AE} = 7\%$; $\dot{P}_t = 9\%$.

If we take the case where in period t 99 of the 100 industries switch to rational expectations, with only a single industry sticking with the adaptive rule, then we find that inflation is extremely high:

$$\dot{P}_t^E = (0.01)(7) + (0.99)(\dot{P}_t^E + 2)$$

$$= 7 + (0.99/0.01)(2)$$

$$= 205\%$$

In this example, the following results obtain:

$$\dot{W}_t^{RE} = 207\% \qquad \dot{P}_t^{RE} = 207\%$$

$$\dot{W}_t^{AE} = \quad 7\% \qquad \dot{P}_t^{AE} = \quad 7\%$$

Economy-wide inflation: $\dot{P}_t = 205\%$.

Hence, while in each sector profit margins are unchanged (the consequence of markup pricing), the outcome for real (consumption) wages is dramatically different: real wages in the RE sectors rise by 2%; real wages in the fraction of the economy remaining with AE have plummeted. Prices in the economy must rise sufficiently to squeeze real wages in the AE industry to the extent necessary to 'pay for' the 2% real wage rise in 99% of the economy.

The simple device of examining a piecemeal transition in the process by which expectations are formed suggests why inflation would be infinite in period t if rational expectations were held throughout the economy. With no sector in which real wages can be squeezed so as to secure the resources for the 2% increase in the real wage up to the bargained real wage level, the incompatibility of real wage and real profit expectations at unemployment rates below the equilibrium rate of unemployment is absolute. The implication of universal rational expectations is that the only feasible rate of unemployment is the NAIRU. Any attempt by the government to expand beyond this rate will be thwarted before it takes effect as inflationary expectations operate to maintain demand at the equilibrium level. Just as in the New Classical model, only an unexpected or *unanticipated* expansion can temporarily reduce unemployment. Once the private-sector participants in wage- and price-setting recognize that an expansion in demand has occurred, inflationary expectations are adjusted and the fall in unemployment below the equilibrium rate of unemployment is reversed.

Thus far, attention has been focused on the implications of generalized rational expectations for the ability of the government to run the economy at a lower rate of unemployment than the NAIRU. Whereas with adaptive expectations this was possible, though at the cost of accelerating inflation, with rational expectations the government can only secure such a fall in unemployment to the extent that it has an informational advantage over the private-sector agents. However, just as was the case with the New Classical model, there is a second important policy implication flowing from rational expectations: the *reduction in inflation* is simple and costless. If the government wishes to reduce the rate of inflation from $y\%$ to $x\%$, then it simply has to announce that henceforth the money supply will grow at $x\%$ rather than at its former rate of $y\%$. Expected inflation will drop immediately from the current $x\%$ to $y\%$. There will be an immediate fall in the price level on the policy announcement as agents anticipate lower inflation and hence raise their demand for money. This will leave the real money supply unchanged. With rational expectations, the short-run Phillips curves showing the short-run trade-off between unemployment and inflation are no longer relevant since, at any rate of unemployment below the equilibrium rate of unemployment, inflation is infinite.

The notion that inflation can be painlessly lowered through an announced policy change was one explanation used for the British government's announced shift to a monetary growth rate rule in 1979. For those economists who believed both that the British economy was characterized by rational expectations and that the announced policy change would be believed by all wage- and price-setters, the output costs associated with disinflation were predicted to be very small. However, as noted in the discussion of the New Classical model, if either of these presumptions is wrong, then the consequences for the real economy will be serious. In Britain, the consequences of the policy change for output and employment were serious.[1] In the presence of adaptive expectations or a lack of credibility of the policy announcement, a sharp reduction in monetary growth creates a sharp reduction in aggregate demand and hence in output and employment. Instead of the swift, costless drop in inflation envisaged, there is a lengthy period of rising unemployment. As we will see

---

[1] We return in pt. III to the way in which the failure of wage- and price-setters to behave as if they had rational expectations and believed the policy to be credible was compounded, in the case of Britain in 1979, by the behaviour of the foreign exchange market. For an excellent discussion of the development of the British economy subsequent to the policy change, see e.g. Buiter and Miller (1983). For an interesting insight into the policy advice with regard to the control of inflation in the UK generated by monetarist and New Classical models and their use of rational expectations, see the House of Commons Committee on the Treasury and Civil Service (1981).

in the final chapter of this book, the period of high unemployment may itself damage the structure of the economy.

Conclusion

The contrast between rational and adaptive expectations is clear: with adaptive expectations the government can run the economy at a rate of unemployment below the equilibrium rate by pursuing an accommodating monetary policy. The cost is rising inflation. Further, should the government wish to reduce the stable rate of inflation at the NAIRU, then with adaptive expectations a lengthy adjustment process will ensue, with unemployment initially rising above the equilibrium rate of unemployment. Under rational expectations, unemployment must be at the equilibrium rate of unemployment even in the short run. Deviations from the NAIRU can occur only as the result of unanticipated changes in government policy. Secondly, with rational expectations the output and employment costs associated with reducing inflation are eliminated: the government simply has to announce a lower growth rate of the money supply, and wage and price inflation will drop immediately to the new equilibrium level.

8.1.2 Wage-Bargaining Institutions and Expectations Formation

As we have seen, adaptive expectations implies that unions are consistently proved wrong in their expectations of price increases and yet do nothing to correct the predictive rule they use. This seems unsatisfactory. The alternative assumption of rational expectations overcomes this flaw. Expectations are formed by 'solving the whole model', i.e. by working out what must happen for the outcome to comply with the behaviour of all the agents. Expectations can then be thwarted only by the occurrence of random events, i.e. by policy or other shocks which by definition cannot be anticipated. Nevertheless, the Rational Expectations Hypothesis produces such powerful results when applied to all agents in the economy that it cannot be accepted uncritically. The issue to be considered here is whether the degree of plausibility for one or other expectations hypothesis depends on the institutional structure of wage-bargaining.

In what sort of economy might rational expectations apply? As noted in Chapter 4, the theory was developed by neoclassical economists of the New Classical school who assumed the atomistic setting of a competitive economy. While none of the industrialized economies resembles a perfectly competitive economy, some are more atomistic and less centrally co-ordinated than others. Paradoxically, the hypothesis of rational expectations is probably more appropriate in economies that are highly co-ordinated in their wage-setting behaviour than in economies with more fragmented decentralized wage-setting practices.

The Rational Expectations Hypothesis may not be a useful empirical model for an economy with an uncoordinated decision-making structure for two reasons. First is the assumption that agents know the structure of the economy. If this is not true, then rational expectations will founder since each agent will have to guess what other agents think the structure is and how those other agents will behave. Secondly, the rational expectations hypothesis makes a common knowledge assumption; in other words, even if everyone knows the structure of the economy, it is necessary to make the further assumption that they are all aware of this.

In a large economy like the USA, where there is little co-ordinated decision-taking, it is inconceivable that most agents know the structure of the economy. The concept of the 'structure of the economy' itself becomes difficult. By contrast, in a highly co-ordinated economy such as Austria or Sweden, there is a large amount of agreement about the structure of the economy and how it works. With a highly centralized wage-bargaining structure, the key wage and price decision-makers are few and are in contact with each other frequently, so that common knowledge is not such an unreasonable assumption.

In practice, it is in small open economies that the assumption of common knowledge of the economic model which lies at the heart of the Rational Expectations Hypothesis is most likely to be justified. The Scandanavian economies and Austria fit this description best. Wage-bargaining there is highly centralized. In a small open economy firms will have little control over the prices at which they can sell their exports or purchase imports. This provides one way of explaining co-ordinated employer behaviour in wage-bargaining. This kind of externally generated cohesion is absent in a large economy (such as the USA).

With highly centralized bargaining, participants are aware that a rate of unemployment below the equilibrium rate of unemployment is unsustainable because of the inconsistency of the claims on output per head associated with it. Inflation this period will not be thought to be equal to its outturn last period unless the economy is at the equilibrium rate of unemployment. This focuses the attention of participants on the possibilities for manipulating the NAIRU itself. Thus, while rational expectations takes away the ability of the government to operate on the level of employment even in the short run by raising aggregate demand, the implied transparency of decision-making may enable shifts to occur in the bargained real wage or price-determined real wage curves to lower the equilibrium rate of unemployment. The obvious example is the negotiation of an explicit or implicit incomes policy which, by lowering the BRW, has the effect of reducing the equilibrium rate of unemployment. This enables the economy to operate at a lower rate of unemployment in the long run as well as in the short run. We return to the question of incomes policies below.

Thus, the reason for the effectiveness of a Keynesian policy of achieving higher employment by raising aggregate demand is completely different in a decentralized economy from that in a centralized economy. In a decentralized economy, such a policy works because there is so-called *nominal inertia* in the economy. By nominal inertia, we mean that an expansion of nominal demand has a real effect on output and employment because it takes some time for prices and wages to adjust. Institutional characteristics of the US economy (apart from its decentralized character) that are often adduced to explain the existence of nominal inertia are the lengthy wage contracts (three years) and absence of wage indexation procedures (see e.g. Okun 1981; Taylor 1979). By contrast, a very high degree of co-ordination and centralization in an economy can render expansionary policies effective. If the key agents have rational expectations, then the bargained real wage curve may be shifted to ensure that higher employment is consistent with constant inflation. In other words, the equilibrium rate of unemployment itself moves into line with lower unemployment. While both institutional settings permit a rise in employment, a long-run expansion is possible only in the centralized case. In the decentralized case, wages and prices will eventually adjust to the rise in demand and the rising inflation will render the expansion untenable.

*8.1.3 Wage Indexation: Institutionalized Adaptive Expectations

While adaptive expectations may be used as a simple way of modelling inertia in wage- and price-setting, it can be found in economic models for a quite different reason. The observation that wage-setting behaviour includes a term in last period's inflation may represent the attempt by unions to recoup the real wage loss arising from the unexpected rise in inflation in the previous period. It is a 'catch-up' element rather than a backward-looking forecast of inflation.[2]

Formal wage indexation procedures have generally taken the form of the *automatic* increase of wages by the rise in the cost of living in the previous period. Agreement by unions to automatic wage indexation can be explained by their desire to prevent real wage gains from being dissipated through inflation. From the management side, indexation may be seen as a way of avoiding extra bargaining sessions during the year whenever prices rise by more than expected. The reopening of negotiations during the tenure of the wage settlement would typically be accompanied by strikes or the threat of strike action.

What are the consequences of a formal wage indexation system for inflation? It is useful to differentiate between two types of wage indexation procedure. On the other hand, indexation can be set up as a procedure that

---

[2] See Modigliani and Tarentelli (1977) for a useful discussion of the consequences of wage indexation for the Italian economy.

simply passes on cost-of-living increases to money wages. In this case, which we will refer to as 'unrestricted bargaining', the annual wage bargain is struck at the beginning of the year and is based on the bargained real wage curve. The negotiated settlement has two elements: (1) an indexation element to raise money wages by last period's cost of living rise, and (2) an element dependent on the level of employment through the BRW function. The indexation element simply makes up for past cost-of-living increases; it does not, for example, provide protection for the real wage in the face of a decline in union bargaining power associated with higher unemployment. We will look at a system of quarterly wage indexation where, at the end of each quarter, a money wage increase is automatically granted to make up for the inflation that occurred in that quarter.

The second type of indexation procedure will be referred to as 'restricted bargaining'. In this case, indexation is applied to the wage bargain itself. This creates a floor to the level of the real wage. The implications of this form of indexation will be investigated and compared with the results of unrestricted bargaining. In both cases, it will be assumed that the wage bargain occurs annually at the beginning of the year and that indexation is quarterly.

Unrestricted Bargaining

Money wages are set at the annual wage bargain as follows:

$$\dot{W} = \dot{W}^I + \dot{W}^R,$$

where $\dot{W}^I$ refers to the indexation component of the bargain and $\dot{W}^R$, to the component that reflects the change in the real wage necessary to take the real wage to w^B. More precisely, $\dot{W}^I = \dot{P}_{-1,\text{IV}}$ where -1 refers to the year and IV to the quarter; $\dot{W}^R = (w_B - w_{-1})/w_{-1}$. As usual, prices are set immediately after wages rise.

Initially, suppose that the economy is at the equilibrium rate of unemployment. At the start of the year 0, expected inflation (equal to last quarter's inflation) is, say, 3% so a money wage rise of 3% is agreed (i.e., with $w = w^B$, $\dot{W}^R = 0$). Prices are immediately marked up by 3%. At the end of the first quarter, an indexation award occurs. Since prices have risen in the quarter by 3%, money wages will be automatically increased by a further 3% at the start of the second quarter. Prices are put up again by 3% immediately. Table 8.1 shows the successive wage and price rises for the year. By the end of the year, money wages and prices have each risen by 12% and the bargained real wage has been attained. In this case, indexation makes no difference to the outcome that would have resulted from the standard adaptive expectations rule.[3] Because the economy is at

---

[3] In fact, there is a slight difference between the outcomes for the annual rate of inflation: in the case of quarterly indexation, inflation over the full year is given by $(1.03)^4 = 1.1255$, i.e. an annual rate of 12.6%. We will ignore this discrepancy.

Table 8.1 Quarterly wage indexation: unrestricted bargaining

Year	Quarter	U	Cost-of-living rise $(\dot{P}_{-1,-Q})$	$\dot{W}^R$	$\dot{W}^I$	$\dot{W}(=\dot{W}^R+\dot{W}^I)$	$\dot{P}$
0	I	U_N	3	0	3	3	3
	II	U_N	3	0	3	3	3
	III	U_N	3	0	3	3	3
	V	U_N	3	0	3	3	3
						Annual $\dot{P}=12\%$	
1	I	U_1	3	2	3	5	5
	II	U_1	5	0	5	5	5
	III	U_1	5	0	5	5	5
	IV	U_1	5	0	5	5	5
						Annual $\dot{P}=20\%$	
Annual indexation							
1	I–IV	U_1	12	2	12	14	14
						Annual $\dot{P}=14\%$	

the equilibrium rate of unemployment with $w^B=w^P$, prices rise as expected and there is no unexpected real wage loss to make up through indexation. Indexation merely replicates what would have happened in its absence. Note that a procedure of *annual* wage indexation is formally identical to our standard model with adaptive expectations (i.e. with $\dot{P}^E=\dot{P}_{-1}$).

However, when unemployment is not at the equilibrium rate, indexation procedures alter the inflationary dynamic. Suppose that at the beginning of the following year, year 1, the government boosts the level of demand, reducing unemployment to U_1. With lower unemployment, the unions arrive at the wage-bargaining sessions at the start of the year in a stronger position. They negotiate a wage rise of the previous quarter's inflation rate of 3% plus 2% to take the real wage up to the now higher w^B. This gives a settlement of 5% for the first quarter. Prices rise by 5%. At the start of the second quarter, automatic indexation raises money wages by 5%. Hence by the end of the year (see Table 8.1) wages and prices will have risen by 20%. This compares with the 14% inflation outcome in the standard adaptive expectations case, or equivalently, in an economy with *annual* indexation. The more frequent are the indexation intervals, the more rapid will be inflation at levels of unemployment below the equilibrium rate of unemployment.

Restricted Bargaining

A different wage indexation system is one that not only recoups last period's price increase but which also protects the real wage—we will call this restricted bargaining. If the government adopts a tighter aggregate demand policy and pushes unemployment up, the bargained real wage, w^B, would be lower, reflecting the diminution in union bargaining strength. But with the restricted type of indexation, the expected real wage cannot fall. In the wage–employment diagram, this means that the BRW curve becomes flat to the left of the current expected real wage. Let us examine the implications for inflation.

In year 1, with unemployment below the equilibrium rate, the two indexation systems produce identical outcomes (Table 8.2). Annual inflation is 20%. Suppose that the government decides to halt the inflationary process by lowering demand and raising unemployment to the NAIRU. Inflation will remain at 20% in the economy with the first type of indexation but will rise in the economy with restricted bargaining. Figure 8.2 illustrates why: an indexation system that protects the existing real wage means that the BRW becomes flat at a real wage 2% above the PRW. There is therefore a 2% gap between the w^B and w^P at E_2. In other words, restricted bargaining has eliminated the equilibrium rate of unemployment. Inflation will continue to rise indefinitely at E_2. To stabilize inflation, restricted bargaining must be abolished.

The problems created for an economy by the adoption of a restricted bargaining procedure are highlighted by considering the impact of a shock to the economy which has the effect of shifting the PRW curve downwards. One example would be an external shock raising the real cost of imports—e.g. the OPEC oil price shocks of the 1970s. With higher imported materials costs and an unchanged profit margin, the real wage implied by pricing decisions is reduced: the PRW shifts downwards. In Fig. 8.3, the PRW shifts to PRW′. If the economy was initially at E_N with stable inflation and a real wage of w_0, the effect of the OPEC shock would

Table 8.2 Restricted and unrestricted bargains with quarterly wage indexation

Year	Quarter	U	Unrestricted bargain					Restricted bargain				
			$\dot{P}_{-1,-Q}$	$\dot{W}^I$	$\dot{W}^R$	$\dot{W}$	$\dot{P}$	$\dot{P}_{-1,-Q}$	$\dot{W}^I$	$\dot{W}^R$	$\dot{W}$	$\dot{P}$
1	I	U_1	3	3	2	5	5	3	3	2	5	5
	II		5	5	0	5	5	5	5	0	5	5
	III		5	5	0	5	5	5	5	0	5	5
	IV		5	5	0	5	5	5	5	0	5	5
			Annual inflation = 20%					Annual inflation = 20%				
2	I	U_N	5	5	0	5	5	5	5	2	7	7
	II		5	5	0	5	5	7	7	0	7	7
	III		5	5	0	5	5	7	7	0	7	7
	IV		5	5	0	5	5	7	7	0	7	7
			Annual inflation = 20%					Annual inflation = 28%				

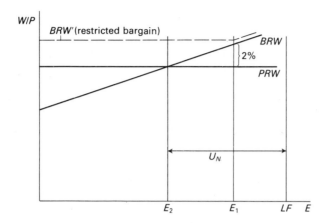

Fig. 8.2 Wage indexation: restricted bargaining

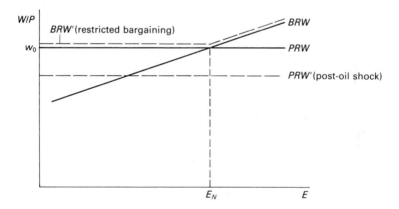

Fig. 8.3 Oil shock and restricted bargaining

be to push down the PRW. Restricted bargaining would require that the real wage remain at w_0, creating a horizontal BRW to the left of E_N. The shock has transformed the situation at E_N from stable to rising inflation, and moreover, the existence of restricted bargaining means that a rise in unemployment will not reduce inflation. There is no longer an equilibrium rate of unemployment.

*8.1.4 Shifts in the Expectations Formation Process

When applied to models in which there is a unique equilibrium rate of unemployment, the Rational Expectations Hypothesis produces very strong results. In the analysis of some economic situations, it may be preferable to use a modification of the Adaptive Expectations Hypothesis. For example, in a period such as the 1930s, when inflation was low (sometimes positive and sometimes negative), the assumption that expected inflation is equal to last period's inflation is not very plausible. It is much more likely that people will predict that the *price level* this year will be equal to last year's price level. At the other extreme, in economies with rapidly accelerating inflation and prices changing on a daily basis, such as Brazil or Argentina in 1989, it would be equally implausible to suggest that individuals assume that inflation this year will be equal to its value last year.

Starting out from the idea. that adaptive expectations are based sometimes on last period's price level and sometimes on last period's rate of inflation, economists have suggested that the adaptive formation of expectations resembles a process of changing gears.

To illustrate, we will assume that unions and firms use the experience of the previous five years as the basis for the gear they use to form their expectations. For example, if an initial rule of using the previous period's price level to forecast the price level is in use, it would take five years of rising prices before the rule was changed to using the price change in the previous period to predict this period's price change. In the absence of a consistent experience of the price level rising, forecasts of *inflation* seem improbable. As shown in Table 8.3, unions simply predict that the price level this period will be the same as it was last period: $P^E = P_{-1}$. Now, suppose that, after five periods without much change in the price level, the government boosts aggregate demand pushing the bargained real wage (w^B) 2% above the current real wage. With five periods' experience of an unchanged price level, expectations will continue to be formed according to the initial rule ($P^E = P_{-1}$). However, during periods 5–9 the price level rises when it was expected to remain constant; i.e., money wages rise by 2% each period as unions seek to secure the bargained real wage associated with the higher level of employment; prices are put up in line to keep the real wage equal to w^P.

Unions will begin to view their expectations formation rule with scepticism, and it is likely that at some stage attention will switch from forming expectations of the price level to forming expectations of its rate of change, i.e. of the rate of inflation. So we assume that, with five years' experience of inflation at 2% (see Table 8.3), inflation would be expected to continue at 2% in the year ahead. In period 10, with expected inflation of 2%, unions will secure an overall money wage increase of 4% to take the expected real wage up to w^B. This is the familiar adaptive expectations case where $\dot{P}^E = \dot{P}_{-1}$.

But what happens when current inflation is consistently underpredicted by last period's inflation? After five periods (periods 10–14 in Table 8.3) in which the inflation outturn exceeds expected inflation, the expectations

Table 8.3 Shifts in adaptive expectations: 'changing gears'

Expectations rule	Period	P^E	$\dot{P}^E$	$\ddot{P}^E$	Gap $\equiv \dfrac{w^B - w_{-1}}{w_{-1}}$	$\dot{W}$	$\dot{P}$	$\ddot{P}$
$P^E = P_{-1}$	0	100	n/a	n/a	0	0	0	0
	1	100	n/a	n/a	0	0	0	0
	2	100	n/a	n/a	0	0	0	0
	3	100	n/a	n/a	0	0	0	0
	4	100	n/a	n/a	0	0	0	0
		Policy change: rise in aggregate demand						
$P^E = P_{-1}$	5	100	n/a	n/a	2	2	2	0
	6	102	n/a	n/a	2	2	2	0
	7	104	n/a	n/a	2	2	2	0
	8	106	n/a	n/a	2	2	2	0
	9	108	n/a	n/a	2	2	2	0
		Change gear to $\dot{P}^E = \dot{P}_{-1}$						
$\dot{P}^E = \dot{P}_{-1}$	10	n/a	2	n/a	2	4	4 •	2
	11	n/a	4	n/a	2	6	6	2
	12	n/a	6	n/a	2	8	8	2
	13	n/a	8	n/a	2	10	10	2
	14	n/a	10	n/a	2	12	12	2
		Change gear to $\ddot{P}^E = \ddot{P}_{-1}$						
$\ddot{P}^E = \ddot{P}_{-1}$	15	n/a	14	2	2	16	16	4
	16	n/a	20	4	2	22	22	6
	17	n/a	28	6	2	30	30	8
	18	n/a	38	8	2	40	40	10
	19	n/a	50	10	2	52	52	12

rule of $\dot{P}^E = \dot{P}_{-1}$ is now under pressure from the experience of *rising* inflation. Once more, unions may 'change gear' in their expectations formation process. The first change was from expectations based on last period's price level to the expectation that prices would rise at the same rate as they did last period. The second gear change is from expectations of inflation based on past inflation to the view that the inflation rate will *change* at the same rate as it did previously (i.e. $\ddot{P}^E = \ddot{P}_{-1}$, where the double-overdot refers to the change in the rate of change of the variable).

It is easy to generalize this process of changing gears further still. However, as Table 8.3 shows clearly, the shift from standard (first-gear, i.e. $\dot{P}^E = \dot{P}_{-1}$) expectations to second-gear (i.e. $\ddot{P}^E = \ddot{P}_{-1}$) expectations results in accelerating inflation. In this example, inflation rises from 16% to 52% in the five years following the switch to the second-gear rule. This may provide a model for how a process of hyperinflation gets going.[4] Of course, this modification to adaptive expectations does not address the very important shortcoming of the hypothesis that it is entirely backward-looking and does not permit the direct incorporation of new information about policy changes or changes in objective economic conditions such as the occurrence of an oil shock.

8.2   Incomes Policy: Problems with Implementation

As presented in Chapter 7, an incomes policy appears to be a highly desirable policy instrument since it enables a costless reduction in the equilibrium rate of unemployment. Yet incomes policies have had a chequered history in the advanced economies.[5] One important reason for the tendency for such policies to break down, and hence for the declining willingness of governments to use them, can be traced to a co-ordination problem between the unions involved in the pact. Consider the situation represented in Fig. 8.4. The economy is at the new equilibrium rate of

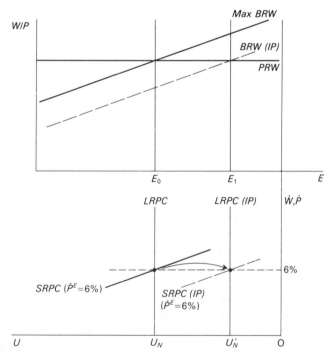

Fig. 8.4 Expanding employment with an incomes policy in place

[4] For a useful introduction to the issue of hyperinflation, see Cagan (1987).
[5] See Flanagan *et al.* (1982), Faxen (1982), and Schelde-Andersen and Turner (1980).

unemployment (U'_N) at employment level E_1 as the consequence of the incomes policy. The problem is that for each individual union there is a temptation at E_1 to seek the real wage associated with the pre-incomes policy Max BRW curve. However, acting in its own perceived best interests and succumbing to temptation, the union may end up in a situation in which it is worse off than it would have been had it stuck to the incomes policy agreement. The problem has the character of the famous Prisoner's Dilemma (see the accompanying box). In other words, by succumbing to the temptation to break the incomes policy, a single union expects to secure a higher real wage for its members. Instead, the incomes policy collapses as other unions act in the same way. The consequence is rising inflation and the likelihood of restrictive measures to cut aggregate demand and hence employment back to E_0. The unions will end up in no better position in terms of wages and will have lost the higher level of employment associated with the incomes policy.

The Prisoner's Dilemma and incomes policy

The Prisoner's Dilemma (PD) is an example of a variable-sum game. Unlike the simpler zero-sum game in which one player's gain is the other player's loss, in a variable-sum game *both* players may gain (or lose) from the pursuit of a particular pair of strategies. The simplest way to explain the essence of the PD game and to highlight its relevance for incomes policy is to return to the original formulation. There are two prisoners, both of whom have been arrested in possession of stolen goods. Although known by the police jointly to have committed a burglary, a lack of evidence means that confession is required for a successful conviction. Without a confession, conviction is possible only on the lesser charge of possession of stolen goods.

The prisoners are held in separate cells for interrogation and are unable to communicate with each other. The interrogator gives each prisoner the following information. We know you have committed the burglary. If you confess, and your accomplice does not, you will be freed in return for your co-operation and your accomplice will be gaoled for the maximum 20 years. If you both confess, then you each get a reduced sentence of 10 years. If neither of you confesses, we have insufficient evidence to convict you of burglary and you will each be gaoled for 2 years on the lesser offence. How does each prisoner respond?

We can represent the choices available in the form of a pay-off matrix; the pay-off (years of gaol) to prisoner A is in the left-hand corner of each cell, and to prisoner B in the right.

		PRISONER B	
		confess	not confess
PRISONER A	confess	10 ⟍ 10	20 ⟍ 0
	not confess	0 ⟍ 20	2 ⟍ 2

Let us follow A's reasoning. Whether B confesses or not, A will always receive a shorter sentence by confessing, 10 rather than 20 or 0 rather than 2 years. Hence he will confess. B will reason just the same, with the result that each prisoner is gaoled for 10 years. The crucial insight of the PD is that *both* would have been better off if they had not confessed. This preferable strategy is not chosen, however, even if each believes the other will not confess . Note that had communication between the parties been possible, *and* had they trusted each other not to cheat, it would still have paid each of them to confess.

The chosen *dominant strategy* is the one that is preferred irrespective of the strategy chosen by the other party. While rational for each individual, it does not provide the utility-maximizing outcome for the prisoners taken together.

This game provides a powerful model for the relationship between separate industry unions engaged in wage negotiations in the context of an incomes policy. Suppose the government sets aggregate demand so as to secure its desired unemployment rate but states as a condition to the unions that rising inflation will not be accommodated. We set out the pay-offs to union A as it considers the choices available to the rest of the unions. In each case, the union can go for the maximum wage increase (on the Max BRW) or it can exercise restraint by bargaining along BRW(IP) (refer back to Fig. 8.4). We represent these strategies as 'maximum' and 'restraint'.

We rank the outcomes for union A from 1 (best) to 4 (worst) as it considers each strategy of B in turn. Thus, A does best if it pursues a

B (THE REST OF THE UNIONS)

	maximum	restraint
maximum	3	1
restraint	4	2

UNION A

maximum wage strategy while the rest show restraint: A would secure higher real wages and there would be little change in employment. Second-best for A is restraint on both sides—in this case employment would remain high and there would be no change in wages. Ranked third by A is when all seek the maximum wage increase; in this case there would be no real wage effect for A although employment would fall. The worst outcome for A is if it shows restraint and the others do not; it would then lose out in terms of both wages and employment. With each union seeing the problem this way, each will opt for the maximum wage increase whatever the strategies the rest follow. Just as in the original PD, the dominant strategy does not coincide with maximizing the utility of the parties.

The Prisoner's Dilemma model suggests that we should not expect the behaviour of independent unions to lead to an incomes policy outcome. If a policy is agreed, then the model indicates the strength of the internal pressures towards defection which will tend to lead it to collapse. In other words, even if each union recognizes the character of the Prisoner's Dilemma, it is still in its interest to break the incomes accord. This is because of its justified fear that, if other unions seek to use their bargaining power to the full, then a union that sticks by the pact will see its members losing out in terms of wage relativities. To prevent the breakdown of the incomes policy through this mechanism, a guarantee is required that other unions will not break the agreement. This raises once more the role of the institutional structure of wage-bargaining. Economies characterized by highly centralized wage-bargaining or where there is a single acknowledged leader union will find the achievement of an incomes policy agreement for wage restraint easier than economies in which there are a number of large unions, because the institutional structure of the former will help to prevent the Prisoner's Dilemma from arising. With a small number of unions, communication between them is easier; complete centralization overcomes the problem entirely, since there is a single decision-taker which chooses the best outcome for the unions as a whole.

*8.3   Wage-bargaining and Productivity Growth

In the context of a growing economy, it is reasonable to assume that unions enter wage negotiations seeking a particular growth rate of real wages rather than a specific real wage level. Whether or not this requires a fundamental change to the earlier analysis depends crucially on how the real wage growth 'target' is formulated. Consideration of two extreme cases illuminates the point at issue.

- *Case (i)*   If the unions seek (and are able to negotiate) a growth in real wages equal to the rate of productivity growth, then the simplifying assumption used in the analysis up to this point is valid. Assuming zero productivity growth and bargaining for a real wage level dependent on the rate of unemployment is a straightforward simplification of a more general aspiration—of securing real wage growth equal to productivity growth plus a component dependent on the rate of unemployment.
- *Case (ii)*   An alternative assumption is that unions have a real wage growth 'target' which is independent of the rate of productivity growth. If this is so, then serious qualifications to the earlier analysis will be required.

Although it will be argued below that case (i) is probably correct, we cannot ignore the implications of the second case. The reason is that, if we think of a situation in which the growth of productivity declines, there may well be a transitional period before union wage growth expectations are adjusted downward to reflect the new conditions. A contemporary example is the decline in productivity growth which characterized the major OECD economies in the period since the mid-1970s. In the transitional period, phenomena associated with case (ii) will be encountered.

Let us set out wage- and price-setting behaviour for each case and deduce the implications for the equilibrium rate of unemployment.

Case (i): Productivity-related Real Wage Growth Target

In this case, wage-bargaining behaviour can be represented as a straightforward modification of the original analysis. In wage-bargaining, there will be three components to the money wage rise:

1   an amount to cover expected inflation ($\dot{P}^E$);
2   an amount to cover expected productivity growth ($\dot{L}P$);
3   an amount related to the labour market situation.

This third component is most easily represented by adding to money wage increases an amount which is a linear function of the gap between actual unemployment and a reference rate of unemployment, U_R, i.e. $B(U_R - U)$, where B is a positive constant. The higher is unemployment relative to U_R, the lower will be money wage increases, *ceteris paribus*.

Money wages will rise according to the following equation:

$$\dot{W} = \dot{P}^E + \dot{L}P + B(U_R - U). \qquad \text{[wage inflation]}$$

Prices will be raised to cover the rise in unit costs, so as to maintain an unchanged profit margin:

$$\dot{P} = \dot{W} - \dot{L}P. \qquad \text{[price inflation]}$$

We can substitute the wage inflation equation into the price inflation equation to get

$$\dot{P} = \dot{P}^E + \dot{L}P + B(U_R - U) - \dot{L}P.$$

The terms in productivity growth drop out, and in a stable inflation situation where $\dot{P} = \dot{P}^E$ we have

$$0 = B(U_R - U).$$

This implies that there is a unique rate of unemployment at which inflation is constant; this is unemployment equal to U_R, which we can identify as the unique equilibrium rate of unemployment, U_N. Any rate of unemployment below U_N will be associated with rising inflation in exactly the same way as before. Note that the real wage grows at exactly the rate of growth of productivity. At unemployment below the equilibrium rate this is insufficient to satisfy union wage expectations, since a gap always remains between the bargained real wage and the actual real wage.

Case (ii): Constant Real Wage Growth Target

In this case, we assume that there is a fixed target growth rate for real wages, β, independent of the rate of productivity growth, $\dot{L}P$. Bargained money wage increases have the following components:

1   an amount to cover expected inflation;
2   an amount to bring real wages up to the real wage target;
3   an amount related to the labour market situation.

As shown in the starred box, if the target real wage is persistently

growing faster than productivity, there will be an increasing divergence
between the BRW and the PRW. In effect, workers are bargaining for an
increasing share of output per head; continuously rising unemployment is
required to damp down these aspirations.

*Fixed Target Wage Growth and Equilibrium Unemployment

We can show how the rise in equilibrium unemployment depends on
the difference between productivity growth and the wage growth
target and on the sensitivity of the bargained real wage to
unemployment in the following way. Because we are working with
growth rates, it is simplest to use logarithms of w^B and w^P. Let us
assume that

$$\ln w^B = a - bU + g_\beta t,$$

where g_β is the target real wage growth rate and t is time; and

$$w^P = LP(e^{g_{LP}t})(1 - m),$$

where g_{LP} is the growth of labour productivity and LP its initial
value. Thus

$$\ln w^P = \ln LP + g_{LP}t + \ln(1 - m).$$

Equating $\ln w^B$ with $\ln w^P$ determines U_N:

$$a - bU + g_\beta t = \ln LP + g_{LP}t + \ln(1 - m)$$

or

$$U_N = \frac{a - \ln LP - \ln(1 - m)}{b} + \frac{g_\beta - g_{LP}}{b}t.$$

Hence,

$$\Delta U_N = \frac{g_\beta - g_{LP}}{b}[t - (t - 1)] = \frac{g_\beta - g_{LP}}{b}.$$

The rise in equilibrium unemployment each period will be higher, the
larger is the gap between the wage growth target and productivity
growth $(g_\beta - g_{LP})$, since each period a higher level of unemployment
will be required to dampen bargaining power. The less responsive is
the bargained wage to unemployment (i.e. the lower is b), the higher
will unemployment have to rise each period to secure the required
reduction in bargaining power to offset the 'excessive' wage growth
aspirations.

Having set out alternative ways in which wage growth expectations are formed, there are two issues to address. First, what are the implications in each case of a fall in the rate of productivity growth? Second, can a reduction in taxation, or a reduction in the bargained real wage at each level of employment as the consequence of an incomes policy, reduce the equilibrium rate of unemployment?

8.3.1 Fall in Productivity Growth

Case (i): $\beta = \dot{L}P$

In case (i), where one component of the wage bargain is an increase to reflect the growth of labour productivity, the implicit assumption is that lower productivity growth will simply result in an equal reduction in that component of the wage bargain. In other words, wage growth aspirations adjust in line with productivity growth. Of course, the growth of actual real wages will also fall into line with the new lower rate of productivity growth. There will be no further ramifications for inflation since the equilibrium rate of unemployment will be unaffected.

Case (ii): β constant

With a fixed real wage growth target, a fall in productivity growth will have implications for equilibrium unemployment. The equilibrium rate of unemployment will now be continuously increasing. This is because higher unemployment will be required each period to dampen wage aspirations by the increasing divergence between the target real wage and productivity.

A simple example illustrates the point. Suppose that w^B (the bargained real wage) equals w^P (the price-determined real wage) in period 0 at 5% unemployment. The BRW now shifts up by 3%—the target real wage growth—and the PRW shifts up by 2%—the growth in labour productivity. Thus, in period 1 there will be a 1% gap between w^B and w^P at 5% unemployment. Let us assume that the slope of the BRW is such that a 1.5% increase in unemployment is needed to eliminate the 1% gap; then the equilibrium rate of unemployment in period 1 will be 6.5%. Now consider period 2: the BRW shifts up by 3% and the PRW by 2%, so that at 6.5% unemployment there is *again* a 1% gap between the BRW and the PRW. Hence unemployment has to rise to 8% to eliminate the gap. This shows that, if target real wage growth is above labour productivity growth, the equilibrium rate of unemployment has to rise each period.

Clearly, it is unrealistic to suppose that this situation could last for any long period of time. But the failure of wage growth aspirations to adjust *immediately* to a decline in productivity growth may have been one element in explaining the rise in equilibrium unemployment in the 1970s.

It is evident from the above example that the size of the increase in equilibrium unemployment each period depends on (i) the difference between the target real wage growth and labour productivity growth and (ii) the slope of the BRW with respect to unemployment. The bigger is (i) and the smaller is (ii), the larger will be the per-period increase in equilibrium unemployment. This result is shown explicitly in the box.

8.3.2   Using Tax Cuts and Incomes Policy to Reduce the Equilibrium Rate of Unemployment

In the earlier analysis of Part II, where zero productivity growth was assumed, the government was able to achieve a reduction in the equilibrium rate of unemployment by using policy to manipulate the bargaining curve or the price-determined real wage curve. In the case of tax cuts, the reduction of the government's share of output per head (the wedge) meant that private-sector claims were reconcilable at a higher level of employment. If we consider now case (i), where money wages grow by expected inflation, productivity growth, and a component determined by the labour market, in the face of a tax cut the first two components will be unchanged. However, lower income taxes (or indirect taxes) will reduce the gross wage increase required at each level of employment. Hence the equilibrium rate of unemployment will be reduced.

In case (ii), however, the reduction in equilibrium unemployment is not so simple. Suppose that the economy is at the equilibrium rate of unemployment but that the wage growth target exceeds productivity growth. Unemployment has to be rising sufficiently fast to offset the 'excessive' wage aspirations associated with the wage growth target. A lower rate of taxation will dampen gross wage demands and hence will mean that a lower rate of unemployment will be temporarily consistent with constant inflation. But the gap between w^B and w^P reappears each period, since w^B is rising faster than w^P. Therefore taxes have to be cut each period to sustain a constant equilibrium unemployment rate. A one-off cut in taxation or a one-off incomes policy which shifts the BRW (or PRW) would have the effect of lowering equilibrium unemployment only for one period. The following period the gap between wage growth aspirations and productivity growth would recur, and it would be necessary once again to lower taxation or negotiate further wage restraint to prevent equilibrium unemployment from rising. This is clearly unrealistic as a long-term policy option.

PART III

Imperfect Competition Macroeconomics in the Open Economy

9

Extending *IS/LM* to the Open Economy

In Parts I and II of this book, macroeconomic problems presented themselves in the form of unemployment and inflation. Once the economy is opened up to trade with the rest of the world, there is the additional problem of external balance. This part of the book is devoted to the analysis of how foreign trade and flows of capital affect the way the economy operates and the use of policy. As in Part II, the microeconomic foundations for the analysis are imperfect competition in both the labour and the product market. Firms producing in contemporary industrialized economies are not generally faced with perfectly competitive markets at the world level in which it is possible to sell at the going price as much of a product as is desired.[1] Just as is the case in the closed economy, producers will generally respond to an increase in the demand for their output by raising production. In other words, the typical situation for the product markets is one of demand constraint. Of course, in the open economy, an important constituent of demand is exports, which will be affected by the competitiveness of domestic production relative to that of foreign suppliers. Similarly, competition from imports can restrict demand for domestically produced goods.

After running through the way in which the *IS/LM* model must be modified to take account of exports, imports, and flows of capital, we will be in a position to extend the imperfect competition model to the open economy. The principal task is to show how endogenous wage- and price-setting behaviour affects the economy's competitiveness and its external balance. It is then possible to examine the constraints on the achievement of low unemployment and the policy tools available to governments.

---

[1] See Goldstein and Khan (1985) for a survey of the evidence supporting the use of an imperfect substitutes model for the bulk of traded goods of the OECD economies.

9.1 Goods Market Equilibrium

9.1.1 The *ISXM* and *BT* lines

Before introducing the determinants of international competitiveness into the analysis, it is helpful to hold prices and wages fixed and concentrate on the extension to the open economy of the *IS/LM* model. In the closed economy without a government, equilibrium in the goods market was characterized by the equality of planned expenditure and output:

$$y^D = y \qquad \text{[goods market equilibrium]}$$

where $y^D = c + i$. In the open economy, output demanded will be augmented by the demand by foreigners for output (exports), and reduced by the extent to which domestic consumers and enterprises purchase output from abroad (imports); i.e., c and i record the total volume of consumption and investment goods demanded by agents in the domestic economy, some of which will be met by foreign suppliers. Thus, it is necessary to add export demand and subtract import supplies in order to arrive at the total planned expenditure on domestically produced output. Hence

$$y^D = c + i + x - m,$$

where x is real exports and m real imports. At this stage, it is adequate to assume that the demand for exports is fixed exogenously (by the level of world trade, for example) and that the demand for imports depends simply on the level of domestic output:

$$x = \bar{x} \qquad \text{[export function]}$$

$$m = m_y y \qquad \text{[import function]}$$

where m_y is the propensity to import; $0 < m_y < 1$. The volume of imports is positively related to the level of output for several reasons. Some proportion of consumer goods will be imported, and since consumption depends positively on income, so will the level of imports. In addition, some proportion of the inputs to domestic production will be imported. Substituting the import and export functions, along with the consumption and investment function, into the goods market equilibrium condition gives

$$y = \bar{c} + c_y y + i(r) + \bar{x} - m_y y.$$

Hence in goods market equilibrium, the *IS*, which is now called the *ISXM* to emphasize the inclusion of exports and imports, is defined by

$$y = \frac{1}{1 - c_y + m_y} [\bar{c} + i(r) + \bar{x}]. \qquad \text{[ISXM equation]}$$

The closed economy multiplier is reduced by the marginal propensity to import and the elements of autonomous expenditure are augmented by exports. This is illustrated in Fig. 9.1. The *ISXM* will be steeper than the closed economy *IS* because a given reduction in the interest rate will require a smaller rise in (domestic) output to restore equilibrium in the goods market, since some of the extra output demanded will come from abroad in the form of imports.

Trade balance requires that exports are equal to imports:

$$\bar{x} = m_y y, \qquad \text{[trade balance equation]}$$

and defines a unique level of output, y_{BT}, at which balance occurs:

$$y_{BT} = \bar{x}/m_y.$$

As Fig. 9.2 illustrates, the level of output fixed by goods market equilibrium does not necessarily coincide with y_{BT}. In the case shown, there is a trade deficit at output level, y_0. A balance of trade equilibrium line (BT) can be drawn on the *IS/LM* diagram. Since there is a unique level of output, y_{BT}, at which trade is balanced, the BT line will be vertical at $y = y_{BT}$. At levels of output greater than y_{BT}, there will be a deficit on the trade balance as imports exceed exports (see upper panel). Similarly, for $y < y_{BT}$, the trade balance will be in surplus.

Suppose that, as the result of a boom in world trade, exogenous exports rise from a value of x_0 to x_1. It is clear from the upper panel of Fig. 9.3 that trade will be balanced at a higher level of output; a higher level of income will be required to generate imports equal to the new higher level of exports. The rise in exports will also have the effect of shifting the *ISXM* to the right. However, the *ISXM* will not shift by as much as does the *BT* because, for goods market equilibrium, output must rise so as to generate additional imports *and savings* equal to the increase in exports. Hence, at the original interest rate of r_0, output rises from y_0 to y_1; and y_1 is a position of trade surplus.

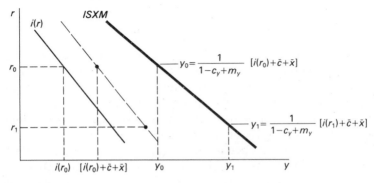

Fig. 9.1 The open economy *ISXM* curve

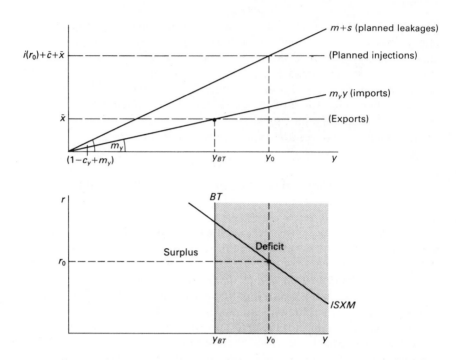

Fig. 9.2 Equilibrium output (planned injections = planned leakages); balanced trade output

Shaded area denotes trade deficit.

9.1.2 Correcting Deficits: Reducing Absorption, Increasing Savings

A common way of highlighting the sources of trade disequilibrium is to rewrite the goods market equilibrium condition as follows:

$$y = c + i + x - m$$

i.e.

$$y - (c + i) = x - m,$$

where $(c + i)$ is referred to as *domestic absorption*. Trade balance is equal to output less domestic absorption. Thus, a trade deficit means that domestic absorption exceeds output, with the implication that an improvement requires a reduction in absorption, on the assumption that $\bar{x}$ and m_y are fixed. Lower absorption would be achieved by a higher domestic savings propensity or by lower investment.

This simple analysis lies behind the oft-quoted formula that, to eliminate an external deficit, it is necessary to raise domestic savings. By including the government sector, we can see the relationship between domestic savings and investment, the external deficit, and the budget deficit as

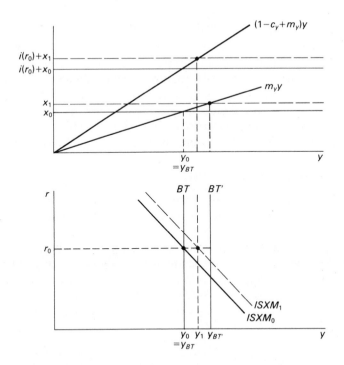

Fig. 9.3 A rise in exports improves the trade balance

follows. With the inclusion of the government sector, the equilibrium level of output will be

$$y^D = y,$$

where

$$y^D = c + i + g + x - m;$$

i.e., $y = c + i + g + x - m$; output is equal to domestic absorption $(c + i + g)$ plus the trade balance. Since private sector saving $s = y - c - t$, we can write $y = s + c + t$. Thus, we have

$$s + c + t = c + i + g + x - m,$$

which can be rearranged to form

$$s - i + t - g \quad = x - m$$

$$\underbrace{\text{Net private} + \text{Govt.}}_{\text{savings} \quad \text{savings}} \quad \begin{array}{l} = \text{Trade surplus} \\ \text{(net investment abroad)} \end{array}$$

Domestic savings

Alternatively, we can write

$$i - s + g - t \quad = m - x,$$

i.e. domestic investment less savings plus the government deficit is equal to the external deficit. If there is an external deficit (i.e. if $m > x$), then its reduction (given $\bar{x}$, m_y fixed) requires higher domestic savings. To advocate a rise in domestic savings to reduce a balance of trade deficit is a statement that no one should disagree with. But there are two very different implications of the statement depending on whether or not *output* is assumed to be held constant, while the rise in domestic savings occurs.

Expenditure-reducing Policy

In the model here, if the level of exports is fixed and imports are simply a function of the level of output, with the propensity to import also fixed, then domestic savings are equal to $\bar{x} - m_y y$. The *only* way that domestic savings can be increased is by reducing output, y. Thus, in this case advocating an increase in domestic savings, whether by cutting government spending, raising taxation, or inducing a rise in the savings propensity, is simply a somewhat disguised call for a *deflationary* policy.

Expenditure-switching Policy

Alternatively, an increase in domestic savings may be advocated within *either* a policy context designed to ensure that the level of output remains fixed *or* a theoretical framework implying that y remains fixed. In the first case, policy is used to improve the trade balance by diverting a larger percentage of output abroad; i.e., net exports are increased. For example, a devaluation of the exchange rate will have this effect. For the level of output to remain unchanged in the face of the fall in imports and rise in exports, there must be an equivalent rise in domestic savings. (We discuss this policy combination again later.)

In the second case, in a New Classical model for example, the real output in the economy is fixed uniquely by the clearing of the labour market (i.e. at the natural rate of unemployment). In this context, an increase in domestic savings simply means that a larger proportion of output is sold abroad. Thus, the New Classical model does not assume that the level of exports or the import propensity is fixed.

The arguments in the USA from the middle of the 1980s about the policies required to reduce the trade deficit reflect each of these three positions.

9.2   The *LM* Curve and the Balance of Trade: Zero Capital Mobility

In the closed economy, when drawing the *LM* curve, it is assumed that the money supply is exogenous. In the open economy, the payments associated with the flows of imports and exports affect the amount of money remaining in the hands of domestic residents: the supply of money can no longer be considered exogenous. More generally, in the open economy, the role of monetary flows in the short-run when prices are fixed depends on (1) whether there is a fixed or flexible exchange rate and (2) whether financial assets other than money (such as bonds or equities) can move between countries, i.e. whether there is 'capital mobility'. In this chapter we are assuming (1) that exchange rates are fixed; in this subsection, we are assuming (2) that there is no capital mobility.

A major way in which the world economy has changed in the last decades is through the development of highly mobile international capital. Most of Part III concentrates therefore on the assumption of perfect capital mobility; here we introduce a number of important issues by assuming zero capital mobility. Focusing on the case of fixed exchange rates and zero capital mobility, the money flows associated with exports and imports work as follows. A fixed exchange rate means that the central bank undertakes to buy and sell foreign currency at a fixed rate. Suppose that a UK company imports a German machine for £200. The German manufacturer wants to be paid in Deutschmarks (DM). Assume the exchange rate is £0.33 to DM1. The UK company exchanges £200 at the Bank of England for DM600. (In fact, the transaction occurs via the company's own bank.) Assuming that the Bank of England takes no further action, the monetary base (the stock of high-powered money), H, has fallen by £200; and the Bank of England's foreign exchange reserves, R have fallen by DM600.

In the closed economy, the change in the monetary base is equal to the public-sector deficit (PSD) less government sales of bonds; i.e., to the extent that the government deficit is not financed by bond sales, it must be financed by an increase in the money supply:

$$\Delta H = PSD - \text{sales of bonds.}$$

In the open economy (fixed exchange rates, zero capital mobility), there will be a further determinant of the change in the money base: the net purchase of foreign reserves by the central bank:

$$\Delta H = PSD - \text{sales of bonds} + \text{net purchase of foreign reserves } (\Delta R).$$

In the case in which the public-sector deficit is entirely financed by bond sales (PSD = sales of bonds), the money base will change by exactly the change in reserves. With zero capital mobility, the only determinant of changes in reserves is the trade balance:

$$\Delta H = \Delta R = X - M.$$

Hence any discrepancy between exports and imports will see the domestic monetary base rising or falling in line with movements in the foreign exchange reserves of the central bank. If we assume a highly simplified banking system[2] in which the money supply is related to the monetary base by a 'banking multiplier', i.e. $M^S = aH$, then the money supply will be fixed only when trade is balanced.

When we put this result together with the extended *ISXM*, we find that the model works quite differently from the closed economy. The *LM* curve shifts according to whether the economy is in trade surplus or deficit. Suppose, as in Fig. 9.4, that the pre-existing *LM* and *ISXM* curves intersect to give an equilibrium level of output y_0 which is above y_{BT}. The economy is running a balance of trade deficit and the money supply is falling. With imports in excess of exports, more pounds are being absorbed by the Bank of England as domestic agents purchase foreign exchange to pay for their imports than are being paid out by the Bank in exchange for foreign currency export receipts. The *LM* curve shifts leftwards until $LM = LM_1$. As interest rates rise, economic activity falls.

The adjustment of the money supply in response to any balance of trade surplus or deficit ensures that the economy will operate at y_{BT}, where *ISXM* intersects *BT*. When exports and imports are equal, the change in the money supply is zero and the *LM* remains fixed. In other words, the *LM* curve is not under the control of the monetary authorities; it will shift to coincide with the intersection of the *ISXM* and the *BT* curves.

The implications of this result are enormous. In a fixed exchange rate system, the inflows and outflows of money will eventually ensure that the economy is in balance of trade equilibrium. The government is required to do nothing to achieve trade balance (provided it has sufficient reserves). This result applies to a world without capital mobility. It is one illustration

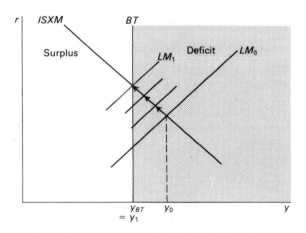

Fig. 9.4 Equilibration of the economy at balanced trade output

[2] For clear discussion of the more complex relationship between the money supply and the monetary base in a sophisticated banking system see Chick (1977), Goodhart (1975).

of the critical role that monetary flows play in the open economy. The role of monetary flows in achieving external balance has been developed further in the monetary approach to the balance of payments. This approach was important in policy debate in the 1970s, in particular in the 'International Monetarist' model. Irrespective of its association with 'monetarism', the mechanism through which monetary flows in a fixed exchange rate economy can have a domestic impact is indisputable. The mechanism continues to play a role even when the restrictive assumptions of this subsection are dropped.

9.2.1   Macroeconomic Policy: Sterilization and the Control of Domestic Credit Expansion; Fiscal Policy

In the very simple model introduced above, the money supply is related to the stock of high-powered money (the monetary base) through the banking multiplier, a, so that

$$\Delta M^S = a(PSD - \Delta B + \Delta R).$$

This equation suggests that the government may be able to place a wedge between changes in foreign exchange reserves and the domestic money supply, thus offsetting the shifting *LM* curve when the economy is in external surplus or deficit. To do this it would either have to adjust the public-sector deficit or bond sales (through open market operations) or the banking multiplier.

The use of open market operations in the bond market to this end is known as *sterilization*. Why would the authorities wish to do this? A good

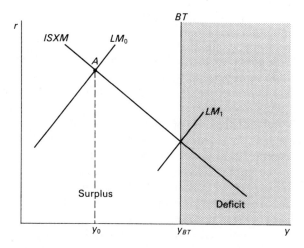

Fig. 9.5 Sterilization by the central bank enables the economy to remain at point *A* in trade surplus

example comes from the West German economy in the 1960s and is depicted in Fig. 9.5. The economy initially is in balance of trade surplus at y_0 (point A). The money supply is rising as a result of the external surplus and the LM is moving towards LM_1. However, the authorities do not wish the economy to operate at output level y_{BT} as they believe this would overheat the economy and result in inflationary pressure. In order to prevent this, the central bank must engage in open market operations to sell bonds to the public, thereby mopping up the liquidity that is entering the economy through the external surplus. To completely offset the effect on the money supply of the trade surplus, i.e. for ΔM^S to equal zero, the government must sell bonds equal to the value of $PSD + \Delta R$. This process is called sterilization of the incoming flows of money. The LM will remain at LM_0, with output at the desired level, y_0 below y_{BT}.

A quite different reason for the central bank to play an active role under the conditions of fixed exchange rates is to *restore* the direct link between changes in the domestic money supply and changes in foreign exchange reserves. In other words, the authorities may wish to *control* other forms of credit creation to prevent their offsetting the effects on the money supply of a deficit, and to ensure therefore that the economy adjusts automatically to balance of trade equilibrium, i.e. that $y = y_{BT}$. The IMF has traditionally been associated with this approach to macroeconomic policy[3] and has coined the term *domestic credit expansion* (DCE) for the excess of changes in the money supply over changes owing to variation in foreign exchange reserves,

$$DCE = PSD - \Delta B$$

so that

$$\Delta M^S = DCE + a\Delta R.$$

A policy to control domestic credit expansion could involve both a reduction of the public-sector deficit and an increase in bond sales. Both would contribute to generating a reduction in the level of output back to the level consistent with balance of trade equilibrium, y_{BT}. As Fig. 9.6 illustrates, in the absence of sterilization the LM shifts leftward, reflecting the external deficit; the $ISXM$ shifts left, reflecting the fall in the public-sector deficit; the economy moves to a lower level of activity at B.

Up to this point, fiscal policy has been discussed only in so far as the contraction of the public sector deficit can contribute to the reduction of domestic credit expansion as part of a programme to eliminate an external deficit. Can fiscal policy be used in the traditional Keynesian manner of changing the level of output to secure a goal such as full employment? It is implicit from the earlier analysis that, under fixed exchange rates with zero capital mobility, the level of output is uniquely fixed at y_{BT}, unless the

[3] See Williamson (1983a: 167–70).

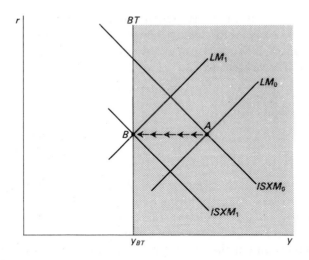

Fig. 9.6 Adoption of a policy of control of domestic credit expansion forces the economy to operate at point *B*

government can successfully engage in sterilization. For example, from an initial equilibrium with balanced trade, a rise in government spending shifts the *ISXM* to the right. Unless the central bank engages in sterilization of the outflow of foreign reserves associated with the trade deficit at the new higher level of activity, the *LM* will shift leftward and return the economy to the initial output level. The only effect of the expansionary fiscal policy will have been a shift in the composition of output: because of the higher interest rate at the new equilibrium, there will be less private investment and a higher level of government expenditure.

9.3   Implications of Capital Mobility for Macro Policy

So far, the external sector of the economy has been confined to trade in goods and services and the monetary flows associated with trade. It is now appropriate to examine the implications of international flows of non-monetary assets such as bonds and equities. The balance of payments is defined by the sum of the current account and the capital account. The current account is the balance of trade in goods and services augmented by net property income from abroad, e.g. the interest payments received on foreign assets owned by UK residents (bonds, equities, etc.) less interest due abroad on UK assets owned by foreigners. To simplify the exposition, we assume that the only internationally traded assets are currency and the bond.

The capital account records the net capital inflow to the economy, i.e. changes in the stock of foreign assets owned by UK residents less changes in the stocks of UK assets owned by foreigners. Hence the balance of payments can be written as

$$BP = [\underbrace{(X - M)}_{} + \text{net interest}] + \text{Net capital inflows}$$

$$\underbrace{\underbrace{\text{Trade balance}}_{\text{Current account}}}_{} \qquad \underbrace{\phantom{\text{Capital account}}}_{\text{Capital account}}$$

$$\therefore \Delta R = [(X - M) + \text{net interest}] + \text{Net capital inflows.}$$

Why would foreigners wish to purchase UK bonds? Presumably because they expect to earn at least as high a return from holding UK bonds as from holding other bonds. Assuming that potential bond-holders are risk-averse, and since by assumption the exchange rate is fixed, foreigners will buy UK bonds only if the interest rate on them is at least as high as on bonds in other countries. This is the case of perfect capital mobility: foreign and domestic bonds are considered perfect substitutes. Hence with perfect capital mobility, interest rates across countries *must* be equal. With perfect capital mobility, there will be a positive capital inflow if the domestic interest rate exceeds the world interest rate; a capital outflow if the domestic interest rate is below the world interest rate. Capital will flow until the interest rate discrepancy is eliminated.

What are the implications of perfect capital mobility? Suppose the economy is in balance of trade equilibrium with output y_{BT} and interest rate r_0 (point A in Fig. 9.7). Since $r_0 > r^*$ (the world interest rate), there will be an inflow on capital account as foreigners purchase UK bonds.

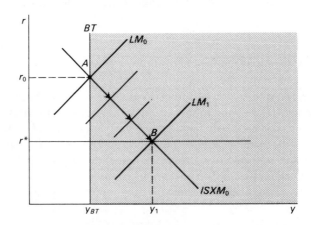

Fig. 9.7 Perfect capital mobility: the economy can remain at point B in trade deficit

Hence foreign exchange reserves will be rising, pushing up the stock of high-powered money and boosting the domestic money supply: the *LM* shifts to the right. This will continue until the domestic interest rate has fallen to the level of the world interest rate (point *B*). The deficit on the balance of trade at y_1 is offset by a surplus on the capital account.

9.3.1 Mundell–Fleming Results: Fixed Exchange Rates, Perfect Capital Mobility

In this short-run analysis, *monetary policy* is powerless to affect the level of output since the interest rate is fixed by the world rate of interest. A decrease in the money supply shifting the *LM* from LM_1 to LM_0 in Fig. 9.7, for example, would result in capital inflows generated by the temporarily higher interest rate. The capital inflow would be reflected in a build-up of reserves as the Bank of England purchased the foreign exchange and an increase in the money supply as overseas residents used the sterling they thereby acquired to purchase bonds from UK residents. The *LM* would shift back to LM_1.

By contrast, *fiscal policy* becomes extremely powerful. The equilibrium level of output is given by

$$y = \frac{1}{1 - c_y(1 - t_y) + m_y} [\bar{c} + i(r^*) + g + \bar{x}].$$

[*ISXM* equation]

Since the interest rate is given by the world interest rate, a fiscal expansion through an increase in government spending, for example, would result in the full multiplier expansion of output. The increase in transactions demand for money associated with higher incomes would be met through

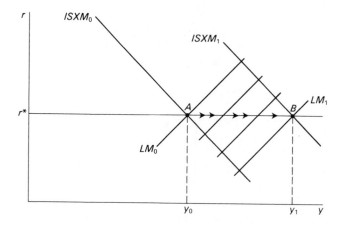

Fig. 9.8 Perfect capital mobility and the powerful effect of fiscal policy

capital inflow, attracted by the tendency for interest rates to rise above the world level. Figure 9.8 shows a fiscal expansion shifting the *ISXM* to *ISXM*$_1$ with output rising from y_0 to y_1.

9.4 Conclusions for the Role of Monetary and Fiscal Policy in the Short Run with Fixed Prices

The most striking conclusion from the short-run analysis of a fixed exchange rate economy concerns monetary policy. Monetary policy is ineffective in altering either the level of output or the interest rate. This conclusion holds both if there is zero capital mobility and if capital is perfectly mobile. As we have seen, in each case domestic monetary policy measures simply call forth offsetting monetary flows from abroad, either over time as the counterpart of a trade deficit or surplus (zero capital mobility), or instantaneously in response to an interest differential *vis-à-vis* the rest of the world (perfect capital mobility).

The ability of fiscal policy to affect the level of activity depends on the mobility of capital. With zero capital mobility, the level of output is fixed uniquely by y_{BT}: fiscal measures can have no lasting effect. The role of fiscal policy is simply to set the interest rate. Since the level of output is fixed, higher government spending can occur only if private spending is lower; the mechanism through which this comes about is by an increase in the rate of interest which crowds out an equivalent amount of private investment expenditure.

With perfect capital mobility, by contrast, fiscal policy becomes immensely powerful as a tool for changing the level of output. Any balance of trade deficit associated with a fiscal expansion is offset in the balance of

Table 9.1 Summary of monetary and fiscal policy

Policy	Zero capital mobility		Perfect capital mobility
	DCE proportional to ΔR (no sterilization)	Sterilization	
Monetary	No effect on y or r in equilibrium; but monetary flows equilibrate the economy	Determines y	No effect on y or r in equilibrium, but monetary flows equilibrate the economy
Fiscal	Determines r; no effect on y ($= \bar{x}/m_y$).	Determines r	Determines y; no effect on r ($= r^*$).

payments by the capital inflow associated with the temporarily higher interest rate. In equilibrium, the interest rate is set by the world interest rate.

As we have seen above, with immobile capital, the central bank can take an active role in order to offset the automatic equilibrating effects of balance of trade surpluses or deficits. The central bank can regain the ability to set the level of output if it is prepared to engage in open market operations of selling or buying bonds to offset the monetary flows associated with the external deficit or surplus. Such sterilization is not possible when capital mobility is perfect as the authorities lose any control over the domestic interest rate.

Table 9.1 presents a summary of the role of monetary and fiscal policy under the different conditions considered above.

10

Competitiveness and External Balance

This chapter forms a short bridge between the standard textbook analysis of the fixed exchange rate open economy, in which prices and wages are constant, and the extension of the imperfect competition model to the open economy. Here, the concept of competitiveness is introduced in conjunction with a discussion of price-setting in the markets for tradeable goods and services. Having defined price competitiveness, its relationship to the balance of trade is examined: under what conditions does a rise in competitiveness lead to an improvement in the trade balance? The famous Marshall–Lerner condition that higher competitiveness will improve the trade balance as long as the sum of the price elasticities of demand for exports and imports exceeds one is derived. Finally, we begin to set up the apparatus for conducting policy analysis in the open economy by introducing the Salter–Swan diagram.

10.1 The Determinants of Exports and Imports: the Role of Competitiveness

Once we relax the assumption that prices are fixed, it is necessary to incorporate a more realistic approach to the determinants of imports and exports. So far, exports have been assumed exogenous and imports, a simple function of the level of domestic income. But the competitiveness of our exports and of import-substitutes would also be expected to affect trade. UK exporters are assumed to secure a share of the exogenously given level of world trade where the share depends on their competitiveness. Export volume will be

$$x = F(\overset{+}{\theta}, \overset{+}{y}{}^*), \qquad \text{[export volume]}$$

where θ is competitiveness and y^*, world output. Import volume will depend both on competitiveness and on the level of domestic income:

$$m = G(\overset{-}{\theta}, \overset{+}{y}). \qquad \text{[import volume]}$$

The definition of competitiveness depends on the type of good and in particular on how prices are set in the markets in which it is sold. There is no general rule which applies to all commodities and all markets. For example, the price of UK manufactured exports may be set by the prices prevailing in the markets in which they sell. If this is the case, then a relative cost concept of competitiveness will be required. Alternatively, the exporter may set the export price equal to the price in the home market using a mark-up formula. In this case, a relative price *or* relative cost definition of competitiveness will suffice. Corresponding alternatives exist for import pricing.

Rather than cataloguing a series of cases, a convenient pricing assumption and associated definition of competitiveness will be adopted. (Section 11.5 below develops a more realistic approach but one which is less commonly used.) The standard elementary analysis of industrialized economies (defined as economies that export mainly manufactured goods and import both manufactures and raw materials) assumes that prices are set on a mark-up basis. As we have seen earlier, this is a reasonable assumption for domestic sales but, as discussed later in Chapter 11, it is less reasonable for export sales. The reason is simple: in order to maintain its market share in foreign markets, the exporter will generally have to take account of the prices prevailing for competing goods in those markets.

In spite of this objection, the standard assumption of mark-up pricing for exports will be maintained here. The corresponding assumption from the viewpoint of the foreign producer) for imports is that import prices will be equal to the world price in terms of domestic currency. Hence

$$P_x = P \qquad \text{[export price equation]}$$

$$P_m = P^*e, \qquad \text{[import price equation]}$$

where P_x is the domestic currency price of exports, P_m the price of imports in pounds sterling, P the domestic price level, P^* the world price level, and e the exchange rate defined as £(domestic currency)/$(foreign currency).[1] These pricing assumptions mean that the dollar price of a UK export item can differ from the price of a good with which it is competing in the US market. Similarly, the price of a home-produced item can differ in price from the price in pounds sterling of a competing import from the USA. In other words, the so-called *Law of One Price* does not hold. The Law of One Price states that the exchange-rate-adjusted price of a given good is identical in different countries (neglecting transport costs); i.e., $P = P^*e$. Suppose that $P_i > P_i^*e$, i.e. that the price of good i is higher in the UK than abroad. The Law of One Price states that good i would flood into the UK until the price was equalized. There is abundant empirical evidence

---

[1] This is now the conventional way of defining the exchange rate; it means that a rise in e represents a depreciation of the pound as there are more pounds per dollar. This conventional definition can be confusing to start with! A rise in e is a depreciation; a fall in e is an appreciation.

that the Law of One Price does not hold (e.g. Kravis and Lipsiy 1978; Isard 1977).

Given these pricing assumptions, a natural definition of competitiveness is in terms of relative prices; i.e.,

$$\theta_x = P^*e/P_x \qquad \text{for exports}$$
$$\text{[export price competitiveness]}$$

$$\theta_m = P_m/P \qquad \text{for import-substitutes}$$
$$\text{[import price competitiveness]}$$

From the pricing equations, $P_x = P$ and $P_m = P^*e$. Thus, both export and import competitiveness are defined by

$$\theta = P^*e/P. \qquad \text{[price competitiveness]}$$

θ is also known as the *real exchange rate*. A rise in competitiveness is synonymous with a depreciation of the real exchange rate. Under the Law of One Price, foreign prices in sterling terms would always equal domestic prices $(P^*e = P)$, so that competitiveness is fixed at the value of one. Under our assumptions, price competitiveness can vary. In nominal terms, the demand for exports and imports will be as follows:

$$X = P_x\sigma(P^*e/P_x)y^* = P\sigma(P^*e/P)y^* = P\sigma(\overset{+}{\theta})y^*$$
$$M = P_m m_y(P_m/P)y = P^*em_y(P^*e/P)y = P^*em_y(\bar{\theta})y.$$

The UK share of world exports (σ) depends positively on the price of UK exports (P_x) relative to foreign goods (P^*e), all measured in terms of pounds sterling. Higher UK competitiveness means a higher share of world exports.[2] Similarly, m_y, the marginal propensity to import, depends negatively on the price of imports relative to the price of domestic goods: higher UK competitiveness means a lower propensity to import.

In nominal terms, the balance of trade is now

$$\text{Nominal } BT = P_x\sigma(\theta)y^* - P_m m_y(\theta)y$$
$$= P\sigma(\theta)y^* - P^*em_y(\theta)y.$$

In real terms, i.e. dividing through by the domestic price level,[3] real

---

[2] More precisely, the *'volume'* share of UK exports in world exports rises with a rise in competitiveness; i.e., the volume of UK exports rises relative to the volume of world trade. The effect on the *value* of UK exports measured in dollars, for example, depends on whether the elasticity of demand exceeds unity. Suppose competitiveness rises because of a devaluation which reduces the dollar price of UK exports. The value share will rise if the volume of exports rises by more than the fall in UK export prices relative to those of the rest of the world.

[3] The focus of attention is on the implications for the domestic economy of changes in competitiveness. It is therefore appropriate to define the real trade balance in terms of the domestic price level. As Dernburg shows, the Marshall–Lerner condition, which we derive below in terms of the implications of a change in competitiveness for the trade balance deflated by the domestic price level, is exactly the same when deflating by the foreign price level (Dernberg 1989: sect. 8.2).

exports and imports are defined as follows:

$$\text{Real exports:} \quad x = \sigma(\theta)y^*$$

$$\text{Real imports:} \quad m = \theta m_y(\theta)y.$$

Thus, the real trade balance is

$$BT = \sigma(\theta)y^* - \theta m_y(\theta)y.$$

[trade balance in real terms]

In Chapter 9 above, the real balance of trade was defined by

$$BT = x - m_y y.$$

Balance of trade equilibrium, i.e. $BT = 0$, implied a unique level of output, $y_{BT} = x/m_y$. Now, the level of output consistent with trade balance will vary with the level of competitiveness, θ. Intuitively, a higher level of competitiveness, by increasing the level of exports and reducing the level of imports, will enable a higher level of output consistent with balance of trade equilibrium. However, this intuition is not always correct. The Marshall–Lerner condition establishes when this will be so.

10.2 The Marshall–Lerner Condition

The so-called Marshall–Lerner condition spells out the circumstances under which increased competitiveness improves the balance of trade. Although an increase in competitiveness unambiguously improves exports, it has two effects on imports: (1) it reduces the volume of imports demanded since home-produced goods become more attractive relative to imports, i.e. $m_y(\theta)y$ falls; but (2) it raises the real price of imports (the real price of imports is P_m/P, i.e. P^*e/P, i.e. competitiveness). Hence an increase in competitiveness will result in an improvement in the balance of trade as long as the increase in exports combined with the reduction in the volume of imports outweighs the effect of the increased real cost of imports. This in turn requires that the sum of the price elasticity of demand for exports and the price elasticity of demand for imports exceeds one (as long as we begin from a situation of balanced trade). This is the Marshall–Lerner condition.

An example helps illustrate this famous result. Suppose that initially exports plus imports equal 100. The elasticity of demand for exports is 0.75 and for imports is 0.50. Consider the implications of a 1% rise in competitiveness arising for example from a rise of 1% in foreign relative to domestic prices:

- exports rise by 0.75 to 100.75;
- import volume falls by 0.50 to 99.50;

- the real price of imports rises by 1, pushing the import bill up to 100.50. In this case, the balance of trade improves because

$$BT = 100.75 - 100.50 = 0.25.$$

If, on the other hand, export demand elasticity was considerably lower at just 0.25, the following results would occur:

- exports rise by 0.25 to 100.25;
- import volume falls by 0.50 to 99.50,
- the real price of imports rises by 1, pushing the import bill up to 100.50. The balance of trade deteriorates because

$$BT = 100.25 - 100.50 = -0.25.$$

It should be noted that the pricing assumptions that have been made imply that neither export nor import prices are affected by changes in the volume sold (within the range of variation considered). This is the traditional assumption made in the proof of the simple Marshall–Lerner condition that supply elasticities are infinite.

The Algebra of the Marshall–Lerner Condition

Since $BT = \sigma(\theta)y^* - \theta m_y(\theta)y$, the change in the trade balance in response to a change in competitiveness is

$$\frac{dBT}{d\theta} = \sigma'(\theta)y^* - \theta m_y'(\theta)y - m_y y$$

$$= \sigma y^* \frac{\sigma'(\theta)}{\sigma} - \theta m_y'(\theta)y - m_y y.$$

But, by assumption, $BT = 0$, i.e. $\sigma y^* = \theta m_y y$, and therefore

$$\frac{dBT}{d\theta} = \theta m_y y \frac{\sigma'(\theta)}{\sigma} - \theta m_y'(\theta)y - m_y y.$$

Dividing through by $m_y y$,

$$\frac{1}{m_y y} \frac{dBT}{d\theta} = \frac{\theta \sigma'(\theta)}{\sigma} - \frac{\theta m_y'(\theta)}{m_y} - 1.$$

Since $m_y y > 0$, $dBT/d\theta$ is positive if and only if

$$\frac{\theta \sigma'(\theta)}{\sigma} - \frac{\theta m_y'(\theta)}{m_y} > 1.$$

Now, $\theta \sigma'(\theta)/\sigma$ is *minus* the elasticity of demand for exports, since θ is the inverse of the real price of exports. Similarly, $\theta m_y'(\theta)/m_y$ is the elasticity of demand for imports. The Marshall–Lerner condition for an improvement in the balance of trade to follow from a rise in competitiveness is that the sum of the absolute values of the demand elasticities is greater than one; i.e.,

$$\left|\frac{\theta\sigma'(\theta)}{\sigma}\right| + \left|\frac{\theta m_y'(\theta)}{m_y}\right| > 1.$$

10.3 Policy Analysis and the Salter–Swan Diagram

If the Marshall–Lerner condition holds, then an improvement in competitiveness will be reflected in an improvement in the balance of trade. Hence the BT line on the $ISXM/LM$ diagram will shift to the right with an increase in competitiveness (see Fig. 10.1), indicating that a higher level of output is consistent with trade balance if the level of competitiveness is higher. For open economy macroeconomics, it is more convenient to use a diagram that allows us to depict the relationship between output and competitiveness (the real exchange rate) directly.

With output and competitiveness on the axes, the balance of trade locus is upward-sloping as long as the Marshall–Lerner condition holds. A high level of output (which boosts imports) is consistent with trade balance as long as the level of competitiveness is also high. The θ–y diagram is called the Salter–Swan diagram after two Australian economists who used a similar diagram to illustrate the choice of policy to achieve internal and external balance (Salter 1959; Swan 1960).

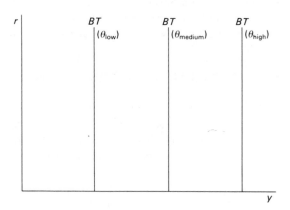

Fig. 10.1 Competitiveness and the trade balance

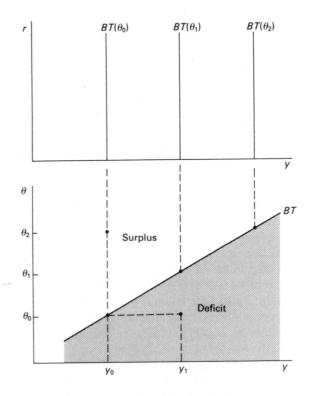

Fig. 10.2 Introducing the Salter–Swan diagram
Shaded area denotes trade deficit.

In the Salter–Swan diagram in Fig. 10.2, to the right of the BT locus,[4] there is a balance of trade deficit, and to the left, a surplus. With competitiveness equal to θ_0 and output y_0, trade is balanced; with a higher output level such as y_1 and the same competitiveness θ_0, there will be a deficit since imports will be higher while exports are unchanged.

When the Marshall–Lerner Condition Does Not Hold

If the Marshall–Lerner condition does not hold, the BT locus in the Salter–Swan diagram is downward-sloping. In this case, the volume effect of changes in competitiveness is so weak that the increase in the real cost of imports associated with a rise in competitiveness results

---

[4] In the original Salter–Swan model, domestic absorption rather than output was on the horizontal axis. They used the term 'external balance' to refer to the BT locus. We discuss fully the differences between the original analysis and our 'modernized' version in sect. 12.1.

in a worsening of the trade balance. An economy for which the Marshall–Lerner condition did not hold would be in a fortunate position, since trade balance would be consistent with the combination of low competitiveness and high output. We will return to this possibility in the next chapter, where the relationship between competitiveness and real wages is discussed.

To show the negative slope of the BT line in θ–y space in the case where the Marshall–Lerner condition (M–L) does not hold, we fully differentiate the balance of trade expression setting dBT equal to zero:

$$BT = \sigma(\theta)y^* - \theta m_y(\theta)y.$$

For $dBT = 0$,

$$d\theta(\sigma'y^* - \theta m_y'y - m_y y) - \theta m_y dy = 0.$$

In the case when M–L does not hold, $dBT/d\theta < 0$ and this is the term in parentheses above. Thus we have

$$d\theta/dy = \theta m_y/(\sigma'y^* - \theta m_y'y - m_y y),$$

in which the numerator is positive and the denominator is negative. Hence the slope of the BT line in θ–y space is negative.

The BT curve will be shifted by any change in world aggregate demand, y^*. For a given level of competitiveness, θ_0, a higher y^* will boost exports and thus permit balanced trade to occur at a higher level of output y_1. The BT curve shifts to the right with a rise in world trade and vice versa.

10.3.1   The Aggregate Demand Curve in the Salter–Swan Diagram

For policy analysis, it is necessary to represent the equilibrium level of output, i.e. where $y = y^D$, in the Salter–Swan diagram. From Chapter 9 above, we know that

$$y = y^D$$
$$= c + i(r) + g + x - m$$

and therefore

$$= \frac{1}{1 - c_y(1 - t_y) + m_y} [\bar{c} + i(r) + g + \bar{x}].$$

Using the export and import functions which include competitiveness, we have in equilibrium

$$y = \frac{\bar{c} + i(r) + g + \sigma(\theta)y^*}{1 - c_y(1 - t_y) + \theta m_y(\theta)}.$$

[goods market equilibrium]

With perfect capital mobility, the interest rate r is set equal to the world interest rate, r^*, and there is a unique locus showing the combinations of y and θ for which output is equal to aggregate demand:

$$y = \frac{\bar{c} + i(r^*) + g + \sigma(\theta)y^*}{1 - c_y(1 - t_y) + \theta m_y(\theta)}.$$

This locus is called the aggregate demand (AD) curve in the Salter–Swan diagram. As long as the Marshall–Lerner condition holds, this will be upward-sloping because a high level of output generates large leakages and therefore high competitiveness is required to ensure that injections are equally high. The AD curve will be less steep than the BT locus. Figure 10.3 illustrates how the points of intersection between the *ISXM* and *LM* curves are mapped into θ–y space to derive the AD locus. (Note for future reference that the AD curve will be derived differently under flexible exchange rates.)

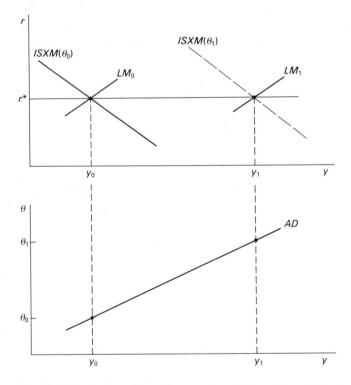

Fig. 10.3 Derivation of the AD curve in the Salter–Swan diagram

Why the Slope of BT is Flatter than that of AD

To demonstrate that the BT curve will be flatter than AD, consider an increase in competitiveness. For trade balance, the level of output must increase to generate sufficient extra imports to offset the improvement in the balance of trade associated with the increase in competitiveness (assuming the Marshall–Lerner condition holds). However, the equilibrium level of output will increase by less than this since there are other leakages (savings and taxation) in addition to imports to offset the injection of demand owing to the rise in competitiveness.

It is useful to note that the aggregate demand locus and the BT curve coincide in an economy with zero capital mobility and without sterilization by the central bank. The intuition is that in this case monetary flows always ensure that the economy is in balance of trade equilibrium, i.e. that $y_{BT} = y$. By contrast, as we have seen earlier, if the central bank is able completely to sterilize the monetary flows associated with a payments imbalance, the BT and AD loci again diverge, with the BT curve flatter than AD for the same reason as given above.

10.3.2 Policy Analysis

In the present setup of fixed prices, the government is presumed to pursue the policy objectives of high employment and external balance. The Salter–Swan diagram is a particularly clear way of illustrating that in general the use of two policy instruments will be required to meet both objectives. More precisely, it is sufficient for the targets to be related to the instruments by two independent linear relations. There are two simultaneous linear equations in the two unknowns of g, the indicator of fiscal stance, and e, the exchange rate, to produce the outcome of (θ_1, y_F). We will see in the next chapter that the introduction of a third equation relating the targets and instruments means that in general the targets cannot both be achieved. Let us take a situation in which the full employment output level is y_F, but the economy is operating at a lower output and hence lower employment level, y_0. In addition, there is a trade deficit. The economy is at point A in Fig. 10.4. Both policy objectives are met at point C. The question is how to shift from A to C.

Government demand management policy measures will be reflected in shifts in the AD curve. With perfect capital mobility, it was shown in the previous chapter that monetary policy is ineffective since such policy

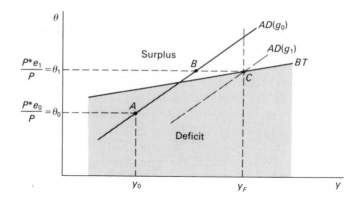

Fig. 10.4 The use of two instruments (*e, g*) to achieve two targets: full
employment and trade balance
$A \rightarrow B$: instrument 1 (*e*)
$B \rightarrow C$: instrument 2 (*g*)

operates on demand by changing the interest rate, and any deviation of the
interest rate from the world interest rate elicits an inflow or outflow of
foreign exchange reserves until the discrepancy is eliminated, i.e. until the
effect of the initial monetary measure is totally offset. However, fiscal
policy (changes in government spending or taxation) will change the level
of output. Fiscal policy measures will be reflected in a shift in the aggregate
demand schedule in the Salter–Swan diagram: AD will shift to the right in
response to a fiscal expansion, as a given level of competitiveness will be
associated with a higher level of output (see Fig. 10.4).

According to the assumptions of the Salter–Swan analysis, both the
domestic and the world price levels (P and P^*) are given. The only way
that competitiveness can be changed is to alter the exchange rate. Looking
at point A in Fig. 10.4 on the aggregate demand curve reflecting the initial
level of government spending g_0, a devaluation of the exchange rate will
take the economy to point B: at a higher level of competitiveness, goods
market equilibrium will occur at a higher output level because of the boost
to net exports. At B the trade deficit has been replaced by a surplus;
however, there is still a shortfall in output below the full employment level,
y_F. While the use of one policy instrument, the exchange rate, produced a
higher output level and an improvement in the trade position, the use of
the second, fiscal policy, is required to take the economy to point C with
full employment and balanced trade. An expansion of government
spending from g_0 to g_1 shifts the AD curve to the right, and, with the new
exchange rate of e_1 and thus competitiveness of θ_1, the economy moves
from B to C.

Once the point is taken that the number of instruments must equal the
number of targets, then at least conceptually the problem for the

government of achieving internal and external balance in the Salter–Swan model is straightforward. Fiscal policy is used to adjust the level of aggregate demand, and exchange rate policy is used to adjust competitiveness. Only in the case of zero capital mobility and sterilization can monetary policy play any role in the achievement of policy objectives.

11

The Imperfect Competition Model in the Open Economy

In this chapter, we bring the competing-claims behaviour characteristic of imperfectly competitive labour and product markets into the open economy. And we will see that, by dropping the assumption of fixed prices, the simplicity of using policy to achieve high employment along with external balance discussed in the last chapter disappears. The move to the open economy introduces an additional claimant on the output per head produced in the economy. In addition to the claims of real wages, real profits, and taxation, real imports must be included.

The introduction of real imports provides an interesting extra dimension to the imperfect competition model. We will see that under fixed exchange rates the claims of the *domestic* agents—unions, firms, and government—can be made consistent at *any* rate of unemployment because of the possibility of squeezing the real cost of imports. Thus, there is no longer a unique competing-claims equilibrium rate of unemployment. Nevertheless, the economy will be constrained as to the rate of unemployment it is able to sustain because of the consequences of squeezing the real cost of imports. We will see that a lower real cost of imports means lower *international competitiveness* for the economy. Thus, the ability of the government to run the economy at low unemployment is constrained by the weak competitiveness associated with low unemployment and its consequences for the balance of trade.

We define the unique rate of unemployment that is consistent both with competing-claims equilibrium and with trade balance as the *sustainable rate of unemployment* or *long-run equilibrium rate of unemployment*. To minimize confusion, we will use the term 'sustainable rate of unemployment'. At the sustainable rate of unemployment, inflation is constant and equal to world inflation and trade is balanced. Should the government choose a lower rate of unemployment, there will be constant inflation in the medium run — once the real cost of imports has been squeezed to the extent required to bring the price-determined real wage into line with the bargained real wage — but competitiveness will be lower and hence there will be a trade deficit. We argue that a trade deficit cannot be sustained indefinitely and that this establishes the uniqueness of the minimum sustainable rate of unemployment.

It is possible to convey in a simple diagram the new dimension that is added to the imperfect competition model by opening the economy. The bar charts in Fig. 11.1 depict the available output per head. As before, we assume that labour productivity does not vary with the level of employment so that, at both high and low unemployment, the columns are the same height. In each column, the claim of firms in terms of real profits per head is identical, while the real wage claim of unions is higher when unemployment is lower, reflecting the shift in bargaining power associated with falling unemployment. The residual in each column is the real cost of imports to the economy, i.e. the output per head that is claimed by foreigners. This part of the column is smaller at low unemployment.

The ability of domestic firms to set prices on their overseas as well as their domestic sales accounts for the ability of the domestic economic agents to reduce the real cost of imports to the economy.[1] By increasing

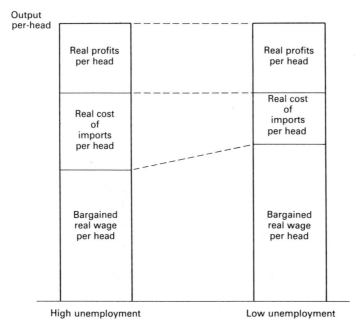

Fig. 11.1 Comparison between claims on output per head at high and low unemployment

[1] In the final section of this chapter, we examine the implications of a quite different competitive situation facing firms. If firms have to follow the price that is set by their overseas competitors, then we see that it is firms' profits that are squeezed at low rates of unemployment, rather than the real cost of imports.

their prices to protect their profit margins in response to the higher wage settlements achieved by unions at lower unemployment, the real cost of imports is reduced. Of course, higher prices will put domestic firms at a disadvantage in international trade, both in the domestic market in competition with imports and in the export market. This deterioration in competitiveness, along with the usual detrimental effect of higher activity on the trade balance, means that at low unemployment there will be a trade deficit. In spite of the consistency of the competing claims in each of the two columns of Fig. 11.1, and hence the absence of accelerating inflation, the economy cannot remain at low unemployment indefinitely. A trade deficit is not a sustainable position in the long run.

We can show the equilibrium rates of unemployment and the unique sustainable rate of unemployment in the familiar real wage–employment diagram (Fig. 11.2). As ever, there is an upward-sloping bargained real wage (BRW) curve. The total amount of output per head available at each level of employment is shown as usual by the labour productivity (LP) line. But the price-determined real wage line is not the same as before. The price-determined real wage is the amount left for real wages once real profits and real import costs per worker to firms have been deducted. Thus, the PRW will shift about as the real cost of imports changes. As we will show, the PRW always shifts—as the result of changes in the real cost of imports—so that it intersects the BRW at whatever is the current rate of unemployment (Fig. 11.2). The balance of trade can be shown on the same

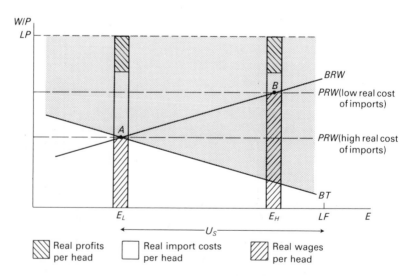

Fig. 11.2 Defining the lowest long-run sustainable rate of unemployment, U_S, in the fixed exchange rate open economy

Shaded area denotes trade deficit.

diagram. It will be downward-sloping because trade will be balanced when competitiveness is low (real wages are high) and output is low, *or* when competitiveness is high (real wages are low) and output is high. At point A, the economy is in balance of trade equilibrium. However, at B, with a higher real wage and, as we will show, lower competitiveness, and with higher output, there is a trade deficit. Thus, the lowest long-run sustainable rate of unemployment is fixed at E_L. We call this U_S.

From Fig. 11.2, it is apparent that there are two routes to achieving a *shift* in the sustainable rate of unemployment to a lower rate. In terms of lines on a diagram, the most obvious solution is to bring about a rightward shift in the balance of trade line. However, we will see that in economic terms there are few instruments available to the domestic economy through which the BT line can be shifted. Typically, the BT line will be shifted by *exogenous* changes in the volume of world trade. More promising is the second line of attack; this is to use policy to shift the bargained real wage curve. A downward shift in the BRW, achieved for example through a reduction in income taxes or the negotiation of an incomes policy, would produce a lower sustainable rate of unemployment. With a lower bargained real wage at each level of employment, real import costs would not have to be squeezed to such an extent to render domestic claims consistent, with the result that competitiveness would be higher at each rate of unemployment, enabling trade balance and competing-claims equilibrium to occur at lower unemployment.

Having sketched the basic modifications to the imperfect competition model required by opening the economy in a fixed exchange rate regime, the remainder of this chapter is devoted to spelling out the details. We shall focus on how the model works—i.e. on the behaviour of wages and prices and their effects on competitiveness, on the way in which competing claims are rendered consistent at each rate of unemployment, and on the determinants of the unique sustainable rate of unemployment. The question of using policy to shift the sustainable rate of unemployment is also addressed. In the following chapter, there is a detailed discussion of the role that changes in the exchange rate can play in macroeconomic policy. In stark contrast to the open economy model with fixed prices and wages of Chapter 10, we see that changes in the exchange rate can play a strictly limited role in the achievement of lower unemployment. The discussion of exchange rate changes paves the way for the move to flexible exchange rates in Chapter 13.

In summary, the characteristics of an open economy with fixed exchange rates and imperfectly competitive product and labour markets can be stated as follows:

R1   Any rate of unemployment is a potential competing-claims equilibrium rate of unemployment; i.e., any rate of unemployment is consistent with stable inflation.

R2 In competing-claims equilibrium, domestic inflation is equal to world inflation. A sharp way of depicting this result is to construct the long-run Phillips curve which is horizontal.

R3 There is a *unique* sustainable rate of unemployment associated with balanced trade. Unemployment below this rate is associated with the existence of a trade deficit. There is a trade deficit for two reasons: on the one hand, competitiveness is lower, and on the other, output and hence imports are higher. Competitiveness is lower at lower unemployment because the increased bargaining power of unions pushes up the real wage at the expense of a loss of competitiveness.

11.1 Price-setting, Wage-setting, the Real Cost of Imports, and International Competitiveness

We begin by summarizing price- and wage-setting in the open economy, and introduce the concept of the real cost of imports which plays a key role in the analysis. Since there is no change to the analysis of wage-setting, we simply recall the wage equation from the closed economy model.

11.1.1 Wage-setting

The wage-setting process in the open economy will be just as it was in the closed economy. The bargained real wage, w^B, rises with the level of employment:

$$w^B = W/P^E = b(U),$$

[bargained real wage equation]

where $db/dU < 0$.

11.1.2 Price-setting, the Real Cost of Imports, and Competitiveness

In the previous chapter, the standard assumption of mark-up pricing for exports was introduced; import prices are set by world prices. We can summarize price-setting as follows:

- *domestic prices*: mark-up;
- *export prices*: also mark-up, i.e. equal to domestic prices;
- *import prices*: equal to world prices in domestic currency terms.

Once the economy is importing raw materials, materials will figure as an element of costs along with labour costs. The domestic price level can be written as

$$P = mP + W/LP + P^*e/MP.$$

[open economy pricing equation]

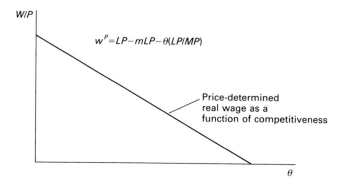

Fig. 11.3 The open economy price-determined real wage and competitiveness

The third term is unit imported materials costs, which is defined as the cost of materials in terms of domestic currency, where $1/MP$ units of materials are used per unit of output. MP (materials productivity) is assumed constant. As in Part II, P refers to the market price, i.e. the price paid by the consumer.

Dividing the pricing equation through by P, substituting θ for P^*e/P, and rearranging gives the expression for w^P, the price-determined real wage:

$$1 = m + w/LP + \theta/MP$$

$$LP = mLP + w + \theta(LP/MP)$$

$$\therefore w^P = LP - mLP - \theta(LP/MP).$$

[open economy price-determined real wage]

Price-setting implies a real wage equal to w^P, after real profits per worker (mLP) and real imported materials costs per worker $(\theta(LP/MP))$ are deducted from labour productivity. (The box shows exactly why $\theta(LP/MP)$ measures the real cost of imports per worker.) With the profit mark-up m, and labour and materials productivity (LP and MP) constant, there is an inverse relationship between w^P and θ (Fig. 11.3). This implies that the only way that the price-determined real wage can increase, *ceteris paribus*, is if the level of competitiveness is reduced.

Why $\theta(LP/MP)$ Measures the Real Cost of Imports per Worker

$P_m \equiv$ price of 1 unit of imports in £ terms.
$P^* \equiv$ price of 1 unit of imports in foreign currency terms.

$$P_m = P^*e.$$

$P^*e/P = \theta$ is the real price/cost of 1 unit of imports in the UK, i.e. measured in terms of the UK consumer price index, P.

θ/MP is the real cost of imports needed to produce 1 unit of output; 1 unit of imports produces MP units of output, so 1 unit of output requires $1/MP$ units of imports.

$(\theta/MP)LP = \theta(LP/MP)$ is the real cost of imports per worker since each worker produces LP units of output and each unit of output has import cost of θ/MP.

As noted earlier, competitiveness and the real cost of imports are both measured by θ, since $\theta = P^*e/P = P_m/P$. This enables a more transparent interpretation of the inverse relationship between w^P and θ: the only way in which the price-determined real wage can increase (given the fixed mark-up and constant labour and materials productivity) is if the terms of trade improve, i.e. if the real cost of imports declines. The terms of trade for an economy is defined as the ratio of export prices to import prices (where both are measured in terms of the same currency):

$$\text{Terms of trade} = P_x/P_m = P/P^*e = 1/\theta.$$

The terms of trade improve if the export price level (i.e. the domestic price level) rises relative to the import price level (i.e. the foreign price level), in other words if competitiveness declines.

If we think of a classic 'workshop economy' (Rowthorn and Wells 1987), which imports *only* raw materials and exports manufactures in competition with other countries, real wages can increase only because of a rise of the money wage relative to the world price of materials, while what reduces competitiveness is the rise in export prices relative to the world price of manufactures. If the economy imports substantial amounts of manufactures which enter directly into the cost of living, then the rise in money wage relative to manufacturing prices as a whole contributes to the higher real wage. In what follows, we will assume the workshop economy model—i.e. that only raw materials are imported. This allows the central arguments to be conveyed without unnecessary distraction.

11.2 Equilibrium Rates of Unemployment and the Sustainable Rate of Unemployment[2]

The reason for the disappearance of a single rate of unemployment at which competing claims are consistent and hence inflation is constant has

---

[2] These arguments are set out in Carlin and Soskice (1985).

been sketched above. At any level of employment, there are three claimants on output per head: profits, real wages, and imports. As the level of employment rises, the real cost of imports can be squeezed through the exercise of market power by domestic wage- and price-setters. This provides the mechanism through which higher expected wages at higher levels of employment are reconciled with an unchanged profit margin. The reconciliation of competing claims eliminates the pressure for accelerating inflation. Thus at any rate of unemployment, in equilibrium, inflation will be constant and equal to the world rate of inflation.

Suppose that in Fig. 11.4 the economy is initially at point A. Since there is an inverse relationship between w^P and θ (Fig. 11.3), the PRW curve now has to be indexed by the level of competitiveness (initially, θ_0). The BRW curve remains as before. At E_0, with the bargained real wage equal to the price-determined real wage, inflation is constant; the unemployment rate U_0 is an equilibrium rate of unemployment. However, at a higher level of employment, E_1, there will be a new equilibrium also characterized by constant inflation. Constant inflation requires that $w^B = w^P$, i.e. that the expected real wage that unions are able to negotiate through collective bargaining is consistent with the real wage resulting from business pricing decisions. For w^B to equal w^P at E_1, the PRW curve must rise. The PRW shifts up to PRW (θ') because competitiveness falls. The lower level of competitiveness represents a reduction in the real cost of imports. The lower real cost of imports is what permits a higher real wage, $w' = w^P = w^B$ at E_1. Hence E_1 is an equilibrium rate of employment.

However, although point A in Fig. 11.4 with real wage, w_0, and employment of E_0 and point B, with a higher real wage and higher

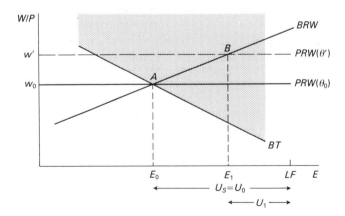

Fig. 11.4 Non-unique equilibrium rates of unemployment with fixed exchange rates: the minimum sustainable rate of unemployment
At both U_0 and U_1, inflation is constant.

employment, are equilibrium positions in the sense that inflation is constant, trade will not be balanced in both cases. As noted earlier, we can construct a balance of trade line in the labour market diagram to show positions of trade balance, of deficit, and of surplus. The balance of trade line will be downward-sloping: a high real wage implies low competitiveness and therefore, for balance of trade equilibrium, a low level of output and hence of employment is required. Conversely, a low real wage means high competitiveness, and for trade balance, a high level of employment is necessary. Above the BT line, the trade balance will be in deficit since, for a given employment level, the real wage is higher and hence competitiveness is lower than consistent with balanced trade: this is indicated by the shaded area in Fig. 11.4. While point A is a situation of balanced trade, point B clearly is not—both because the real wage is higher (and therefore competitiveness is lower) and because the level of activity is higher which pushes imports up. The lowest sustainable rate of unemployment is that associated with point A, i.e. unemployment of U_s. To pursue the analysis further, it is necessary to shift to the Salter–Swan diagram.

11.2.1 The Salter–Swan Diagram and the Sustainable Rate of Unemployment

For policy analysis in the open economy, the Salter–Swan diagram with its axes of output and competitiveness proves to be very useful. It is quite straightforward to transfer the key features of price- and wage-setting behaviour from the real wage–employment diagram to the Salter–Swan diagram. Since we have already derived the balance of trade line for the Salter–Swan quadrant with competitiveness and output on the axes, the remaining task is to transfer the competing-claims behaviour to that diagram. We construct a locus in θ–y space which shows the combinations of output and competitiveness at which $w^B = w^P$, i.e., at which the claims for real profits by firms are compatible with the claims for real wages by

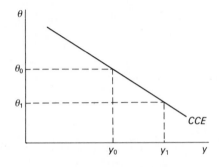

Fig. 11.5 The competing-claims equilibrium locus (CCE)

workers, given the level of labour productivity. To emphasize that a constant inflation equilibrium requires the consistency of real income claims of businesses and workers, the locus is called the competing-claims equilibrium (CCE) locus.

The CCE will be downward-sloping in θ–y space since at a high level of output employment will be high, generating a high w^B as the balance of bargaining power lies in favour of employees (Fig. 11.5). For w^P to be high, and hence for the actual real wage to equal w^B, competitiveness must be low; the real cost of imports must be low, reflecting favourable terms of trade for the economy. A high real wage is consistent with fixed real profits per worker only if real import costs are low. Conversely, at a low level of output, w^B is depressed. For w^P to be correspondingly low consistent with a fixed real profit margin requires high real import costs. Hence the terms of trade are unfavourable and competitiveness is high.

Figure 11.6 illustrates the explicit construction of the CCE curve from the wage–employment diagram. The quadrant to the left of the real wage–employment graph shows the inverse relationship between the price-determined real wage and competitiveness (refer back to Fig. 11.3). Let us consider the way in which a shift in the bargaining curve will be reflected in the Salter–Swan diagram. Suppose that the government manages to negotiate an incomes policy with the unions. This shifts the

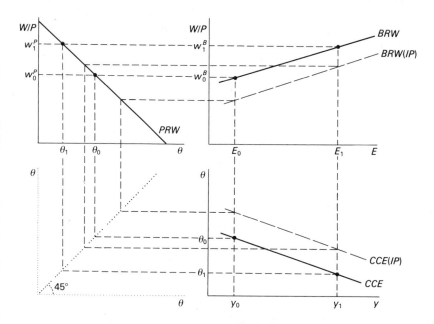

Fig. 11.6 Derivation of the CCE locus; the effect on CCE of an incomes policy: CCE → CCE(IP)

BRW downwards as unions are prepared to accept lower expected real wages at each level of employment (refer back to Section 7.1). In an entirely mechanical fashion, Fig. 11.6 illustrates that a lower BRW will be represented by an upward shift in the CCE locus. The intuition is that the negotiation of an incomes policy which has the effect of reducing w^B for each level of employment and output will permit a higher level of competitiveness consistent with any output level, since imported materials costs can rise by the amount by which the bargained real wage has fallen.

To pin down the sustainable level of output and hence the sustainable rate of unemployment, it is necessary to bring together the external balance and competing-claims relationships. In Fig. 11.7, the downward-sloping CCE and the upward-sloping BT curves are shown. These two lines divide the space into four zones: as we have seen earlier, to the left of the BT line there is a trade surplus, since for a given level of competitiveness output is lower than in consistent with trade balance. To the right of BT there is a trade deficit. Moving down the CCE line to the right, the level of competitiveness is declining. However, at no point on the line is there any tendency for competitiveness to change, since at each point output and real import costs (competitiveness) are such that $w^B = w^P$.

It is not difficult to see that there will be just one point (θ, y combination) at which there is trade balance *and* constant competitiveness, i.e. inflation constant at the world rate of inflation. Indeed, this point fixes the unique level of output and unemployment that is sustainable in the long run; although any rate of unemployment is consistent with constant inflation (along the CCE), only one will also be associated with

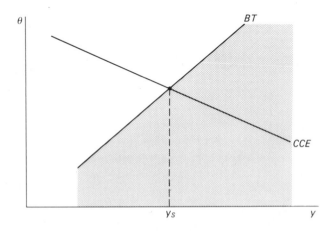

Fig. 11.7 The unique level of output consistent with constant inflation and balanced trade, y_S

Shaded area denotes deficit.

trade balance. This is the sustainable rate of unemployment U_s, and the associated level of output is y_s (Fig. 11.7). Before looking at how this result affects government policy choices, it is necessary to spell out more clearly why, under conditions of perfect capital mobility, the government should be concerned with the trade balance.

11.2.2   The Sustainable Rate of Unemployment and the Trade Balance

Why, under conditions of perfect capital mobility, should a trade deficit act as a constraint preventing the economy from remaining at a lower rate of unemployment? Surely the assumption of perfect capital mobility means that any trade deficit will be financed at the world rate of interest by an equivalent capital inflow to maintain balance of payments equilibrium. In principle, this is true. However, in practice it seems to break down. The simplest way to think of the unsustainability of a balance of trade deficit beyond the short run is to note that the economy must pay interest on its overseas borrowings. As the stock of external liabilities arising from a persistent capital inflow to finance a trade deficit builds up, the burden of interest payments rises. The interest payments push the current account (= trade balance + interest payments) further into deficit, requiring ever-increasing capital inflows. At some point, foreign currency holders are likely to get nervous about whether the exchange rate will be maintained. The government then finds itself confronted by a classical foreign exchange market situation, where holders of the currency become nervous because they believe other holders of the currency are nervous. If large-scale selling of the domestic currency then starts, the government may be unable to maintain the currency's value except by offering exceptionally high interest rates. Thus, the feed-back from the external debt to the financing of the interest payments leads eventually to the breakdown of perfect capital mobility in the sense that funds cease to be available to the economy at the world rate of interest.

Even in the 1980s, with greatly increased capital mobility, governments have been forced to respond to current account difficulties. Frequently they have had to take preventative action when the balance of trade has gone into deficit, to the extent that the deficit was not covered by long-term capital inflows. It is therefore appropriate to consider the balance of trade exerting a binding constraint on the economy in the medium run. In Chapter 19, we discuss the implications for the sustainable rate of unemployment of the pursuit of a policy which in the short run implies the running of a trade deficit (see Section 19.5).

It should be noted that this argument applies properly to the *current account* of the balance of payments: we have been using the trade balance as a proxy for the current account.

It is usually argued that countries with a tendency towards current account surplus, such as West Germany and Japan, are under less pressure to adjust towards trade balance than are economies with deficits. It may be possible for countries in such a situation to remain away from the sustainable rate of unemployment (e.g. at point B in Fig. 11.8), with higher than the sustainable rate of unemployment, for some time. Concern about the *temporary* rise in inflation above the world rate which would be associated with the shift to the sustainable rate of unemployment may explain the willingness of the authorities to hold unemployment above the sustainable rate.

11.3   Using Policy to Shift the Sustainable Rate of Unemployment

The policy dilemma for the economy can now be summarized in Fig. 11.9. With the prevailing structure of wage-bargaining and price-setting, and the level of productivity, the CCE is given. The level of world trade y^* fixes the position of the BT line. The intersection of BT with CCE fixes the maximum level of output that is sustainable, y_s. This in turn fixes the minimum sustainable rate of unemployment. At a lower rate of unemployment, associated for example with point B in the figure, there is a trade deficit. The fundamental problem is that at that level of unemployment workers demand and are able to achieve a level of real wages that makes exports insufficiently competitive to balance imports.

A sustainable lower rate of unemployment can be secured only through policies that succeed in shifting either the CCE or the BT curves. As we have seen already, supply-side fiscal and incomes policy measures can play some role in lowering the sustainable unemployment rate through their

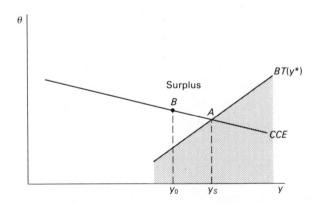

Fig. 11.8 The surplus-prone economy
Economy can remain at B with higher than sustainable unemployment. The BT constraint may be less binding for a surplus than for a deficit economy.

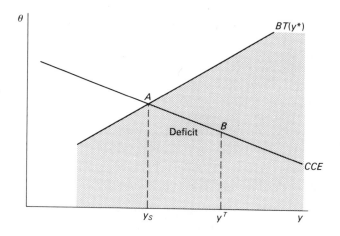

Fig. 11.9 The policy dilemma: target unemployment is associated with y^T, sustainable unemployment with y_S

effect on the CCE. An incomes policy or lower taxation is reflected in a rightward shift of the CCE and hence a reduction in the sustainable rate of unemployment. Of course, should there be an exogenous shock to the economy in the form of a change in world aggregate demand, y^*, then the BT line will be shifted. A positive external demand shock will shift the BT line outwards, with the effect of lowering the sustainable rate of unemployment.

11.3.1 Supply-Side Fiscal Policy

In this section we look first in a more systematic way at the potential for tax policy to shift the CCE curve and thereby influence the sustainable rate of unemployment. We then turn to a second example of supply-side fiscal policy—government expenditure on training. Here, it seems plausible to propose that increased expenditure on training could have the effect of shifting the *balance of trade* line, and in this way could enable the economy to move to a lower sustainable rate of unemployment.

Tax Policy and the CCE Locus

The use of tax changes to shift the BRW or PRW, and thereby to reduce the equilibrium rate of unemployment in the closed economy, relied on reducing the government's share of output per worker so as to be able to reconcile real wage and real profit claims at a lower rate of unemployment. In the fixed exchange rate open economy, the analogous policy renders real wage and profit claims consistent at a higher level of activity *without* the necessity of a deterioration in competitiveness and the balance of trade: the CCE curve is shifted to the right. The example of income taxation illustrates this.

For exactly the same reason as in the closed economy, a reduction in the rate of income tax would be expected to shift the BRW curve in the real wage–employment diagram downwards, as employees receive unchanged take-home pay in spite of a reduction in the pre-tax wage. This in turn means a rightward shift in the CCE locus in the Salter–Swan diagram and a reduction in the sustainable rate of unemployment.

Government Expenditure on Training and the BT Line

It can be argued that increased government expenditure on industrial training would result in higher net exports at a given level of price competitiveness. The UK's share of world exports will depend on structural characteristics reflecting product quality, design, etc. At each level of competitiveness, an improved industrial training system, by contributing to the speed and successful implementation of new products, will imply higher net exports, and hence a balance of trade consistent with a higher level of output, and lower unemployment. These arguments suggest that the government can effect a rightward shift of the BT curve and hence a fall in sustainable unemployment by undertaking such an expenditure programme.

It could also be argued that an expenditure programme on training would shift the CCE curve to the right by reducing mismatch in the labour market. Increasing training may lower the bargained real wage at each level of employment by increasing the skilled labour supply and reducing the mismatch between job vacancies and the unemployed.

11.3.2 Incomes Policy

Just as in the closed economy, the ability of the government to 'buy' a higher sustainable level of output through the reduction of taxation is constrained by the amount of government expenditure it wishes to carry out for social policy reasons and the size of public-sector deficit that is sustainable. If fiscal tools are not available, then the achievement of the target unemployment rate depends on the *negotiation* of a reduction in the competing claims on output as between profits and wages, or on the imposition of changes in industrial relations legislation that reduce union bargaining power. Let us consider an incomes policy that embodies the negotiation of a reduction in competing claims. Its functioning under fixed exchange rates is directly analogous to the closed economy (Chapter 7 above).

An incomes policy that is reflected in a downward shift in the BRW curve translates into a rightward shift in the CCE line. With the incomes policy in place, the economy can operate at a lower rate of unemployment with balanced trade. The ability to do so relies on the increase in competitiveness, and higher competitiveness is possible because of the agreement of the unions to reduce their expected real wage claims.

However, there is one extremely important difference between the working of an incomes policy in the open and the closed economy. In the closed economy, the incomes policy works by reducing the *expected* real wage; i.e., money wage claims relative to expected inflation are lowered. The *actual* real wage was unchanged by the implementation of the policy, since the real wage in the closed economy is fixed by the PRW and the PRW is horizontal.[3] Under fixed exchange rates, however, as we have seen above, the real wage is set by the BRW: the PRW shifts with changes in competitiveness to ensure that $w^B = w^P$ at every level of employment. The implication of this is that, under fixed exchange rates, an incomes policy that lowers the BRW will mean a *reduction* in the actual real wage. This is shown in Fig. 11.10: the real wage falls from w_0 to w_1. The move from A to B in the lower panel corresponds with that from A' to B' in the upper panel.

If, as we have been assuming throughout, labour productivity is constant, then a fall in the real wage will be necessary for the achievement of the target unemployment rate. Since by assumption labour productivity is constant, the reason cannot have anything to do with the declining marginal productivity of labour—a lower real wage being required to make additional employment profitable. Rather, the real wage is lower because higher competitiveness is required in order to have higher output consistent with trade balance, and since higher competitiveness means more expensive imports, a real wage cut is necessary. The requirement for an actual cut in real wages may make the negotiation of an incomes policy more difficult. To the extent that labour productivity is rising (reflecting the trend of technical progress), real wages may not have to be reduced in absolute terms; a reduction in wage growth relative to trend may suffice.

If an economy suffers a negative external demand shock, then an incomes policy can enable employment to be protected. Suppose that world aggregate demand declines from y_0^* to y_1^* (Fig. 11.11); this causes the BT curve to shift to the left, since for a given level of domestic output higher competitiveness will be required to secure trade balance. If the economy was initially in equilibrium at the target output level, y^T (position A in the figure), the fall in world demand will have two immediate effects:

---

[3] In the closed economy, a fall in the real wage will be required for the successful operation of an incomes policy if the PRW slopes downward. If it is the case that firms are able to raise their profit margins as the level of capacity utilization rises (or if the price was set as a mark-up on marginal costs in a situation in which marginal costs increased with employment), then a higher level of employment consistent with stable inflation requires a lower real wage.

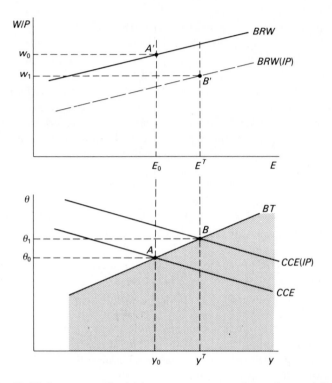

Fig. 11.10 Incomes policy in the open economy: the real wage falls

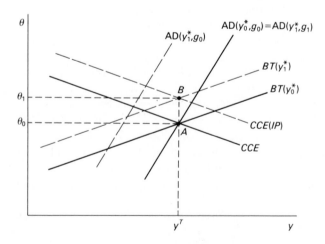

Fig. 11.11 Incomes policy as a response to a negative external demand shock

first, aggregate demand will fall as a result of the decline in net exports from $AD(y_0^*, g_0)$ to $AD(y_1^*, g_0)$; and secondly, the BT line will shift to the left. The government could always offset the aggregate demand effects by raising government spending from g_0 to g_1, (at least in the short run), thus shifting AD right to $AD(y_1^*, g_1)$ so that the economy could remain at A; however, it will be in trade deficit. With the lower level of world trade, one way that employment can be maintained in a sustainable way is through the negotiation of an incomes policy, which would shift the CCE curve to the right to CCE(IP). The economy would remain at output level y^T with lower real wages (point B).

11.4 Inflation and Employment in the Fixed Exchange Rate Open Economy

Having set out the equilibrium relationships under fixed exchange rates, it is appropriate to look at how the economy adjusts from one equilibrium to another. An examination of the adjustment process of the economy from A to Z in Fig. 11.12 helps to clarify the reason why inflation is constant at both E_0 and E_1. Assume initially that the economy is operating at E_0 with a constant rate of inflation equal to the world rate of inflation. If the level of employment rises from E_0 to E_1 as the result of higher demand, money wages will rise relative to expected inflation since w^B has increased, reflecting the rise in union bargaining power. (Note that we assume throughout that expected inflation is equal to the rate of world inflation; the alternative assumption of adaptive expectations produces the same result in the new equilibrium, but the adjustment process is different and messier.) This increase in unit labour costs will prompt firms to raise their

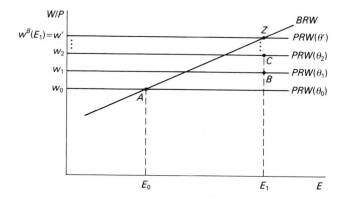

Fig. 11.12 Adjustment from one equilibrium rate of unemployment (E_0) to another (E_1)

prices in order to protect their profit margins. The result of this rise in domestic (and therefore export) price inflation is a deterioration in competitiveness, since world inflation remains unchanged. Since the real cost of imports is reduced, the PRW moves upward, say to $\text{PRW}(\theta_1)$, and the real wage rises to w_1 (point B in Fig. 11.12).

Unlike the situation in the closed economy, where a rise in money wage inflation followed by a rise in price inflation will leave the real wage unchanged, the real wage in this case has increased. Why? The reason is that domestic prices will have risen proportionately less than wages, since only the labour component of unit costs was affected by the rise in employment. Since the price level is a function of unit labour *and* unit materials costs, price inflation is a weighted average of labour cost inflation (ϕ_{lc}) and materials cost inflation (ϕ_{mc}). (The box on the price inflation expression explains the derivation of this equation.)

$$\dot{P} = \alpha\dot{\phi}_{lc} + (1 - \alpha)\dot{\phi}_{mc}, \qquad \text{[price inflation]}$$

where α is the share of labour costs in total unit costs; unit labour costs, $\phi_{lc} = W/LP$; and unit materials costs, $\phi_{mc} = P^*e/MP$. With LP, MP, and e (the exchange rate) constant,

$$\dot{P} = \alpha\dot{W} + (1 - \alpha)\dot{P}^*.$$

Deriving the Expression for Price Inflation

The price is set according to

$$P = mP + W/LP + P^*e/MP,$$

and since the exchange rate is fixed, it makes matters simpler if we take $e = 1$. Rearranging, we have

$$(1 - m)P = W/LP + P^*/MP.$$

Taking first differences of the variables and dividing left- and right-hand sides through by P gives

$$(1 - m)\frac{\Delta P}{P} = \frac{W/LP}{P}\frac{\Delta(W/LP)}{W/LP} + \frac{P^*/MP}{P}\frac{\Delta(P^*/MP)}{P^*/MP}.$$

Therefore

$$\dot{P} = \frac{W/LP}{(1 - m)P}\dot{\phi}_{lc} + \frac{P^*/MP}{(1 - m)P}\dot{\phi}_{mc},$$

where $(1 - m)P$ is total unit cost. Since $(1 - m)P$ is total unit costs and W/LP is unit labour costs, we can write $(W/LP)/(1 - m)P$ as α, the share of unit labour costs in total unit costs. Similarly, $(1 - \alpha)$ is the share of imported materials costs in total unit costs.

Thus, we have $\dot{P} = \alpha\dot{\phi}_{lc} + (1 - \alpha)\dot{\phi}_{mc}$, where α is the share of unit labour costs in total unit costs and $(1 - \alpha)$ is the share of imported materials costs.

In our example, since only wage inflation has increased, price inflation will rise only by the proportion α of the increase in money wages. Thus, $\dot{W} > \dot{P} > \dot{P}*$; real wages increase and competitiveness (and the real cost of imports) declines.

The economy is now characterized by E_1, w_1 (Fig. 11.12). This is not an equilibrium, since although the real wage has risen it is still not equal to $w^B(E_1) = w'$. The domestic price inflation (to restore profit margins) eroded a proportion of the expected real wage gain. Hence money wages will again rise relative to expected inflation as unions attempt to close the gap between w_1 and w'. This will prompt a further rise in domestic inflation relative to world inflation, and once again the PRW will shift up, reflecting the deterioration in competitiveness.

Eventually, the PRW will have shifted up to PRW(θ') and the real wage will be $w' = w^B = w^P$. In the subsequent round of collective bargaining, unions will not seek money wage increases in excess of expected inflation since they have secured the expected real wage $w' = w^B(E_1)$. Inflation will remain constant at the world rate of inflation.

Table 11.1 provides a numerical example to illustrate the period-by-period adjustment of the economy from the original equilibrium rate of

Table 11.1 Numerical example of adjustment to new equilibrium rate of unemployment at lower unemployment

Assumptions: $\dot{P} = \alpha\dot{W} + (1 - \alpha)\dot{P}*$; LP, MP, e fixed; $\alpha = 0.7$; $\dot{W} = \dot{P}^E +$ gap; $\dot{P}^E = \dot{P}* = 0$; Gap $= (w^B - w_{-1})/w_{-1}$

Period	Employment	Gap	$\dot{W}$	$\dot{P}$	Approx. cumulative Δw
0	E_0	0	0	0	0
1	E_1	2	2	1.4	0.6
2	E_1	1.4	1.4	0.98	1.02
3	E_1	0.98	0.98	0.686	1.314
4	E_1	0.686	0.686	0.480	1.520
5	E_1	0.480	0.480	0.336	1.664
6	E_1	0.336	0.336	0.235	1.765
⋮	⋮	⋮	⋮	⋮	⋮
z	E_1	0	0	0	2

unemployment at E_0 to the new equilibrium rate of unemployment at E_1.

The counterpart of the unique equilibrium rate of unemployment in the closed economy is a vertical long-run Phillips curve. The long-run Phillips curve records the combinations of the rate of unemployment and inflation for which inflation is constant (see Chapters 3 and 6 above). There is a single rate of unemployment at which inflation is stable. Since every rate of unemployment is an equilibrium rate of unemployment in a fixed exchange rate economy, the long-run Phillips curve becomes horizontal. It is horizontal at the world rate of inflation (Fig. 11.13).

Suppose the economy is initially at an equilibrium rate of unemployment at E_0 with constant inflation equal to world inflation, and there is an increase in the level of aggregate demand. To show the path of inflation explicitly in response to a boost in demand, we can use short-run Phillips curves. As was the case in the earlier example, it greatly simplifies the analysis to assume that inflation expectations are formed with reference to world inflation:

$$\dot{P}^E = \dot{P}^*.$$

We will see that the short-run Phillips curves shift as competitiveness changes. These short-run Phillips curves work differently from those in the

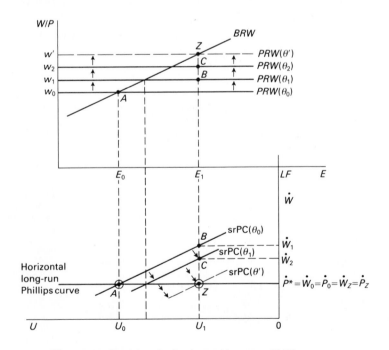

Fig. 11.13 Deriving the horizontal long-run Phillips curve

closed economy. They are indexed by competitiveness rather than by the expected rate of inflation.[4] Let us index the first short-run Phillips curve by the initial level of competitiveness, θ_0. The first point on that curve will be at the unemployment rate U_0 and the current inflation rate, $\dot{W}_0 = \dot{P}_0 = \dot{P}^*$, i.e., domestic inflation is equal to the world rate of inflation. Aggregate demand rises and reduces unemployment to U_1. Wage inflation rises by expected inflation plus an amount to take the expected real wage to $w^B(E_1)$: $\dot{W}_1$ is the second point (point B), allowing us to complete the original short-run Phillips curve (Fig. 11.13). (Since in the short run wage and price inflation differ in the open economy, with price inflation equal to only a proportion of wage inflation, it is easiest just to show wage inflation on the Phillips curve diagram.)

At the beginning of the next period, the real wage has risen to w_1; competitiveness (the real cost of imports) has fallen to θ_1. The new $PRW(\theta_1)$ shows that there is now a smaller gap between the actual real wage and the bargained real wage at E_1. This is reflected in a *shift* in the short-run Phillips curve from $srPC(\theta_0)$ to $srPC(\theta_1)$; money wages will rise by only $\dot{W}_2$ to take the real wage to its expected level. The position of the second short-run Phillips curve is fixed by the rate of unemployment at which $w^P(\theta_1) = w^B$, since this is where inflation will be equal to world inflation; i.e., $w^P(\theta_1) = w^B$ defines where the short- and long-run Phillips curves intersect.

Adjustment proceeds as discussed above, with the PRW shifting up to reflect the falls in competitiveness and the short-run Phillips curves shifting to the right for the same reason. Once the real wage has risen to $w' = w^B(E_1)$, the short-run Phillips curve will show wage inflation equal to world inflation. As long as unemployment remains at U_1, inflation will stay fixed at this level. In other words, the combination of U_1 and $\dot{W} = \dot{P} = \dot{P}^*$ is a point on the long-run Phillips curve. Hence both the initial situation (of $\dot{W}_0 = \dot{P}_0 = \dot{P}^*$, U_0) and the new situation (of $\dot{W}_z = \dot{P}_z = \dot{P}^*$, U_1) represent points on the long-run Phillips curve: it is horizontal.

Let us now translate the analysis of inflation into the Salter–Swan diagram. As we have seen earlier, the CCE line is downward-sloping in the Salter–Swan diagram. Each point along the CCE represents the consistency of competing claims, with the result that inflation is constant and equal to world inflation. The fact that inflation is constant at any level of unemployment (and output) shows up in a horizontal long-run Phillips curve as well as in the CCE line, where at each level of output competing claims are consistent. Points above the CCE line will be associated with falling competitiveness, i.e. with inflation in excess of world inflation. For example, in Fig. 11.14, at a level of competitiveness θ_0, a level of output y_1

---

[4] If the alternative expectations hypothesis of adaptive expectations is used, then the short-run Phillips curves shift with P^E as well as with competitiveness, θ.

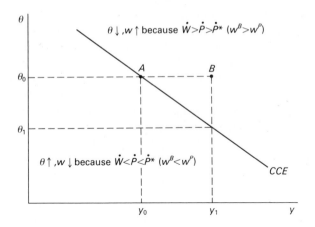

Fig. 11.14 The competing-claims equilibrium locus and inflationary pressure

greater than y_0 implies that wage inflation is greater than price inflation, which in turn means that domestic inflation exceeds world inflation (point B). Hence competitiveness is falling. In other words, employment and hence bargaining power are higher at E_1 (the employment level associated with y_1) than is consistent with competitiveness, θ_0. As long as employment is maintained at that level, endogenous wage- and price-setting behaviour will produce falling competitiveness until it equals θ_1. At θ_1, the real cost of imports will have been squeezed sufficiently to have enabled the real wage to have risen to $w^B(E_1)$. Conversely, points below the CCE locus will be associated with rising competitiveness.

We now have the apparatus with which to examine the interaction of aggregate demand conditions, endogenous price- and wage-setting behaviour, and the external balance. All three relationships can be depicted on the Salter–Swan diagram in the form of the AD, CCE, and BT curves. We concentrate on the central case of perfect capital mobility; in this case, the AD curve is shifted by fiscal policy measures (changes in government spending or taxation) as well as by changes in the exogenous world interest rate, r^* (refer back to Section 10.3). As discussed in Chapter 10, monetary policy is ineffective as a means of changing the level of employment under conditions of capital mobility and fixed exchange rates, since it is impossible for the government to alter the rate of interest and thereby to affect the level of aggregate demand. For reasons of clarity, we will assume that the economy is always on AD; i.e., we neglect the process of adjustment from one ISXM/LM intersection to another.

Assume initially that the economy is at A in Fig. 11.15, i.e. with competitiveness equal to θ_0 and output equal to y_0. Since A is below the

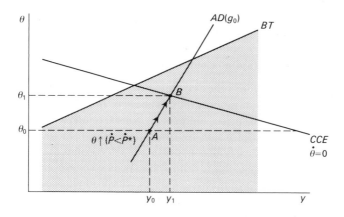

Fig. 11.15 Adjustment of the economy to the competing-claims equilibrium locus

CCE line, competitiveness must be rising. Rising competitiveness in turn implies that ISXM is shifting to the right and therefore that the economy is moving up the AD curve (refer back to Section 10.3) with the level of output rising. The economy will come to rest at point B, where competitiveness is θ_1 and output is y_1. Once the economy is on the CCE curve, inflation is equal to world inflation and competitiveness is constant. The government is able to choose the position of the economy along the CCE through its choice of fiscal policy. By changing the level of government spending or taxation, the government is able to shift the AD curve to secure the desired level of output (refer back to Fig. 10.4). As pointed out in Section 9.3 above, perfect capital mobility rules out any role for monetary policy: the interest rate is set by the world interest rate.

The ability of the government to choose the level of output in the economy, and hence the level of employment and rate of unemployment, without a problem of accelerating inflation is at odds with the situation in the closed economy. Nevertheless, governments will still be frightened of inflation in a fixed exchange rate system for three reasons. First of all, a fall in competitiveness owing to an albeit *temporary* rise in inflation above the world rate may lead speculators to believe that the government will devalue the exchange rate. The government will interpret the belief of the exchange market operators as arising from the presence of the rise in inflation. The second reason for expressed concern with inflation is that the government is worried about a fall in competitiveness but uses the language of inflation. Finally, it may be the case that, when the government observes a rise in price and wage inflation when unemployment falls, it does not understand that if the exchange rate does not fall then price and wage inflation will eventually fall back to the world rate.

*11.5 More Realistic Assumptions about Pricing and Competitiveness: Profit Squeeze

11.5.1 A Broader Notion of Competitiveness

In the previous chapter the concept of price competitiveness was introduced. The international competitiveness of the economy was defined as $\theta = P^*e/P$, i.e. the price of foreign goods relative to domestically produced goods. This definition followed naturally from the price-setting hypothesis adopted, namely that exports are priced on a mark-up basis in exactly the same way as goods for the domestic market are priced, and that imports are priced in a symmetrical way by the producers of those goods; i.e., imports to the UK are priced at the world price level. The implication of such price-setting is that any change in domestic costs is passed on in export prices and reflected in a change in competitiveness.

The merit of this set of assumptions is its simplicity. However, a more realistic model of the open economy would take account of the likelihood that producers of exports, for example, will not only use their own costs (labour costs and imported materials costs) as the basis for price-setting but will also take account of the prices being charged by their competitors in foreign markets. In some markets, producers may set export prices by the world price alone. We can think of export pricing as comprising three alternatives:

1 mark-up
2 world pricing
3 hybrid pricing: a combination of mark-up and world pricing.

It should be noted that, when using the term 'world pricing', we are not confining it to the special case where a UK producer faces a perfectly elastic demand curve for its output at the world price. International markets may be imperfectly competitive and yet characterized by world pricing. Figure 11.16 illustrates the contrast between the world pricing assumption under imperfect competition and the assumption of perfect competition in international markets. In the first case (part (a)), British producers of a range of mechanical engineering equipment will typically not be able to sell at a higher price (for a similar specification) than that charged by other producers. Thus, there may in fact be something like world pricing. This does not mean that British producers can sell as much as they want at the world price. Their market share will be determined by a whole host of factors, of which long-term relations with customers will be important. In the diagram, the UK is able to sell an amount $\bar{q}_{UK}$ in the German mechanical engineering market assuming that it prices in line with the other sellers at price P^*. In other words, there is a kinked demand curve at work. The UK firm's share of the market will depend on the

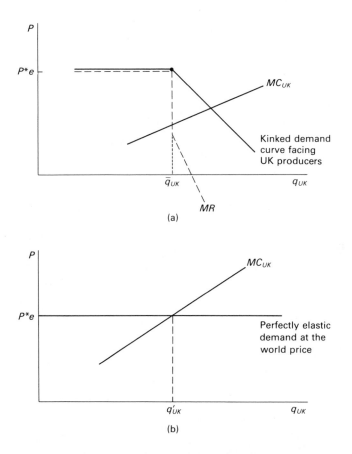

Fig. 11.16 World pricing (imperfect competition) compared with perfect
competition
(a) Imperfect competition in world markets: demand curve kinked at the
world price
(b) Perfect competition in world markets: perfectly elastic demand at the
world price

non-price attributes of its product. By contrast, in a perfectly competitive
world market, the UK is able to sell as much as it finds profitable, q'_{UK}, at
the world price, P^*, where $q'_{UK} > \bar{q}_{UK}$ (Fig. 11.16(b)).

Equally, the world pricing hypothesis does not imply that purchasing
power parity (PPP) holds—prices of cars in any particular category, for
example, may be uniform in the West German market regardless of the
country of origin, but nevertheless at a different level than car prices in the
UK. Under PPP, all cars in the category share the same dollar price,
regardless of the market that is being considered. In other words,

international arbitrage in goods is assumed to eliminate price differentials between countries.

World pricing implies that, for exports, $P_x = P^*e$. If competing imports (final goods) are priced in a symmetrical way, i.e. in line with the price set in the UK, we have for imports, $P_m = P$. Prices for the same good can differ across markets. By contrast, purchasing power parity implies that: $P_x = P^*e = P = P_m \Rightarrow \theta = 1$.

Broadening the pricing possibilities in turn requires a broadening of the concept of competitiveness. We will find that the concept of *cost competitiveness* becomes useful. For example, if export prices are set according to world prices, there is no scope for divergence between the price of exports and the price of goods in foreign markets with which they compete (i.e., $P_x = P^*e$). If domestic costs change relative to foreign costs, this would not be reflected in prices (see Fig. 11.16(a)).[5] Nevertheless, it seems appropriate to speak of a change in competitiveness, since the ability to compete has, in the broadest sense, been affected. In the extreme case where a cost increase renders participation in the foreign market unprofitable, we would say that the firm had been driven out by a lack of competitiveness.

Classical Unemployment in the Open Economy

This is the most natural setting in the imperfect competition model in which to find the occurrence of *classical unemployment* (refer back to Sections 5.4 and 6.4). Suppose there is an upward shift in the bargained real wage line in the UK as the result, for example, of increased militancy in the work-force. As argued in this section, real wages will rise and workers will achieve their bargained real wage. The resources to pay for this will come from the squeezing of export profit margins as exporters are unable to raise the price of their output. In such a situation, the real wage may rise above the marginal product of labour, rendering marginal employment unprofitable. Since sales to the domestic market are demand-constrained, firms cannot divert output from export to the home market to avoid making losses. In other words, firms will drop out of export markets and reduce their employment in line. The unemployment arising from this set of circumstances is clearly classical unemployment.

Since the world pricing hypothesis means that there is no difference between the prices of UK and German goods sold in Germany, how are we

---

[5] A microeconomic model that produces price-setting of the world pricing type is presented in ch. 18.

to interpret the measure of competitiveness, $\theta = P^*e/P$? In other words, P^*e/P no longer represents price competitiveness. With mark-up pricing of exports, an increase in P^*e relative to P implies an improvement in competitiveness since UK exports are cheaper than competing goods in foreign markets. Although price competitiveness is not applicable with world pricing, we find that θ remains a useful indicator of competitiveness *if domestic prices remain set on a mark-up (i.e. cost-plus) basis:* the domestic price level remains an indicator of domestic costs. In that case, with world pricing implying that export prices are set equal to the domestic price of the importing country, θ could have risen because:

1   P^* has increased in response to an increase in costs abroad. This would be the case where a foreign firm is the market leader in the international market and is confident that any price increase that it initiates will be followed by the other sellers in the market. With unchanged costs in the UK, unit profits on export sales must have risen;

2   e has increased; i.e., there has been a devaluation of the pound which raises UK exporters' revenue in pounds;

3   P has fallen because of a reduction in costs in the UK, and with export prices unchanged at the world price level, P^*e, this raises unit profits for UK exporters.

Can the improvement in export profitability relative to non-tradables' profitability at home and/or to the profitability of foreign production be interpreted as an improvement in competitiveness? The answer depends on the role played by changes in profitability in altering the incentive and resources for investment, for product and process innovation, for advertising, and for marketing. For example, higher tradables' profitability would be expected to boost investment in the tradables sector, enabling UK exporters to improve the non-price competitiveness of their products. Similarly, an improvement in the profitability of domestic exporters relative to their foreign competitors would be expected to permit a boost in the non-price competitiveness of UK exports. For a discussion of different concepts and measures of competitiveness, see Bank of England (1982).

In the discussion in previous sections, we have focused on imports of raw materials, assuming that the prices of such goods were set by world pricing ($P_m = P^*e$). If we concentrate instead on imports of final goods, as noted above, the symmetrical assumption to the world pricing of exports is that they are priced exactly in line with the domestic goods with which they compete. This implies that $P_m = P$. When producers of import substitutes face a cost rise of domestic origin, i.e. when their labour costs rise, they put up their price using the mark-up rule. According to the new import pricing rule, the prices of competing imports go up too. This improves the profitability of production of foreigners selling in the UK market; by the same arguments used above, this amounts to a deterioration of UK competitiveness. Similarly, if costs abroad rise, import prices remain fixed and therefore profit margins of foreign firms exporting to the UK are reduced. Therefore the standard definition of competitiveness, $\theta = P^*e/P$, is an indicator of the cost competitiveness of import substitutes.

To summarize, adopting either of the polar-opposite pricing hypotheses for exports and for imports of final goods, i.e. mark-up pricing of exports or world pricing of exports, and world pricing of imports or import prices equal to domestic prices, does not alter the usefulness of the definition of competitiveness, $\theta = P^*e/P$. θ should be interpreted as a measure of *cost competitiveness* under the alternative pricing hypothesis. Where the prices of goods selling in the same market are identical, competitive advantage will derive from non-price attributes. An increase in relative costs for UK producers will reduce their ability to compete on non-price grounds.

The most plausible simple hypothesis about pricing in an industrialized economy is that there is a combination of world pricing and mark-up pricing in place. Some UK firms will be price leaders in both their domestic and foreign markets, others will set prices at home but not abroad, and there will be still other firms for which prices must be followed both in the local and in their overseas markets. In general, both relative price and relative cost differences will determine competitiveness and θ must be interpreted accordingly. In their survey of studies of the elasticity of the export price of manufactured goods with respect to wage costs and to competitors' export prices, Goldstein and Khan (1985) found for example that, for West Germany, a 1% rise in wages leads to a 0.58% rise in export prices, while a 1% rise in competitors' export prices leads to a 0.36% rise. Corresponding figures for the much less open economy of the USA are a 0.85% rise in export prices in response to a 1% wage rise and a 0.09% rise in export prices in response to a 1% rise in competitor's export prices. For further discussion of open economy pricing and the presentation of two simple micro-based models, see Chapter 18.

11.5.2   Non-unique Equilibrium Rates of Unemployment and Profit Squeeze

It is easy to show that, under fixed exchange rates, the choice of pricing hypothesis does not affect the basic results of this chapter. However, the model works in a sufficiently different way for it to be worth presenting. We will assume that exports are priced according to world prices and that all imports are raw materials which are also priced by world prices. This enables the essential difference in operation of the model to be presented without unnecessary complication.

In the imperfect competition basic model presented above, the reason the unique equilibrium rate of unemployment disappeared was that it was possible for the economy to squeeze the real cost of imports and thereby permit a higher real wage and unchanged real profit margin at a higher level of employment. The cost of this was a deterioration in competitiveness and in the trade balance. However, under world pricing of exports and imports, it is not possible for the economy to turn the terms of trade in its favour and reduce the real cost of imports by raising domestic and hence export prices relative to world prices.

World pricing of exports means that export profit margins cannot be protected by the marking up of domestic cost increases. At a higher level of employment, the equation between w^B and w^P is brought about by a *reduction in export profit margins*. The PRW curve shifts upward in the real wage–employment diagram, reflecting a lower level of competitiveness as before. However, the inverse relationship between the price-determined real wage and competitiveness is no longer a reflection of the inverse relationship between the real wage and the real cost of imports. Rather, under these conditions it reflects the inverse relationship between the real wage and export profit margins. At a higher level of employment, real wages are higher, export profit margins are lower, and as a result,

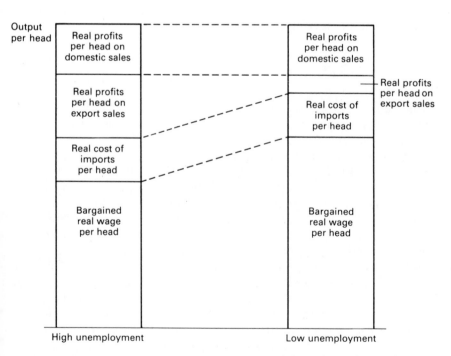

Fig. 11.17 Comparison between claims on output per head at high and low unemployment: world pricing of exports

Export profits are squeezed at low unemployment.

competitiveness is lower. As before, lower competitiveness implies a deterioration in the balance of trade. Figure 11.17 shows the squeeze on export profit margins at a higher level of employment.

An examination of the adjustment path to a new equilibrium rate of unemployment at a higher level of employment assists in understanding the way in which wage- and price-setting responses permit a transfer of real income from export profit margins to real wages. The domestic price level is now

$$P = mP + W/LP + P^*_{rm}e/MP,$$

where P^*_{rm} is the world price level of raw materials defined as

$$P^*_{rm} = (1/\tau)P^*,$$

where τ is the world terms of trade as between manufacturers and raw materials. An increase in the world price of raw materials relative to manufactures would see a reduction in τ. The domestic price level in terms of P^* and τ is

$$P = mP + W/LP + \frac{1}{\tau}\frac{P^*e}{MP}.$$

Rearranging and substituting θ for P^*e/P gives

$$w^P = LP(1 - m) - \frac{\theta}{\tau}\frac{LP}{MP}.$$
$$[\text{price-determined real wage}]$$

This defines an inverse relationship between the price-determined real wage and competitiveness. (Note that the country's terms of trade, tt, are constant since $tt = P_x/P_m = P^*e/(1/\tau)P^*e = \tau$.)

To examine the adjustment process of the economy from A to B in Fig. 11.18, assume as before that $\dot{P}^E = \dot{P}^* = 0$. At the start of period 1, employment rises to E_1 with the result that money wages rise by 10% at the annual wage bargaining round. Firms immediately mark up *domestic* prices by the implied rise in unit total costs: if labour costs comprise a proportion $\alpha = 0.75$ of total costs, then P arises by 7.5%. The sterling price of exports, $P_x = P^*e$, remains unchanged, with the result that export profit margins decline. The real wage rises by 2.5%. In the following period, money wages will rise by 7.5% to take the expected real wage up to $w^B(E_1) = w'$. P rises by $0.75 \times 7.5 = 5.625\%$ to maintain the profit margin on domestic sales unchanged. The process continues until the real wage has risen by the full 10%. Since the terms of trade for the economy have not changed, the real cost of imports to the national economy is unchanged. Profit margins on domestic sales are also unchanged. This implies that the higher real wages represent a *redistribution of national income* away from export profits towards real wages. The decline in

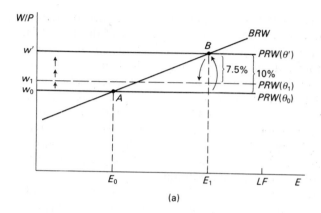

(a)

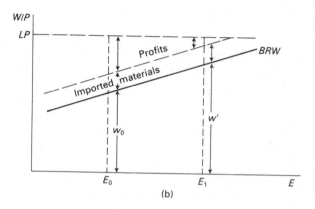

(b)

Fig. 11.18 Non-unique equilibrium rates of unemployment with world pricing behaviour

(a) Adjustment to new equilibrium rate of unemployment at E_1

(b) Lower export profit margin at E_1

competitiveness which is associated with this redistribution as exporting industries are less able to compete over non-price aspects is reflected in the fall from θ_0 to θ'.

11.6 Summary and Conclusions

The main features of the fixed exchange rate open economy with imperfectly competitive product and labour markets can be characterized in the following propositions.

1 The sustainable or long-run equilibrium rate of unemployment in an economy depends on the determinants of wage- and price-setting

behaviour summarized in the CCE curve and by the level of world aggregate demand which fixes the position of the BT. On the one hand, unless the economy is on the CCE, inflation is out of line with that of competitors and hence competitiveness is changing; the economy is not in equilibrium. On the other hand, there will generally be a limit to the length of time for which the economy can sustain a current account imbalance. Thus, the intersection of the CCE and BT in the Salter–Swan diagram (or the corresponding intersection between BRW and BT in the real wage–employment diagram) establishes the maximum sustainable level of output and employment consistent with the structure of the labour market, price-setting, and external conditions.

2   With perfect capital mobility, *monetary policy* is unable to affect the level of aggregate demand even in the short run, since the rate of interest is set by the world rate of interest. Should the government increase the domestic money supply, for example, this simply tends to depress the interest rate below the world interest rate. There is a capital outflow until the extra liquidity has leaked abroad. The interest rate returns to the world level and the economy is left with lower official foreign exchange reserves and a higher stock of foreign bonds in private hands.

3   *Fiscal policy* plays an important role in fixing the level of aggregate demand; the government can use changes in government spending and taxation to shift the AD curve to the desired output level along the CCE. However, the longer-run sustainability of this level of output is constrained by the external position (point 1 above).

4   In the *short run*, the economy will be on an aggregate demand (AD) curve at a position such as A in Fig. 11.19. This is an equilibrium in the short run since output is equal to planned expenditure (aggregate demand); nevertheless, competitiveness is changing and the economy is

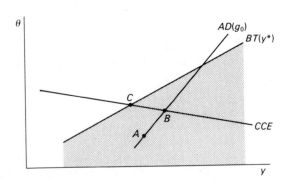

Fig. 11.19 Short-, medium-, and long-run positions for an economy
Shaded area denotes trade deficit.

not in external balance (the economy is on neither the CCE nor the BT curves).

In the *medium run*, the economy will be at the intersection of an AD curve and the CCE at a position such as *B* in Fig. 11.19. The economy moves from *A* to *B* since the real wage is greater than can be sustained by unions through wage-bargaining. This implies that domestic prices rise less rapidly than international prices, resulting in rising competitiveness. As competitiveness rises, net exports rise boosting the level of activity. At *B*, there is a medium-run equilibrium since competitiveness is constant: inflation is equal to world inflation. Nevertheless, the economy is not in external balance because of the trade deficit.

In the *long run*, an economy prone to a current account deficit may be forced to move to the intersection of CCE and BT at a position such as *C* in Fig. 11.19. (A large and powerful economy such as the USA appears to have more leeway in operating with a current account deficit than smaller economies.) There is no automatic mechanism in the model which ensures that position *C* is reached. The shift from *B* to *C* can occur in two different ways:

(a)   if the CCE and BT are taken as fixed. To eliminate the deficit at *B*, it must reduce aggregate demand through fiscal contraction (AD shifts left). The long-run equilibrium sees trade balance but a higher level of unemployment than at *B*;

(b)   if the government uses policy measures to shift CCE (*fiscal policy* or *incomes policy*), or if there is an exogenous change in world aggregate demand which shifts BT. Then *C* will change to the new intersection of CCE and BT; AD will have to change also to intersect the new *C* position.

Note that an economy prone to current account surpluses (such as Germany and Japan) can operate for long periods of time at a position of medium-run equilibrium with a current account surplus. Thus, international financial markets can force deficit countries in the medium run to adjust unemployment upwards until the deficit is eliminated. By contrast, surplus countries have greater freedom to choose their unemployment rate.

5   If there is world pricing of exports, then the reconciliation of the competing claims for output at each level of employment occurs through the squeezing of export profit margins. If firms are unable to alter the price at which they sell exports—because of the expected reaction of their competitors in the market—then, they are unable to protect their profit margins in the face of higher wage claims as the level of employment rises. The deterioration of export profit margins will be reflected in a decline in the competitiveness of the domestic economy since exporters will be less

able to compete on non-price grounds. The deterioration of competitiveness feeds through to the current account and constrains the ability of the economy to stay at the higher level of employment. Finally, with world pricing, classical unemployment can arise from an upward shift in the bargaining curve as exporters are unable to produce profitably for overseas markets.

12

The Exchange Rate as a Policy Instrument

In this chapter, we bring together material from the analysis of devaluation as a policy instrument which was introduced in the context of fixed prices and wages of Chapter 10 with the imperfect competition model analysed in Chapter 11. The central question to be addressed is the limits to the use of discrete changes in the exchange rate to enable the economy to operate at lower unemployment while respecting the external constraint. In the fixed-price world of Chapter 10, devaluation of the exchange rate in conjunction with the use of fiscal policy permitted the achievement of internal and external balance. In the imperfect competition model, no mention was made of the use of exchange rate changes to lower the sustainable rate of unemployment. We show that devaluation of the exchange rate does not permit a lasting improvement in competitiveness and hence lower sustainable unemployment *unless* it is associated with an additional policy which shifts the CCE or BT curves.

The limited potency of devaluation in the imperfect competition model arises because of the existence of *real wage resistance*.[1] Although devaluation provides an immediate boost to competitiveness and therefore tends to improve the external position of the economy, this comes at the cost of a deterioration in the terms of trade. The real cost of imports rises and real wages are reduced. The response of wage- and price-setters to this erodes the competitiveness-boosting effect of the devaluation.

Aside from the question of real wage resistance, which characterizes the imperfect competition model, there has been a long tradition of debate about the effectiveness of exchange rate changes as a policy tool. We review the debate looking at the 'elasticities' and 'absorption' arguments. The elasticities approach focuses on the relationship between the response of quantities of imports and exports to changes in the exchange rate and the price changes involved. The absorption approach focuses on the demand implications of devaluation.

Having run through the twists and turns of the devaluation issue, there are circumstances even in the imperfect competition model in which

---

[1] See e.g. Dornbusch (1980: 71–4).

changes in the exchange rate can provide a very useful policy instrument. We look, for example, at the combination of devaluation with a programme of government expenditure on training and with an incomes policy.

12.1   Devaluation and Real Wage Resistance

Under the Bretton Woods system of fixed exchange rates, economies were able to change their exchange rate unilaterally if they could demonstrate to the IMF that there was a fundamental disequilibrium in their balance of payments position. The use of parity changes was sparing during the Bretton Woods years: following the realignments in Europe in 1949, the UK devalued in 1967 and France in 1958 and 1968, and West Germany revalued in 1961 and 1969. Parity changes became more frequent in the early 1970s as the Bretton Woods system began to break up. The European Monetary System (EMS) is the major contemporary example of a more or less fixed exchange rate system. But the study of exchange rate changes is of interest not only for analysis of policy in the EMS or for the Bretton Woods period; it forms the basis for understanding how a flexible exchange rate system, with its frequent parity changes, works.

In Chapter 10 above, the traditional analysis of the use of policy to attain internal and external balance was described. Exchange rate changes provided an essential adjunct to aggregate demand measures in securing full employment with balanced trade. In Chapter 11, with the reintroduction of endogenous wage- and price-setting, it was concluded that there was a unique level of employment at which inflation would be constant and trade, balanced. The implication was that such an employment level may not coincide with the government's objective for high employment. For a government to achieve the target unemployment rate with external balance, it seemed that it would have to use incomes policies or tax changes to shift the CCE or BT lines; otherwise it would be reliant on an exogenous boost in world trade. The use of exchange rate policy was not mentioned. This should make us wary of the scope for using the Salter–Swan tool of devaluation as a lasting solution to the problem of reducing unemployment while maintaining external balance.

12.1.1   Can Devaluation Permit Higher Employment Consistent with External Balance?

To answer the question of whether devaluation permits a higher level of employment consistent with external balance, it is necessary to examine how changes in the exchange rate affect the three components of the model we are working with: aggregate demand, the balance of trade, and price-

and wage-setting behaviour. The exchange rate enters the model through the definition of competitiveness. As we have seen (Chapter 10 above), as long as the Marshall–Lerner condition holds, the trade balance is directly related to competitiveness and, *ceteris paribus*, inversely related to the exchange rate; i.e., a lower exchange rate (higher e when defined as £/$) is associated with a stronger trade balance. A devaluation boosts competitiveness and the trade balance, and also therefore the level of aggregate demand.

In terms of the Salter–Swan diagram, a devaluation of the exchange rate takes the economy along an aggregate demand curve (the position of which is fixed by the domestic policy instruments of government spending and taxation and by the exogenous levels of world trade and the international interest rate) to a higher level of output. Suppose the economy is originally at A in Fig. 12.1(a), i.e. at the target employment level, by means of fiscal policy g_0 but with an external deficit. The question is whether it is possible

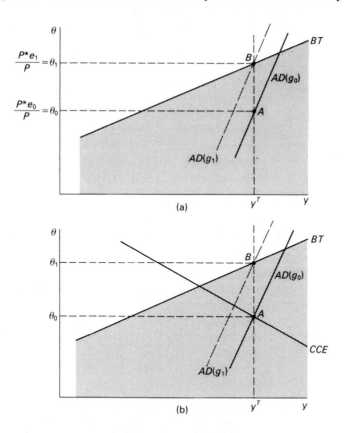

Fig. 12.1 Devaluation as a means of eliminating a trade deficit
Shaded area denotes trade deficit.

to use devaluation to raise competitiveness from θ_0 to θ_1 and eliminate the trade deficit (shift from A to B). Leaving aside the CCE line, the immediate answer is 'yes'. The effect of the devaluation is to raise competitiveness to θ_1. At this level of competitiveness, and with government spending at g_0, output exceeds the target level, y^T, because the rise in competitiveness has increased aggregate demand. Thus, to get to B, it is necessary to reduce government spending to g_1 and shift the aggregate demand line to the left as indicated by the broken AD line.

Although the external deficit has been eliminated, the economy is not in equilibrium once account is taken of labour market behaviour. It is simplest to assume that the government is continually shifting g to maintain y at y^T. This is equivalent to a vertical AD curve, AD' (see Fig. 12.2). Point B lies above the CCE curve, which means that competitiveness is falling (Fig. 12.1(b)). With competitiveness and hence the real cost of imports at θ_1, the amount left for real wages once the fixed profits per worker have been deducted is below the bargained real wage at the level of employment associated with y^T. Wages are rising faster than prices as

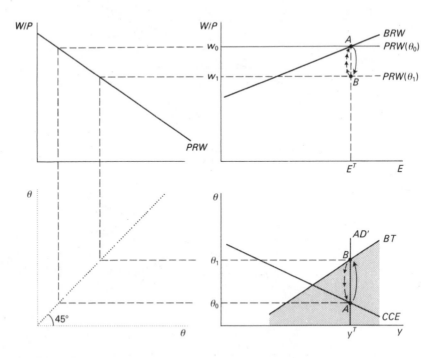

Fig. 12.2 The implications of a devaluation for real wages

The long directional arrows between A and B indicate the effect of *devaluation*, which immediately raises θ and cuts the real wage to w_1. The short directional arrows between A and B indicate the effect of *erosion*: over a period of three to five years, the process of $\dot{W} > \dot{P} > \dot{P}^*$ returns θ to θ_0 and w to w_0.

unions seek to claw back the loss in real wages associated with the devaluation. This prompts wage increases in excess of expected inflation. In other words, the endogenous wage- and price-setting behaviour at B operates to counteract the effect on competitiveness of the devaluation. Figure 12.2 illustrates the situation very clearly; the new level of competitiveness θ_1 at B implies a new real wage, w_1. The labour market is not prepared to accept this real wage—the real wage that unions expect to be able to negotiate at E^T is w_0 (since $w^B(E^T) = w_0$). The consequence of the fall in the real wage to w_1 is to set in train money wage increases in excess of expected inflation. As a consequence, prices rise relative to world prices and competitiveness begins to fall ($\dot{W} > \dot{P} > \dot{P}^*$).

When we write the price equation (refer back to Section 11.1) as

$$LP = mLP \qquad\qquad + w \qquad + \theta(LP/MP)$$

$$\left(\begin{array}{cc} \text{Labour} = \text{Fixed profit margin} + \text{real wage} + \text{real imported materials} \\ \text{productivity} \quad \text{per worker} \qquad\qquad\qquad \text{cost per worker} \end{array}\right)$$

we see that if θ rises (owing in this case to the devaluation), then the real wage w must fall (since LP, MP, and m are fixed). The devaluation brings about a deterioration in the terms of trade and hence a rise in the real cost of imports ($\uparrow e \Rightarrow \downarrow P_x/P_m$ since $P_m = P^*e$). Higher prices for imports reduce the real wage. This occurs either directly, through consumers having to pay increased prices for their imported consumer goods, or indirectly, as a consequence of higher prices for domestic goods as the higher imported raw materials prices are passed on.

The disequilibrium in terms of competing claims at B in Fig. 12.2 is resolved through domestic wages and prices rising relative to world prices until θ has returned to θ_0 (point A). The economy is once again confronted with a trade deficit.

To summarize, a devaluation permits an *immediate* rise in competitiveness and therefore an improvement in the balance of trade. However, because employees are not prepared to accept the cut in real wages implied by the deterioration in the terms of trade associated with the devaluation, the improvement in competitiveness and in the external balance is gradually eroded. In the context of devaluation, the operation of the labour market depicted by the BRW curve is often referred to a *real wage resistance*. Figure 12.2 provides a summary of the process.

In order to underline that it takes time for the competitive benefit of a devaluation to wear off, it is helpful to work through a numerical example of the period-by-period adjustment of the economy. As we have seen before when working with the path of changes in inflation, it is convenient to take advantage of the approximate equality between changes in percentage rates of growth and changes in logs of the variable in question. Rewriting the domestic price inflation equation,

$$\dot{P} = \alpha \dot{W} + (1 - \alpha)(\dot{P}^* + \dot{e}),$$

by subtracting $\dot{P}$ from each side,

$$0 = \alpha(\dot{W} - \dot{P}) + (1 - \alpha)(\dot{P}^* + \dot{e} - \dot{P}),$$

and substituting dln w for $(\dot{W} - \dot{P})$ and dln θ for $(\dot{P}^* + \dot{e} - \dot{P})$ gives

$$\text{dln } w = -\frac{(1 - \alpha)}{\alpha} \text{ dln } \theta.$$

This transformation enables us to show directly the changes in money wage inflation, price inflation, and the exchange rate in the ln w–ln θ quadrant. To enable a direct comparison with the real wage–employment quadrant, real wages are also measured in logs there.

*12.1.2 Illustrative Example of the Erosion of the Effects of a Devaluation through Real Wage Resistance (Fig. 12.3)

The economy is initially at point A with competitiveness θ_0 and employment E^T; there is a trade deficit. Trade is balanced at point Z: (θ^T, E^T). Assume that:

A1 $\dot{P}^* = 0$ and $\dot{P}^E = \dot{P}^* = 0$.

A2 The government manipulates aggregate demand to ensure that output and employment remain at (y^T, E^T) despite changes in competitiveness.

A3 A devaluation of 10% is required to raise competitiveness from θ_0 to θ^T, hence to eliminate the trade deficit.

A4 Imports are only of raw materials—this simplifies the example since real wages will be reduced only indirectly by the devaluation, i.e. once domestic prices have gone up to reflect the higher costs.

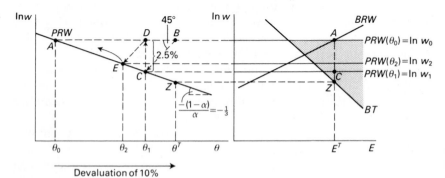

Fig. 12.3 The process through which a devaluation is eroded.
$A \rightarrow B$: devaluation; $B \rightarrow C$: prices rise; $C \rightarrow D$: money wages rise
Note θ is measured in logs, so $\theta \equiv \ln P^* + \ln e - \ln P$.

A5   Labour costs comprise three-quarters of total costs. Thus,

$$\dot{P} = 0.75\dot{W} + 0.25(\dot{P}^* + \dot{e}).$$

In period 1, the following three steps occur (Table 12.1 provides a summary):

1(1)   *Devaluation*   At the start of period 1, the exchange rate is devalued by 10%. This immediately raises competitiveness by 10%. The economy moves from A to B.

1(2)   *Wage-setting*   In the period 1 collective bargaining round, which occurs at the beginning of the year just after the devaluation, money wages will not rise because by A4 the devaluation has had no *direct* effect on real wages: the real wage is still equal to $w^B(E^T)$ i.e. w_0.

1(3)   *Price-setting*   The devaluation raises unit costs by 2.5% through its effect on imported materials costs. Businesses pass this on in their prices: $\dot{P} = (0.75 \times 0) + (0.25 \times 10)$. The domestic price rise reduces competitiveness and the real wage by 2.5%: the economy moves from B to C.[2]

In period 2, wage-setting and price-setting occur once more:

2(2)   *Wage-setting*   Money wages rise by 2.5% to take the expected real wage back to the BRW (C to D).

2(3)   *Price-setting*   The increase in wages raises unit labour costs by 2.5%. Total unit costs and hence prices rise by

$$\dot{P} = (0.75 \times 2.5) + (0.25 \times 0) = 1.875.$$

Competitiveness is eroded and the real wage is cut by the same amount, 1.875% (D to E).

Table 12.1 The erosion of the competitiveness-boosting effect of a devaluation

Period	Percentage growth rates						Levels		Diagram (left panel)
	$\dot{P}$	$\dot{W}$	$\dot{P}^*$	$\dot{e}$	$\dot{\theta}$	$\dot{w}$	w^B	w	
0	0	0	0	0	0	0	w_0	w_0	A
1(1)				+10	+10				$A \to B$
1(2)		0							
1(3)	+2.5				−2.5	−2.5	.	w_1	$B \to C$
2(2)		+2.5				+2.5	.	w_0	$C \to D$
2(3)	+1.875				−1.875	−1.875	.	w_2	$D \to E$
⋮	⋮	⋮	⋮	⋮	⋮	⋮	⋮	⋮	
z	0	0	0	0	0	0	w_0	w_0	A

[2] Note that the line from B to C has a slope of 45° since $\ln\theta = \ln P^* - \ln P$ and $\ln w = \ln W - \ln P$; so the rise in P reduces both axes by the same distance.

In subsequent periods, steps (2) and (3) are repeated until the economy is back at point A. If wage rounds occur annually, then the process of adjustment resulting eventually in the complete erosion of the competitive benefits of the devaluation will take many years. And, in practice, the benefits of devaluation in an economy like the UK would take at least five years to be substantially eroded.

12.2   The Effectiveness of Devaluation: a Summary of the Debate

The effectiveness of devaluation as a policy instrument has long been a subject of contention among economists and policy-makers. It is useful to draw together the arguments, which can be characterized in terms of (1) elasticities, (2) absorption, and (3) real wage resistance.

12.2.1   Elasticities

Given the Marshall–Lerner condition that the sum of the price elasticities of demand must exceed one for a devaluation to improve the trade balance (refer back to Section 10.2), the debate over elasticities was an empirical one. It is worth noting at this point that, should the Marshall–Lerner condition fail, the consequence is positive rather than negative for the economy concerned. The failure of the Marshall–Lerner condition would place the economy in the fortunate position of being able to improve its trade balance by revaluing and therefore benefiting from an *improvement* in the terms of trade. There would be no need for a reduction in domestic incomes in order to secure the improvement of the trade balance.

As noted earlier, the failure of the Marshall–Lerner condition shows up in a downward-sloping BT line in the Salter–Swan diagram (Section 10.3). This translates into an upward-sloping BT curve in the real wage–employment diagram, underlining the point that under these conditions the economy can expand output and employment with *rising* real wages.

Although early estimates of elasticities appeared to suggest that the Marshall–Lerner condition would not be fulfilled, estimates made from the 1950s onwards indicate the typical size of the (absolute value of the) elasticity of export demand at between 1.25 and 2.50 and of the import elasticity at between 0.5 and 1.[3] Williamson (1983a) suggests two reasons for the move away from so-called elasticity pessimism: (1) the early estimates were based on data from the 1930s and 1940s, during which time extensive controls over trade existed with the result that responsiveness to relative price changes was low; and (2) the early estimates omitted consideration of the time lag between price changes and their effect on the trade balance.

---

[3] Goldstein and Khan (1985: 1076)

There may be a lag of some three to four years between a change in competitiveness and its reflection in the trade balance, owing to the need for firms to assess whether the benefits in price that would accrue from a switch of suppliers outweigh the costs of adjusting to a different source of supply.

12.2.2 Absorption

From a Keynesian perspective, concern about the effectiveness of devaluation as an instrument to improve the trade balance was located elsewhere—in the implications of the rise in aggregate demand assumed to be associated with devaluation. In other words, it was *assumed* that the Marshall–Lerner condition held. Given that devaluation would boost net exports, what would be the net outcome for external balance of (1) the initial improvement in the balance of trade and (2) the increased demand for imports as a consequence of the multiplier effects of the improved trade balance? Two situations are considered: the fully employed economy, and the economy at less than full employment.[4]

Taking full employment first, the absorption approach draws attention to the fact that the trade balance is equal to output less absorption (refer back to Section 9.1):

$$x - m = y - (c + i + g).$$

If output is fixed at its full employment level, then a devaluation can improve the trade balance only if there is a cut in absorption. As illustrated in Fig. 12.4(a) the economy is initially at full employment but experiencing a trade deficit (at A). A devaluation with absorption unchanged would take the economy beyond full employment (towards B), presumably unleashing price increases which would negate the improvement in competitiveness. Hence to achieve both targets simultaneously, the government must reduce domestic absorption by lowering government spending from g_0 to g_1 so that the economy can move from A to C.

For an economy at less than full employment, we have already dealt with the question of the net effect on the trade balance of a change in competitiveness. It is precisely the same issue as determines the relative slopes of the BT and AD curves. As shown in Section 10.3, although an improvement in the balance of trade owing to a rise in competitiveness will generate a growth in imports, this will not outweigh the initial improvement in the external balance.

If the economy starts in trade balance at point A in Fig. 12.4(b), the initial effect of the devaluation at a constant output level will move the economy strongly into surplus at B. However, the aggregate demand

[4] This approach is associated with Alexander (1952).

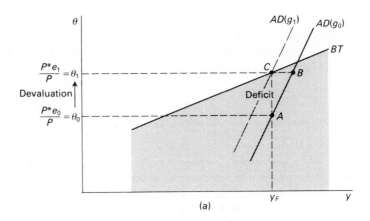

(a)

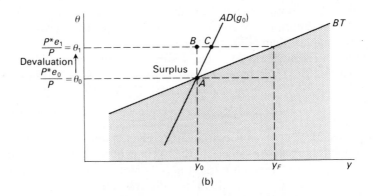

(b)

Fig. 12.4 Devaluation and absorption
(a) Economy at full employment, y_F
(b) Economy at less than full employment, y_0

implications of the higher net exports will move the economy along $AD(g_0)$ to C: the surplus is smaller since imports have risen with the rise in y. Nevertheless, a surplus remains. Of course, as we have seen earlier, the absorption approach is only a part (the optimistic part) of the story—we have to recall once again the problem of real wage resistance.

12.2.3 Real Wage Resistance

The final argument regarding the efficacy of devaluation is the one dealt with earlier in this chapter: namely, the erosion of the competitiveness-boosting effect of a devaluation in an economy where the labour market is characterized by real wage resistance. The devaluation is effective in the short run in raising competitiveness and improving the trade balance. However, this benefit is gradually lost as unions are able to negotiate wage increases to offset the reduction in living standards resulting from the increased cost of imports. It is important to note that the analysis of devaluation in the imperfect competition model that we have developed uses and extends the earlier elasticities and absorption approaches. This is exemplified in the construction of the aggregate demand and balance of trade lines in the Salter–Swan diagram.

12.3 Why Devalue?

The use of devaluation as a policy tool was developed in the original analysis of internal and external balance by Salter and Swan, as well as by Meade.[5] The accompanying box below sets out the way in which those earlier writers presented their argument, so as to make very clear how their analysis differs from the working of the imperfect competition model. The essential difference lies in the notion of internal balance. For the earlier analysts, the level of demand was the sole determinant of inflation. Thus, a situation of internal balance prevailed at the lowest rate of unemployment consistent with acceptable inflation. There was no real wage resistance in the model, with the result that the feedback from changes in competitiveness to real wages and hence to inflation was eliminated. As we have seen, in a model without real wage resistance, devaluation is a powerful tool for improving the trade balance in a sustainable way.

*Comparing the Original Salter–Swan–Meade Analysis of Internal–External Balance with the Imperfect Competition Model

The problem with which Salter, Swan, and Meade were concerned was shifting the economy to the intersection of their external and internal balance curves. External balance was defined in the same way as BT, but internal balance was defined quite differently from CCE. There is an obvious source of confusion between the Salter–Swan–Meade internal–external balance analysis and the present one, so for the sake of clarity it is worth presenting the comparison explicitly.

For those earlier writers, internal balance referred to the highest level of employment consistent with acceptable inflation, and the

[5] Salter (1959), Swan (1960), Meade (1951).

level of demand was the determinant of inflationary pressure. To capture the difference between their analysis and the present one, it is necessary to note that the horizontal axis of the original Salter–Swan diagram was *domestic absorption* (i.e. domestic spending), not output. Internal balance would be achieved at a high level of competitiveness (and therefore high net exports) and low domestic absorption because this would produce the correct level of demand to establish the unique high employment output level. At low competitiveness, domestic spending would have to be high to offset the low level of demand coming from abroad. Hence the internal balance line would have a negative slope (see Fig. 12.5(a)). But internal balance simply refers to the achievement of the correct level of demand; competitiveness is assumed only to affect aggregate demand. In other words, the implications of changes in the level of competitiveness for real wages and hence for domestic inflation at each level of demand are ignored. In terms of our modernized Salter–Swan diagram with competitiveness and output on the axes, the original internal balance line is simply vertical at y_F, the target or non-inflationary high employment level. This is how we presented Salter–Swan in Chapter 10.

As we saw there, a combination of expenditure-changing and expenditure-switching policies was required to take the economy from a position such as B to combined internal–external balance at $C(\theta^T, y_F)$ (see Fig. 12.5(b)). The expenditure-switching policy was required to increase competitiveness and switch expenditure away from imports towards exports (to raise θ from θ_0 to θ^T). The tool that would bring about the required switch in expenditure was devaluation. The expenditure-raising policy (g_0 to g_1) was required to increase total domestic expenditure. The point is that, with the appropriate choice of aggregate demand settings and the exchange rate, the target employment level can *always* be attained. The great contrast represented by the introduction of the CCE is that the combination of the desired level of employment y_F and trade balance (point C) may be inconsistent with the competing-claims equilibrium (see Fig. 12.5(c)). At C, above CCE, the implication is that inflation will be above $\dot{P}^*$, so that θ will be falling.

The existence of real wage resistance certainly reduces the potency of exchange rate changes as policy instruments. Nevertheless, there are circumstances in which devaluation can be an effective tool in the hands of policy-makers. Its usefulness stems from its immediate effect on competitiveness. For example, suppose that, as depicted in Fig. 12.6, the economy

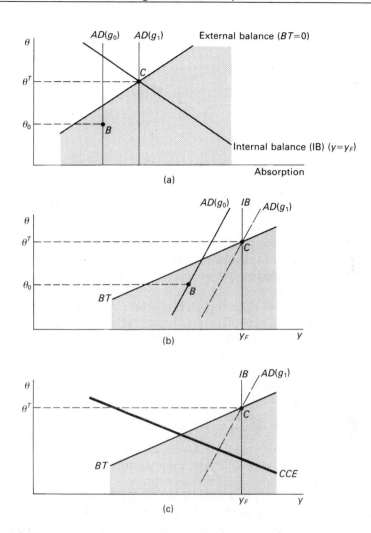

Fig. 12.5 Direct comparison between the Salter–Swan–Meade analysis and the imperfect competition model
(a) Salter–Swan–Meade: internal and external balance
(b) Salter–Swan–Meade in θ–y diagram
(c) Salter–Swan–Meade and the problem of real wage resistance

is initially at point A. With unchanged policies—both for aggregate demand and for the exchange rate—the economy will gradually move along the aggregate demand curve to point B, the sustainable employment level. This will happen because to the left of CCE real wages are above the level of w^B, with the result that, at each round of wage negotiations, money wages increase by less than expected inflation: competitiveness is

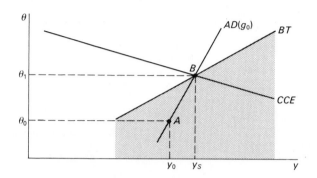

Fig. 12.6 The usefulness of devaluation

rising. However, as illustrated in a different context in the example in Table 12.1, this process could be extended over several years during which the economy is suffering an unnecessary competitiveness loss. The authorities can avoid this loss by devaluing the exchange rate to take competitiveness immediately from θ_0 to θ_1 and the economy from A to B (abstracting from the very short-run J-curve effects[6]). The devaluation reduces the real wage to the level of the bargained real wage, and competitiveness will remain constant with the economy at point B.

Two further examples show why a government, aware of the economic structure summarized in the BT and CCE curves, may choose to devalue.

12.3.1 Combining Devaluation with Incomes Policy

A strong case can be made for combining the implementation of an incomes policy with a devaluation (plus restrictive aggregate demand policy) when the economy is operating at the target rate of unemployment but is in external deficit (point A in Fig. 12.7). The incomes policy operates to shift the CCE upwards to CCE(IP) as discussed in Chapter 11, enabling a sustainable employment level at y^T. To get from A to B rapidly, the government should devalue to raise competitiveness to θ_1 and tighten the fiscal stance to offset the effect of the rise in competitiveness on demand.

Alternatively, the two policies can be combined to move the economy from a higher sustainable unemployment rate y'_s (point A') in Fig. 12.7 to a lower sustainable unemployment rate, y_s (point B). Using an incomes

---

[6] The term 'J-curve' is used to refer to the typical perverse response of the value of the trade balance to a devaluation which can last for up to four or five quarters. The trade balance worsens in the short run, for two reasons. (1) The short-run price elasticity of demand for exports and imports is much lower (approximately one-half) the long-run value. This means that the volume response to the devaluation is weak initially. (2) Since exports are typically invoiced in domestic currency, the dollar value of exports falls immediately, worsening the trade balance, while imports invoiced in foreign currency remain unchanged in dollar terms. In sterling terms, export receipts are unchanged while the import bill rises immediately.

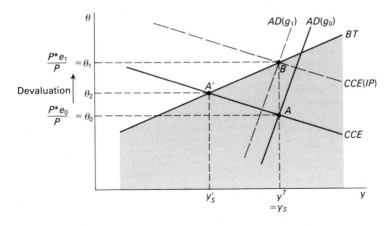

Fig. 12.7 Combining devaluation with an incomes policy

policy alone to enable the economy to move from A' to B in the figure would involve an extended period of adjustment with the full reduction in real wages occurring over a series of wage rounds. The shift to B could be speeded up by combining a devaluation with the incomes policy. Of course, the government must make the necessary modification to aggregate demand. A simple numerical example illustrates the combined effect of devaluation and incomes policy. Suppose that labour costs are 70% of total costs, imported materials costs, 30%, and that a 10% boost to competitiveness is required to take competitiveness from θ_2 to θ_1. By assumption, world inflation is zero. Thus:

$$\dot{P} = 0.7\dot{W} + 0.3(\dot{P}^* + \dot{e})$$

$$= 0.7\dot{W} + 0.3\dot{e}.$$

In period 1, the government devalues by 10% and negotiates an incomes policy simultaneously which involves the reduction of money wages. The objective is to raise competitiveness by the full 10% so that domestic inflation will remain at zero. Thus, the incomes policy must be an agreement for money wages to move so that the following statement for price inflation holds:

$$0 = 0.7\dot{W} + 0.3(10).$$

$$\therefore \dot{W} = -3/0.7 = -4.3\%.$$

If money wages fall by 4.3%, then the fall in labour costs contributes a 3% fall in total costs while materials costs contribute a rise of 3%. Total costs therefore remain unchanged. Domestic inflation will remain at zero and competitiveness will have risen by 10%. Assuming that the appropriate aggregate demand stance is maintained, the economy has moved directly from A' to B in Fig. 12.7. In subsequent periods, as long as the incomes policy holds, real wages will remain unchanged at the new lower level and wage and price inflation will be zero.

12.3.2 Combining Devaluation with Government Expenditure on Training

The economy is initially at A in Fig. 12.8—at the sustainable output level (i.e. on CCE and BT), but with a level of unemployment higher than desired. The government believes that, if it engages in a policy of increased government spending, this will, in the medium run, permit a rightward shift of the balance of trade line from BT to BT'. This would enable a lower sustainable rate of unemployment. The reason for the effect of higher government expenditure on the balance of trade has been set out in Chapter 11 above: by directing government expenditure towards a training programme, improved quality of product would be achieved at each level of price competitiveness.

Devaluation would be a useful adjunct to the policy through its ability to maintain external balance in the short run until the effects of structural measures of training come onstream. The logic of this policy combination can be illustrated in Fig. 12.8. In the short run, the expansionary fiscal policy results in a shift from A to B in the figure. This implies a worsening of the external deficit. In the medium to long run, the effect of the extra expenditure on training feeds through to shift the BT line. If the short-run deterioration in the deficit is unacceptable, then the government can make use of devaluation to *jump* to the original BT line (point C). Note that this will require some fiscal restraint to shift the AD schedule—which otherwise would have gone through B—leftwards so that it intersects C.

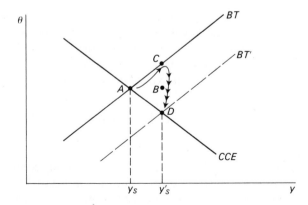

Fig. 12.8 Combining devaluation with a government expenditure programme on industrial training

At the same time, as the effect of the devaluation on competitiveness gradually unwinds through wage and price rises, the benefits of the training programme on the trade balance feed through. The economy ends up at point D. The use of devaluation has eased the transition to the lower sustainable rate of unemployment by offsetting the short run deterioration in competitiveness. Although the effect of the devaluation is not permanent, it provides the economy with a period of years, free of a trade deficit, during which the effects of the new training programme build up to create a permanent improvement in the trade balance.

The policy mix introduced in Sweden in 1982 bears a resemblance to the combination of policies discussed here. The government devalued sharply (by 16%), and this was combined with an implicit incomes policy and additional government expenditure on training, retraining, and research and development. The mixture of policies appears to have had a good measure of success in enabling Sweden to regain competitiveness while maintaining very low unemployment (OECD 1989; Martin 1990; Walters 1985).

12.4   Conclusions

The examination of macroeconomic policy in the imperfect competition model of the fixed exchange rate open economy is now complete. Using the modernized Salter–Swan diagram, it is possible to highlight the limits to the use of devaluation as a policy instrument when there is real wage resistance. Devaluation can be used to provide a temporary boost to competitiveness (i.e. to bring about a shift along an AD line to an improved balance of trade position). Although the improvement in competitiveness will be eroded through subsequent rounds of wage- and price-setting, the rapidity of the effect of devaluation and the time taken for the full erosion of benefits to occur makes it a useful policy tool. We have seen how devaluation can be combined with an incomes policy and with other supply-side measures to enable the more rapid achievement of a sustainable improvement in the trade balance or in unemployment. The analysis of devaluation provides a natural introduction to the analysis of the floating exchange rate economy.

13

Floating Exchange Rates with Zero Capital Mobility

In the early years of the 1970s, it became apparent that the turmoil in the world economy and the absence of a single hegemonic economic power meant that the system of fixed but adjustable exchange rates that had constituted the Bretton Woods system could not be resurrected. In March 1973, the West German government announced that the Deutschmark would be allowed to float freely. This signalled the end of an era. Over the decade and a half since then, experience has gathered of floating exchange rates in a world with highly mobile international capital. Exchange rates proved to be much more volatile than had been expected. The mid-1980s saw the appearance of a number of publications from influential sources[1] calling for the re-establishment of a more or less fixed rate system.

The highly mobile nature of world capital markets is the key to understanding the volatility of exchange rate movements. Most of the rest of Part III will assume perfect capital mobility. This chapter, however, will assume zero capital mobility. This will make it easier to carry through a review of some of the original economic arguments put forward in support of a floating rate system. We will see that under certain conditions floating rates provide the domestic economy with insulation from the effects of external shocks. This is a property that policy-makers find highly desirable, since it suggests the ability to hold employment and inflation rates steady in the face of falls in world demand and rises in world inflation.

However, this result is modified once endogenous price- and wage-setting are introduced. We find that, in contrast to the fixed exchange rate case, a unique equilibrium rate of unemployment reappears. In other words, there is a single rate of unemployment at which competing claims are reconciled and inflation is constant. It is fixed by the intersection of the CCE and BT lines. Thus, the features of the economy that determine the constraints on the achievement of a particular desired level of employment remain the same as in the fixed rate case (represented by the CCE and BT

---

[1] For example from the Washington-based Institute for International Economics: Williamson (1983b); McKinnon (1984).

lines), but the manifestation of disequilibrium is different: the attempt to run the economy at a higher level of output then y_N produces accelerating inflation fuelled by a depreciating exchange rate in the flexible rate case (as long as monetary policy is accommodating) and a trade deficit in the fixed rate case.

Monetary and fiscal policy turn out to be equally effective in shifting aggregate demand in the flexible rate economy when there is zero capital mobility. Once the obligation of the central bank to buy and sell foreign exchange at a fixed rate of exchange is eliminated, it can once more control the amount of high-powered money in the economy. The efficacy of monetary policy then becomes a question of the behaviour of domestic financial institutions, just as it is in the closed economy.

13.1 Why Float the Exchange Rate? Insulation from External Shocks

An influential argument in favour of floating exchange rates is that such a regime protects the economy from external shocks—both demand shocks and price shocks. Recall that, with fixed exchange rates (and zero capital mobility), in the simple case with fixed wages and prices, the level of output is fixed by equilibrium on the trade account. An external demand shock will change domestic output and employment by altering the level of output at which trade is balanced. In the fixed rate economy, inflation is equal to the world rate of inflation with the result that external price shocks feed through into domestic prices.

13.1.1 External Demand Shock

Let us hold prices and wages fixed and concentrate on the effects of a world demand shock under floating exchange rates. A floating exchange rate means that there is no intervention by the central bank in the foreign exchange market. With zero capital mobility, the demand and supply of foreign exchange only reflect trade flows. In other words, the exchange rate (the domestic price of foreign exchange; $e = £/\$$) clears the market for foreign exchange where the demand for foreign exchange ($\$$) comes from those seeking to purchase imports, and the supply from the sellers of exports. A positive world demand shock (an increase in y^*) means that exports rise, shifting the supply curve for foreign currency to the right (see Fig. 13.1). At the existing exchange rate of e_0, there is excess supply of dollars, with the result that the exchange rate appreciates (the pound rises in value relative to the dollar; the value of e falls).

Trade is balanced when exports are equal to imports:

$$x = m;$$

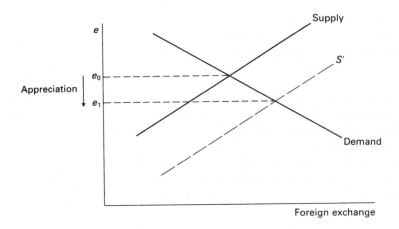

Fig. 13.1 Positive external demand shock and exchange rate appreciation

i.e.,

$$\sigma(\theta)y^* = \theta m_y(\theta)y. \qquad \text{[balanced trade]}$$

Thus the exchange rate will appreciate until competitiveness ($\theta = P^*e/P$) has deteriorated sufficiently to restore trade balance. What is the effect on output? Aggregate demand, y^D, will fall if the trade balance is reduced; but with zero capital mobility the trade balance is always zero. Therefore output does not change. The increase in aggregate demand arising from the effect on exports of the rise in world trade is exactly offset by the fall in net exports associated with the fall in competitiveness as the result of exchange rate appreciation. The external demand shock has no lasting effect on the domestic economy. Figure 13.2 illustrates the adjustment to a change in world trade. The economy is initially at A, with output at y_0, and competitiveness equal to θ_0. Higher world trade shifts the BT curve to the right since the exogenous boost to exports means that trade is balanced at a higher level of domestic output for each level of competitiveness. The economy will move from A to B, with the incipient boost to demand from higher exports (A to A') offset by the decline in competitiveness as the exchange rate appreciates. Or to put it another way, floating exchange rates mean that the aggregate demand curve moves to intersect the BT line exactly at the original output level.

A glance at the implications of a floating exchange rate for the ISXM/LM model confirms this result. Beginning with the ISXM;

$$y = c_y y + i(r) + g + x - m,$$

the export and import functions are written so as fully to reflect their dependence on the exchange rate:

$$y = c_y y + i(r) + g + \sigma(\theta)y^* - \theta m_y(\theta)y. \qquad \text{[ISXM equation]}$$

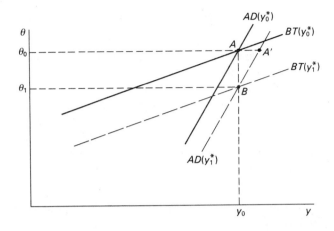

Fig. 13.2 Adjustment to a positive external demand shock

In addition, the exchange rate, e, moves to clear the foreign exchange market, which in the case of zero capital mobility requires e such that

$$\sigma(\theta)y^* = \theta m_y(\theta)y. \qquad \text{[balanced trade]}$$

Substituting balanced trade into the ISXM produces the following result characterizing goods market equilibrium once the exchange rate has adjusted:

$$y = c_y y + i(r) + g$$
[ISXM, floating exchange rate, zero capital mobility]

Money market equilibrium is

$$M/P = L(y, r). \qquad \text{[LM equation]}$$

Thus, a regime of floating exchange rates with zero capital mobility takes us back to the closed economy in terms of the determination of the level of output and the interest rate. Since the exchange rate changes to ensure trade balance, the determinants of trade balance are irrelevant to the determination of the output level. The AD curve reflects the situation in the very short run before the exchange rate has had the chance to adjust. In Fig. 13.2, the economy moves from equilibrium at A to point A' in the very short run as the result of increased demand for exports; at A', there is a trade surplus and this produces the exchange rate appreciation and the move to B.

13.1.2 External Price Shock

Once again, the movement of the exchange rate to ensure balanced trade dominates the analysis. The trade balance equation is

$$\sigma(\theta)y^* = \theta m_y(\theta)y. \qquad \text{[balanced trade]}$$

With world demand fixed at y^* and domestic output set by the chosen combination of fiscal and monetary policies, any change in the world price level, P^*, must produce an offsetting change in the exchange rate to keep the level of competitiveness constant. Suppose that the world price level rises. This produces an increase in competitiveness for the domestic economy. Net exports rise, taking the economy into trade surplus. The excess supply of dollars in the foreign exchange market leads to an appreciation of the pound until competitiveness and external balance are restored. The economy returns to its original position.

13.1.3 Policy Analysis under Floating Rates (Zero Capital Mobility; Fixed Wages and Prices)

To sum up the operation of the floating rate economy in the simple case with fixed prices and zero capital mobility, it is useful to look at the operation of monetary and fiscal policy. The other side of the coin of insulation from external shocks is that the domestic authorities can choose the level of output though their monetary and fiscal stance. Effective use of monetary policy is restored to the authorities because the floating exchange rate equilibrates the supply and demand for foreign exchange, with the result that there are no changes in foreign exchange reserves and hence none in the monetary base arising from the emergence of a temporary surplus or deficit.

Consider the effects of a government decision to increase the money supply so as to raise employment. The economy is initially at point A in Fig. 13.3. An increase in the money supply through open market

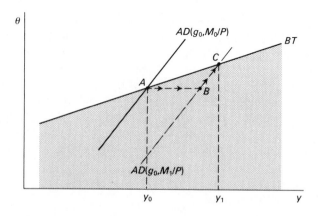

Fig. 13.3 Expansionary monetary policy results in higher output
Shaded area denotes trade deficit.

operations produces a fall in the interest rate and a consequential rise in investment. The AD curve shifts to the right: for each level of competitiveness, goods market equilibrium will occur at a higher output level because of the additional investment demand. We can think of the economy moving initially from A to point B as the result of the extra demand. At B, there is a trade deficit because of the induced rise in imports. A deficit means there is excess demand for foreign exchange which produces a depreciation of the pound. The increase in competitiveness produces a further rise in output as the economy moves along the $AD(g_0, M_1/P)$ curve to point C. A fiscal expansion would have had exactly the same effect.

The contrast with the fixed exchange rate (zero capital mobility; fixed prices) case is striking: there, aggregate demand policy was totally ineffective in changing output. Any tendency towards trade deficit produced an outflow of foreign exchange reserves which lowered the monetary base and offset the initial demand move. The government had to engage in sterilization measures if it was to prevent this. In the floating rate case, demand management policy is particularly effective in altering output: output expands by more than it would in the closed economy because of the induced effect of the exchange rate depreciation on net exports.

A floating exchange rate regime with fixed prices appears to be an attractive one because the government can choose the level of output and hence of unemployment, independent of demand shocks coming from the outside. Secondly, the government can choose the price level and, by extension, the rate of inflation through its monetary policy, independent of external price shocks. (It is worth noting that the analysis has depended on assuming that a depreciation of the exchange rate leads to an improvement in the trade balance and vice versa. Possible qualifications to the stability assumption arise from the failure of the Marshall–Lerner condition and, in the short run, the operation of the J-curve).

13.2 Reintroducing the Competing-Claims Equilibrium: the Reappearance of the Unique Equilibrium Rate of Unemployment

Once prices are allowed to vary according to our standard price- and wage-setting equations reflecting imperfect competition, the competing-claims equilibrium locus is brought back into the analysis. This has the effect of reinstating the unique equilibrium rate of unemployment: there is once more a single rate of unemployment at which inflation is constant. At the equilibrium rate of unemployment, inflation will be equal to the growth rate of the domestic money supply. The equilibrium rate of unemployment is fixed by the intersection of the CCE and the BT curves. Intuitively, the argument is straightforward. Along the CCE curve there is competing-claims equilibrium; i.e., the price-determined real wage is equal to the bargained real wage and there is therefore no tendency for inflation to change. Along the BT line, exports are equal to imports and there is no pressure in the foreign exchange market for the exchange rate to alter. With a constant exchange rate, there is no disturbance to real wages and hence inflation will remain constant. Thus, at the intersection of the BT and the CCE, inflation is constant. This fixes the unique equilibrium rate of unemployment.

A fuller explanation of why constant inflation will occur *only* at a single rate of unemployment in the flexible rate economy requires a step-by-step approach utilizing pieces of analysis we have come across before. The first step is to look at the inflationary pressures that arise from the labour market; secondly, we focus on the pressures in the foreign exchange market for the exchange rate to change; and finally, we put together the labour with the foreign exchange market and identify the source of accelerating or decelerating inflation away from the equilibrium rate of unemployment. Throughout, it is assumed that inflation expectations are formed adaptively.

13.2.1 Inflationary Pressure in the Labour Market

The competing-claims equilibrium locus was derived in Chapter 11 to represent the points in the Salter–Swan diagram where the bargained real wage equals the price-determined real wage, i.e. where the claims on real output per head from wages, profits, and import costs are consistent. At high output levels employment is high and so, therefore, is union bargaining power and w^B. Given the fixed profit margin, this means that import costs must be low if workers are to receive their bargained real wage. A low real cost of imports, low P^*e/P, implies low competitiveness. Hence high output and low competitiveness produce competing-claims equilibrium. Similarly, low output and high competitiveness are consistent with competing-claims equilibrium. At each point on the CCE, with $w^B = w^P(\theta)$, competitiveness has no tendency to change. From the definition of competitiveness ($\theta = P^*e/P$), this means

$$\dot{\theta} = 0 = \dot{P}^* + \dot{e} - \dot{P}.$$

In the flexible rate economy, competitiveness will change with a change in either P, P^*, or e. For constant competitiveness, domestic wage and price inflation must be equal to world inflation plus the rate of depreciation of the exchange rate since a depreciating exchange rate offsets the effect on competitiveness of higher than world inflation. For clarity in this section, let us assume that world inflation is zero so that $\dot{\theta} = 0 = \dot{e} - \dot{P}$. In other words, at each point along the CCE, where competitiveness is constant, the rate of domestic inflation is exactly equal to the rate of exchange rate depreciation (Fig. 13.4). Below the CCE, competitiveness is rising because real wages are above the level of the bargained real wage. Hence inflation is less than exchange rate depreciation. Conversely, above the CCE, inflation exceeds the rate of depreciation because of the upward pressure of money wage claims when the real wage lies below the bargained real wage. Figure 13.4 shows how the CCE divides the θ–y space into zones where inflation either exceeds or falls short of the rate of depreciation.

Precisely, in the labour market with $w > w^B$ (below the CCE), $\dot{W} < \dot{P}^E$ is the outcome of bargaining. Let us assume that

$$\dot{P}^E = \dot{P}^*_{-1} + \dot{e}_{-1} = \dot{e}_{-1},$$

assuming that $\dot{P}^*_{-1} = 0$. Therefore, below the CCE, we have $\dot{W} < \dot{e}_{-1}$. Secondly, mark-up pricing implies

$$\dot{P} = \alpha\dot{W} + (1 - \alpha)\dot{e}_{-1},$$

where it is assumed that there is a lag before higher import prices get passed on in final prices. Thus,

$$\dot{P} = \alpha\dot{W} + (1 - \alpha)\dot{e}_{-1} < \alpha\dot{e}_{-1} + (1 - \alpha)\dot{e}_{-1} = \dot{e}_{-1},$$

so that below the CCE, we also have $\dot{P} < \dot{e}_{-1}$. The opposite is true above the CCE line.

13.2.2 Pressures on the Exchange Rate from Trade Imbalance

Turning from wage- and price-setting to the foreign exchange market, when trade is balanced the real exchange rate will be constant. The real exchange rate is simply a name for competitiveness, θ. Maintaining the

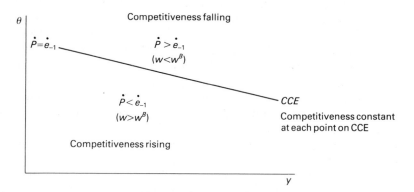

Fig. 13.4 Inflationary pressure from the labour market
$\dot{P}^*$ is assumed to be zero.

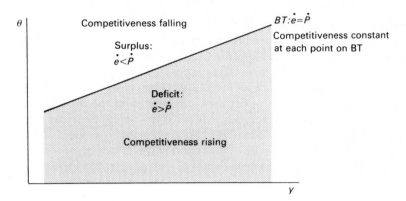

Fig. 13.5 Pressures on the exchange rate from trade imbalance

simplifying assumption of zero world inflation, it is clear that, for competitiveness to remain constant at each point along the BT line, the nominal exchange rate, e, must depreciate at a rate equal to domestic inflation: $\dot{e} = \dot{P}$ (assuming that $\dot{P}^* = 0$). Below the BT line, there is a trade deficit since output is too high at a given level of competitiveness for trade to balance. A deficit means there is excess demand for foreign exchange with the result that the exchange rate is falling. For competitiveness to increase from such a position and eliminate the deficit, exchange rate depreciation must exceed the rate of domestic inflation ($\dot{e} > \dot{P}$). The converse must be true for the surplus position to the left of the BT ($\dot{e} < \dot{P}$). The two zones are depicted in Fig. 13.5.

13.2.3 Putting the CCE and BT Together

Along the CCE and the BT the rate of domestic inflation equals the rate of exchange rate depreciation (remembering the simplifying assumption of zero world inflation). We can identify one point, Z, in Fig. 13.6 where the two lines intersect. Here, competitiveness will be constant since pressure for change is absent from both the labour market and the foreign exchange market. In other words, when the economy is in competing-claims equilibrium and in trade balance, domestic inflation is exactly equal to the rate of depreciation of the exchange rate. For example, with domestic inflation of 3% and world inflation of zero, the exchange rate will depreciate at 3% p.a. This is a stable situation.

But what of positions away from Z? It is best to concentrate first on zones I and II. In each of these zones the combined pressure from the labour market and the foreign exchange market causes competitiveness to change. Let us assume that the government keeps the level of aggregate demand fixed at y_0. Consider a point such as A at output level y_0 in zone I. From the perspective of the labour market, inflation is rising less rapidly

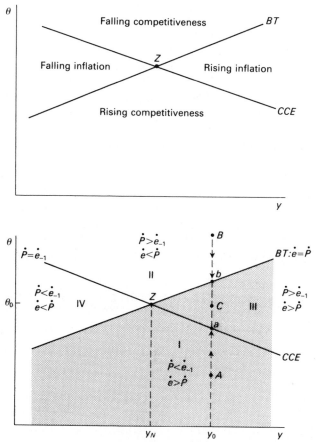

Fig. 13.6 The unique level of output at which inflation and competitiveness are constant: y_N

than the exchange rate depreciates—competitiveness is tending to rise. From the perspective of the foreign exchange market, there is a trade deficit at A, with the result that the exchange rate is depreciating faster than domestic inflation—competitiveness is tending to rise. Hence behaviour in both key markets is consistent and is producing a rise in competitiveness. The economy will move upwards to point a. (Aggregate demand is being held at a level appropriate to y_0.)

An exactly parallel argument in the reverse direction can be made for points in zone II, such as B. At B, both the labour market and the foreign exchange market produce pressure for competitiveness to fall: the economy moves down to point b. Thus, the economy must lie between points a and b. What is true of such points in zone III? Take a position such as C. In the labour market, unions seek a higher real wage—at C, real import costs, θ_0 are higher than is consistent with the real wage equal to

$w^B(y_0)$. Thus, with mark-up pricing, domestic inflation will exceed the lagged rate of depreciation of the exchange rate: $\dot{W} > \dot{P} > \dot{e}_{-1}$. At the same time, the economy is characterized by a trade deficit which generates a rate of depreciation faster than domestic inflation so as to push competitiveness up ($\dot{e} > \dot{P}$). From the labour market side, the rise in inflation has the effect of *reducing* competitiveness, and this is followed by a depreciation in the foreign exchange market to *improve* competitiveness. But the depreciation implies a fall in real wages and initiates a further round of domestic inflation in excess of the rate of depreciation. Of course, the boost to domestic inflation sets off an even faster rate of depreciation in the foreign exchange market. As long as the government maintains the level of demand at y_0—in particular, allows the money supply to rise to accommodate the rise in inflation—the economy will be characterized by rising inflation and a more and more rapidly depreciating exchange rate. In mathematical terms, in zone III $\dot{P} > \dot{e}_{-1}$ and $\dot{e} > \dot{P}$, i.e. $\dot{e}_{-1} > \dot{P}_{-1}$. Putting these two propositions together gives $\dot{P} > \dot{P}_{-1}$ and $\dot{e} > \dot{e}_{-1}$.

*Defining Constant Competitiveness and Inflation Loci

We have illustrated why the economy will move from a point such as A to a in Fig. 13.6 and also the reason for rising inflation in zone III. We can pin down the points in zone III for which competitiveness is constant. This is the line shown in Fig. 13.7 denoted $\dot{\theta} = 0$. We can thus show why there will be just one level of θ at which competitiveness is constant associated with output level y_0. Consider a point just above a in Fig. 13.7, i.e. a point just inside zone III. Inflationary pressure emanates from both the labour market and the foreign exchange market. However, since we are only just above the CCE line, the pressure from the labour market will be relatively weak. Hence we will find that $\dot{e} > \dot{P}$ by more than $\dot{P} > \dot{e}_{-1}$ and competitiveness will therefore still be rising. Taking a point just below b, we find just the converse: $\dot{P} > \dot{e}_{-1}$ by more than $\dot{e} > \dot{P}$ and competitiveness is still falling. There will be some point between a and b at which pressure from each market is exactly equal and this defines point C. The $\dot{\theta} = 0$ line will therefore go through point C, point Z, and the equivalent points at each output level.

By reasoning in exactly the same way, the locus of points through zones I and II along which inflation is constant can be derived.

Only if the level of demand is reduced to that consistent with y_N will the economy operate with constant inflation. y_N is defined as the unique

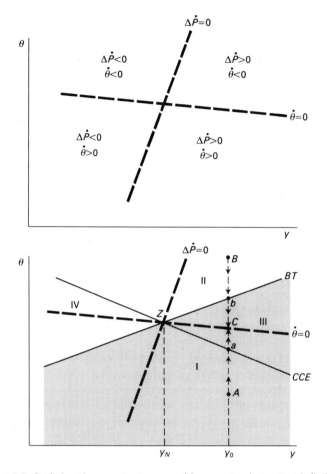

Fig. 13.7 Defining the constant competitiveness and constant inflation loci

non-accelerating inflation rate of output and fixes the unique attainable equilibrium rate of unemployment for the flexible exchange rate economy. Any attempt to run the economy at lower unemployment than U_N will eventually encounter accelerating inflation as inflationary pressure from the labour market is fed by exchange rate depreciation. Should the government refuse to accommodate the rising inflation with an easy money policy, the economy will eventually return to Z as the falling real money supply dampens demand. For stable inflation, the government is constrained to run its aggregate demand policies such that output is at the equilibrium rate defined by the intersection of CCE and BT.

13.2.4 Policy Implications

How does the reappearance of a unique equilibrium rate of unemployment affect the conclusions of the previous section that a floating rate economy is insulated from external demand and price shocks? Taking demand first, let us suppose that there is a negative external demand shock. As ever, this shifts the BT line to the left (Fig. 13.8). When prices and wages are fixed, we saw that a freely floating exchange rate produces a change in competitiveness which exactly offsets the effect of the external shock on domestic output. However, once prices and wages vary, the pressure in the foreign exchange market for competitiveness to change so as to restore external balance feeds back into the labour market. Higher real import costs trigger off higher wage claims. In other words, an external demand shock pushes the economy, initially at Z, into zone III (a negative demand shock) or zone IV (a positive demand shock). In the present example, lower world demand has the effect of raising the domestic equilibrium rate of unemployment (y_N falls to y_N'), since higher unemployment is required to reduce real wage claims so as to permit the higher level of competitiveness required for external balance under the new conditions (at Z'). In other words, a world recession has the consequence of raising equilibrium rates of unemployment in each country. Although the authorities can use fiscal and monetary policy to offset the effects on *demand* of the external shock, this will nevertheless be associated with accelerating inflation.

Unlike demand shocks, there is no need to modify the conclusion of the previous analysis of the effect of external price shocks. Suppose the economy is initially at the equilibrium rate of unemployment with world and domestic inflation of zero. The world price level then rises from P_0^* to P_1^*. If the government holds the nominal money supply constant, the economy tends to move up the AD schedule. Domestic prices, P_0, will not change if the foreign exchange market reacts quickly; the exchange rate will have appreciated at once by the percentage increase in P^*. Competitiveness will return to its original level, as will aggregate demand.

In terms of the possibilities for using domestic policies to choose the rate

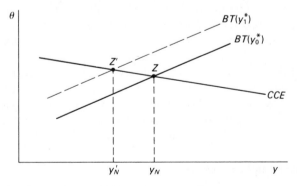

Fig. 13.8 External demand shock shifts the equilibrium rate of unemployment

of unemployment, the situation resembles that of the closed economy more closely than does the fixed exchange rate case. In other words, while monetary and fiscal instruments can be used to shift the AD curve, any move away from y_N will produce a situation of accelerating (or decelerating) inflation. The accelerating inflation, which derives in the closed economy from a higher bargained real wage, will be exacerbated by the balance of trade deficit, which leads to a depreciating real exchange rate and thus to a falling real wage. Unless monetary policy is accommodating, rising inflation will produce a falling real money supply and the eventual return of the aggregate demand curve to its original position. For example, the government adopts an expansionary fiscal policy (g_0 to g_1), which shifts AD rightwards so long as M/P remains constant at M_0/P_0. Rising inflation (P_0 to P_1) shifts AD back (Fig. 13.9(a)). With *fixed* exchange rates and zero capital mobility (Fig. 13.9(b)), a fiscal expansion takes the economy away from y_s to a point such as A on the CCE. After a brief burst of inflation in excess of world inflation as the economy moves from Z to A, inflation remains constant at the world rate. The unsustainability of A is reflected in different processes: the trade deficit means the loss of foreign exchange reserves and the decline in the domestic money supply. *Unless* the sterilization of these outflows is undertaken, the economy will return to Z (Fig. 13.9(b)). With fixed exchange rates and perfect capital mobility (Fig. 13.9(c)), the economy can stay at A for as long as it can borrow on the international market to finance the trade deficit.

It is clear that the introduction of floating exchange rates does not alter the fundamental constraints which determine the sustainable rate of activity in an economy. It simply alters the way in which the constraints are manifested. The phenomenon of accelerating inflation returns to characterize the situation in which the government seeks to hold unemployment below the equilibrium rate by pursuing an accommodating monetary policy. A lower sustainable rate of unemployment in both the fixed and floating exchange rate cases requires the use of supply-side fiscal policy or incomes policy to shift the CCE curve to the right. The use of such techniques is the same as under fixed exchange rates, discussed earlier in Chapter 11. Should the economy be fortunate enough to experience a positive external demand shock which shifts the BT to the right, the equilibrium rate of unemployment will fall automatically.

13.3   Summary and Policy Implications

When domestic prices and wages are fixed, the replacement of fixed by floating exchange rates produces a sharp change in economic behaviour. Effectively, the floating exchange rate means that the re-equilibration of

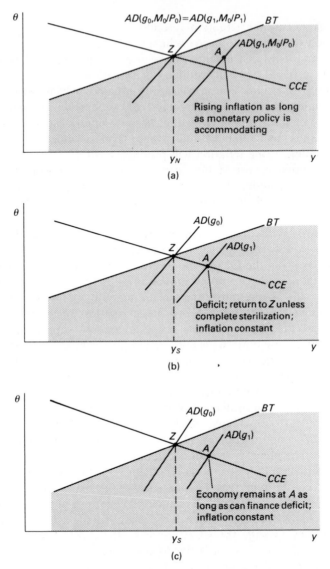

Fig. 13.9 Comparison of policy in different exchange rate regimes
(a) Floating exchange rate; zero capital mobility
(b) Fixed exchange rate; zero capital mobility
(c) Fixed exchange rate; perfect capital mobility

the economy to an external shock occurs through a relative price change (the exchange rate moves to adjust competitiveness in the required way), with the result that quantities (the level of output and employment) are left unaltered. If the exchange rate is fixed, then the only way equilibrium can be restored is if quantities move to recreate trade balance. This produces the famous result that, with zero capital mobility and fixed prices, a floating rate economy is insulated from external demand and price shocks. With fixed exchange rates, an external shock (demand or price) produces a change in the domestic output or prices in the same direction.

Introducing endogenous price- and wage-setting based on imperfect competition reduces somewhat the difference between exchange rate regimes. Regardless of regime, the level of output and employment is constrained by the CCE and BT curves. In each case, a unique sustainable output and unemployment level is determined by the requirements of internal and external balance. At only one level of output, where CCE and BT intersects, will there be both trade balance and consistency of claims on output per head from imports, wages, and profits. Under fixed exchange rates, the attempt to run the economy at lower than sustainable unemployment encounters a trade deficit. Under floating exchange rates, accelerating inflation is the consequence. It remains the case that floating exchange rates leave the domestic economy able to choose its inflation rate; under fixed rates inflation is equal to world inflation.

14

Floating Exchange Rates and Perfect Capital Mobility: Exchange Rate Expectations

In the conduct of open economy macroeconomics, something of a consensus has emerged in the last decade along the lines of the earlier chapters in this part of the book. Assumptions of purchasing power parity and perfectly competitive markets are generally viewed as over-restrictive for the short- to medium-run analysis that dominates policy discussion.[1] But once we extend the analysis to include internationally mobile capital, as we must to get any purchase on reality, then there remain substantial areas of disagreement.[2] When financial assets are mobile internationally, the movement of the exchange rate in the short run is dominated by the asset market. Purchases and sales of financial assets can occur at the touch of a switch and will dominate the effects on the exchange rate of the demand and supply of foreign exchange coming from trade flows.

The source of disagreement about how such an economy works hinges on the question of how exchange rate expectations are formed. How do exchange market operators decide on the level of the exchange rate that they expect to prevail in one month, three months, or a year's time? They have to form such an expectation in order to decide on the currencies in which to hold their portfolio of international financial assets. Since the question is still an open one, it seems appropriate to present several alternative hypotheses of exchange rate expectations and to look at the implications for macro policy of each. This will be done in a consistent framework based on the earier chapters of the book, so as to make clear the implications of differences in assumption about exchange rate expectations.

We begin the discussion with a look at the foreign exchange market itself, assuming initially that the expected exchange rate is fixed at a particular value. With exchange rate expectations uniform across dealers at a fixed rate, arbitrage in international financial markets will eliminate the possibility of profits being made from holding assets denominated in one

---

[1] See e.g. Dornbusch (1987b).
[2] Dornbusch (1987a) has an excellent summary of many of the areas of disagreement.

currency rather than another. We will see how the process of arbitrage (buying and selling of assets until the possibility of profit accruing from holding one rather than the other is eliminated) determines the short-run movement of the exchange rate. If the domestic interest rate is equal to the international rate, then the exchange rate will remain equal to its expected value. Dealers will be indifferent between holding assets denominated in sterling or dollars.

If, however, the domestic interest rate diverges from the international one, then the exchange rate will change immediately as the result of arbitrage behaviour to ensure that any expected interest rate gain from holding assets in one currency rather than another will be exactly offset by an expected exchange rate loss from holding the assets in the chosen currency. The assumption of perfect capital mobility requires that assets denominated in different currencies are perfect substitutes. Note however that risk-averse agents will seek to maintain a diversified portfolio even if expected returns on assets are unequal. Nevertheless, we will maintain the assumption of perfect capital mobility since the attempt to deal with the question of portfolio choice introduces many complications into an already difficult area.

After introducing the perfect interest arbitrage condition (also known as the *uncovered interest parity condition*) to define exchange market equilibrium, discussion turns to macroeconomic policy in the simple case where prices, wages, and exchange rate expectations are fixed. This provides the groundwork for the presentation of the famous Mundell–Fleming model,[3] where adaptive exchange rate expectations replace the assumption of a fixed expected exchange rate. Mundell and Fleming produced the striking result that fiscal policy would be quite ineffective in raising output and monetary policy very effective. The Mundell–Fleming assumptions mean that a fiscal expansion, which tends to raise the domestic interest rate relative to the world rate, produces an exchange rate appreciation. The appreciation reduces competitiveness and dampens demand. By assuming adaptive expectations, the sequence of appreciation and falling competitiveness continues until the economy is back at its initial position. Higher government demand has crowded out an equivalent amount of export demand through exchange rate appreciation.

In the same model, monetary policy is especially effective in raising output because it has just the opposite effect on the exchange rate and competitiveness. But these results turn out to be dependent on the assumptions of fixed prices and adaptive exchange rate expectations.

As a first step to showing the sensitivity of the Mundell–Fleming results to the assumptions made, we show how Sachs (1980) turned the results on their head by replacing the assumption of fixed prices by a fixed real

---

[3] Mundell (1958), Fleming (1962).

consumption wage. When the real wage is fixed, it is fiscal policy that is effective and monetary policy, ineffective. We show how Sachs's analysis can be extended to the general case of labour market behaviour depicted in the competing-claims curve. This produces what we will refer to as the 'fiscalist' model.

Attention is then turned to the implications of exchange market expectations based on real factors in the economy. It can be shown that, if the expected exchange rate is a function of real variables in the economy, then a unique equilibrium rate of unemployment exists. An example would be if the expected exchange rate was set so as to produce current account balance. If this is the case, then the government is unable to shift the economy to a lower rate of unemployment by a fiscal expansion *without* inflationary consequences.

14.1   Exchange Market Equilibrium

Just as was the case with fixed exchange rates, perfect capital mobility alters the working of the floating rate economy significantly. Any balance of trade surplus can be matched by an outflow of funds on capital account, and any deficit by an inflow. There is no longer any need for the exchange rate to appreciate to eliminate a trade surplus; the surplus can be lent abroad. The second implication of perfect capital mobility is that flows on the capital account as asset portfolios are adjusted can easily dominate trade flows, with the result that the exchange rate can be thought of as being set in the market for international financial assets.[4]

Holders of financial assets are concerned not simply with the interest rate differential between assets denominated in different currencies but also with the yield from holding the asset, i.e. including any change in the exchange rate.[5] For the holder of short-term financial assets that are potentially switchable between currencies, arbitrage in foreign exchange markets means that the interest rate differential in favour of sterling bonds as compared with dollar bonds must be equal to the expected depreciation of the pound against the dollar. Until this so-called *uncovered interest parity condition* holds, it will be profitable for dealers to switch their holdings of assets from pounds to dollars or vice versa.[6] Let us look at a simple example. Suppose that the interest rate on sterling Treasury bills is equal to 6.5% while on the equivalent US bond the interest rate is only

---

[4] This is known as the asset market approach to exchange rate determination. For the early development of this view see contributions to the volume edited by Herin *et al.* (1977).

[5] Remember that in what follows it is assumed that holders of financial assets are risk-neutral.

[6] Williamson (1983a: 246–8) gives a very clear explanation of why it is not necessary to include the analysis of forward markets in the *macro*economics of exchange rates.

4%. The *interest gain* from holding sterling rather than dollar bonds on an annual basis is therefore

$$\text{Interest gain: } r - r^* = 6.5 - 4 = 2.5\%.$$

If the current exchange rate is £0.635/\$ and it is expected to be equal to 0.65 in a year's time, then the *expected exchange rate loss* from holding sterling rather than dollars owing to the expected depreciation of the pound on an annual basis is

$$\text{Expected exchange rate loss: } (e_{t+1}^E - e_t)/e_t = (0.65 - 0.635)/0.635$$
$$\approx 2.5\%.$$

With the interest differential equal to the expected exchange rate depreciation, the investor is indifferent between holding US or UK bonds. Of course, if the exchange rate were currently 0.6 and the expected exchange rate still 0.65, the expected loss from pound depreciation would be over 8%, a loss that would not be compensated for by the 2.5% interest differential in favour of pound bonds. Buying and selling of dollar and pound bonds will ensure that the interest differential exactly equals the expected exchange rate depreciation.

As we have seen before, $(e_{t+1}^E - e_t)/e_t$ is approximately equal to $\ln e_{t+1}^E - \ln e_t$. Thus, assuming uncovered interest parity, we can write the condition for *exchange market equilibrium* as

$$r - r^* = \ln e_{t+1}^E - \ln e_t.$$
[exchange market equilibrium condition (EME)]

In a diagram with the interest rate on the vertical axis and (the log of) the exchange rate on the horizontal axis, the exchange market equilibrium (EME) condition can be depicted as a line through the point (r^*, e^E) with a slope of $-45°$ (see Fig. 14.1). In the rest of the chapter, e will refer to the log of the exchange rate so EME will be written $r - r^* = e_{t+1}^E - e_t$. With the interest rate, r_1, above r^*, the EME line shows that the current exchange rate must be at e_1 in order that the *expected depreciation* over the year back to e^E will be exactly equal to the interest differential. To the left of the EME, at point A for example, with the interest rate at r_1, the current exchange rate is far too high for exchange market equilibrium. In other words, dealers will be selling pounds in order to buy dollar securities. This will have the effect of taking the exchange market to equilibrium at B on the EME as the pound depreciates in value. At a position such as C to the right of the EME, the opposite pressure will characterize the foreign exchange market: there will be excess demand for pounds. There will be a capital inflow until the exchange market equilibrium is restored once more. Thus, to the left of the EME there is capital outflow and depreciation of the exchange rate; to the right, capital inflow and appreciation.

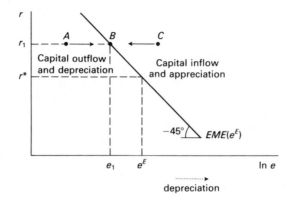

Fig. 14.1 Exchange market equilibrium

14.2   An Introduction to Policy Analysis: Fixed Prices, Fixed Wages, and Fixed Expected Exchange Rate

We make these restrictive assumptions to ease entry to the analysis of policy under capital mobility. The assumptions mean that we are considering the very short run: exchange rate expectations are not allowed to change, and no account is taken of the implications of changes in the actual exchange rate for demand or for wage- and price-setting.

Fiscal Policy

The economy is initially characterized by an equilibrium in which the interest rate equals the international rate and the current exchange rate coincides with its expected value. A fiscal expansion tends to raise the interest rate above r^*, taking the economy from A to B in Fig. 14.2. But at B there is no exchange market equilibrium, as there are gains to be had from holding pound securities. The resulting capital inflow immediately pushes up the exchange rate to the point on the EME curve where the expected loss from holding assets in pounds (the expected depreciation of the exchange rate from e_1 to e^E) exactly matches the gain in interest rate terms. In other words, the expected *yield* from holding pound or dollar bonds is equal. The economy is at C.

It is worth noting at this point that the *trade* balance will be worse in the new situation, both because of the effect of the higher level of activity on imports and because of exchange rate appreciation reducing net exports. Hence, fiscal expansion reinforces the negative effect on the trade balance associated with any expansion arising from higher domestic absorption by appreciating the exchange rate.

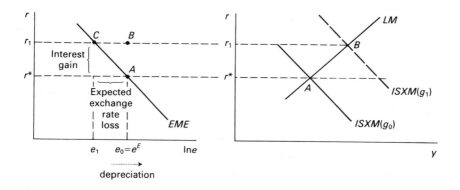

Fig. 14.2 Short-run effects of fiscal expansion

Monetary Policy

In this case, the interest rate tends to fall as the result of the expansionary policy. Thus, the exchange rate depreciates (owing to the capital outflow), and as a result, the implications for the trade balance of a higher level of activity tend to be offset by the rise in competitiveness associated with depreciation (see Fig. 14.3).

The very short-run analysis is clearly incomplete—the ramifications of the change in competitiveness induced by the policy measure have been ignored. However, it points the way to the Mundell–Fleming results in so far as fiscal expansion appears to have the counter-productive effect of reducing competitiveness, while monetary expansion creates a reinforcing effect via depreciation.

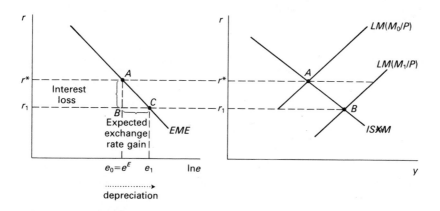

Fig. 14.3 Short-run effects of monetary expansion

14.3 Exchange Rate Expectations and Macro Policy: a Guide to the Major Results

There are three sharply contrasting sets of results for the effectiveness of macroeconomic policy as a means of raising output in the floating rate economy with perfect capital mobility. On the one hand, there is the famous Mundell–Fleming result that, while monetary policy could be used successfully to raise output, fiscal policy would be completely ineffective. The diametrically opposite result that only fiscal policy could raise output is also derived, producing the 'fiscalist' position. The third result is that neither monetary *nor* fiscal policy can raise output in a sustainable way, i.e. without the consequence of accelerating inflation. We will see that assumptions both about prices and wages and about exchange rate expectations are important in accounting for these contrasting results. We will look at two different assumptions about prices and wages:

A1 P, W fixed;
A2 P, W set so as to achieve real objectives, e.g. according to price and wage determination behaviour in the imperfect competition model.

There are two assumptions about the formation of exchange rate expectations which help to pin down what is generating the different results:

B1   adaptive expectations: $e^E = e_{-1}$;
B2   expectations based on real factors; e.g., the expected exchange rate is based on the view that a particular level of competitiveness will be maintained, or that the current account must be in equilibrium.

By putting these different assumptions into a grid, it is possible to identify the combinations which produce three contrasting results (see Table 14.1).

Table 14.1 Major results for the effectiveness of macro policy

Assumption about prices and wages	Assumption about the expected exchange rate	
	Adaptive (B1)	Real factors (B2)
Fixed P, W (A1)	Monetary effective (R1) Mundell–Fleming	
P, W set according to real objectives (A2)	Fiscal effective (R2) 'fiscalist'	Neither effective (R3) 'unique equilibrium rate of unemployment'

R1 monetary policy can raise output; fiscal policy cannot;
R2 fiscal policy can raise output; monetary policy cannot;
R3 neither monetary nor fiscal policy can raise output beyond a certain level without the consequence of accelerating inflation. In such circumstances, an accommodating monetary policy would be required.

Historically, the debate started in cell 1 with the Mundell–Fleming analysis. Following a demonstration of the result that monetary policy alone is effective in raising output (R1), we turn to the results based on prices and wages set according to real objectives, an example of which is the imperfect competition model. Results of the R2 and R3 type are associated with the names of Sachs and Dornbusch. Sachs provided a clear demonstration of how the Mundell–Fleming results could be overturned, and his analysis will be shown to be a special case of R2. Finally, the adoption of an assumption that ties the expected exchange rate to *real* variables produces the unique equilibrium rate of unemployment result.

14.4 The Mundell–Fleming Results

Assumptions: A1—P, W fixed

B1—adaptive expectations: $e^E = e_{-1}$

Results: R1—monetary policy can raise output; fiscal policy cannot

In separate contributions written in 1958 and 1962 respectively, Mundell and Fleming developed an argument to show that the impotence of monetary policy in a fixed exchange rate economy is radically overturned if exchange rates float. As compared with a fixed exchange rate system under conditions of perfect capital mobility, both authors came to conclusions, now known as the Mundell–Fleming results, that with flexible rates:

• monetary policy is successful in raising output;
• fiscal policy is unsuccessful in raising output.

The results depend on three assumptions, namely that nominal wages and prices are fixed; that expectations of the exchange rate are formed in the simple adaptive manner:

$$e^E = e_{-1};$$
[adaptive exchange rate expectations]

and that equilibrium is characterized by fulfilled exchange market expectations:

$$e = e^E = e_{-1}.$$
[equilibrium: fulfilled exchange market expectations]

Although maintaining the fixed W, P assumption, the Mundell–Fleming model goes beyond the very short run discussed in Section 14.2: full adjustment to the consequences of induced exchange rate changes is examined.

Fiscal Policy

The impact effect of a fiscal expansion is exactly as discussed in Section 14.2; looking at Fig. 14.4, and assuming realistically that exchange market equilibrium is restored very rapidly, the economy moves from A to B. The appreciation of the exchange rate from e_0 to e_1 reduces competitiveness and produces a leftward shift in the ISXM curve from ISXM(g_1, θ_0) to ISXM(g_1, θ_1). Now is the time to bring in the assumption of adaptive exchange rate expectations. Since the actual exchange rate appreciated from e_0 to e_1 in period 1, its expected value in period 2 will be equal to e_1:

$$e_2^E = e_1.$$

Thus, it is necessary to redraw the exchange market equilibrium line since an interest rate equal to the world interest rate will now represent an exchange market equilibrium position when the exchange rate is equal to its new expected value, e_2^E.

With the interest rate in period 2 equal to r_2 (point C in the ISXM/LM diagram), the exchange rate in period 2 will appreciate further as indicated by point C in the r–ln e diagram. In other words, since the expected exchange rate has risen *and* the interest rate is still above the world rate, the exchange rate must appreciate further if the interest gain from holding

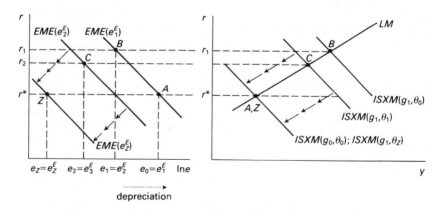

Fig. 14.4 Ineffectiveness of fiscal expansion: Mundell–Fleming

pounds is to be equal to the expected exchange rate depreciation (from e_2 to e_2^E). In the next period, there is the same feedback channel from exchange rate appreciation to a decline in competitiveness and a leftward shift in the ISXM. Adaptive expectations produce a further shift in the EME and, as long as the interest rate remains above r^*, a further appreciation will ensue. Finally, declining competitiveness will have shifted the ISXM right back to its original position, i.e. ISXM(g_1, θ_Z) coincides with ISXM(g_0, θ_0) since, with the money supply fixed, that is the level of income where the interest rate has returned to the original level. Output is back at the level of y_0. With the interest rate equal to the world rate once more, the new equilibrium EME in period Z will be characterized by r^*, $e_Z^E = e_Z$. In Fig. 14.4, the economy is at Z.

Since output is at the original level, with government expenditure higher and competitiveness lower, the expansionary effect of fiscal policy has been nullified by 100% crowding-out of net exports.[7]

Monetary Policy

By contrast, an expansionary monetary policy works as a method of raising output because the induced exchange rate changes *reinforce* the expansion, rather than offset it. Initially in Fig. 14.5, the economy moves from A to B just as in the previous discussion of monetary policy. In this case the ISXM will be shifted rightwards by the demand-stimulating effect of the depreciation of the exchange rate from e_0 to e_1. Output rises further from B to C in the ISXM/LM diagram. Because exchange rate expectations are adaptive, the EME line shifts to reflect the new expected exchange rate, $e_2^E = e_1$. There is a further depreciation as the economy moves to point C,

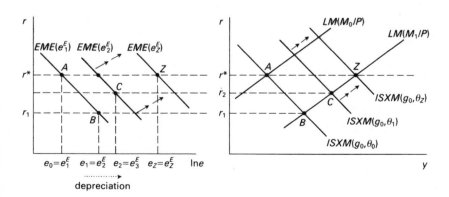

Fig. 14.5 Effectiveness of monetary expansion: Mundell–Fleming

---

[7] Domestic expenditure is not crowded out—in effect, the extra government expenditure is borrowed from abroad.

reflecting the fact that the interest rate remains below the world rate. The process of expansion and depreciation continues until the interest differential is eliminated. At point Z, the economy is in a new equilibrium with higher output and a lower exchange rate. Beyond the initial effects of monetary policy in reducing the interest rate and inducing higher private investment, the policy has created additional demand from net exports through the rise in competitiveness.

*An Algebraic Demonstration of the Mundell–Fleming Results

By assuming simple linear functions to capture the essential elements of the ISXM and LM equations, the Mundell–Fleming results can be shown easily. The real money supply is written as m; imports are not shown explicitly in this box, so there is no chance of confusion. Net exports are written as $a_\theta\theta$. The relevant equations are as follows:

$$y = a_\theta\theta + a_g g - a_r r \qquad \text{[ISXM equation]}$$

$$\bar{m} = b_y y - b_r r \qquad \text{[LM equation]}$$

$$r - r^* = \ln e_{t+1}^E - \ln e_t \qquad \text{[EME equation]}$$

$$e_t^E = e_{t-1}. \qquad \text{[adaptive exchange rate expectations]}$$

Equilibrium is defined by the exchange rate being unchanged from one period to the next; i.e., $e_t = e_{t-1}$. From the EME condition and adaptive expectations, this implies that in equilibrium,

$$r = r^*. \qquad \text{[equilibrium condition]}$$

Therefore

$$y = a_\theta\theta + a_g g - a_r r^* \qquad \text{[ISXM](14.1)}$$

$$\bar{m} = b_y y - b_r r^* \qquad \text{[LM](14.2)}$$

It is clear from (14.2) that, with fixed money supply $\bar{M}$ and price level $\bar{P}$, along with r^*, there is a unique output level for money market equilibrium. In other words, the level of output is fixed solely by the LM curve and the international interest rate:

$$y = (\bar{m} + b_r r^*)/b_y. \qquad (14.3)$$

Thus the multiplier associated with an increase in the money supply is

$$\mathrm{d}y/\mathrm{d}m = 1/b_y.$$

Since output is fixed by (14.3), the ISXM equation (14.1) shows that any sustained rise in g must be associated with a fall in θ. Thus,

$$dy = 0 = a_\theta d\theta + a_g dg$$

and

$$d\theta/dg = -a_g/a_\theta < 0.$$

A change in government expenditure has no effect on output because it has an exactly offsetting negative effect on competitiveness. The positive effect of monetary policy on competitiveness can be seen as follows. Comparing equilibria before and after a monetary expansion results in

$$dy = a_\theta d\theta$$

and

$$dy = dm/b_y.$$

Equating the changes in equilibrium output leads to

$$dm/b_y = a_\theta d\theta;$$

i.e.,

$$d\theta/dm = 1/a_\theta b_y > 0.$$

14.5   The 'Fiscalist' Model: the Reversal of Mundell–Fleming

Assumptions: A2—P, W set according to real objectives
 B1—adaptive expectations: $e^E = e_{-1}$
Results: R2—fiscal policy can raise output; monetary policy cannot

In Mundell and Fleming's analysis, the assumption that the money wage, W, and the price level of domestic production, P, were fixed meant that real wages fell on each occasion of a rise in competitiveness (owing to depreciation) and there were no repercussions of this. Using the definition of competitiveness ($\theta = P^*e/P$), any change in e produces a change in θ since by assumption both P^* and P are fixed. The higher real cost of imports associated with depreciation must be paid for by some mixture of falling real wages and profits (and we assumed for simplicity that it is paid for entirely by lower real wages). Similarly, an appreciation reduces the real cost of imports and raises real wages even though the bargaining situation is unchanged.

A more realistic assumption than the Mundell–Fleming one of unresponsive wages and prices would be that prices and wages are set by domestic
firms and unions in such a way that real profit margins and real wages are
protected—i.e. the imperfect competition model. We will return to the
implications of price- and wage-setting summarized in the BRW and PRW
curves a little later. First, it is useful to look at a simple special case which
illustrates Sachs's reversal of the Mundell–Fleming results.

14.5.1 Sachs's Special Case (a Modified Version of Sachs 1980)

Assumptions: A2—fixed real wage, i.e. horizontal CCE
B1—adaptive expectations: $e^E = e_{-1}$
Results: R2—fiscal policy can raise output; monetary policy
cannot

We illustrate the thrust of Sachs's argument by looking at a modified
version of his model, couching it in terms of the analytical apparatus that
we have built up. It is possible to highlight the role of the Mundell–Fleming
assumption of a fixed price level by making the opposite assumption that
the effect on competitiveness of exchange rate changes is fully offset by
changes in domestic wages and prices. More precisely, we assume that
competitiveness is an inverse function of the real wage,

$$\theta = \theta(\bar{w}),$$

and we focus on the special case in which the real wage is fixed at the
level, w_0;

$$w = w_0;$$

thus we have $\theta = \theta(w_0) = \theta_0$.

The essence of Sachs's case can be conveyed by assuming a constant real
wage modelled by a constant bargained real wage line (see Fig. 14.6); the
inverse relationship between the price-determined real wage and competitiveness is also depicted. Since the real wage is fixed, there is a unique level
of competitiveness consistent with constant inflation: $w^B = w^P$ at θ_0 only.
This can be represented by a horizontal CCE line as in Fig. 14.6. If
competitiveness is pushed above this level by an exchange rate depreciation, then this means a fall in the real wage below w^B (e.g., position A).
This will produce a situation in which money wages and prices will rise
faster than the depreciation so as to restore the real wage and
competitiveness to their original levels.

Fiscal Policy

Let us now pursue the policy implications of wage and price behaviour
which ensure that the level of competitiveness is unchanged in conse-

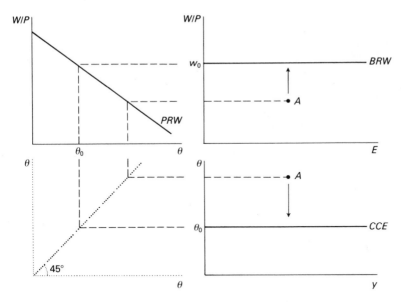

Fig. 14.6 The assumption of a fixed real wage, w_0, implies a flat CCE at θ_0

quence of exchange rate changes. As we have seen before, a fiscal expansion leads initially to a rise in output and the appreciation of the exchange rate. This *lowers* the real cost of imports and raises real wages. With a constant bargained real wage, money wages will adjust downward to reflect the boost to real wages provided by the fall in import costs. Prices will fall as well, reflecting lower costs, until competitiveness returns to its original level; there is a unique θ for which

$$LP = m(LP) + w + \theta(LP/MP)$$

Output/worker = Real profits/worker + real wages

+ real import costs/worker.

Thus there will be no induced shift in the ISXM as the result of exchange rate appreciation since its effect on competitiveness has been fully offset by falling domestic prices. In Fig. 14.7 the ISXM remains at ISXM(g_1, θ_0). However, a lower price level, P, will raise the real value of the money supply and cause the LM to shift to the right, *reinforcing* the expansion of output. (Remember that, by assuming a flat BRW in this special case, only the endogenous wage and price responses to exchange rate changes are taken account of; there are no wage/price responses to changes in the level of output and employment.) The economy moves from point B to C in Fig. 14.7.

Adaptive exchange rate expectations come into play exactly as before, shifting the EME to the left and evoking a further appreciation. This

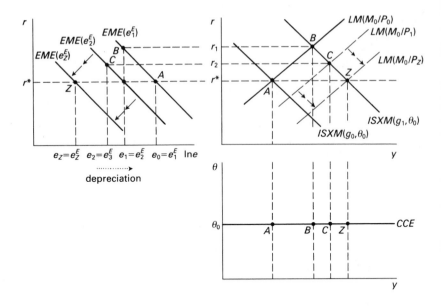

Fig. 14.7 Fiscal expansion is effective: a modified version of Sachs (1980)

produces a repetition of the previous pattern of events as before: W falls, P falls until θ is returned to θ_0; the fall in P raises M/P and shifts LM rightward; output rises; the EME shifts left to reflect the new expected exchange rate; ... Eventually, in period Z, the interest rate will have returned to r^* and there will be no further exchange rate changes to be offset with price falls; hence the LM remains fixed at $LM(M_0/P_Z)$.

In Mundell–Fleming, fiscal policy is ultimately ineffective because appreciation dampens demand via falling competitiveness. In a Sachs-type setup competitiveness cannot fall. Fiscal policy becomes highly effective in raising output because of its effect in lowering prices and therefore boosting demand via a higher real money supply and falling interest rates. In such a world, fiscal policy holds the key to an anti-inflationary expansion of output and employment.

Monetary Policy

It is hardly surprising that there is a symmetrical reversal in the efficacy of monetary policy in the move from Mundell–Fleming to a model with a fixed real wage. The heart of the matter is once more the consequences of exchange rate changes. Recall that it was the ability of a monetary expansion to secure higher competitiveness through depreciation of the exchange rate which created output-enhancing effects. Once real wage resistance in the form of a fixed w^B is introduced, the implications of

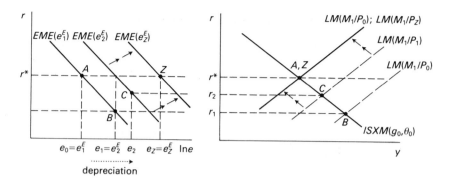

Fig. 14.8 Monetary expansion is ineffective: a modified version of Sachs (1980)

depreciation (higher real import costs) for wage- and price-setting must be pursued. With the economy at point B in Fig. 14.8 following the monetary expansion, depreciation is followed by higher wage increases as workers seek to restore their pre-existing real wage. Since costs for business are pushed up, prices rise as well. Wages and prices must go up sufficiently to restore both the previous real wage and the real profit margin. This will have occurred when competitiveness has been reduced to its original level. Just as with fiscal expansion, endogenous wage and price behaviour rules out the change in competitiveness which, in Mundell–Fleming, brought about an induced shift in the ISXM. Instead, it is the change in the price level that holds centre-stage—in the case of monetary expansion, the *rise* in prices reduces the real money supply and shifts the LM back in a leftward direction. The economy moves from B to C. The remainder of the adjustment path from C to Z introduces no new elements. It is clear that monetary policy is quite ineffective in altering the level of output.

Because monetary expansion causes depreciation and reduces real wages, it triggers off inflation, which with a fixed money supply implies a decline in aggregate demand as interest rates rise. The short-run inflation has *nothing* to do with the fact that activity in the economy has been expanded. It is solely a function of the change in the exchange rate. Another way of putting the same point is that, should the government choose to expand from point A with a balanced mix of fiscal and monetary measures keeping the interest rate fixed at the world rate, there would, in a model with a fixed real wage, be no change in the price level at all.[8]

---

[8] It may be useful to note that the reversal of Mundell–Fleming does not rest on the assumption of a constant real wage—a horizontal BRW line. As a second example, it could be generated by an alternative assumption such as that international markets for traded goods impose purchasing power parity such that competitiveness is always equal to the constant 1. The combination of the standard positively sloped BRW with PPP produces a horizontal CCE—a unique level of competitiveness regardless of output level—and this is all that is required to generate the above results.

14.5.2   The 'Fiscalist' Position in the Imperfect Competition Model

Assumptions: A2—*P, W* set according to real objectives; downward
             sloping CCE
             B1—adaptive expectations: $e^E = e_{-1}$
Results: R2—fiscal policy can raise output; monetary policy
             cannot

The discussion of the special case with a constant real wage gives us a hint as to the implications of monetary and fiscal expansion in the more general imperfect competition model. In the imperfect competition model, the bargained real wage curve is upward-sloping—expected real wages rise with employment. Now, because a fiscal expansion produces exchange rate appreciation and a decline in the real cost of imports, this will make room for a higher expected real wage at a higher level of output, enabling the economy to move to a new equilibrium rate of unemployment at lower unemployment. This analysis strikes a chord in common with the fixed exchange rate case where a higher level of employment was a new equilibrium rate of unemployment because competitiveness (and hence the real cost of imports) was squeezed by endogenous wage and price increases. Under flexible exchange rates, only a *fiscal* expansion can succeed in shifting the economy to a new equilibrium rate of unemployment at lower unemployment. This is because competitiveness is depressed by the exchange rate appreciation owing to the rise in the interest rate above the world interest rate associated with fiscal expansion. Hence, the real wage can rise.

Before going through the fiscal expansion more carefully to show, in particular, the role played by exchange rate expectations, let us look in a preliminary way at monetary expansion. Monetary expansion pushes down the exchange rate. By *increasing* the real cost of imports (increasing competitiveness), the monetary expansion produces inflationary pressure additional to that associated with the higher bargained real wage at higher employment. With a fixed nominal money policy, the economy will move back to the original equilibrium rate of unemployment. An accommodating monetary policy would see accelerating inflation.

Thus, in a floating exchange rate world with capital mobility, it is possible for the economy to move to a new lower equilibrium rate of unemployment as long as expansion is undertaken using fiscal rather than monetary means. In the next section, limitations to the use of fiscal policy in this way will be examined. The *trade* balance is worsened at the new equilibrium rate of unemployment by both the effect of higher output and the appreciation. The lasting current account disequilibrium associated with the new higher level of output raises questions as to the plausibility of maintaining the assumption that the expected exchange rate is equal to its previous value *irrespective* of the trend in the current account. An answer will be given to the question, Will the trade deficit eventually affect exchange rate expectations, rendering the new equilibrium rate of unemployment untenable?

Fiscal Policy

We can simplify the illustration of the fiscalist result and concentrate on the essentials by assuming that investment is interest-insensitive. This gives us a vertical ISXM. Secondly, we note that the competing-claims equilibrium defines a relationship between competitiveness and the level of output; i.e., for equilibrium at any level of output, a specific level of competitiveness is implied so that $w^B(U(y)) = w^P(\theta)$. Let us write the CCE equation as

$$\theta = \bar{\alpha} - \alpha_y y. \qquad \text{[CCE]}$$

We can incorporate the requirement that competitiveness must be at a specific level for constant inflation at each level of output into the ISXM equation. This modifies the multiplier:

$$y \quad = a_y y + a_\theta \theta + a_g g \qquad \text{[ISXM]}$$

$$\theta \quad = \bar{\alpha} - \alpha_y y \qquad \text{[CCE]}$$

$$\therefore \quad y \quad = a_y y + a_\theta \bar{\alpha} - a_y \alpha_y y + a_g g$$

$$\Rightarrow \quad y \quad = \frac{1}{1 - a_y + a_\theta \alpha_y} (a_y \bar{\alpha} + a_g g)$$

$$\text{[ISXM incorporating CCE]}$$

In Fig. 14.9 we show the initial vertical $\text{ISXM}(g_0, \theta_0)$ and the new

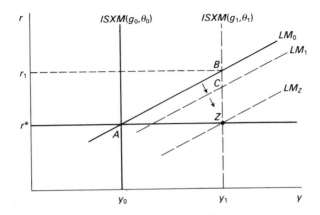

Fig. 14.9 Fiscalist model: fiscal policy effective

$ISXM(g_1, \theta_1)$ following the rise in government spending. It is simplest (although unrealistic) to think of the economy adjusting to the fiscal boost in two sequential steps.

Step 1 The labour market adjusts fully to the rise in government spending, with the result that output rises to y_1 and competitiveness falls to θ_1. The economy moves from A to B. In other words, we assume that the exchange rate remains fixed, and we have the rise in real wages to $w^B(y_1)$ and associated squeeze on competitiveness occurring immediately.

Step 2 With the interest rate at r_1 above r^*, there will be pressure for the exchange rate to appreciate. Exchange rate appreciation reduces competitiveness. The reduced real cost of imports will be passed on in lower prices by firms, and this will have the effect of raising real wages above the level consistent with $w^B(y_1)$. Hence wages will fall as well. The fall in prices causes the LM to shift to the right. (The economy moves from B to C.) Adaptive exchange rate expectations will operate as usual to create further appreciation and falling inflation until the LM has shifted to the right sufficiently to bring the interest rate back into line with the world interest rate, r^*.

Thus the economy traces the path from A to B to C to Z. At Z there is a non-inflationary equilibrium since the economy is on the CCE curve with the bargained real wage equal to the price-determined real wage. The foreign exchange market is in equilibrium since $r = r^*$ and $e^E = e$. It is useful to note that a more realistic adjustment process than that of the two sequential steps used above produces the same outcome. If we suppose that the exchange rate reacts first to the fiscal boost, then prices fall initially. This downward pressure on prices is then counteracted by rising inflationary pressure from the labour market as the result of higher activity. However, as long as the interest rate remains above the world interest rate $(r > r^*)$, appreciation will continue and eventually falling prices will shift the LM to the right.

Monetary Policy

To allow monetary policy to have any chance of raising output, we must reinstate an interest-sensitive ISXM (Fig. 14.10). In this case, an expansionary monetary policy elicits exchange rate depreciation. The real cost of imports rises and is passed on in higher prices. At the same time, the higher level of output generates higher wage claims. Thus, from both the foreign exchange and the labour markets, prices are being pushed upward. The LM shifts back to the left, and with adaptive exchange rate expectations, the economy returns via point B and C to Z, the original output level with the interest rate equal to the world rate.

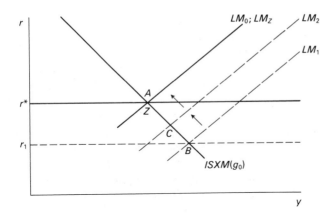

Fig. 14.10 Fiscalist model: monetary policy ineffective

14.6 Bringing Back the Unique Equilibrium Rate of Unemployment: Exchange Rate Expectations

Assumptions: A2—P, W set according to real objectives

B3—expectations based on real factors; e.g., the expected exchange rate is based on the view that a particular level of competitiveness will be maintained, or that the current account must be in equilibrium

Results: R4—neither monetary nor fiscal policy can raise output without the consequence of accelerating inflation; in such circumstances, an accommodating monetary policy would be required

The last section reported the rather optimistic 'fiscalist' result that an economy characterized by price- and wage-setting behaviour incorporating real wage resistance is able to secure a reduction in unemployment without the consequence of accelerating inflation as long as the chosen policy instrument is fiscal rather than monetary expansion. But this result rested on the adaptive formation of exchange rate expectations. And this leads to a central problem: although the economy has moved to a stable inflation position at lower unemployment, the sustainability of the situation depends on the persistence of *unchanged exchange rate expectations*. If the reduction in unemployment and the associated lower competitiveness generate a trade deficit, and if the trade deficit begins to affect the formation of exchange rate expectations, then the exchange rate is likely to depreciate. Higher real import costs will cut the real wage and release higher wage claims in response. The economy will face either falling output and employment as the government raises interest rates and the real money supply falls, or accelerating inflation if the authorities allow the nominal money supply to rise with inflation.

The reappearance of a unique equilibrium rate of unemployment under perfect capital mobility depends on the expected exchange rate being a function of *real* variables. Dornbusch and Fischer (1980) argue that ultimately the expected exchange rate depends on real variables. For example, exchange rate expectations are formed in such a way that the actual exchange rate will move to ensure equilibrium in the current account of the balance of payments. An alternative hypothesis which would also produce a unique equilibrium rate of unemployment is that the exchange rate is expected to arrive at an equilibrium eventually, defined for example by a specific level of competitiveness (e.g. Sachs 1985). The intuition of this result is not difficult because broadly speaking it simply reimposes the constraint on the choice of a sustainable stable-inflation unemployment rate from the case of zero capital mobility.

Let us set out the argument by distinguishing first of all between two of the assumptions about exchange rate expectations, either of which will produce the unique equilibrium rate of unemployment result. The first is that the exchange rate is expected to change so as to ensure a specific level of competitiveness, θ^T:

$$e^E = \theta^T + P^E$$

[exchange rate expectations](14.4)

where all variables are in logarithms. In other words, for the expected exchange rate to move so as to achieve θ^T, it must be expected to be at a value higher than θ^T by the level of domestic prices. (The international price level, P^* is normalized to a value of 1 ($\ln 1 = 0$) for convenience.)

The second, and alternative, assumption is that the expected exchange rate moves so as to ensure current account equilibrium. We can express this as follows.

$$BT(y, y^*, \widetilde{\theta}) = 0,$$

where $\widetilde{\theta}$ is defined by

$$\widetilde{\theta} = e^E - P^E$$

(where θ, e, and P are measured in logarithms); i.e.,

$$BT(y, y^*, e^E - P^E) = 0.$$

[exchange rate expectations](14.5)

One justification for forming expectations on this basis is that θ^T and $\widetilde{\theta}$ are the values that foreign exchange market operators believe will hold in the long run. An alternative justification is that they believe the government will ensure that these values hold in the medium or even short run (if the market does not).

*14.6.1 Exchange Rate Expectations Assumption (14.4): $e^E = \theta^T + P^E$

We will begin by using assumption (14.4). Note that the assumption that the exchange rate moves to ensure $\theta = \theta^T$ is a generalization of the purchasing power parity condition that $\theta = 1$. To focus attention on this issue, it is useful to reduce the remainder of the model to its bare bones. The model is as follows:

$$y = a_\theta \theta + a_g g - a_r r \qquad \text{[ISXM equation]}$$

$$m = b_y y - b_r r \qquad \text{[LM equation]}$$

$$\theta = \bar{\alpha} - \alpha_y y \qquad \text{[CCE equation]}$$

$$r - r^* = e^E - e \qquad \text{[exchange market equilibrium]}$$

$$e^E = \theta^T + P^E \qquad \text{[exchange rate expectations](14.4)}$$

$$\theta = e - P \qquad \text{[definition of competitiveness]}$$

$$r = r^* \ (\text{i.e., } e^E = e). \qquad \text{[fulfilled expectations]}$$

The exchange rate, e, competitiveness, θ, and price level, P, are all measured in logs. Matters are simplified by focusing only on potential equilibria by assuming that the real money supply is always adjusted to keep the interest rate equal to the international rate: $r = r^*$. This means that the LM equation can be dropped and we are left with

$$y = a_\theta \theta + a_g g - a_r r^* \qquad \text{[ISXM equation]}$$

$$\theta = \bar{\alpha} - \alpha_y y \qquad \text{[CCE equation]}$$

$$e^E = \theta^T + P^E \qquad \text{[exchange rate expectations](14.4)}$$

$$\theta = e - P. \qquad \text{[definition of competitiveness]}$$

Let us assume that inflation expectations are formed adaptively:

$$\dot{P}^E = \dot{P}_{-1}. \qquad \text{[inflation expectations]}$$

Using the definition of last period's competitiveness ($\theta_{-1} = e_{-1} - P_{-1}$) and rearranging the equations for e^E and θ_{-1}, we have

$$\theta^T - \theta_{-1} = e^E - e_{-1} - (P^E - P_{-1})$$

or

$$e^E - e_{-1} = (\theta^T - \theta_{-1}) + \dot{P}^E,$$

where $\dot{P}^E \equiv P^E - P_{-1}$. Using adaptive inflation expectations,

$$e^E - e_{-1} = (\theta^T - \theta_{-1}) + \dot{P}_{-1},$$

and since $r - r^* = e^E - e$ and with $r = r^*$, this implies that $e^E = e$. Therefore $e^E - e_{-1} = \dot{e}$ and we have

$$\dot{e} = \dot{P}_{-1} + (\theta^T - \theta_{-1}).$$

The target exchange rate, θ^T, defines a horizontal line in the Salter–Swan diagram, and the expression above for $\dot{e}$ explains what happens on and off this line. When the level of lagged competitiveness (θ_{-1}) is equal to θ^T, $\dot{e} = \dot{P}_{-1}$; for positions *above* this line (see top panel of Fig. 14.11), the rate of depreciation of the exchange rate is less than last period's inflation: competitiveness is falling ($\dot{e} < \dot{P}_{-1}$ in zones II and IV). The converse holds for positions below θ^T. θ^T defines *full exchange market equilibrium*

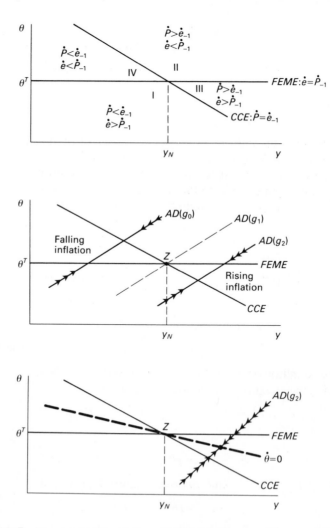

Fig. 14.11 Exchange rate expectations tied to target competitiveness, θ^T; unique equilibrium rate of unemployment at y_N

(FEME) since $r = r^*$ *and* $e^E = e$. Along the competing-claims line, inflation is equal to the lagged rate of depreciation of the exchange rate; to the right of the CCE, inflation exceeds the lagged rate of depreciation, and to the left, $\dot{P} < \dot{e}_{-1}$.

Figure 14.11 depicts the model: the space divides into four zones, depending on the implications for inflation of the state of the foreign exchange market and labour market relative to changes in the exchange rate. The lower panel of the figure includes the constant competitiveness line $(\dot{\theta} = 0)$, indicating the set of points at which internal and external pressures on inflation and the exchange rate are equal. (For the derivation of this line, refer back to the box in Section 13.2.)

Demand management policies can be represented by the lines defined by the ISXM equation (assuming as before that monetary policy is adjusted to ensure that $r = r^*$). If we take an aggregate demand stance defined by the line g_0 to begin with, then an economy beginning in zone I will be pushed along line g_0 by the ensuing rise in competitiveness. Similarly, from a position on line g_0 in zone II, competitiveness will be falling. Thus, we will eventually arrive in zone IV. Here the economy is characterized by falling inflation, since the downward pressure on inflation coming from the labour market is reinforced by a tendency for the exchange rate to appreciate relative to last period's inflation.

Taking a rather higher level of aggregate demand represented by g_2 produces the same pressures for movement along g_2 from zones I and II. Once the economy enters zone III, though, inflation increases. The need for the exchange rate to depreciate relative to last period's inflation so as to push competitiveness back up to θ^T is met by pressure emanating from the labour market for wages and prices to rise faster than the exchange rate depreciates to take the expected real wage up to w^B.

It is only when the authorities set demand policies at g_1 that a situation of stable inflation will be achieved—at the intersection of the CCE and FEME. This defines the unique equilibrium (constant inflation) rate of unemployment.

14.6.2 Exchange Rate Expectations Assumption (14.5): BT(y, y^*, $e^E - P^E$) = 0

The second example of exchange rate expectations, being based on real variables, recreates the constraints on the achievement of stable inflation exactly as they were under floating rates with zero capital mobility: the economy must be at the intersection of the CCE and the BT curves. The latter coincides with the exchange market equilibrium line under (14.5) about exchange rate expectations. Since the expected exchange rate will move so as to create current account balance, expectations can be fulfilled only along the BT line.

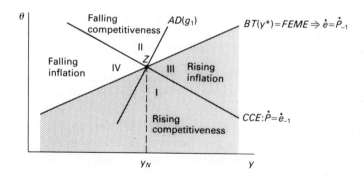

Fig. 14.12 Exchange rate expectations tied to BT = 0; unique equilibrium rate of unemployment

Figure 14.12 shows the diagram for (14.5). The space is divided up into zones I–IV in an exactly analogous way, with the unique equilibrium rate of unemployment fixed by y_N. An important difference between the two cases is that under the second assumption, since the BT = FEME line will shift with a change in world aggregate demand, y^*, the equilibrium rate of unemployment will be a function of y^*.

To conclude this section, it is sufficient to highlight once more the centrality of the issue of how exchange rate expectations are formed. If they are formed in a simple backward-looking way through a process of adaptive expectations such as has been described, then it is possible for the authorities to *choose* their desired employment level by selecting a point along the CCE. Only fiscal measures will be successful in securing a higher target employment rate, since exchange rate appreciation is required to reduce the claims on output per head of imports and enable competing-claims equilibrium to occur at higher output. The assumption of simple adaptive expectations implicitly excludes any feedback to the exchange rate from the deterioration in the current account which must accompany a fiscal expansion. We will return to the question of the pursuit of such a policy by *several* economies when policy interdependence is examined in Chapter 15.

By contrast, tying down exchange rate expectations to a real variable, be it a specific level of competitiveness or current account equilibrium, rules out the choice of any desired employment level along the CCE. The range of possible stable inflation outcomes is reduced to the single unemploy-ment rate associated with the intersection of CCE and FEME. If this is the exchange market behaviour that characterizes the economy, then the authorities will have to turn to policy tools that operate on the position of the CCE itself if they wish to move to a lower equilibrium rate of unemployment. These policies were discussed earlier in Chapter 13.

14.7 A Summary of the Floating Exchange Rate Models (Perfect Capital Mobility)

We can summarize the different models discussed in this chapter using the Salter–Swan diagram. The starting position is at point C. The original Mundell–Fleming result, of monetary policy having a strong impact on output but fiscal policy having no ultimate effect, rests on the change in the interest rate associated with a monetary versus fiscal expansion. The monetary expansion creates exchange rate depreciation by putting downward pressure on the interest rate. Thus the economy moves up the aggregate demand curve (AD' in Fig. 14.13) to a higher level of output as net exports rise: point A. Now reinterpret AD' as the result of a fiscal expansion. With a fiscal expansion, the exchange rate appreciates and the boost to demand from the higher government spending is offset as net exports are crowded out: the economy moves down AD' to point B. The assumption of adaptive exchange rate expectations means that there is no feedback to the exchange rate from the trade position—although the economy is in trade surplus at A and in deficit at B, there is no tendency in

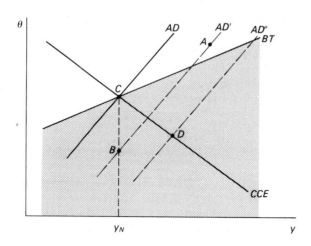

Fig. 14.13 Summary of the floating exchange rate models (perfect capital mobility)

Assumptions
  Initial position is C; monetary or fiscal expansion AD to AD'
Results
  Mundell–Fleming model: monetary expansion → point A
                fiscal expansion → point B
  Fiscalist model: monetary expansion → point C
                fiscal expansion → point D
  Section 14.6 model (i.e., real wage resistance and exchange rate expectations based on real factors):
                unique equilibrium output, y_N, at point C

the Mundell–Fleming model for the exchange rate to react to this. The assumption of fixed wages and prices means that there is no feedback from the real wage implied by the real exchange rate at point A or point B. At point A, real wages are much below the level of the bargained real wage associated with that level of unemployment (A lies well above the CCE). Similarly, at point B the real wage is above the level of the bargained real wage. By mapping the Mundell–Fleming case into the Salter–Swan diagram, the restrictive assumptions on which it is based are highlighted.

In the same way, we can look at the fiscalist model. In this case, a monetary expansion, by creating exchange rate depreciation and therefore pushing the real wage below the bargained real wage, leads to rising inflation as unions seek to secure w^B. The ensuing inflation depresses the real value of the money supply, offsets the expansionary effect of the policy, and produces the outcome of an unchanged output level (point C in Fig. 14.13). By contrast, a fiscal expansion creates exchange rate appreciation and therefore a rise in the real wage above the bargained real wage. Falling inflation feeds back to boost the real money supply and aggregate demand (AD″) and takes the economy to a position such as D. Although point D is on the CCE line, it lies well below the balance of trade line: the economy is in trade deficit. This highlights the fact that the fiscalist model rests on adaptive exchange rate expectations, which rules out any feedback from the trade position to the exchange rate and hence to inflation. If, as in the last sub-section, the expected exchange rate is tied to the trade balance, position D becomes untenable: the trade deficit would generate a depreciating exchange rate and, as a consequence, rising inflation. The economy would drift back toward point C.

14.8   Unique Equilibrium Rate of Unemployment or Asymmetry?

In the models producing a unique equilibrium rate of unemployment discussed in Section 14.6, although we concentrated on the problem of accelerating inflation if the authorities attempted to run the economy at a level of unemployment below the equilibrium rate, the assumption was that the model was symmetrical. In other words, the attempt to run the economy at unemployment *higher* than the equilibrium rate would see falling inflation as the exchange rate appreciated to eliminate the trade surplus. Unless the money supply declines in line with falling inflation, the level of demand would rise and the economy would move to the unique equilibrium rate. However, there is no compelling reason why the exchange rate should be expected to *appreciate* to eliminate a current account surplus. This is the exact parallel of the case discussed under fixed exchange rates where the economy may remain for much longer in a situation of surplus than in one of deficit.

Note that, in the world economy as a whole, to the extent that deficit countries are forced to move towards the equilibrium rate and eliminate the deficit, the corresponding surplus countries will find themselves also moving towards the equilibrium rate. If, as seems to be the case in reality, the USA is able to run a current account deficit much more easily than any other economy, then the possibility of asymmetry with a surplus economy such as West Germany able to remain with unemployment above the minimum achievable becomes explicable.

Thus, the assumption that exchange rate expectations are formed on the basis of the requirement for current account balance has some weight in pinning down the *lowest* attainable rate of unemployment the economy can achieve consistent with constant inflation and exchange market equilibrium. It does not, however, set an upper limit on equilibrium unemployment. As indicated in Fig. 14.14, a government may choose an unemployment rate associated with output levels to the left of y_N along the CCE. The economy can remain at a position such as A with constant inflation and a constant exchange rate. The output level, y_N, is associated with the *minimum* equilibrium rate of unemployment.

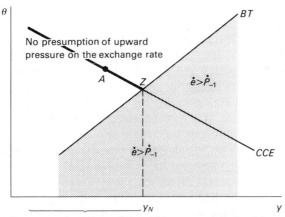

Any output level is consistent with constant inflation (along *CCE*).

Fig. 14.14 Asymmetry: non-unique equilibrium rates of unemployment for $U > U_N$, owing to the absence of the expectation of exchange rate appreciation when the current account is in surplus

Shaded area denotes trade deficit.

15

Further Open Economy Topics

In this chapter, we address a number of loosely connected problems which face policy-makers in the open economy: problems of exchange rate overshooting, the role of government policy in the formation of exchange rate expectations, the analysis of a raw materials price shock and of policy interdependence. We begin with the empirical puzzle of how to explain the large jumps in the exchange rate which appeared to accompany unanticipated changes in monetary policy in the 1970s and 1980s. Why did nominal exchange rates jump by much more than required to establish the new equilibrium level? This is the phenomenon of exchange rate 'overshooting' investigated first by Dornbusch (1976). It brings in both the issue of rational expectations of the exchange rate and the implications of the slower adjustment of wages and prices than of the exchange rate to a tightening of monetary policy.

We then move from concentrating on the formation of exchange rate expectations in an abstract way to the connection between the beliefs that agents have about government behaviour and the way they form their exchange rate expectations. We show that the course of the exchange rate can differ very sharply according to exchange market operators' views about the government's policy objectives.

The second part of the chapter concentrates on the relationship between the open economy and the world economy. Economic interdependence between nations has increased markedly since the end of the Second World War. One simple indicator of this is that world trade has grown much faster than output over this period. We will look first at the impact of a rise in the price of an essential raw material. Secondly, we turn to the consequences of policy interdependence, where we begin by outlining the Keynesian analysis of unilateral versus multilateral expansion. By defining the concept of the world equilibrium rate of unemployment, the shortcomings of the Keynesian analysis are highlighted.

15.1 Rational Exchange Rate Expectations: Dornbusch's Overshooting Model

Dornbusch (1976) wanted to investigate the implications for exchange rate behaviour of the differential pace of adjustment of the key markets in the economy to a change in monetary policy, on the assumption that expectations about the exchange rate are formed rationally. He looked at the realistic case where goods and labour markets react much more slowly to a change in monetary policy than does the foreign exchange market. Within a few years, his model was used to explain the *empirical* phenomenon that changes in monetary policy appeared to elicit much larger changes in the exchange rate than are justified by the new equilibrium price level.

As we saw in Section 14.6, there is a unique real money supply in equilibrium, say $\bar{m}$, because the LM curve must intersect $r = r^*$ at the equilibrium level of income, y_N. If, at the initial equilibrium, $\bar{m} = M_0 - P_0$ (working henceforth in logs of variables M, P, θ, and e), then a reduction of the money supply to M_1 (by 5%) implies an eventual fall in the price level by 5% to P_1. This in turn tells us what the new equilibrium (nominal) exchange rate must be since the equilibrium level of competitiveness (the so-called equilibrium *real* exchange rate, $\bar{\theta}$), will not have been altered by the nominal policy change. The initial equilibrium exchange rate is $e_0 = \bar{\theta} + P_0$. The new equilibrium exchange rate in the long run, after the fall in the money supply has fully worked itself out in a proportionate fall in prices, is $e_1 = \bar{\theta} + P_1$ and is therefore 5% below e_0: a 5% appreciation.

It has been argued that the rise in sterling in 1979 after the Conservative government adopted a tight monetary policy was very much greater than could be accounted for by the increase in the equilibrium value of the pound. This extra appreciation is called *overshooting* the new long-run equilibrium value. Dornbusch seeks to explain how exchange rate overshooting happens and how the exchange rate gradually returns to equilibrium. In order to do this, he assumes that

- exchange market expectations are formed rationally—or at least sensibly;
- the product and labour markets adjust slowly, with the result that the price falls to its new equilibrium value of P_1 only slowly.

He maintains that the existence of slow price adjustment (captured in the second assumption), in combination with a rapidly operating foreign exchange market, is responsible for creating overshooting.

The simple rational expectations way of forming the expectation of the exchange rate, e^E, is to work out the new equilibrium e; as we have seen, this falls (e appreciates) by the percentage drop in the money supply. Now, if there are rational expectations in all markets—product and labour as well as exchange—then this method of calculating e^E may indeed be rational and correct. The economy will jump immediately from point A to point D in the left-hand panel of Fig. 15.1 and there will have been no *real* change in the economic variables. (Points A and D coincide in the right-hand panel.) In other words, all nominal variables have changed proportionately. This must be equal to the long-run equilibrium position.

If, however, the price level adjusts slowly, and if exchange market participants are aware of this, then the economy will deviate in the short run from this long-run equilibrium position. A slow moving price level means that it is not rational for them to expect the exchange rate to appreciate at once by exactly the percentage fall in the money supply. Rather, they will expect a much larger immediate appreciation in order that the exchange rate will depreciate over the length of time for which the interest rate lies above the world interest rate. It is the sluggish adjustment of prices that is responsible for keeping the interest rate higher than the world rate. The importance of the Dornbusch result for policy-makers is that, in the period during which the exchange rate lies away from its equilibrium value, the economy experiences a fall in its real competitiveness.[1]

Rather than presenting Dornbusch's full analysis of overshooting (for which, see Dornbusch 1980), it is useful to give a flavour of the process by using a simple example. We take as our starting point the situation sketched above: the government cuts the money supply by 5% and, although the price level will eventually fall by 5%, it remains fixed for

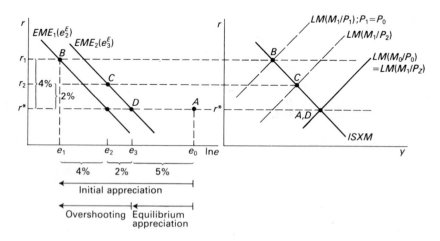

Fig. 15.1 Example of exchange rate overshooting

we return in ch. 19 to the possibility of lasting repercussions of overshooting. As Dornbusch has put it, 'A period of overvaluation or undervaluation thus changes the industrial landscape in a relatively permanent fashion' (1987a: 9).

period 1 and falls by 2.5% in period 2, arriving at the new equilibrium price only in period 3. To make things as simple as possible, we will assume that the ISXM remains fixed throughout, with the government adjusting its own expenditure to offset the demand effects arising from changes in competitiveness. This allows us to concentrate on the shifts in the LM curve—first as a result of the reduction in the money supply, and secondly in response to the changes in the price level. In the example below, it is assumed that the interest rate is pushed up by 4% as the result of the initial decline in the real value of the money supply. The magnitude of this effect obviously reflects the interest elasticity of the demand-for-money function.

The LM curve initially shifts sharply left, up the ISXM, pushing up the interest rate in period 1 by 4%, and raising unemployment so that in period 2 prices fall by 2.5%. This fall in prices partially restores the cut in the real money supply, so the interest rate falls from $r^* + 4\%$ to $r^* + 2\%$; in turn, unemployment moves some of the way back to its original level. In the next period, 3, there is a further fall in prices, so that prices have now fallen 5%, fully restoring the real money supply back to its original level, and hence re-establishing the original rate of interest, $r = r^*$, and original level of output and unemployment. It is this set of facts that exchange market operators can work out for themselves in period 1 as soon as they receive news that the nominal money supply has been cut by 5%.

Given the information in Table 15.1, it is straightforward to follow the calculations that will be made by dealers. The only trick is to see that they must work backwards from the situation that they expect to prevail from period 3 onwards in order to calculate their expectations of the exchange rate in period 2 so as to decide on their portfolio choice for period 1.

Table 15.1 An example of overshooting

Situation: 5% reduction in M from M_0 to M_1
Facts known to exchange market operators:
(a)   ISXM remains fixed at $ISXM_0$
(b)   Path of price level and interest rate:

Period	Price level	Interest rate
0	P_0	$r_0 = r^*$
1	$P_1 = P_0$	$r_1 = r^* + 4\%$
2	$P_2 = P_0 - 2.5\%$	$r_2 = r^* + 2\%$
3 onwards	$P_3 = P_0 - 5\%$	$r_3 = r^*$

Problem for exchange market operators: how will the exchange rate move in period 1?
Assumption: exchange market operators use all available information on which to base their portfolio decisions—they are equipped with *rational expectations*.

In period 3, the price level will have fallen by 5% to its new equilibrium value, and this means that the interest rate will once more equal the world interest rate. Hence the nominal exchange rate will be 5% below its original value (representing an appreciation of 5%). Competitiveness and output will be at their original levels. This fixes the position of the exchange market equilibrium line for period 2 (see $EME_2(e_3^E)$ in Fig. 15.1). *In period 2*, the partial adjustment of prices in response to lower employment in the economy means that the LM is at $LM(M_1/P_2)$ with the interest rate above the world rate at r_2. With an interest rate of r_2 and an expected exchange rate, e_3^E, the dealer can work out that the actual exchange rate in period 2 must be e_2 (the economy at point C). Since exchange rate expectations are formed rationally, this outturn for the exchange rate in period 2 must have been expected; i.e., $e_2^E = e_2$. This fixes the position of the exchange market equilibrium line for period 1 (see EME_1 (e_2^E) in Fig. 15.1). *In period 1*, with the interest rate equal to r_1 and with the exchange rate in period 2 expected to be e_2^E, the exchange rate must have jumped from e_0 to e_1.

Thus, the path travelled by the economy on the announcement of the reduction in the money supply is: from A to B to C to D. The initial appreciation of the exchange rate of 11% is considerably greater than the 5% that would have been predicted by calculation of the long-run equilibrium adjustment. An appreciation of 5% would have occurred in the short run only if rational expectations had been applied by foreign exchange operators in a world where product and labour markets were known to adjust immediately and fully to an announced policy change. Because the interest rate is expected to be above the world rate by 4% for a year and then by 2% for another year, the total expected depreciation of the pound must be equal to 6% for the exchange market arbitrage condition to hold. This is what accounts for the initial appreciation of 6% *in addition* to the equilibrium jump of 5%. Had the pound appreciated by any amount less than 11%, exchange market operators would have made abnormal profits, reaping a gain from holding sterling securities in excess of the expected foreign exchange loss.

This example suggests that the initial jump in the exchange rate depends on the length of time over which exchange market operators believe the interest rate will stay above the world rate. As we have seen, this depends crucially on the time taken for wage and price behaviour to adjust to the lower growth rate of the money supply. We have looked in detail earlier in the book at the very considerable time it may take for prices and wages to be adjusted downward in such a situation when price expectations are formed adaptively and wage negotiations occur only once a year. To illustrate, suppose that a reduction in the money supply of 5% produces a rise in the interest rate from the pre-existing level of 5% (equal to the world rate) to a level of 9% (Fig. 15.2). Each period, the interest rate falls

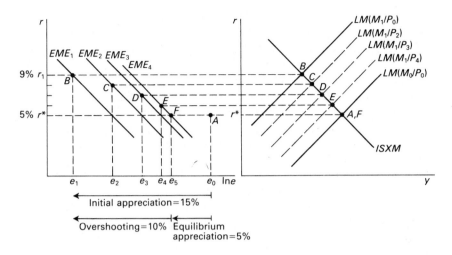

Fig. 15.2 Exchange rate overshooting: very slow price adjustment in response to tight monetary policy

just one percentage point, reflecting slowly adapting prices. Only in period 5 will the interest rate have fallen back to 5%. Cumulatively, the excess of the interest rate above the world level is 10%. Figure 15.2 shows the leap (appreciation) in the exchange rate in period 1 by 15%. This puts the exchange rate 10% points above the new equilibrium level, which is only an appreciation of 5%.

*15.2   Exchange Rate Expectations and Government Behaviour

Four ways of forming exchange rate expectations have been presented in Chapters 14 and 15: (1) the case of static expectations, where the expected exchange rate is assumed fixed at a specific nominal value, $e^E = e^T$; (2) adaptive expectations ($e^E = e_{-1}$); (3) a real anchor for the expected exchange rate, such as a specific level of competitiveness or the requirement for current account balance; and (4) the sophisticated rationality and knowledge implied by overshooting. The range of possibilities and lack of consensus about the appropriate way to model exchange rate expectations is bewildering. The problem is eased somewhat if we try to link up beliefs about government behaviour with expected exchange rate formation.

Suppose that it is believed that the government will raise or lower interest rates as necessary to maintain a target nominal exchange rate, $e = e^T$. Suppose further that in the current period, period 1, the exchange rate is equal to the target value and that this has been produced by setting $r_1 = r^* + e_2^E - e^T$. Now, what will e_2^E be if it is believed that the government will set r_2 such that $e_2 = e^T$? Obviously, the expected exchange rate for period 2 will equal the target: $e_2^E = e^T$. Similarly, for period 3, complete credibility of the government's policy will ensure that $e_3^E = e^T$. This means that any incipient rise in e_3^E as the result of fear of the effect of an external deficit on the market or on government behaviour will be neutralized by the belief in government policy. If the government is completely credible, then the expected exchange rate will always be equal to the target rate, with the result that the government will not have to raise the interest rate above the world rate. In such a case, $e^E = e^T$ will be a fully rational belief.

It is also possible to provide a justification for the assumptions that base exchange rate expectations on real factors. For example, the premise that the exchange rate is expected to move to a level at which there is current account balance can be justified if it is believed that the government itself will set r_2 so as to ensure that the exchange rate is sufficiently competitive to maintain external balance.

In general, however, foreign exchange market operators are unlikely to have any clear idea at all about government behaviour beyond at most a two- or three-year horizon. One way of modelling this is as follows. From, say, year 3 on, we assume the expected exchange rate will be some weighted average of the current exchange rate and what the exchange rate is expected to be in year 2. Specifically: we assume that the government embarks on an expansionary fiscal policy in period 1; there are firm beliefs about how it will behave in period 2; but uncertainty about what will happen from period 3 onwards.

Assumption 1: $e_3^E = \alpha e_2 + (1 - \alpha)e_0, 0 \le \alpha \le 1$.
This assumption reflects the view that, in conditions of uncertainty, people forming their expectation of the exchange rate in period 3, e_3^E, will attach some importance to the current exchange rate, e_0, and to what the exchange rate will be in period 2, e_2.
Assumption 2: Government reaction function.
(a): r_2 will be set to maintain a specific level of competitiveness, $\theta = \theta^T$. Let us call such government 'Socialist'. Such a government, in other words, will allow the exchange rate to change to maintain θ, rather than let unemployment rise.
(b): r_2 will be set to maintain the interest rate unchanged at r_1. Let us call such a government 'Conservative'. By contrast, this government will maintain the higher rate of interest.

We begin with the policy change in period 1: a fiscal expansion results in a rise in the interest rate from r_0 to r_1. The following statements hold:

$$r_1 - r^* = e_2^E - e_1$$
$$r_2 - r^* = e_3^E - e_2$$

$$e_3^E = \alpha e_2 + (1 - \alpha)e_0.$$

The question is, What happens to the exchange rate in period 1 relative to its initial level?

With rational expectations, we can assume that the expected exchange rate in period 2 is equal to the actual exchange rate in period 2:

$$e_2 = e_2^E.$$

If this is the case, then the exchange rate in period 1, e_1, is

$$e_1 = (r^* - r_1) + e_2^E,$$

and, using the above equations,

$$r_2 - r^* = e_3^E - e_2^E$$
$$e_3^E = \alpha e_2^E + (1 - \alpha)e_0.$$

Therefore

$$r_2 - r^* = [\alpha e_2^E + (1 - \alpha)e_0] - e_2^E$$
$$= (1 - \alpha)(e_0 - e_2^E);$$

hence

$$e_2^E - e^0 = [1/(1 - \alpha)](r^* - r_2). \tag{15.1}$$

Therefore

$$e_1 = (r^* - r_1) + e_0 + [1/(1 - \alpha)](r^* - r_2),$$

and the change in the exchange rate from period 0 is

$$\Delta e = (r^* - r_1) + [1/(1 - \alpha)](r^* - r_2).$$

15.2.1 'Socialist' Government

Let us look in turn at the implications of each of the government reaction functions, taking the 'Socialist' government first. The 'Socialist' government adopts a policy to ensure that the level of competitiveness remains fixed at the target level, θ^T. Assumption 2(a) implies that the interest rate in period 1 lies above the world rate as the result of the fiscal expansion, but that this must be followed in period 2 by an interest rate *below* the world rate; i.e.,

$$r_1 > r^* \text{ and } r_2 < r^*.$$

The reason that the interest rate must be below the world rate in the second period is that this is the only way that the government can secure its competitiveness target. The increase in government spending will have boosted output and exerted downward pressure on competitiveness through the effect of rising inflation.

At e_0, $\theta^T = e_0 - P_0$ and is at its target level. Now P_0 has risen; hence e_2 must be above e_0 to restore competitiveness to its target level. From (15.1) above, r_2 must be pushed below r^*. If we assume for simplicity that the magnitude of the interest rate deviations from the world rate are identical and equal to β, then

$$|r_2 - r^*| = |r_1 - r^*| = \beta. \tag{15.2}$$

Thus, using the expression for the change in the exchange rate in period 1 and substituting β,

$$\Delta e = -\beta + \beta/(1 - \alpha) = \beta[1/(1 - \alpha)] - 1 = \beta[\alpha/(1 - \alpha)] > 0.$$

In other words, if (15.2) holds, the exchange rate will *depreciate* in period 1, in spite of the initial rise in the interest rate. The known commitment of the government to hold competitiveness at θ produces an immediate depreciation, since exchange market operators work on the fact that the government would have to engineer a depreciation in period 2 if they were to achieve their competitiveness target. As less and less weight is placed on the original level of the exchange rate in forming the expected exchange rate in period 3 ($\alpha \to 1$), the depreciation of the exchange rate in period 1 becomes greater.

15.2.2 'Conservative' Government

We turn to the alternative government policy reaction function, which we have dubbed 'Conservative'. The 'Conservative' government will set policy so that the interest rate in period 2 is exactly the same as in the first period. Assumption 2(b) implies that $r_1 > r^*$ owing to the fiscal expansion and $r_2 = r_1$. If we substitute $r_1 = r_2$ into the Δe expression above, we get

$$\Delta e = (r^* - r_1) + [1/(1 - \alpha)](r^* - r_1)$$
$$= [(2 - \alpha)/(1 - \alpha)](r^* - r_1) < 0,$$

since $0 < \alpha < 1$ and $r^* < r_1$. The exchange rate *appreciates* in period 1. As less and less weight is placed on the original level of the exchange rate in the formation of exchange rate expectations ($\alpha \to 1$), the appreciation in period 1 will become greater.

In the above example, it has been shown that uncertainty about the future combined with two alternative government reaction functions produces the 'rational expectation' of very different levels of the exchange rate in the period subsequent to a fiscal expansion. The result is that one reaction function is associated with an immediate depreciation of the exchange rate; the other with an immediate appreciation. Perhaps examples suggestive of each type of reaction would be the Mitterrand fiscal expansion of 1981, which produced exchange rate depreciation (Sachs and Wyplosz 1985), and the Reagan fiscal expansion in 1982, which produced exchange rate appreciation (Sachs 1985).

15.3 The Impact of a Raw Materials Price Shock

In the last section some of the implications for the national economy of the burgeoning international market in financial assets have been investigated. Here we return to the real side of the economy, looking at the implications of an external shock in the form of higher prices for essential raw materials. Such a price shock will affect the distribution of income at the international level with the result that, at least in the short run, demand in the domestic economy is affected. Secondly, there will be a cost effect of the rise in raw materials prices. The question is, Who bears the cost, and what are the implications for employment?

Great interest in the analysis of the impact of raw materials price shocks on the economy was generated by the commodity price boom of the early 1970s, the two oil price shocks of 1973 and 1979, and the fall in oil prices in the mid-1980s.[2] In general terms, for an economy that imports raw materials, a rise in the world price of those materials imposes an exogenous deterioration in the terms of trade for the economy. For a given level of employment and competitiveness, this means, *ceteris paribus*, that imports take a large share of output per head.

The competing-claims approach to the operation of labour and product markets provides an insight into the alternative adjustments of the economy to the increased claim from imported materials. For the economy to continue to operate at the same level of employment, the increase in the share of imported materials in output per head must be offset by a reduction in real wages or a reduction in real profits (or a combination of the two). The only other alternative is if the externally imposed deterioration in the terms of trade is reversed by the marking up of the higher import costs in export prices; this implies a fall in competitiveness. The assumption that wage bargaining occurs along the BRW curve means that workers will secure compensation in money wage rises for the rise in prices associated with the price shock. Hence, unless the BRW can be shifted through, for example, the negotiation of an incomes policy, it will be either profits or competitiveness that bears the brunt of the increased raw materials costs.

On our standard assumption of mark-up pricing for exports, profit margins will be protected by the marking up of the higher materials costs. Thus the downward shift of the CCE reflects the lower level of competitiveness consistent with a given output level. If, on the other hand, exports are priced by the level of world prices (as in Section 11.5), then exporters will be unable to pass on their increased costs in their prices, with the result that their profits will be reduced. The lower θ associated with any

---

[2] Bruno and Sachs (1985) provide a detailed theoretical and empirical analysis of the impact of the oil shocks on the OECD economies.

level of output (the post-shock CCE) then represents the lower profits of exporters at each level of output and the associated lower level of non-price competitiveness.

In terms of the Salter–Swan diagram (Fig. 15.3), an exogenous rise in the cost of imported materials has the effects outlined in the box. In summary, such a rise implies

1 a downward shift of the CCE curve (from CCE to CCE′ (post-shock)) because of the fall in the price-determined real wage associated with each level of competitiveness;
2 a simultaneous leftward shift of the BT curve as, on the one hand, higher prices of imports have to be paid for by more competitive exports and, on the other hand, the level of world aggregate demand will have fallen;
3 a leftward shift in the AD curve, for two reasons:
   (a) as the result of the fall in world aggregate demand: y^* will have fallen because of the redistribution of income at an international level from raw materials importing to exporting countries; at least in the short run, the world propensity to save will rise as raw materials producers are unable to spend their additional revenues;
   (b) because a higher proportion of income is absorbed by expenditure on imports and hence is diverted away from expenditure on domestically produced goods.

Figure 15.3 shows the implications of the shock: originally the economy could remain at point Z with output y_N; in the wake of the shock, the sustainable position for the economy is at the lower output level y'_N (post-shock).

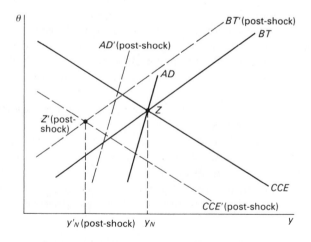

Fig. 15.3 The impact of an increase in the world price of raw materials

The Effects of Higher Raw Materials Prices on CCE, BT, and AD

(1) CCE: Assuming for simplicity that all imports are of raw materials and that the prices of domestic output including exports are set on a mark-up basis,

$$P = mP + \frac{W}{LP} + \frac{1}{\tau}\frac{P^*e}{MP},$$

where $P_m = P^*_{rm}e = (1/\tau)(P^*e)$ where P^*_{rm} is the world price index for raw materials (in dollars) and τ is the world terms of trade between manufactures and raw materials: $\tau = P^*/P^*_{rm}$. Hence, the price-determined real wage, w^P, is

$$w^P = LP(1 - m) - \frac{\theta}{\tau}\frac{LP}{MP}.$$
[price-determined real wage]

Any fall in τ as the result of a rise in world raw materials prices lowers the price-determined real wage for each value of θ. This implies a leftward shift of the CCE to CCE (post-shock). (For instance, at a given level of output and employment, a specific level of competitiveness and of the real wage is implied; after the shock, the same real wage implies via the PRW, a lower level of competitiveness.)

(2) BT: The inclusion of the world terms of trade between manufactures and raw materials enters the balance of trade equation straightforwardly through the definition of imports, and the level of world aggregate demand is shown explicitly as a (positive) function of τ:

$$BT = x - m$$

$$= \sigma(\theta)y^*(\tau) - \frac{\theta}{\tau}m_y(\theta)y. \text{ [trade balance]}$$

For $BT = 0$, a lower τ as the result of a rise in world raw materials prices will require a lower level of domestic output, y. The BT line shifts to the left.

(3) AD: Assuming perfect capital mobility, planned expenditure y^D is

$$y^D = c_y y + i(r^*) + g + \sigma(\theta)y^*(\tau) - \frac{\theta}{\tau}m_y(\theta)y.$$

Goods market equilibrium requires

$$y = \frac{1}{1 - c_y + (\theta/\tau)m_y(\theta)} \left[i(r^*) + g + \sigma(\theta)y^*(\tau) \right].$$

[ISXM/LM]

A lower τ reduces the size of the multiplier because of the increase in $(\theta/\tau)m_y(\theta)$, the propensity to import, and lowers exports at each level of competitiveness because of the fall in y^*: the AD line shifts to the left.

With an unchanged domestic demand management stance, the economy will move from the original aggregate demand curve to a point on AD' (post-shock). At the level of output at A, y_1, the post-shock price-determined real wage lies below the bargained real wage, reflecting the higher claim of imported materials (see Fig. 15.4, where $w^P(y_1) < w^B(y_1)$). Higher wage claims will be submitted. The precise pattern of developments at A will depend on the exchange rate regime. Under fixed

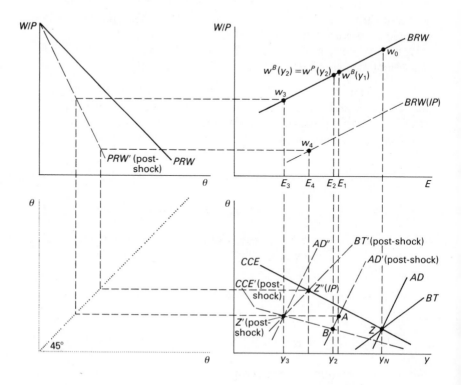

Fig. 15.4 Policy options in the face of a raw materials price shock

exchange rates, competitiveness is falling at A with the result that the economy moves along the new aggregate demand curve to point B on the CCE' (post-shock). At B there is a trade deficit which can be removed only by the implementation of a tighter fiscal stance, taking the economy to Z' (post-shock). With floating exchange rates and either with zero capital mobility or with exchange rate expectations tied to the trade balance, the economy experiences accelerating inflation at A (assuming an accommodating monetary policy); the government will have to tighten demand to shift to the new equilibrium rate of unemployment at higher unemployment (Z' (post-shock)).

Regardless of exchange rate regime and of the specific determinants of the expected exchange rate, to the extent that price- and wage-setting behaviour is represented by the CCE curve, there will be a unique new underlying *sustainable* level of output and associated rate of unemployment at Z'(post-shock), i.e. at the intersection of the post-shock CCE and post-shock BT lines. Given this constraint, let us consider three contrasting policy responses by the government to the raw materials shock:

1 the government uses its aggregate demand tools to protect employment;
2 the government uses its aggregate demand tools to maintain the trade balance and to eliminate the inflationary pressure;
3 the government negotiates an incomes policy which, when combined with an appropriate aggregate demand policy, enables it to minimize the damage to employment.

The first policy reflects the exclusive concentration of the government on the deflationary implications of the raw materials price shock. It raises domestic demand so as to return the aggregate demand curve to its original position. However, this policy sees a widening of the trade deficit and an increase in inflationary pressure. Such a policy is clearly unsustainable. The economy is at a point such as Z, whereas the new sustainable position is Z' (post-shock).

The second policy reflects the concern of the authorities with the balance of payments implications of the shock. The government tightens its domestic policy stance to take the economy to the new sustainable position at Z' (post-shock), by shifting AD leftwards to AD". Trade balance is restored and inflationary pressure eliminated. However, the economy suffers from considerably higher unemployment and lower real wages (see Fig. 15.4, where the real wage at Z' (post-shock) is w_3 as compared with the original real wage of w_0).

The third policy reflects the attempt of the authorities to attain the most favourable position in terms of employment along the new BT' (post-shock) curve. They negotiate an incomes policy (IP) to shift the CCE to the right. Let us suppose that they are able to gain agreement to a downward shift in the bargaining curve (BRW) sufficient to take the CCE back to its original position. This will enable the attainment of the sustainable position $Z''(IP)$ with balanced trade (Fig. 15.4). Real wages will have been sharply reduced to w_4 but unemployment is lower than under option 2.

In the light of our discussion in Chapter 8 of wage-bargaining institutions, it would be expected that different economies would show different reactions to a raw materials price shock. For example, in an economy with highly centralized bargaining, an exogenous deterioration in the terms of trade would be interpreted as *requiring* a downward shift in the bargained real wage if the level of employment consistent with constant inflation was to be maintained.[3]

15.4 Policy Interdependence and the World Equilibrium Rate of Unemployment

In the years of slower growth since 1973, the issue of the interdependence of policy-making within the industrialized economies has become a pressing one. Starting from a generalization of Keynesian ideas to the international level, it was argued that, whereas economies may be *individually* constrained from expanding because of their external position, a concerted expansion would overcome the constraint. The argument for a concerted expansion arose from the simple idea that balance of payments equilibrium for a system of economies as a whole can occur at many different levels of activity. If the system as a whole is operating at a low level of activity with high rates of unemployment, then welfare would be improved by shifting to another equilibrium at lower unemployment. However, for each economy operating individually, a policy of expansion is not possible because of a balance of payments constraint.

The simplest case to consider is where all n identical economies in the system are initially in current account equilibrium but with unemployment higher than desired. For simplicity, we assume zero capital mobility and fixed exchange rates. Economy A is constrained from expanding because this would produce an unsustainable current account deficit as its imports rose faster than exports. Each economy is in the same position, with the result that none expands. Had they undertaken a co-ordinated expansion, unemployment in all economies would have been reduced and payments equilibrium maintained as demand for each economy's exports rose in line with its imports. This is the essence of the international Keynesian approach to the co-ordination of macroeconomic policy.

---

[3] We return in ch. 17 to the issue of the implications of the *steepness* of the BRW for the equilibrium unemployment impact of supply shocks; there are some reasons to believe that steepness is related to the centralization of wage-bargaining institutions.

However, we will see that the international Keynesian approach provides only a partial analysis of the problem. The key omission is the role of price- and wage-setting. Let us consider economy A again and assume that, in line with all other economies, it is initially in external equilibrium with constant competitiveness; i.e., it is at output level y_0^A at the intersection of the BT and the CCE lines (point 1 in Fig. 15.5).

With a unilateral expansion, we know from Chapter 11 that the economy will move along the CCE line to a point such as 2 as competitiveness is lowered by the inflationary pressure associated with a higher level of output. The problem for economy A is that at point 2, while there is constant inflation, there is a trade deficit. Now, the international Keynesian analysis steps in to suggest that a co-ordinated expansion would eliminate the trade deficit since world trade, y^*, would rise and the BT line would shift rightwards. However, if all economies in the system expand together, it will be impossible for economy A's competitiveness to decline relative to the others. In other words, competitiveness must remain constant at θ_0^A with the result that the position of trade balance is now at point 3. But a glance at Fig. 15.5 shows immediately that point 3 lies above the CCE line and represents a position of inflationary pressure in the labour market, since

$$w^B(y_2) > w^P(\theta_0).$$

At point 3, in economy A money wages will rise by the percentage gap between the bargained real wage and the price determined real wage with $\theta = \theta_0$. Assuming that pre-existing inflation is zero, we have wage inflation;

$$\dot{W} = \text{gap}.$$

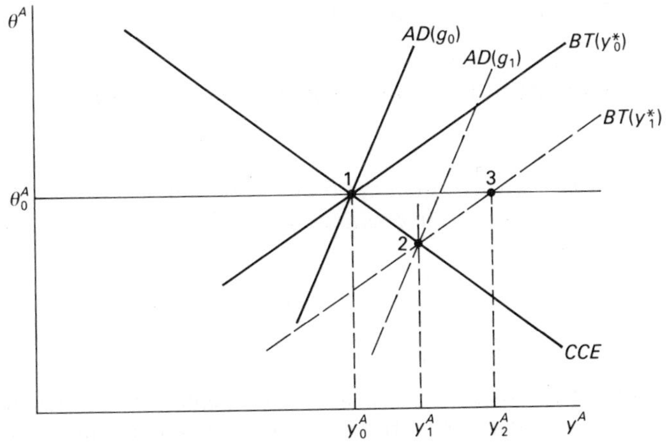

Fig. 15.5 Concerted expansion: trade balance but accelerating inflation at point 3

Prices will rise according to $\dot{P} = \alpha \dot{W} + (1 - \alpha)\dot{P}^*$, assuming constant labour productivity, and where α is the share of labour costs in total unit costs. In each of the other economies, wages and prices and hence $\dot{P}^*$ will be rising according to the same rules with the result for A:

$$\dot{P} = \alpha \dot{W} + (1 - \alpha)\dot{P}^*$$

$$= \alpha \times \text{gap} + (1 - \alpha)[\alpha \times \text{gap} + (1 - \alpha)(\alpha \times \text{gap} + \ldots)]$$

$$= \{1/[1 - (1 - \alpha)]\}(\alpha \times \text{gap})$$

$$= \text{gap} = \dot{W}.$$

In other words, in economy A and elsewhere, price inflation will be equal to wage inflation, with the result that the gap between the bargained real wage and the price-determined real wage will not be reduced. In the next period, with $\dot{P}^E = \dot{P}_{-1}$, money wages will rise by $\dot{P}_{-1} + \text{gap}$. Prices will rise by the same amount. Economy A and all the other economies are in a situation of accelerating inflation. Thus, the effect of the co-ordinated expansion has been to take the *system of economies* from a position of stable inflation to one of accelerating inflation. In the initial situation the system was at the 'world equilibrium rate of unemployment'. In the new situation, unemployment has been pushed down below the world equilibrium rate of unemployment with the result of accelerating inflation throughout the system. Although the economies are in balance of payments equilibrium in the new situation, it is not a stable position because of the rising inflation.

The following section provides a more formal diagrammatic demonstration of the accelerating inflation consequent on a co-ordinated expansion when the 'world' is initially at an equilibrium rate of unemployment. It also gives a particularly sharp illustration of the partial nature of the international Keynesian analysis.

*15.4.1   The Limits to International Policy Co-ordination

The Keynesian Approach

Let us begin with the Keynesian approach in its simplest form. We assume a two-economy system with economies A and B. For each economy, planned expenditure is

$$y^A = c_y y^A + g^A + x^A - m^A y^A$$

$$y^B = c_y y^B + g^B + x^B - m^B y^B,$$

where to minimize subscripts the common propensity to consume is c_y; superscripts A and B refer to the economies A and B; and g stands for autonomous spending. In a closed two economy system, the exports of A must be the imports of B and vice versa; i.e.,

$$x^A = m^B y^B$$

and

$$x^B = m^A y^A.$$

Thus, for goods market equilibrium, we have

$$y^A = \frac{1}{1 - c_y + m^A} (g^A + m^B y^B) \qquad [\text{AD}^A]$$

$$y^B = \frac{1}{1 - c_y + m^B} (g^B + m^A y^A) \qquad [\text{AD}^B]$$

In Fig. 15.6, the aggregate demand lines depicting goods market equilibrium for each country are shown in a diagram that has the output of economy A on the vertical axis and that of B on the horizontal axis.

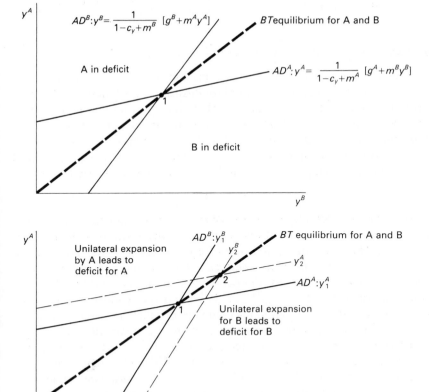

Fig. 15.6 Concerted expansion, leading to a new balanced trade equilibrium at point 2

We can also show the line representing balance of trade equilibrium for the two countries. This is defined by the balanced trade equations for each country:

$$BT^A = 0 \Rightarrow x^A = m^A y^A, \qquad \text{and by definition, } x^A = m^B y^B$$

$$BT^B = 0 \Rightarrow x^B = m^B y^B, \qquad \text{and by definition, } x^B = m^A y^A.$$

Therefore $m^A y^A = m^B y^B$, and in $y^A - y^B$ space (Fig. 15.6) balanced trade for *both* economies is defined by the line

$$y^A = (m^B/m^A)(y^B). \qquad \text{[BT equilibrium]}$$

With the initial levels of autonomous spending, g, the two-economy system is in balance of trade equilibrium at y_1^A and y_1^B (point 1 in Fig. 15.6). If both economies undertake an expansionary policy, the AD lines will shift outwards and the system will be in a new trade equilibrium at y_2^A, y_2^B (point 2 in Fig. 15.6).

Is There a Unique World Equilibrium Rate of Unemployment?

We can incorporate the competing-claims constraint for each country into the same diagram that we have used to illustrate the Keynesian argument. As noted earlier, the key difference when moving from the consideration of policies for a single economy to an economic system is that it is not possible for all economies in a system to lower (or raise) their competitiveness simultaneously. We can illustrate this in Fig. 15.7. In a two-economy system, $\theta^A = 1/\theta^B$, and if we take logs of both sides, we get

$$\ln \theta^A = -\ln \theta^B.$$

This provides a definitional relationship between competitiveness in the two countries: the system must be on this line (the north-west quadrant) at all times. The competing claims lines for each economy are shown in the north-east (for A) and south-west (for B) quadrants. Combined with the definitional relationship, the two CCEs define the world CCE in the south-east quadrant (see Fig. 15.7). Points on the world CCE show the only combinations of output in the countries at which inflation is constant. For example, when output is high in economy A, competitiveness is low and real wages are high. But this requires that in B competitiveness be high and real wages, low. Points on the world CCE line represent world equilibrium rates of unemployment, i.e. the various combinations of unemployment in the two countries which are consistent with constant inflation.

The remaining task is to show why a concerted expansion by the two economies which takes the system to the south-east of the world CCE (and to a new balanced trade position) implies that there will be accelerating

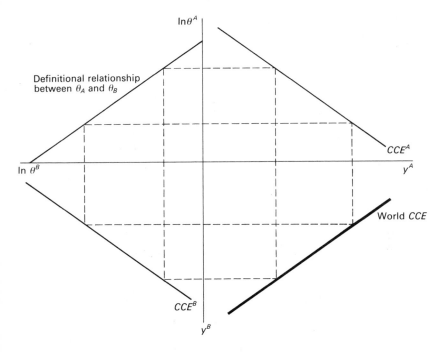

Fig. 15.7 Constructing the world competing-claims equilibrium line

inflation in each economy and that inflation in each economy will be the same. Let us begin at point 1 outside the world CCE line (Fig. 15.8). From the definitional relationship, this is consistent with a pair of points such as the point 1^A *inside* A's CCE and point 1^B outside B's CCE. In this situation inflation in A is *falling*, while it is rising in B. We can show, however, that the economies will move from points 1^A and 1^B to a position of accelerating inflation in both economies at points $2^A, 2^B$.

Looking first at economy A at point 1^A, we see that inflation in A is falling. Since it is rising in B, A's competitiveness is rising and economy A is moving upwards as shown by the arrows. Simultaneously, B's competitiveness is falling and it moves rightward. The critical point is that A reaches CCE^A *before* B reaches CCE^B. This is because both A and B cannot be inside CCE^A and CCE^B respectively, and outside the world CCE at a point such as 1. Once A crosses its CCE, its inflation is rising but still less fast than is B's. Thus A's competitiveness continues to increase. This will go on until point $2^A, 2^B$ is reached when inflation in each economy is identical. Competitiveness is then constant, and in each economy we have $\dot{P}^A > \dot{P}^B_{-1}$ and $\dot{P}^B > \dot{P}^A_{-1}$. Thus, any position to the south-east of the world CCE is associated eventually with accelerating inflation: the system has been pushed to a rate of unemployment below the world equilibrium rate of unemployment. Hence the adoption of an

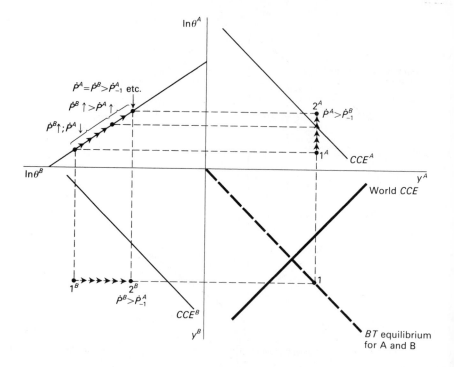

Fig. 15.8 The limits to concerted expansion

international Keynesian-style co-ordinated expansion which takes the system to point 1 is unsustainable because it is associated with accelerating inflation.

*Rolling Back the Limits: Co-ordinated Incomes Policies and Co-ordinated Aggregate Demand Management

This gloomy assessment can be reversed if the governments of both A and B can agree appropriate incomes policies. This can be shown simply using Fig. 15.9. With the new world CCE shown by CCE(IP), economies A and B can now move to point 2 by increasing aggregate demand in a co-ordinated manner. How difficult might the negotiations of such incomes policies be? Obviously, a major problem is that a requirement for sustaining incomes policies is the existence of sufficiently strong macro and micro industrial relations systems. Such systems exist only in certain countries.

Let us leave the institutional problem to one side. It is important to note that the wage restraint that is required is simply that the real wage remains constant as unemployment falls. And, if labour productivity rises as

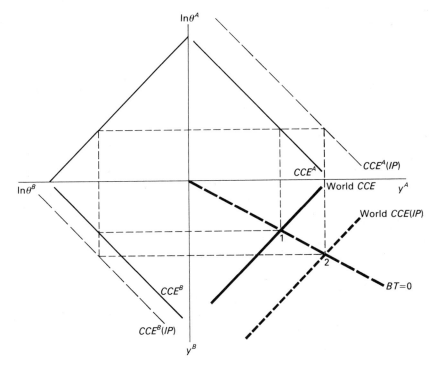

Fig. 15.9 Co-ordinated incomes policies and co-ordinated aggregate demand policies, enabling lower world equilibrium unemployment to be achieved at point 2

unemployment falls, then the requirement is yet weaker: the real wage can rise in line with labour productivity.

The limited nature of the requirement is evident once we see what the wage restraint is needed for. The need is to hold competitiveness constant as output in economies A and B rises. Constant competitiveness requires a constant real wage; not a declining one. Note the contrast here with the situation of *unilateral* expansion by one of the economies; in that case, as we have seen in Section 11.3, because of the tightening of the external constraint, a *rise* in competitiveness is required and hence a fall in real wages.

PART IV

Macroeconomic Models, Stylized Facts, and Microeconomic Foundations

16

Macroeconomic Models and the Stylized Facts of Macro Performance

The task of this brief chapter is to confront macroeconomic models with some stylized facts of macroeconomic performance, some of which have become especially evident in the 1970s and 1980s. It serves both as a conclusion to the first three parts of the book and as an introduction to the fourth part. In short, we argue that the imperfect competition model built up in Parts II and III provides a fairly good starting point for accounting for the stylized facts. It will be suggested that it provides a better basis than either of the other two major directions of research effort in macroeconomics which were identified in part I: the New Classical macroeconomics and the non-Walrasian equilibrium rationing approach of Malinvaud. In other words, the imperfect competition model can be seen as a way of addressing the key issues in macroeconomic analysis which existed at the outset of the 1980s: 'In the early 1980s, the Keynesian view of business cycles was in trouble. The problem was not new empirical evidence against Keynesian theories, but weakness in the theories themselves' (Ball *et al.* 1988: 1).

There is not the scope in this book to conduct a thoroughgoing empirical analysis or survey of macroeconomic behaviour. Rather, we will rely on the device of presenting a set of 'stylized facts'. We conclude that the imperfect competition model goes quite some way to providing a consistent explanation for these stylized facts. There are nevertheless aspects of macroeconomic behaviour that require further development of the model. Part IV is devoted to examining recent research on two major issues that arise: the so-called persistence or hysteresis of the unemployment rate, and the relationship between unemployment performance and wage-bargaining institutions. In addition, it pursues the question of the microeconomic foundations of the basic wage and price relationships underlying the imperfect competition model.

16.1　Six Stylized Facts of Macro Behaviour in Contemporary Industrialized Economies

Stylized fact (i)　There is no strong pattern in the movement of the real wage over the business cycle. However, there is some tendency for the real wage to rise as output and employment rise, i.e. for real wages to be procyclical.

Stylized fact (ii)　A large proportion of unemployment in the 1980s is involuntary and cannot be explained either in terms of mistaken expectations about the rate of inflation or monetary growth, or in terms of search activity.

Stylized fact (iii)　Firms generally would like to produce more if the real wage remained constant. They are constrained in their output by the level of aggregate demand.

Stylized fact (iv)　Changes in nominal aggregate demand provoke changes in quantity, i.e. of output and employment, in the same direction, and only subsequently changes in prices and wages.

Stylized fact (v)　Shifts in unemployment arising from changes in aggregate demand do not roll back to their original level, or do so only very slowly. This is because a rise (say) in unemployment above the equilibrium rate of unemployment does not produce permanently falling inflation—and hence does not produce eventual increases in aggregate demand. Approximately constant inflation is observed at many different rates of unemployment.

Stylized fact (vi)　There is a range of unemployment rates across countries in the 1980s which appears to be related to bargaining structures. There is a dispute about measuring bargaining structures, but one influential view is that low equilibrium unemployment seems to be attainable with either a highly centralized system of wage bargaining or with very decentralized wage-setting.

16.1.1　The Malinvaud–Keynesian Model and the Stylized Facts

The Malinvaud–Keynesian model presented in Chapter 5 above is consistent with the first four stylized facts, as long as the economy is in a state of Keynesian unemployment. Let us go through each 'fact' in turn.

(i) Real Wages over the Cycle

In *Keynes*'s original model, he derived *counter*-cyclical real wages; in recession, with a rigid nominal wage, the real wage rises above the market-clearing level as prices fall to clear the goods market. There is therefore a fall in employment associated with a rise in the real wage. Similarly, in a boom, the real wage will fall and employment will rise; prices rise in response to higher demand, and with a rigid money wage, the real wage falls.

However, as we have seen in Chapter 5, an economy characterized by Keynesian unemployment in the Malinvaud model will operate rather differently. Suppose we begin at a position such as A in Fig. 16.1 with a real wage W_0/P_0 and employment of E_0. If we ask what happens in response to a rise in aggregate demand (the EAD shifts to EAD_1), then in the Malinvaud model the real wage remains constant (by assumption) and the economy moves to higher employment of E_1. Employment rises because firms find it profitable to expand their output at the given real wage. Hence the model is consistent with the finding that there is no strong relationship between real wages and employment as output changes: if employment changes because of a change in aggregate demand, then no relationship will be found between the real wage and employment.[1]

(ii), (iii) Involuntary Unemployment and Rationing in the Product Market

In the regime of Keynesian unemployment there is always involuntary

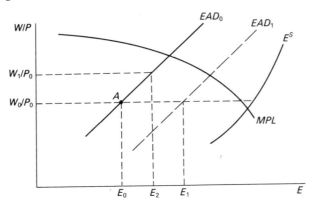

Fig. 16.1 The cyclical pattern of real wages in the Malinvaud model

[1] Note that the Malinvaud model is capable of explaining *pro*-cyclical real wages in the case where there is an exogenous rise in the real wage. There is an upward-sloping EAD schedule, reflecting the positive effect of a change in the real wage on aggregate demand because of the greater propensity to spend out of wage income than out of profit income. From position A in Fig. 16.1, a rise in the real wage will produce a movement upward and to the right along the EAD_0 curve with employment rising as the result of the higher consumption demand associated with the rise in the real wage. There is no supply-side constraint on the move to higher employment since the real wage W_1/P_0 still remains below the marginal product of labour. However, it is unlikely that Malinvaud would wish to suggest that cyclical employment fluctuations are the *consequence* of exogenous changes in real wages.

unemployment and the rationing of firms. Unemployed workers are constrained from gaining employment by the lack of jobs available; firms are unable to increase employment because of the lack of demand for the output that they would produce. A position such as A lies to the left of both the labour supply curve and the marginal product of labour schedule.

(iv) Quantity rather than Price Responses to Nominal Aggregate Demand Changes

By assumption, money wages and prices are held constant. Thus, a change in aggregate demand evokes a quantity response.

Although the Malinvaud–Keynesian model is *consistent* with the first four of the stylized facts, there is no explanation of why individuals and firms, who are assumed to be operating under competitive conditions, behave as they do. Why do individuals and firms feel quantity-constrained if their individual contribution to a perfectly competitive market is atomistic? How did the money wage and the price get set? Finally, the model does not itself provide an answer to the question of why the regime of Keynesian unemployment should be more likely than any other regime.

16.1.2   The New Classical Macroeconomic Model and the Stylized Facts

This approach suffers from exactly the opposite problems to Malinvaud–Keynes. The microeconomic behaviour on which the model relies is quite consistent with the assumption of perfect competition. However, the New Classical model (NCM) does not appear to be able to provide a coherent explanation of many of the stylized facts.

(i) Real Wages over the Cycle

In the models that were precursors to the NCM—such as Friedman's model—the prediction was that real wages were *counter*-cyclical. Shifts in aggregate demand produced shifts in the labour supply curve in the same direction, reflecting misperception on the part of workers. The labour supply curve would, in the face of a positive demand shock, shift to the right and the real wage would fall; the economy would move down the labour demand curve (the marginal product of labour).

In the simple New Classical model presented in Chapter 4, anticipated changes in nominal aggregate demand *do not* cause changes in employment, because the existence of rational expectations prevents misperceptions occurring on the part of workers and therefore keeps output and employment at the natural rate. If there are unanticipated changes in aggregate demand, then the NCM predicts counter-cyclical real wages since the model temporarily operates just like Friedman's.

However, there are New Classical models of the business cycle which argue that cycles arise from *shifts in the labour demand curve*. To the extent that this is so, procyclical real wages can be expected. (Figure 16.2 compares the effect of shifts in the effective labour supply curve and in the labour demand curve.) Shifts in the labour demand curve are suggested as arising, say from autonomous shifts in technology. For example, a positive shock to technology shifts the labour demand curve to the right and raises employment, output, and real wages. However, such models (e.g. Kydland and Prescott 1982) have not been able to explain the size of the technological shocks that are presumed to have led to business cycles in reality, nor to give an explanation for the symmetrical negative shifts in the labour demand curve necessary to explain downward cyclical movements (Hoover 1988: 48–52). Furthermore, 'real equilibrium business cycle' models of this kind have not been able to explain the empirical correlation between fluctuations in money and output.

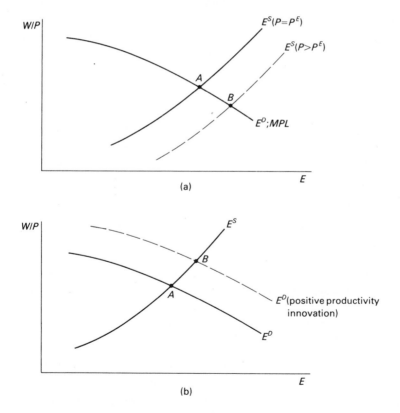

Fig. 16.2 Cyclical real wage patterns in New Classical models
(a) Counter-cyclical real wages from a 'monetary shock'
(b) Pro-cyclical real wages from a 'real shock'

To conclude, the standard New Classical model and NCM monetary business cycle models predict counter-cyclical real wages. Although alternative theories within the New Classical paradigm have been developed which suggest procyclical real wages, there are serious problems in accepting them as descriptions of observed cyclical fluctuations in output and employment.

(ii), (iii), (iv) Involuntary Unemployment and Rationing in the Product Market; Quantity rather than Price Responses to Aggregate Demand Changes

At the core of the New Classical macroeconomics is the clearing of markets and the full use of available information by all agents. Only unanticipated shocks will lead to a deviation of employment and output from their natural rates. Observed unemployment is identified as voluntary; individuals have chosen to engage in search activities and/or leisure. An anticipated change in aggregate demand has an immediate effect on prices and no effect on output and employment. The assumption of rational expectations strictly limits the extent to which there can be temporary deviations from the natural rate in response to changes in aggregate demand: only unanticipated shocks have real effects.

Once again, the new classicals have built so-called 'monetary equilibrium business cycle' models to account for the observed cyclical fluctuations in output apparently arising from demand shocks. The models are based on the idea that *random* demand shocks can generate cycles in output and employment as the result of limitations on the information-processing capacities of individual agents. Hoover discusses Lucas's 1975 model as a paradigm of this approach (1988: 40–2). The fluctuations in output in the model arise because firms are unable to separate out changes in real demand for their product from changes in aggregate demand arising from a monetary shock. Thus, nominal shocks are accompanied by real changes. These quantity effects persist through time because of the investment decisions made by firms on the basis of such imperfect information.

But note that employment fluctuations that occur in such models do not *unemployment.* At all times, workers are optimizing; reservation wage equal to the marginal disutility of s exceeds all wage offers then they are voluntarily the New Classical models cannot explain is 'the real re sometimes being a pool of qualified workers who are obs that currently pay wages at rates that they would ame time those wage rates showing no tendency to fall'

16.2   The Imperfect Competition Model and the Stylized Facts

In Part II above, the perfectly competitive microfoundations of the Malinvaud–Keynesian model were put aside. We outlined how wages and prices are set under imperfect competition and how quantities are set. With imperfectly competitive microfoundations, it is also straightforward to show why there is generally involuntary unemployment of a 'Keynesian' type when unemployment is at the equilibrium rate. However, it should be noted that the meaning of Keynesian unemployment as defined by Malinvaud is not clear once real wages are endogenous as they are in the imperfect competition model; the relevant point is that, at the equilibrium rate of unemployment in the imperfect competition model, there is the 'Keynesian unemployment' combination of involuntary unemployment (employment is less than the labour supply at the prevailing real wage) and firms that are 'rationed' (employment is less than the level associated with the marginal product of labour curve at the prevailing real wage).

16.2.1   Persistent Involuntary Unemployment in Equilibrium

Let us run through the way in which the imperfect competition model deals with the stylized facts. We do this in three steps. First, assuming that we can justify wage- and price-setting of the kind implied by the price-determined real wage curve and the bargained real wage curve, and the associated output and employment behaviour, then we can have persistent involuntary unemployment in equilibrium. The labour supply curve shows the real wage at which individual workers would be prepared to accept a job; the bargained real wage curve shows the real wage that unions expect to secure through collective bargaining at each level of employment. The bargained real wage curve lies above the labour supply curve. Similarly, the price-determined real wage curve shows the real wage that is implied by businesses pricing decisions under imperfect competition and which lies below the marginal product of labour curve. Equilibrium unemployment is fixed by the intersection of the BRW and the PRW and will therefore occur in the region defined by Malinvaud as Keynesian unemployment. There is involuntary unemployment (stylized fact (ii)), and firms would like to produce more output *if the real wage remained constant* (stylized fact (iii)); see Fig. 16.3.

In the next two chapters, we will attempt to show how the price-determined real wage curve and the bargained real wage curve (along with its analogue in the absence of unions, the 'efficiency real wage curve') can be justified on the basis of the behaviour of optimizing economic agents. In other words, attention is focused on the microeconomic bases of the imperfect competition model which combine to produce outcomes consistent with 'facts' (ii) and (iii).

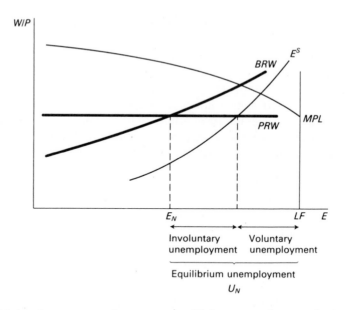

Fig. 16.3 Involuntary unemployment at equilibrium unemployment in the imperfect competition model

16.2.2 Nominal Inertia, Quantity Adjustments, and the Cyclical Pattern of Real Wages

Coming to the second step, if in addition to the unique intersection between the price-determined real wage and the bargained real wage, either (a) there is an adjustment cost to wage and/or price changes; and/or (b) there are wage- and price-setters who use adaptive expectations rather than rational expectations, then stylized facts (i) and (iv) can be explained. As a matter of casual empiricism, there is no doubt that both prices and wages are set at intervals: continuous adjustment in the face of changes in the economic environment does not occur. Why that should be so is a matter of considerable dispute. On the one hand, the physical or technical cost of changing nominal prices and wages would seem minimal, so why is there not a system that automatically changes prices and or wages as, for example, industry demand or unemployment changes? (Such systems partially exist with automatic cost-of-living adjustment (COLA) clauses in wage agreements.)

(a) Adjustment Costs of Changing Prices and Wages

A series of explanations for the existence of adjustment costs have been developed. For example, Akerlof and Yellen (1985) use the concept of *near-rationality* to argue that imperfectly competitive firms have little to gain from frequent price adjustments and may therefore refrain from doing so. While the loss to the firm from failure to adjust prices is a 'second-order' one and must be offset against the physical costs of actually changing the prices, the cost for the economy as a whole is 'first-order' in the sense that nominal rigidity permits the translation of nominal shocks into real changes in output and employment. By focusing on the discrepancy between the cost to the individual firm and the cost to the economy as a whole, the Akerlof–Yellen argument helps throw light on the paradox of why firms do not adopt a more flexible approach to price-setting, the effect of which in aggregate would be to reduce the amplitude of the business cycle. There are large macroeconomic fluctuations because the private incentives for flexibility are so small.

A similar type of argument is presented by Blanchard and Kiyotaki (1987), who stress the existence of external effects. If, for example, a recession occurs as the result of the pursuit of a tight monetary policy, then the demand curve facing each individual imperfectly competitive firm shifts to the left. Of course, the firm would like the demand curve to return to its original position, but it cannot achieve this by lowering its price. Just as in the Akerlof–Yellen case, lowering its own price will only make possible a second-order gain—to the extent that it is the optimal response to the depression in industry demand. If all firms did lower their prices, then the recession would end, but for each individual firm the gains from so doing are small.

As another example, from the point of view of the unions, there is a bureaucratic interest in not having automatic adjustments; if a union literally worked out a comprehensive bargain on day 1, it would then be out of business.

Clearly, an ideal microeconomic theory of imperfect competition in product and labour markets would explain costs of adjustment as an integral part of the theory. But at the present time, the debate is proceeding along many different tacks at a technical level and no clear conclusions have yet emerged. For this reason, we simply acknowledge the existence of adjustment costs to prices and wages and the *nominal inertia* that is therefore entailed. We do not discuss the theoretical work on this issue further. (For a survey of the current state of play, see for example Blanchard and Fischer 1989: ch. 8.)

(b) Adaptive Expectations

We have already discussed at length the implications of the existence of adaptive expectations and have argued that adaptive expectations may describe behaviour when there is incomplete information about the structure of the economy (refer back to Chapter 8).

How does the existence in the imperfect competition model of elements of nominal inertia resulting from price and wage adjustment costs and/or from adaptive expectations relate to the explanation of the stylized facts relating to the cyclical behaviour of real wages (i) and to the predominance of quantity over price adjustments in the face of demand changes (iv)? Explaining quantity adjustments is straightforward. In the presence of nominal inertia arising from either (a) or (b), a rise in aggregate demand is not associated with an immediate rise in wages and or prices—or if it is, wage and price rises will be limited by expected inflation being equal to past inflation. The demand shock is not immediately absorbed in full price/wage adjustment.

However, in addition to the nominal inertia, the size of wage and price responses will be determined by the size of the gap that has opened up between the price-determined real wage and the bargained real wage. The smaller the gap, the smaller will be the resulting price changes (after whatever lag is implied by the degree of nominal inertia). In other words, the *flatter* are the BRW and the PRW, the greater will be the quantity response to a change in aggregate demand. (We take up the issue of the flatness of the BRW/PRW in Section 16.2.3 below.)

Turning to the question of the cyclical pattern of real wages, in setting out the imperfect competition model in Part II, it was assumed for simplicity that there were no adjustment costs in price-setting, with the result that the actual real wage was always equal to the price-determined real wage. Since the PRW was horizontal, changes in aggregate demand that produced fluctuations in output and employment were associated with no change in the real wage: prices adjusted immediately to changes in money wages. However, a degree of procyclicality in real wages is introduced once allowance is made for costs of adjustment in prices as well as in wages. In such a case, the real wage will lie between the bargained

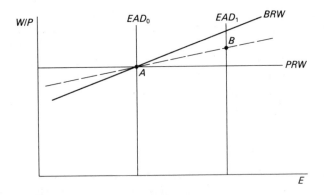

Fig. 16.4 Cyclical pattern of real wages in the imperfect competition model
With nominal inertia in wage- and price-setting, a rise in aggregate demand (EAD_0 to EAD_1) leads to a shift from A to B; real wages are pro-cyclical.

real wage and the price-determined real wage, so that a positive demand shock will see a rise in the real wage. The rise will be smaller, the flatter is the BRW (see Fig. 16.4).[2]

16.2.3 Nominal Aggregate Demand Changes and Persistent Unemployment

The third task is to explain stylized fact (v): a change in nominal aggregate demand produces a rise in unemployment which is persistent in the sense that, at the new level of unemployment, inflation may fall but at a very slow rate, or it may level out at a lower *but constant* rate after an initial fall. In other words, the experience in the 1980s is that not only can there be involuntary unemployment which persists at an equilibrium rate of unemployment in the sense that there is constant inflation, but also that a fall in aggregate demand from such a position leads to a higher rate of unemployment, which either is a new equilibrium rate—with constant (lower) inflation—or is associated with very slowly falling inflation. There is a major disagreement about whether the new situation is best captured by a model that explains it in terms of very slowly falling inflation or in terms of constant inflation.

We can identify three broad approaches.

(1) The price-determined real wage is fairly flat, the bargained real wage becomes flattish at high rates of unemployment, and there are significant nominal inertia effects of types (a) and (b) above. If all these conditions obtain, then inflation falls at high unemployment, but very slowly. Blanchflower and Oswald (1989) have provided convincing statistical evidence for the UK and certain other countries that the bargained real wage curve indeed becomes very flat at high rates of unemployment. To date, there is little in the way of a *theoretical explanation* for the confluence of these factors, and we will therefore not pursue this explanation further. Of course, this should not be interpreted as ruling out such an account.

(2) The bargained real wage and/or price-determined real wage curves shift as a result of a change in aggregate demand, but move back eventually to their long-run positions. Figure 16.5 illustrates this case. With this type

---

[2] This can be seen algebraically in a simple model as follows. In period -1, unemployment is at an equilibrium rate, so $w^B = w^P = W_{-1}/P_{-1}$ and inflation is assumed to be zero. In the next period, U falls because of a rise in aggregate demand and $w^B > w^P$. The unions set W so that $W/P^E = w^B$, where $P^E = \alpha P + (1 - \alpha)P_{-1}$. ($\alpha = 1$ is equivalent to unions being able to achieve $w = w^B$.) Thus, $W/P = w^B(P^E/P) = w^B[\alpha + (1 - \alpha)P_{-1}/P] < w^B$ if $0 < \alpha < 1$ and if $P > P_{-1}$. Businesses set P so that $W^E/P = w^P$, where $W^E = \beta W + (1 - \beta)W_{-1}$. ($\beta = 1$ implies $w = w^P$.) Thus, $W/P = w^P(W/W^E) = w^P\{1/[\beta + (1 - \beta)W_{-1}/W]\} > w^P$ if $0 < \beta < 1$ and $W > W_{-1}$. Since $P > P_{-1}$ and $W > W_{-1}$, $w^P < w < w^B$ when $0 < \alpha$, $\beta < 1$. So long as the PRW is horizontal, and w^P is the same in both periods, the increase in w^B implies w will have increased—real wages will tend to be procyclical. Clearly, the less the increase in w^B, the smaller the rise in w.

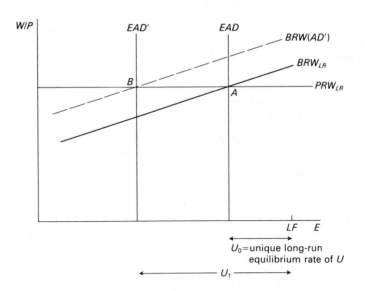

Fig. 16.5 Aggregate demand changes and persistent unemployment
BRW shifts in response to a shift in aggregate demand; constant or slowly falling inflation is observed at unemployment above the unique long-run equilibrium rate, U_0.

of explanation, it is usually argued that the fall in aggregate demand and employment leads initially to falling inflation, but that the fall in employment has consequences for the position of either the bargained real wage or the price-determined real wage. Thus, in the figure, the bargained real wage curve shifts upward and the phase of rapidly falling inflation ceases. However, eventually the bargained real wage curve returns to its long-run equilibrium position. Thus, while unemployment can persist at levels higher than U_0 in the medium run *without* falling inflation (point B), in the long run there remains a unique equilibrium rate of unemployment. Models of this type that have been developed are (a) the long-term/short-term unemployment model of Layard and Nickell (1986), in which the BRW shifts in the medium run as the proportion of long-term unemployed changes; and (b) a model of capital scrapping, in which the PRW shifts in the medium run as the size of the capital stock changes. Both of these models are explained in Chapter 19.

(3) There are *permanent* shifts in the bargained real wage or price-determined real wage curves consequent on changes in aggregate demand. This is the case that has come to be known as *pure hysteresis*. When there is pure hysteresis, there is no unique equilibrium rate of unemployment; the equilibrium rate simply follows the actual rate of unemployment. This kind of model provides the extreme opposite vision of the economy to the New Classical model: aggregate demand is all-powerful in determining not only

actual employment but also equilibrium employment. A particularly well-known example of such a model is the *insider–outsider model* (Lindbeck and Snower 1986; Blanchard and Summers 1986), in which employed workers are able to dictate wages. In the face of unanticipated demand shocks, actual levels of employment change; in the next period the employed workers (insiders) set the wage so as to just maintain their employment. This creates an equilibrium rate of unemployment at the current level of employment which will remain unchanged until another demand shock occurs. This model is explained in Chapter 19.

From an analytic point of view (though for quite different reasons), the argument is similar to the analysis of a range of possible equilibrium unemployment rates in an open economy with fixed exchange rates. In Chapter 19 we therefore also review the argument described in detail in Part III. The price-determined real wage curve shifts about in response to changes in aggregate demand, enabling the economy to experience constant inflation at any unemployment rate. There remains a unique minimum sustainable rate of unemployment determined by the current account balance.

Each of these models provides predictions that are consistent with observations on unemployment and inflation in the 1980s. However, on the evidence available from research to date, it is not possible to discriminate clearly between the hypotheses, or indeed to reject them all. Research continues.

16.2.4 Bargaining Structures and Employment Outcomes

Finally, we turn briefly to the sixth stylized fact: the possibility of a systematic relationship between wage-bargaining structures and employment outcomes. A model that assumes perfect competition would find it difficult to account for such cross-country differences. The finding to be investigated is that the extremes in terms of centralization of wage-bargaining produce lower equilibrium rates of unemployment than does an intermediate form of organization. In other words, it has been argued that low equilibrium unemployment can be associated either with a highly centralized system of wage bargaining (economy-wide) or with a highly decentralized one (firm-level). The intermediate form (industry bargaining) tends to produce a worse employment outcome. There is some empirical evidence in support of this relationship and there are also theoretical reasons for predicting it.

Several studies of cross-country unemployment performance in the 1980s have found that economies organized in highly centralized union and employer institutions—sometimes referred to by the ill-defined term of *corporatism*—have performed very creditably in terms of unemployment outcomes. Good employment performances have also been recorded by countries with apparently decentralized structures. Typical examples of the first case—the economies with centralized wage-setting and low unemployment—are the Scandinavian economies (excluding Denmark) and Austria. Examples of the latter—decentralized wage-setting and low unemployment—are the USA, Japan, and Switzerland (Calmfors and Driffill 1988). Fitting in the middle group with an intermediate level of centralization of bargaining and poor unemployment records are the economies of the European core: West Germany, France, Italy, and the UK. Of course, there are many economies that fail to fit the story neatly; for example, Denmark has a fairly centralized wage-setting structure but a poor unemployment performance. Nevertheless, there appears to be something in the 'hump-shaped' relationship.

In Chapter 17, we use a simple model to illustrate why such a 'hump-shaped' relationship (Fig. 16.6) would be expected. The focus is on the knowledge by the centralized union of the *economy-wide* constraints on employment. Thus, the centralized union chooses the real wage in such a way that unemployment in the economy is minimized. By contrast, bargaining at firm or industry level occurs on the basis of partial equilibrium considerations. The difference in outcome between the two lower levels of centralization then arises from the perceived difference between the elasticity of the labour demand curve at firm level as compared with industry level. In a system where firm-level bargains are struck, the local union will be highly sensitive to the effect of its wage claim on the firm's product price and therefore on demand for the firm's output.

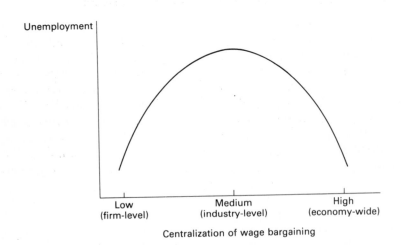

Fig. 16.6 The 'hump-shaped' relationship between unemployment and the centralization of wage-setting

This will produce wage moderation since the union is presumed to care about both wages and employment. By contrast, at industry level there is much less substitutability between the output of different industries, and this produces less wage moderation.

16.3 Conclusion

In this chapter we have argued that the imperfect competition model provides a promising starting point in terms of accounting for a set of stylized facts which appear to characterize the macroeconomic behaviour of the contemporary industrialized economies. While the use of union bargaining throughout Parts II and III reflects a more European focus in terms of institutional structure, it seems that the stylized facts also relate to the US economy (e.g. Okun 1981; Ball *et al.* 1988; Blanchard and Fischer 1989: ch. 1; Greenwald and Stiglitz 1988; Barsky and Solon 1989). The task of providing coherent *micro*economic foundations for the macroeconomics of the USA is a more difficult one, given the much smaller role of unions. In Chapter 17, the idea of *employer-set* efficiency wage as a way of generating a wage curve analogous to the bargained real wage curve, and hence able to account for the existence of involuntary unemployment, is discussed.

The remainder of the book is addressed to putting flesh on the bones of the microeconomic structure assumed as the basis for the macro model in Parts II and III. We try to give a flavour of the kinds of models that are being developed to account for the price-determined real wage, the bargained real wage, and the sort of open economy pricing behaviour that has been assumed. Finally, Chapter 19 follows up the issue of the apparent persistence of unemployment in the face of aggregate demand shifts which has become such an important subject of research in the late 1980s.

The models presented in Part IV are simplified versions of models found in the literature and provide a bridge to ease readers into the research literature and to relate it to a basic macroeconomic model founded on imperfect competition. Simplification necessarily involves the use of unrealistic assumptions, but these have been chosen so as to convey more directly the essential arguments of the more complex material.

17

Wage-Setting in Imperfectly Competitive Labour Markets

A major theme in this book is the importance of wage-setting behaviour for macroeconomic analysis. The bargained real wage curve plays a central role in the analysis of the imperfect competition model in Part II and in the derivation of the competing-claims equilibrium schedule in the open economy analysis in Part III. As argued in Chapter 16, the stylized facts of the contemporary industrialized economies are consistent with a bargained real wage curve which lies above the neoclassical individualistic labour supply curve. Such a curve plays a major part in the arguments about the existence of involuntary unemployment when unemployment is at the equilibrium rate. Much of this chapter is concerned with the microeconomic foundations of the bargained real wage curve in union bargaining behaviour. We will also argue that in a non-union environment—as in the USA—employer wage-setting in the presence of imperfect information creates a wage curve above the labour supply schedule analogous to the BRW. We will refer to this as the efficiency real wage curve, the ERW.

The second focus of the chapter relates to the apparent absence of a simple relationship between unemployment and union bargaining power of the kind that would be predicted from standard models of wage-bargaining. As we will see, the standard models predict that an increase in union bargaining power will be associated with a higher bargained real wage curve. A higher bargained real wage curve in turn means a higher equilibrium rate of unemployment. Thus, we would expect to observe higher (equilibrium) unemployment in those economies in which the trade unions are stronger.

However, there is now a growing belief in a more specific hypothesis. Instead of seeing union power as the key, the focus is on the *level* at which wage negotiations are conducted. A hump-shaped relationship between unemployment and the extent to which wage-bargaining is centrally organized is proposed (Fig. 16.6). Low equilibrium unemployment is consistent with *either* a highly centralized wage determination system or a very decentralized one. In other words, the argument is that it is inadequate to conceive of there being a single route through which union power (as measured for example by membership density or the extent to which the work-force is covered by trade union wage bargains) affects bargaining. Two economies in which trade unions are equally powerful in the above sense would be expected to have very different unemployment outcomes if the unions in one economy are centrally organized (or co-ordinated) while in the other they operate non-cooperatively. We show in a simple model why a hump-shaped relationship between the level of centralization of wage-setting and equilibrium unemployment results. Thus, it is quite possible for an economy with a very high degree of union bargaining power as conventionally measured to have low equilibrium unemployment.

17.1   Microfoundations for the Bargained Real Wage Curve

The bargained real wage curve depicts an inverse relationship between the expected real wage that unions are able to secure through their money wage negotiations and the level of unemployment:

$$W = P^E[b(U)]$$

$$w^B = b(U) \qquad \text{[bargained real wage BRW]}$$

where $db/dU < 0$.

It was suggested in Chapter 6 that higher unemployment would reduce the bargained real wage because union members would be less prepared to go on strike in support of their wage claim. At a time of high unemployment, the prospects of securing temporary work during a strike would be lower and the probability that a strike would result in the permanent loss of jobs through the firm going out of business would be higher. In addition, it was presumed that the BRW would lie above the conventional labour supply curve, representing the willingness of individuals to supply labour at each real wage. In other words, the monopoly power conferred on labour as the result of wage negotiations taking place through collective organizations would produce at each level of employment an expected real wage higher than would be acceptable to workers on an individual basis, in the sense of the minimum necessary to induce them to work.

The task in this section is to provide a more rigorous basis[1] for the existence of an upward-sloping BRW that lies above the individualistic labour supply curve. Although we follow the mainstream approach to the analysis of union wage-setting with its primary building block of utility

[1] For an excellent survey of theories of trade union bargaining behaviour, see Oswald (1985).

maximization by union members, it is important to acknowledge different traditions which provide alternative routes to the derivation of a bargained real wage curve. In particular, there is a rich tradition of analysis of class conflict from Marxian economists. As noted earlier, it was Marx after all who developed the concept of the reserve army of the unemployed, the role of which was to regulate the capitalist system. Marxists have argued that falling unemployment increases the power of workers to press not only for higher wages but also for improved state benefits and less arduous working conditions.[2]

Within the utility-maximizing approach we find that there are two basic models for analysing bargaining: the so-called 'right-to-manage' model and the 'efficient bargains' model. In the right-to-manage model, the firm is able to set the employment level unilaterally, once the wage has been decided. In the simplest variant, there is a monopoly union so the union chooses the wage, given the firm's labour demand curve. Bargaining can be introduced so that the union and the firm bargain over the wage in the knowledge that the firm will set the level of employment on the demand-for-labour curve. In the efficient bargains model, the starting point is the observation that the outcome of a right-to-manage bargain will not necessarily be Pareto-efficient; both parties can gain from moving off the demand-for-labour curve. The essence of the efficient bargains model is that bargaining occurs over *both* the wage and the level of employment.

Both models generate a bargained real wage curve at the aggregate level of the type defined above. More emphasis is placed on the right-to-manage model, since it appears that in reality bargaining does not occur over the level of employment. It is easy to show that a right-to-manage bargain is efficient if unions care only about the wage, and there are some plausible reasons why this may be the case.

17.1.1 The Right-to-Manage Model of Wage-Setting

The Monopoly Union Model

We begin with the simplest model—that of the monopoly union—and show that, if unions have preferences over both the level of employment and the real wage, it is straightforward to derive an upward-sloping BRW above the labour supply curve. This model looks at the case where there is a single union, and for simplicity, we assume also a single firm in each industry in the economy. It is assumed that workers are divided among industries and that industry-specific training means that they are immobile between industries. Each union maximizes the expected utility of the

---

[2] Writers in the Kaleckian tradition have also developed ideas about the effect of changes in labour market conditions on the power of workers. However, Kalecki himself represented the increase in worker power associated with a boom by a decline in the mark-up in the *pricing* equation (Kalecki 1971b).

representative worker. Utility is assumed to depend positively on the real wage in the industry and on employment in the industry. The usual justification for this is that the union is thought of as maximizing the expected utility of their employed *and* unemployed members where members have a random chance of being employed. The randomness of the employment outcome for an individual gives the result that the union utility function will depend both on the real wage and on employment. The expected utility of the representative worker in the ith industry (v_i) which the union in the ith industry maximizes is

$$v_i = (E_i/L_i)\, v(W_i/P) + (1 - E_i/L_i)\, v(z)$$
[union utility function]

where E and L are respectively employment and membership in the ith industry and z is the 'reservation' or 'outside' wage. The reservation or outside wage plays an important part in the story to follow, and this is a good point at which to clarify its meaning. It is the 'wage' that the union member would expect to get if he or she were not employed in the ith industry. It is a weighted average of the wage available elsewhere in the economy and the unemployment benefit. The simple case we will take is where the probability of getting a job elsewhere is the ratio of employment to the total labour force in the overall economy, that is, one minus the overall unemployment rate: $(1 - U)$. Thus, we assume that z is

$$z = (1 - U)w^* + Ub,$$

where w^* is the wage available elsewhere in the economy and b is the state unemployment benefit. Higher unemployment raises the probability that the representative member will be out of work if not employed in the ith industry and reduces the value of the reservation wage z.

The ith union has to juggle two effects in choosing W_i to maximize v_i. Raising W_i increases W_i/P, the real consumption wage of its members, since the ith union believes that the wage it chooses in the ith industry has little or no effect on the aggregate price level. But raising W_i raises P_i, the industry price level, and that in turn reduces demand for the industry's output and hence employment, E_i.

This latter inverse relation between W_i/P and E_i is just the ith industry's demand-for-labour curve. It is downward-sloping even if labour productivity is constant. We will introduce standard diminishing marginal productivity later in this chapter, but here we can derive the downward-sloping labour demand curve using the simple assumptions of constant labour productivity and constant mark-up pricing. These two assumptions tell us that $P_i = (1 + \mu)(W_i/LP)$ or $W_i/P_i = LP/(1 + \mu)$; in other words, a 1% rise in W_i implies a 1% rise in P_i. To see the effect of a 1% rise in W_i on E_i, and at the same time to see the trade-off between W_i/P, the real consumption wage, and E_i, note first from the previous equation that

$$W_i/P = [LP/(1 + \mu)](P_i/P);$$

i.e., a rise in W_i/P implies a rise in P_i/P, the industry's relative price. E_i falls because this reduces the demand for the industry's output. Let $y_i = f(P_i/P, \overset{+}{y}{}^D)$ be the industry's demand curve. Since

$$E_i = y_i/LP,$$

$$E_i = f(P_i/P, y^D)/LP$$

$$= \frac{f\left[\left(\dfrac{1 + \mu}{LP} \dfrac{W_i}{P}\right), y^D\right]}{LP}.$$

This is the ith industry's labour demand curve in the simple case of constant mark-up pricing and constant labour productivity. For convenience, this will be written

$$E_i = E(W_i \,\overline{/}\, P, \overset{+}{y}{}^D).$$

The union maximizes the expected utility of its representative member subject to the labour demand curve:

$$\max v_i = (E_i/L_i)\, v(W_i/P) + (1 - E_i/L_i)v(z)$$

$$\text{subject to } E_i = E(W_i/P, y^D), \tag{17.1}$$

where L_i is set equal to 1 and real aggregate demand y^D is held constant.[3]

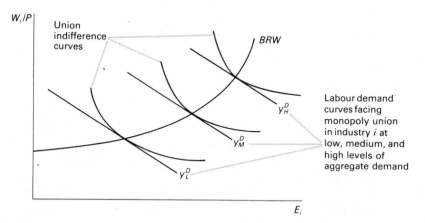

Fig. 17.1 The monopoly union model
Choosing the real wage to maximize the utility of a randomly selected union member, subject to the industry demand-for-labour curve, at three different levels of aggregate demand.
The BRW is the locus of tangencies between union indifference curves and industry demand-for-labour curves.

[3] Note that setting $L_i = 1$ implies that E_i is in effect a percentage between 0 and 1 showing the proportion of the ith labour force employed.

(Figure 17.1 illustrates the wage chosen by the union at three levels of aggregate demand.) Writing W_i/P as w_i, and assuming that the representative union member is risk-neutral, we can rewrite (17.1) as

$$\text{Choose } w_i \text{ to max } E(w_i)w_i + [1 - E(w_i)]z. \qquad (17.2)$$

The assumption of risk neutrality means that the expected utility of the variable x is equal to the money value of x. To find a maximum, we differentiate equation (17.2) with respect to w_i and set equal to zero:

$$w_i\, E'(w_i) + E = E'(w_i)z. \qquad (17.3)$$

Dividing through by E' and substituting the expression for z derived above gives

$$w_i + E/E' = z = (1 - U)w^* + Ub.$$

If we assume that all industries behave in the same way, then $w_i = w^* = w$. Hence

$$w + w(E/wE') = (1 - U)w + Ub.$$

Defining the absolute value of the elasticity of the labour demand curve as

$$\eta = |(dE/dw)(w/E)|,$$

we get

$$w^B\left[1 - \frac{1}{\eta} - (1 - U)\right] = Ub$$

i.e.

$$w^B = \left(\frac{U}{U - 1/\eta}\right)b.$$

[bargained real wage curve](17.4)

Equation (17.4) defines the bargained real wage curve in the monopoly union model under the simplifying assumptions made here. The intuition is straightforward. The real wage set by the monopoly union is a mark-up on the reservation wage z, and in aggregate this produces an inverse relationship between the real wage the union sets and the rate of unemployment. Higher unemployment reduces the value of the reservation wage and therefore reduces the wage that the union can set.

From (17.4), we can see first that the bargained real wage rises as unemployment falls: a one-unit fall in U reduces $(U - 1/\eta)$ by a larger percentage than U; hence $U/(U - 1/\eta)$ rises as unemployment falls.[4] The

---

[4] Note that we look only at cases in which $\eta > 1$. If $\eta < 1$, i.e. if the demand for labour is inelastic, then the union would choose an infinite wage since a 1% rise in the wage would be associated with a less than 1% fall in the wage times the probability of employment in the ith industry.

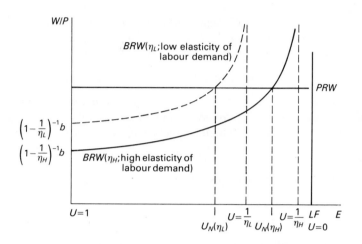

Fig. 17.2 BRW curves derived from monopoly union model
b = unemployment benefit; η = absolute value of elasticity of the labour demand curve

bargained real wage curve becomes vertical at $U = 1/\eta$. Furthermore, since η is the elasticity of the labour demand curve, a more elastic demand for labour implies a lower equilibrium rate of unemployment (see Fig. 17.2). Another way of making the same point is that with a high η, the 'mark-up' of the real wage over the unemployment benefit is less at each rate of unemployment. When η is very high, $1/\eta$ is close to zero, so the mark-up is close to unity; i.e., w is not much greater than b (though the mark-up rises as U falls).

We return to this relationship between the elasticity of the demand for labour curve and the BRW in Section 17.3 below when we look explicitly at the degree of centralization of wage-bargaining and its implications for unemployment. At this point, it is sufficient to emphasize the genesis of the bargained real wage as a mark-up on the reservation wage and therefore as inversely related to the rate of unemployment, holding the elasticity of the demand for labour constant.

The Right-to-Manage Model with Bargaining

There are serious objections to the monopoly union approach if we are trying to model how wages are actually set. In the monopoly model, no bargaining takes place; the union is able to set the wage unilaterally (given of course the constraint of the demand for labour). For a more realistic and interesting approach, we must turn to the idea of bargaining.

There are many different models of the process of bargaining between unions and employers. The most familiar is that of Nash, who modelled bargaining as a co-operative game. The Nash solution can best be thought of as arising from a situation in which the two parties agree to set up an arbitration procedure and lay down the general principles that the procedure must uphold. However, it bears no relationship either to any actual process of arbitration of *a fortiori* to the negotiation of wages through collective bargaining. Since this is not the place to conduct a survey of bargaining theory, we simply choose an approach that seems to capture the essence of the bargaining process most realistically. It is reassuring to note that, although the different approaches to bargaining solutions use quite different arguments, they turn out to produce similar results.

We look at an approach originally proposed by Zeuthen (1930), and put into rather persuasive form by Jackman *et al.* (1989). Suppose the employer makes a wage offer, w_f. The question that then faces the union is what would be the longest time for which it would be prepared to strike in order to get a better offer, w_u. Suppose that the utility obtained by members during a strike is z, the outside wage, and the longest time the union would strike for is s_u. The union's discount rate is r_u. Thus the union has to weigh up the costs of going on strike against the benefits from an increased wage offer that would accompany a strike. The longest strike the union will contemplate is determined by finding the s_u that equates the present value of the employer's wage offer (right-hand side of the expression below) with the sum of the present value of utility gained during a strike (first term on left-hand side) and the present value of utility associated with the achievement of the union's wage claim calculated from the end of the strike (second term on left-hand side). Thus we have[5]

$$(z/r_u)(1 - e^{-r_u s_u}) + (w_u/r_u)(e^{-r_u s_u}) = w_f/r_u.$$

If we cancel the r_u from each side, we get

$$z - w_f = (z - w_u)(e^{-r_u s_u}),$$

and taking logs of each side leads to

$$s_u = \ln[(w_u - z)(w_f - z)^{-1}]^{1/r_u}.$$

Hence we have an expression for the length of time for which the union

[5] The RHS, the discounted value of w_f from now ($t = 0$) to $t = \infty$, comes from

$$\int_0^\infty w_f(e^{-r_u t} dt) = w_f[(1/r_u)(e^{-r_u \cdot 0}) - (1/r_u)(e^{-r_u \cdot \infty})] = w_f/r_u.$$

The discounted value of z for the length of the strike, $t = 0$ to $t = s$ is

$$\int_0^s z(e^{-r_u t} dt) = z[(1/r_u)(e^{-r_u \cdot 0}) - (1/r_u)(e^{-r_u \cdot s})] = \frac{z}{r_u}(1 - e^{-r_u \cdot s}).$$

The discounted value of getting w_u from the end of the stike onwards, from $t = s$ to $t = \infty$, is

$$\int_0^\infty w_u(e^{-r_u t} dt) = w_u[(1/r_u)(e^{-r_u \cdot s}) - (1/r_u)(e^{-r_u \cdot \infty})] = \frac{w_u}{r_u} \cdot e^{-r_u \cdot s}.$$

would be prepared to strike, dependent on the employer's wage offer, the union's wage claim, the utility available to the union during a strike, and the union's discount rate.

By applying exactly the same logic to the employer, it is possible to calculate the maximum duration of a strike that the firm would contemplate rather than accept the union's wage claim. For the firm, the relevant determinants of its decision are—appropriately discounted—the profits per period it would derive if its wage offer is accepted ($\pi(w_f)$), the profits per period, possibly negative, during the course of a strike ($\bar{\pi}$), and the profits per period associated with the award of the union's wage claim ($\pi(w_u)$). The employer chooses the length of strike, s_f, that equates the present value of the union's wage offer (right-hand side of the expression below) with the sum of the present value of profits gained during a strike (first term on left-hand side) and the present value of profits associated with the achievement of the employer's wage claim calculated from the end of the strike:

$$(\bar{\pi}/r_f)(1 - e^{-r_f s_f}) + [\pi(w_f)/r_f](e^{-r_f s_f}) = \pi(w_u)/r_f.$$

Using exactly the same derivation as above, we get the expression for s_f:

$$s_f = \ln\{[\pi(w_f) - \bar{\pi}][\pi(w_u) - \bar{\pi}]^{-1}\}^{1/r_f}.$$

In order to move towards a solution of the bargaining game, it is necessary to make an assumption about how the balance of bargaining power is determined. In the Jackman *et al.* version of a Zeuthen model, it is assumed that the side that is keener to reach an agreement is the one with the weaker bargaining power.[6] Thus, the side in the weaker bargaining position is the one that alters its position (in the sense of its wage offer), and in our model is the one therefore that would strike for a shorter time. Hence, the company will improve its offer if the length of time for which it is prepared to put up with an interruption to production is less than the period for which the union would be prepared to wait: $s_f < s_u$, i.e., if

$$\ln\{[\pi(w_f) - \bar{\pi}][\pi(w_u) - \bar{\pi}]^{-1}\}^{1/r_f} < \ln[(w_u - z)(w_f - z)^{-1}]^{1/r_u}.$$

Eliminating logs on each side and raising each side to the power of r_f, the above expression simplifies to

$$(w_f - z)^{r_f/r_u}[\pi(w_f) - \bar{\pi}] < (w_u - z)^{r_f/r_u}[\pi(w_u) - \bar{\pi}].$$

The union will lower its offer to the extent that $s_u < s_f$. Thus, the party that improves its offer has the smaller value of Ω where

$$\Omega = (w - z)^{r_f/r_u}[\pi(w) - \bar{\pi}].$$

---

[6] This way of characterizing relative bargaining power is given a formal basis by Rubinstein (1982).

Hence negotiations will continue with each side raising Ω until it cannot be raised any further. We can therefore summarize the bargaining rule as:[7]

Choose w which maximizes Ω.

To make finding the solution easier, let us assume that the profits received by a firm during the course of a strike, $\bar{\pi}$, are zero:

$$\bar{\pi} = 0.$$

The bargaining solution requires that we find the wage that maximizes the value of Ω (or, equivalently, log Ω):

$$\ln \Omega = (r_f/r_u) \ln (w - z) + \ln \pi(w).$$

To find the maximum, we differentiate log Ω with respect to w and set $d\ln \Omega/dw$ equal to zero:

$$d\ln \Omega/dw = (r_f/r_u)[1/(w - z)] + \pi'(w)/\pi(w) = 0.$$

Two further simplifications can be made to this formula. Firstly, we can simplify the expression for the wage further by defining r_f/r_u as *labour's bargaining power*, β. The intuition behind such a definition is that the lower is r_u relative to r_f, the longer the union can survive during a strike. This raises its bargaining power. We then have

$$\beta/(w - z) + \pi'(w)/\pi(w) = 0. \qquad (17.5)$$

Secondly, to evaluate $\pi'(w)$,

$$\pi = p[Q(p)] - w[E(Q(p))] = \pi(w, p), \qquad (17.6)$$

where $p \equiv P_i/P$ and $w \equiv W_i/P$. Since the employer is profit-maximizing, p will be set to maximize profits. We need to find $d\pi/dw$. Now,

$$d\pi = \pi_p dp + \pi_w dw$$

for small changes in p and w, where π_p is the partial derivative of π with respect to p and similarly for π_w. Hence

$$d\pi/dw = \pi_p (dp/dw) + \pi_w.$$

Since p is always set at a profit-maximizing level, $\pi_p = 0$, so $d\pi/dw = \pi_w$. Returning to (17.6), we can see that $\partial \pi/\partial w \equiv \pi_w = -E$. Therefore (17.5) can be written

[7] This is identical to the Nash bargaining solution when union and employer discount rates are equal. If the discount rates are identical, the solution is produced by choosing the value of the decision variable that maximizes the product of the utility gains available from avoiding a strike. In this case, with identical discount rates, we have the wage w being chosen which maximizes the product of the gains to the union from receiving w as opposed to the z that arises if there is a strike, and to the firm from getting profits associated with the wage, w, as compared with the profits available during a strike.

$$\beta/(w - z) - E/\pi = 0 \quad \text{or } \beta(\pi/E) = w - z \quad \text{or } w^B = z + \beta(\pi/E).$$
(17.7)

This is illuminating because it states that the bargained real wage is the sum of two factors: the 'outside' wage z, and labour's relative bargaining strength, β, multiplied by profits per employee. But we can go further than this:

$$\pi/E = [pQ(p) - wE]/E = w[(p/w)(Q/E) - 1].$$

For the standard formula for profit maximization,

$$p = \frac{\varepsilon}{\varepsilon - 1} \frac{w}{Q'(E)},$$

where ε is the elasticity of demand, so

$$\frac{\pi}{E} = w\left(\frac{\varepsilon}{\varepsilon - 1} \frac{1}{\alpha} - 1\right)$$

where $\alpha \equiv (dQ/dE)(E/Q)$, the elasticity of output with respect to employment. Returning to (17.7),

$$w = z + \beta w\left(\frac{\varepsilon}{\varepsilon - 1} \frac{1}{\alpha} - 1\right)$$

$$= \frac{z}{1 - \beta\left(\dfrac{\varepsilon}{\varepsilon - 1} \dfrac{1}{\alpha} - 1\right)}$$
(17.8)

Recall that $z = p(E)w^* + [1 - p(E)]b$, where $p(E)$ is the probability of gaining alternative employment during a strike at wage w^* and b is the unemployment benefit that can be claimed during a strike. If all firms are bargaining in a similar way, $w = w^*$. If the probability of gaining alternative employment is the same as the probability of being employed, or one minus the probability of being unemployed, $p(E) = 1 - U$, where U is the unemployment rate, then

$$z = (1 - U)w + Ub,$$

and substituting into (17.8) and rearranging gives

$$w^B = \frac{b}{1 - \dfrac{\beta}{U}\left(\dfrac{\varepsilon}{\varepsilon - 1} \dfrac{1}{\alpha} - 1\right)}$$

[bargained real wage](17.9)

Equation (17.9) shows that five factors will influence the outcome for the bargained real wage:

1 *the unemployment benefit, b*: an increase in b, by reducing the cost of striking, raises the bargained real wage;

2   *the relative strength of the union to endure a strike, β*: an increase in β
    raises the bargained real wage;
3   *the rate of unemployment, U*: an increase in the rate of unemployment,
    by reducing the value of the 'outside' wage and therefore raising the
    cost of job loss in the course of a strike, reduces the bargained real
    wage;
4   *the product market elasticity of demand, ε*: note that an increase in ε
    lowers $\varepsilon/(\varepsilon - 1)$ (since $\varepsilon/(\varepsilon - 1) = 1/(1 - 1/\varepsilon)$). Thus an increase in
    product market demand elasticity reduces the bargained real wage.
    This is because an increase in the wage will have a more depressing
    effect on profits the greater is the reduction in demand as a result of the
    increase in prices consequent on an increase in the wage;
5   *the output elasticity of employment, α*: An increase in α reduces the
    bargained real wage. The more elastic is output with respect to
    employment, the bigger will be the reduction in profits as a result of an
    increase in the wage and hence a reduction in employment. Therefore
    the more strongly will firms resist an increase in the wage.

The Jackman model has the merit of integrating the determinants of
relative union bargaining power into the bargaining model itself. By
focusing on the reasoning behind the union and employer offers, and on
the crucial importance of the relative eagerness of the parties to settle, it
has been possible to pin down the determinants of the wage bargain in a
relatively straightforward way.

17.1.2   Efficient Bargains

The second class of models that have been used in the analysis of
wage-bargaining are the so-called efficient bargains models, the best
known example of which is due to McDonald and Solow (1981). Efficient
bargain models take as their starting point the question as to whether it is
in the interests of both sides to restrict bargaining to the demand-for-
labour curve. Let us maintain the assumption that the union is concerned
both with real wages and with employment producing indifference curves
as shown in Fig. 17.3. Thus, $v = 100$ is one union indifference curve; it
slopes downwards to represent the trade-off for the union between lower
wages and a higher probability of employment; $v = 150$ represents a higher
level of union utility. The firm maximizes profits, and we can draw
isoprofit curves on the same diagram. Since the demand-for-labour curve
depicts the profit-maximizing level of employment at a given real wage,
points along it must correspond to a zero slope on isoprofit curves. A
simple way of understanding why isoprofit curves are shaped as shown is to
look at point A in Fig. 17.3. The firm is able to raise its profits above the

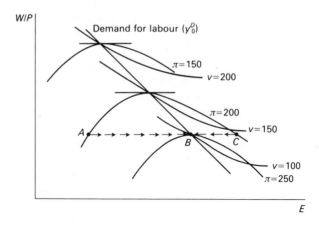

Fig. 17.3 Isoprofit and indifference curves

level corresponding to the isoprofit curve at point A by raising employment until point B is reached. This means that isoprofit curves corresponding to higher and higher levels of profit are crossed on the way from A to
B. Exactly the same pattern is repeated from point C to B. There must be
a series of isoprofit curves with rising levels of profits as one moves down
the labour demand curve.

With both isoprofit and indifference curves, as in Fig. 17.4, we are in a
position to assess the Pareto efficiency of bargains struck along the
demand-for-labour curve. It is clear that bargains at points A', B', or C'
are inefficient in the sense that both sides could be made better off by
moving away from the demand-for-labour curve. Both parties will be
better off at any point in the lens-shaped areas to the right of points A', B',

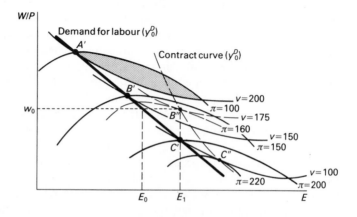

Fig. 17.4 Efficient bargains

and C'. The set of Pareto-superior points available from A' is shaded. For an employer to move off the demand-for-labour curve means that she must be prepared to employ more workers than would maximize profits at that wage. For example, at point B'', with $w = w_0$, $E = E_1$, profits and utility are higher than at B' ($v(B'') = 175$; $\pi(B'') = 160$, compared with $v(B') = 150$; $\pi(B') = 150$), but with wage w_0 the firm would maximize profits by employing only E_0 workers. The points such as B'' and C'', which show the tangency between isoprofit and indifference curves, are joined up to form the contract curve associated with the demand-for-labour curve at aggregate demand y_0^D.

Each level of aggregate demand will define a labour demand curve and a set of isoprofit curves. Thus, with the indifference curves unchanged, there is a new contract curve associated with each level of aggregate demand. Bargaining is the process by which a point on the contract curve is chosen. Any available point on the contract curve will be a Pareto-efficient bargain since it is impossible to make either party better off without making the other worse off. The stronger is the union, the further towards the top of the contract curve the outcome will be and vice versa. As ever, assume that higher unemployment means less union power. In other words, comparing two contract curves, one associated with low and the other with high aggregate demand (Fig. 17.5), in the case of low aggregate demand ($CC(y_L^D)$), union bargaining power will be relatively weak, so that position on the contract curve towards the lower end is achieved. By contrast with high aggregate demand the union has the upper hand in bargaining and will be able to secure a position towards the upper end. By joining up the two bargains, we derive the BRW associated with efficient bargaining. The BRW lies below the monopoly union BRW since the union is deliberately agreeing to a lower real wage to allow a higher level of employment. *Ceteris paribus*, a lower BRW means a lower equilibrium rate of unemployment. However, the price-determined real wage will generally

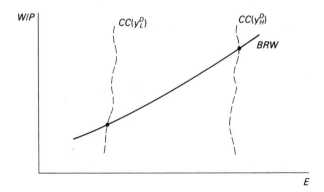

Fig. 17.5 Efficient bargaining and the BRW

also shift down in the face of efficient bargaining since labour productivity is now lower. Hence the final result for the equilibrium rate of unemployment of efficient bargaining as opposed to the monopoly union setting is not predictable.

Although the idea of efficient bargaining where a Pareto improvement is achieved through the negotiation of a wage–employment package off the demand-for-labour curve is appealing, it appears not to reflect what happens in reality.[8] Although there is quite a bit of empirical evidence which supports the notion that bargains are struck along the demand-for-labour curve—i.e. that bargaining over the level of employment as well as the wage does not take place—this issue has by no means been exhaustively tested. Of course, such bargains will be *efficient* if union indifference curves are horizontal. In other words, if for whatever reason the union cares only about the wage, then its indifference curves are horizontal, and the point of tangency with the isoprofit curves of the firm occurs on the labour demand curve (Fig. 17.6).

Explanations for the existence of flat union indifference curves relate to the institutional structure of unions, relying for example on unions using a majority voting rule. Since the median voter will virtually never be in danger of losing his or her job as the result of a wage increase, the union's goal will be purely one of raising wages. Labour turnover data suggests rates of turnover of 20–25% p.a., which means that enforced redundancies are rare with the result that employment may typically not figure in the union utility function. If lay-offs that do occur are not random but follow a seniority rule such as 'last in–first out' (LIFO), then a union maximizing

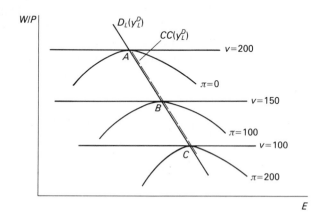

Fig. 17.6 Efficient bargains along the demand-for-labour curve when union indifference curves are flat

[8] See in particular Oswald (1987).

the utility of the median voter would have indifference curves that were flat beyond the point at which the median voter is employed. For these kinds of reasons, greater emphasis has been placed in this chapter on bargaining models based on the right-to-manage idea.

17.2   Employer Wage-Setting: the Efficiency Wage Analogue to the Bargained Real Wage Curve

This section looks at a set of arguments that have developed in the past decade to account for wages being set *by the employer* above the labour market-clearing wage. Such models play a very important role in accounting for the existence of involuntary unemployment in economies in which unions play little role in wage-setting, since the theory explains why it is not profitable for firms to cut the wage in the presence of involuntary unemployment. The general name given to this phenomenon is *efficiency wages*.[9] As we will see, several different explanations for the existence of efficiency wages have been put forward, ranging from the desire of employers to reduce costs of turnover of labour to the objective of reducing shirking by employees. In each case, productivity is directly related to the real wage so the employer is willing to pay a wage in excess of the labour market-clearing wage as a means of reducing total labour costs. Efficiency wages provide an explanation for the existence of a wage-setting curve analogous to the bargained real wage curve for situations in which unions do not participate in wage-setting.

An example helps to illustrate the basic idea. For workers who have the same given level of a marketable skill, a real wage of w_0 per hour would ensure that all workers in that marketable skill class who wished to work at some level of aggregate demand could do so. Figure 17.7 illustrates the situation. With a wage of w_0, point C is on the labour supply curve. If in fact the real wage paid in this situation is w_1, then the result will be involuntary unemployment to the extent of AB. It seems that this empirical fact as to levels of wages holds for all levels of aggregate demand. Thus, we can trace out empirically a wage curve analogous to the BRW schedule, but derived from pay-setting by the employer. The wage curve is $A'AA''$ and shown in Fig. 17.7.

If we assume that there is empirical support for the existence of the $A'AA''$ curve, how can it be explained in terms of rational employer behaviour? The non-market-clearing wage set by the employer has been labelled the *efficiency wage* to indicate that it is efficient for the employer to set a high wage because a higher wage raises productivity.[10] The idea

---

[9] Efficiency wages are not related in any way to efficient bargains.

[10] A very useful collection of major articles on efficiency wages is Akerlof and Yellen (1987).

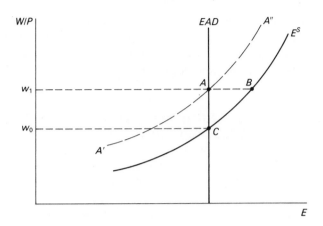

Fig. 17.7 Efficiency wages and the labour supply curve

that labour is a special type of commodity which cannot be bought in the same way as a gallon of a given grade of fuel oil has a long history in economic thought. Marx spent much of the first part of *Capital* drawing the distinction between labour power, the commodity the employer purchased, and labour, the actual work performed by the worker. He highlighted the fact that hiring a worker for eight hours does not entail the specification of exactly how much work is to be produced by the worker. The ability of workers to vary the amount of effort they put into their standard day's work means that it might not be efficient for an employer to buy labour as cheaply as possible, i.e. at the market-clearing wage.

We will look at two of the many explanations that have been put forward in the literature to account for profit-maximizing employers paying a premium above the market price. The common thread is that the payment of a higher wage by the employer *reduces* total labour costs. The first is due to Salop (1979) and focuses on the desire of the employer to reduce the costs of turnover of labour. A higher wage is paid with the intention of reducing the quit rate. The second approach (Shapiro and Stiglitz 1984) is concerned with the use of higher wages to reduce the incentive of employees to shirk on the job. In each case, we show the derivation of a positively sloped 'BRW-like' curve above the labour supply curve. We will call this wage-setting curve the ERW, or efficiency real wage curve.

17.2.1   Reducing Turnover Costs (Salop 1979)

When new workers are hired by a firm, they have to be trained in firm-specific skills and the training cost per new worker is τ. The second key feature of the model is that a certain percentage, q, of the existing work-force quits the firm each period. There are many reasons for the quits, but it is assumed that the higher the wage, w, which the firm pays relative to the reservation or outside wage, z, the smaller will be the percentage of quits. What Salop shows (and what we will show here in a simple version of his model) is that there will be a wage premium which it is just worth while for the employer to offer in order to reduce quits and hence lower training costs.

If N is the number of new hires by the firm each period, total training costs per period are

$$T = \tau N.$$

If the existing work-force is E, then total quits per period are Q;

$$Q = q(\overset{-}{w}, \overset{+}{z})E,$$

where the proportion of workers who quit, q, depends inversely on the wage paid by the employer and directly on the reservation wage. It is assumed that the firm wants a constant work-force, so that quits are equal to new hires:

$$N = qE.$$

It is easy to see that if the wage is low (i.e. close to z), the firm will benefit from a low wage but lose out because there will have to be a lot of new hires and hence high training costs, and therefore high total labour costs. Of course, with a high wage relative to z, quits will be low, reducing training costs, but direct labour costs will be high. The firm will choose the wage, w, to minimize total costs, C:

$$C \equiv wE + T$$

$$= wE + \tau q(w, z)E.$$

Thus, for a minimum, set $\partial C/\partial w$ equal to zero:

$$\partial C/\partial w = E + \tau q_w E = 0;$$

i.e.,

$$1 + \tau q_w = 0 \Rightarrow 1 = -\tau q_w.$$

The employer will want to increase the wage until the extra wage cost per worker of a one-unit increase in w (left-hand side) is equal to the right-hand side, i.e. the saving in training costs from a one-unit rise in w. The rise in wage of one unit reduces the probability of quitting per worker of q_w, which leads to a saving of training costs of $-\tau q_w$.

Let us assume that the function $q(w, z)$ takes the specific form of

$$q = a - cw^\alpha z^{1-\alpha},$$

where a, c are positive constants and α ($0 < \alpha < 1$) is the elasticity of the quit rate with respect to w/z. Now, we have the cost-minimizing equation,

$$1 = -\tau q_w,$$

and

$$q_w = -\alpha c(w/z)^{\alpha-1},$$

$$\therefore 1 = \tau \alpha c(w/z)^{\alpha-1} \quad \Rightarrow \quad w = z(\tau \alpha c)^{1/(1-\alpha)};$$

i.e., the efficiency real wage $w^{EFF} = kz$, where $k = (\tau \alpha c)^{1/(1-\alpha)}$.

The real wage paid by the firm is a mark-up on z, the reservation wage. In the turnover model, the optimal mark-up over the reservation wage rises with an increase in α and in τ. Higher training costs will obviously raise the incentive of the employer to lower the quit rate by raising the wage. In addition, the higher is α, the more sensitive is the quit rate to the differential between the wage and the market-clearing wage, with the result that w will be raised.

To bring in the rate of unemployment explicitly, we substitute the familiar expression for z:

$$z = (1 - U)w^* + Ub,$$

where U is the unemployment rate, w^* the wage available elsewhere in the economy, and b the unemployment benefit. If all firms are similarly motivated, $w = w^*$ and therefore by substitution we get

$$w = k[(1 - U)w + Ub],$$

and

$$w^{EFF} = \frac{kU}{1 - k(1 - U)} b = \left[\frac{U}{U - (1 - 1/k)} \right] b.$$

[efficiency real wage curve]

It is interesting to note that this gives exactly the same form of relationship between the real wage and the unemployment rate as was obtained in the monopoly union model. Thus, the efficiency real wage curve that comes out of the turnover model behaves just as the bargained real wage curve in the monopoly union model (see Fig. 17.8). The efficiency real wage curve, ERW, plays the same role as the BRW in macroeconomic analysis.

17.2.2 Reducing the Incentive to Shirk (Shapiro and Stiglitz 1984)

As noted in the introduction, it has long been known that employment contracts can seldom ensure that the employee works hard.[11] This is

---

[11] For an interesting comparison between the Marxian and so-called neo-Hobbesian approaches (e.g. Shapiro and Stiglitz) to the role of unemployment as a 'disciplining device' in dealing with shirking, see Bowles (1985).

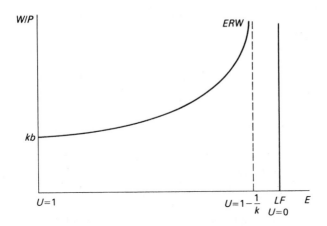

Fig. 17.8 The efficiency real wage curve, derived from the turnover cost model

because continuous monitoring is too costly and also because it is difficult legally to define 'hard' or 'effective' work. A further problem arises from the complexity of production processes characterized by the division of labour. It is often difficult to identify the product of an individual worker engaged in team production. In order to illustrate why the possibility of shirking may lead an employer to raise the wage above the market-clearing level, let us begin by identifying the conditions under which a worker might not work hard.

1   We assume that workers prefer not working hard to working hard:

$$v(\overset{+}{w}, \overset{-}{e}) = w - g(e),$$

where v is the total utility of the worker and depends positively on the wage, w, and negatively on effort, e. A simple explicit utility function is shown on the right-hand side and we will assume further that

$e = 0$ is a situation in which no effort is made, i.e. shirking;
$e = 1$ represents hard work; and
$g(0) = 0$.

Thus the utility associated with shirking equals the wage paid by the employer. For simplicity, we will write $g(1)$ as e, the value to the worker of the disutility of effort (measured in the same units as the real wage).

2   If an employee is hired for one period, and paid the minimum necessary to induce him or her to turn up for work, i.e. b, the unemployment benefit, then, whether he or she is monitored or not, it will pay to shirk, i.e. to set $e = 0$. This is because he or she will get b and will be able to get b next period from another employer, as long as b is the minimum wage at which people will turn up for work. For the worker not

to shirk, the employer must pay a wage greater than this. In addition, there must be monitoring of effort so that there is some probability of getting caught, and if caught shirking, the employee must be sacked. These three conditions create an incentive not to shirk. The problem for the employer is to set the wage, w, so as to prevent shirking, and the level this has to be set at depends on what the worker could get if she shirks and is caught (the outside wage, called z):

$$z = p(E) w^* + [1 - p(E)] b,$$

where w^* is the wage other firms are thought to be paying, $p(E)$ is the probability of finding another job, and b is the minimum wage workers would accept (i.e. to compensate them for the disutility of turning up for work) which is equal to the utility they receive whilst unemployed. We are assuming this is equal to the value of the unemployment benefit, b.

If the worker shirks, then assuming a probability of being caught shirking of π, he or she will get:

$$(1 - \pi)w + \pi z;$$

which is

$(1 - \pi)w$	$+$	$\pi p(E)w^*$	$+$	$\pi[1 - p(E)]b$
Probability of not being caught (does not get caught, so continues to get w)	$+$	Probability of being caught, but times probability of getting another job at w^*	$+$	Probability of being caught and becoming unemployed times the unemployment benefit

If, as usual, we assume for simplicity that the probability of getting another job is equal to one minus the unemployment rate, U, then

$$p(E) = 1 - U$$

The utility available from shirking is then

$$\upsilon_{shirking} = (1 - \pi)w + \pi(1 - U)w^* + \pi Ub,$$

and the utility from not shirking is

$$\upsilon_{not\,shirking} = w - e.$$

Thus, the employer sets the wage so that the utility from not shirking exceeds that which arises if the employee shirks:

$$w - e > (1 - \pi)w + \pi(1 - U)w^* + \pi Ub.$$

If all employers behave in this way, then w^* is equal to w:

$$w - e > w - \pi w + \pi w - \pi Uw + \pi Ub.$$

If we change signs and rearrange,

$$e < (w - b)\pi U.$$

So

$$w > b + e/\pi U.$$

The minimum wage consistent with the discouragement of shirking is the efficiency real wage, w^{EFF}:

$$w^{EFF} = b + e/\pi U.$$

[efficiency real wage curve]

If πU is equal to one, i.e. if people are certain to get caught if they shirk and are certain to be unemployed if they are caught, then $w = b + e$; i.e., everyone pays workers just enough to compensate them for turning up, b, and for the effort involved, e. However, if $\pi < 1$—i.e. if there is not perfect monitoring and this is the typical case—then a premium has to be added by the employer to discourage shirking. If for example your chance of losing your job and remaining unemployed were one-half, then you would need to be paid twice your true effort premium to induce you to exert effort, as there would be a 50% chance of your still earning the premium even if you shirked. Thus, to make the worker's expected loss from shirking greater than the disutility of working, the actual premium would have to be worth double. Figure 17.9 illustrates the efficiency real wage curve and shows the premium that must be paid to induce hard work. For any rate of unemployment, the efficiency real wage will be higher, the more disutility is attached to working hard (the value of e) and the lower is π, the probability of being caught shirking. As unemployment falls, the cost of

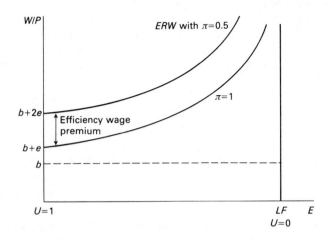

Fig. 17.9 The efficiency real wage curve, derived from the shirking model
The efficiency wage premium must be paid in the presence of imperfect monitoring of effort.

job loss diminishes and a higher efficiency real wage must be paid to prevent shirking. This is the sense in which unemployment can be viewed as a 'worker discipline device'.

17.3 Wage-Bargaining Institutions and Equilibrium Unemployment Outcomes

As outlined in Chapter 16, interest has developed in the past decade as to the relationship between the institutional structure of wage bargaining and the outcome for equilibrium unemployment. The traditional view in the economics literature has been that decentralization of wage- and price-setting (the competitive model) is necessary for efficiency. This has led to the presumption that more decentralized structures are more conducive to economic efficiency and to the creation of full employment at the aggregate level.

However, a separate strand of argument has emerged from the apparent empirical relationship between a highly centralized wage-bargaining system and the maintainence of low unemployment. The two supply-side shocks of the 1970s threw into sharp relief the comparative ability of different economies to maintain low unemployment. It seemed that countries with highly centralized bargaining structures and those with highly decentralized wage- and price-setting were best able to cope with the supply shocks and to contain the rise in unemployment consequent on the shocks. In order to explain this 'hump-shaped' relationship, attention turned towards imperfectly competitive labour markets. It has been argued that in democratic societies interest groups tend to form to defend their members' interests. If this is so, then there appear to be two paths towards efficiency: either to increase the size of the interest groups so that they become large enough to take account of the social interest, or to decentralize and thereby render the interest groups unable to affect the social outcome.

As noted earlier, a number of studies have attempted to divide the major industrialized economies into groups according to the degree of centralization of wage-bargaining. Economies are called centralized when employees and employers are organized into nationwide unions, where the rate of 'unionization' of both employers and employees is high, and where wages are negotiated at the central level. The decentralized group is characterized by wage- and price-setting at firm level, while in the intermediate group wage negotiations occur at industry level. Austria and the Nordic countries are found in the first group; the USA, Canada, Japan, and Switzerland are in the decentralized group, and the UK, France, Italy, West Germany, the Netherlands, Australia, and Belgium are in the intermediate group. Figure 17.10 illustrates the hump-shaped relationship

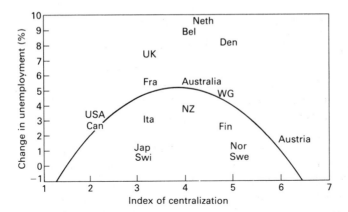

Fig. 17.10 The centralization of wage-bargaining in OECD economies and the rise in unemployment from 1968–73 to 1980–85
Source: Pohjola (1989)

between the rise in unemployment from the early 1970s to the mid-1980s, and the index of centralization.

Calmfors and Driffill (1988) have presented the clearest theoretical argument in support of the existence of a hump-shaped relationship. It is clearest to begin by considering why low equilibrium unemployment would be expected from the two extremes of organization of wage-bargaining, i.e. firm-level bargaining and a very centralized system of bargaining. In each case, it is assumed that the union's utility function includes both the level of employment and the real wage. The fundamental idea is that both the decentralized union and the centralized union perceive a very adverse trade-off between the real wage and employment. The explanation differs in each case. In the case of the decentralized union, if the union sets a high money wage, this is passed on in the firm's price. Given the high degree of substitutability between the products of firms in an industry, the firm in question would lose a substantial amount of demand. As a consequence, it would cut back employment sharply. Thus, any real wage gain to union members would be at the expense of a considerable decline in employment. This chain of reasoning prevents the firm-level union from pushing up wages and therefore at the level of the economy as a whole, assumed to consist of many firms, results in a low equilibrium rate of unemployment. One way of thinking about this outcome is that, although the union has the ability to set the wage in the firm, its effective market power is highly limited.

Paradoxically, the effective market power of a highly centralized union is also tightly circumscribed. In this case, if the union sets a high money wage, it knows that this will be passed on by all firms in higher prices. Real wages will not rise. Moreover, if the government is known to pursue a non-accommodating demand management policy, the union will know that unemployment will rise in the face of the rise in prices. (For example, with a fixed growth rate of the money supply, a rise in inflation as the result of the union setting higher money wages will produce a fall in the real money supply and therefore a fall in real aggregate demand and employment.) Hence, there is nothing for the union to gain from the pursuit of an aggressive wages policy. The result is a low equilibrium rate of unemployment.

It is in the intermediate case of industry-level wage bargaining where the perceived market power of the union is at its greatest. Higher wage and price rises at the industry level will result in a relatively limited reduction in demand and employment since the degree of substitutability between the products of different industries is small. Moreover, the impact on the general inflation rate of faster price rises in an individual industry is relatively small. This means that their real wages will rise by almost all the increase in nominal wages. (Also, the deflationary effect of a non-accommodating monetary policy will be perceived to be rather small.) For all of these reasons, the industry union believes it faces a relatively advantageous trade-off between higher real wages and reduced employment. The result is the adoption of an aggressive wage policy. This is reminiscent of our earlier discussion of the Prisoner's Dilemma problem in a system of unions operating in a non-cooperative manner (refer back to Section 8.2). The outcome at the level of the economy as a whole is a high equilibrium rate of unemployment.

To permit a more precise analysis, we use the simple monopoly union model introduced in Section 17.1 above. Recall that the bargained real wage curve was of the form

$$w^B = \frac{U}{U - 1/\eta}\, b, \quad \text{[bargained real wage curve]}$$

where η is the absolute value of the elasticity of the demand-for-labour function. As noted when the bargained real wage curve was derived, a low η (i.e. the elasticity of the demand for labour curve is low (close to 1)) means a high bargained real wage curve and a high η (a more elastic labour demand curve), a low BRW.

Decentralized wage bargaining, where the bargaining occurs at firm level, will take place in the context of a highly elastic demand-for-labour curve. For the reasons discussed above, the aggregate outcome for an economy where wage-setting occurs at firm level is a low bargained real wage curve. Given the price-determined real wage, the equilibrium rate of unemployment is therefore low (see U_N^D, Fig. 17.11).[12]

---

[12] Refer forward to sect. 18.3 for a discussion of the relationship between the individual firm's demand-for-labour curve (a partial equilibrium concept) and the price-determined real wage curve (a general equilibrium concept).

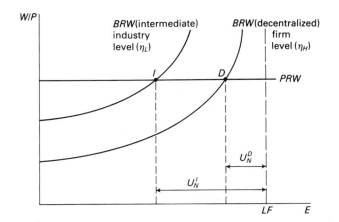

Fig. 17.11 The degree of centralization of wage-bargaining and the BRW curve

Let us contrast the case of firm-level wage-setting with industry wage-setting. The key difference between the two cases lies in the relative elasticity of the labour demand curves, which in turn reflects the relative price elasticity of the product demand curves. There is much less substitutability between the output of different industries than there is between the output of different firms. Therefore the industry demand curve is less elastic. The bargained real wage curve is high (see Fig. 17.11). For the economy as a whole, this is reflected in a high rate of equilibrium unemployment (U_N^I in Fig. 17.11).

In Fig. 17.12, union indifference curves are drawn. Assume that at each level, unions are in a monopoly position. The bargained real wage curves in the cases of firm- and industry-level wage-setting are derived by joining the points of tangency between the indifference curves and the appropriate labour demand curves. Each labour demand curve is indexed by the level of aggregate demand. For the firm-level union, the optimal point, given the level of aggregate demand, is on the relatively flat section of the indifference curve. For the industry union, the optimal point is on the relatively steep section of the indifference curve. The diagram makes clear that, at equilibrium unemployment in the economy with firm-level bargaining, the union is on a much higher indifference curve (point D) then with industry-level bargaining (point I). Nevertheless, the outcome of point I under industry-level bargaining is *rational* given the institutional structure of wage-setting.

But what of a centralized wage-setting structure? If wages are set for the economy as a whole, the union is aware of the requirement that at the equilibrium rate of unemployment the real wage must equal the price-determined real wage. Thus, the union will choose its most preferred point

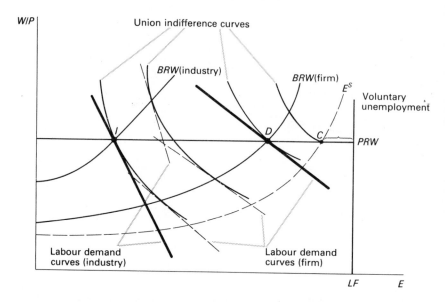

Fig. 17.12 Centralization of wage-bargaining and equilibrium unemployment outcomes

along the PRW curve. The highest indifference curve will be that consistent with the maximum level of employment attainable, i.e. in principle at an unemployment rate of zero; to be a little more precise, the union will choose the point where the labour supply curve crosses the price-determined real wage curve. Only *voluntary unemployment* will remain (point *C* in Fig. 17.12).

One further argument (Calmfors and Driffill 1988) can be made to suggest that fully centralized bargaining will produce lower equilibrium unemployment than any alternative structure. This relates to the issue of so-called *fiscal externalities*. An economy-wide union recognizes that its members will have to pay for the unemployment benefits that are paid to the unemployed—through taxation. This provides an additional incentive to hold the rate of unemployment down.

Calmfors–Driffill: a Qualification

The Calmfors–Driffill argument represents a major intellectual advance. It is the first persuasive attempt to relate unemployment rates in different countries to a properly articulated microeconomic theory of wage-bargaining. The following qualifications should not detract from the importance we attach to their approach.

The argument assumes that, if bargaining takes place at firm level, no external pressures are put on firms to hold down wage increases, so that it is the presumed high elasticity of product demand that maintains the wage restraint. But for one of the 'star performers' in the 'decentralized' wage-setting category, Japan, there is considerable co-ordination between large companies in the wage-setting process. As we will see in the accompanying box, one way of modelling such co-ordination is to assume that employers collectively are able to impose a sanction on an individual employer who concedes too large a wage increase. It may be more plausible to argue that it is the *co-ordination between employers* that holds down wage increases rather than a high product elasticity of demand. Another star performer in the decentralized wage-setting category, Switzerland, has very powerful employer organizations and so may also owe its wage restraint to employer co-ordination. If Japan and Switzerland are removed from the 'decentralized' category on the basis that their low equilibrium rates of unemployment derive not from the *level* at which wage-setting occurs but from a quite different aspect of the wage-setting process, namely the extent of employer co-ordination, then the statistical basis for the hump-shaped relation is much weaker.

*Modelling Wage Co-ordination among Employers

One way of modelling wage co-ordination among employers is to suppose that employers can collectively sanction the individual employer who concedes too large a wage increase. In terms of Jackman's bargaining model (Section 17.1 above), assume that a term $C(W_i/P) = C(w)$—the cost of sanctions—is associated with any given money wage increase W_i relative to the general price level P. Assuming that P_i relative to P is always set to maximize profits, π, the effect of a wage increase on π is given by

$$\partial\pi/\partial w = (\partial/\partial w)\{p\,Q(p) - w\,E[Q(p)] - C(w)\} = -E - C'(w).$$

The implicit formula in the Jackman model for determining the bargained wage is:

$$\beta/(w - z) + \pi'(w)/\pi = 0.$$

Substitution of our expanded term for $\pi'(w)$ gives

$$\frac{\beta\pi}{E + C'(w)} = w - z.$$

Hence

$$\frac{\beta[pQ - wE - C(w)}{E} \quad \frac{E}{E + C'(w)},$$

and since from the standard formula for profit maximization

$$p = \frac{\varepsilon}{\varepsilon - 1} \frac{w}{Q'(E)},$$

this implies

$$\frac{w\beta\left(\frac{\varepsilon}{\varepsilon - 1} \frac{1}{\alpha} - 1 - C/wE\right)}{1 + C'(w)/E} = w - z,$$

where ε is the price elasticity of demand and α the employment elasticity of output. Using the usual expression for z, $z = Ub + (1 - U)w$, as in the original derivation, we get

$$w^B = b\left(1 - \frac{\beta}{U} \frac{\{[\varepsilon/\varepsilon - 1](1/\alpha) - 1 - C/wE\}}{1 + C'(w)/E}\right)^{-1}$$

Thus, the larger is C, the cost of sanctions which can be imposed by the group of employers or employers' organization, relative to the wage bill and the greater is C' per employee, the lower will the bargained real wage be.

17.3.1 Bargaining Structures and Supply-Side Shocks

Finally, it is useful to note the difference in reaction of economies with differing bargaining structures to a supply shock. Recall that the simplest way of representing a supply shock (such as a rise in the price of imported raw materials, e.g. oil) in the wage–employment diagram is as a downward shift of the price-determined real wage curve. Taking the centralized system first, we will find little change in equilibrium unemployment as the result of a supply shock; the union chooses the highest indifference curve consistent with the *new* price-determined real wage curve. The equilibrium rate of unemployment moves from C to C'. In the case of decentralized bargaining, the bargained real wage curve is very steep at high levels of employment. As a result, the supply shock leads to relatively little change in the equilibrium unemployment rate. By contrast, in the intermediate system with industry-level bargaining, the bargained real wage curve is much flatter where it intersects the price-determined real wage curve. Equilibrium unemployment therefore rises much more sharply in the presence of a supply shock than in either of the other two wage-setting systems. Figure 17.13 gives an illustration of the relative impact of a supply shock in the three different cases. Attempts to estimate the responsiveness

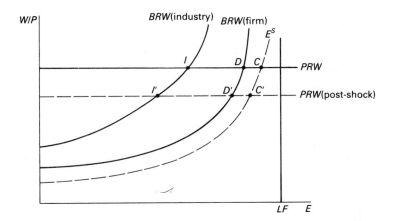

Fig. 17.13 Bargaining structures and supply shocks
The centralized and decentralized systems of wage-bargaining produce a small rise in equilibrium unemployment consequent on a supply shock (downward shift of the PRW), since wage curves are very steep at high employment; the industry-level system leads to a much greater rise in equilibrium unemployment.

of real wages to unemployment (refer back to Table 6.1) suggest that the six low unemployment countries[13] (Austria, Finland, Japan, Norway, Sweden, Switzerland) have the six highest measures of the responsiveness of wages to unemployment. This set of countries represents both centralized and decentralized systems of wage-bargaining (Alogoskoufis and Manning 1988: 443).

*The Slope of the BRW at Equilibrium Unemployment and the Elasticity of Demand

The algebra relating the industry bargained real wage curve and the firm BRW demonstrates the above points clearly. In equilibrium,

$$w^P = w^B = \left(\frac{U}{U - 1/\eta}\right)b.$$

Call η_F the (high) elasticity of labour demand in the case of the firm and U_F the equilibrium unemployment rate for the firm; η_I and U_I correspondingly for industry bargaining. Then,

---

[13] The USA is the exception—the role of nominal rigidities (adjustment costs to changing wages and prices) appears significant in this case.

$$w^P = \left(\frac{U_F}{U_F - 1/\eta_F}\right)b = \left(\frac{U_I}{U_I - 1/\eta_I}\right)b.$$

(1) We show that $U_I > U_F$ if $\eta_I < \eta_F$; i.e., equilibrium unemployment is higher for industry-level bargaining than for firm-level if the demand is more elastic at firm level. Derive U_F:

$$(U_F - 1/\eta_F)w^P = U_F b$$

$$U_F w^P - w^P/\eta_F = U_F b.$$

Therefore

$$U_F = \frac{w^P}{\eta_F}(w^P - b)^{-1}.$$

Similarly

$$U_I = \frac{w^P}{\eta_I}(w^P - b)^{-1}.$$

These imply that

$$U_I/U_F = \eta_F/\eta_I.$$

(2) We now derive the slopes of the two BRW curves at U_I and U_F respectively. For both I and F,

$$\frac{dw}{dU} = \frac{(U - 1/\eta)b - Ub}{(U - 1/\eta)^2} = -\frac{b/\eta}{(U - 1/\eta)^2}$$

or

$$\frac{dw}{dE} = \frac{b/\eta}{(U - 1/\eta)^2} > 0$$

(for $U > 1/\eta$, i.e., in the relevant range of U). So

$$dw/dE \ (I \text{ at } U_I) = (b/\eta_I)/(U_I - 1/\eta_I)^2$$

$$dw/dE \ (F \text{ at } u_F) = (b/\eta_F)/(U_F - 1/\eta_F)^2.$$

From (1), $U_I = (w^P/\eta_I)/(w^P - b)$, so

$$dw/dE \ (I \text{ at } u_I) \equiv \frac{(b/\eta_I)}{\left(\dfrac{w^P}{w^P - b}\dfrac{1}{\eta_I} - \dfrac{1}{\eta_I}\right)^2}$$

$$= \frac{(b/\eta_I)}{\left(\dfrac{1}{\eta_I}\right)^2 \left(\dfrac{b}{w^P - b}\right)^2}$$

$$= \frac{(w^P - b)^2 \eta_I}{b}.$$

Similarly, for the slope of F's BRW at U_F,

$$dw/dE \ (F \text{ at } U_F) = \frac{(w^P - b)^2 \eta_F}{b}.$$

Hence the ratio,

$$\frac{dw/dE \ (F \text{ at } U_F)}{dw/dE \ (I \text{ at } U_I)} = \frac{\eta_F}{\eta_I}.$$

This shows that the slope of the firm-level bargaining BRW is steeper when it cuts the PRW (i.e. at equilibrium unemployment) than the industry-level bargaining BRW.

18

The Behaviour of Firms and Product Markets under Imperfect Competition

In this chapter, the aim is to fill out the analysis of firm behaviour and product markets under imperfect competition which was presented in Part II. As we have seen in Chapter 16, the stylized facts of contemporary industrialized economies suggest that, given the money wage, prices adjust rather little to demand shocks, real wages change little over the cycle—if anything, real wages are slightly procyclical—and firms are typically demand-constrained. These 'stylized facts' are quite consistent with a model in which the price-determined real wage curve is fairly flat; a rise in aggregate demand will not provoke a price response—prices rise only as a consequence of the response of money wages to the reduction in un-employment associated with higher aggregate demand. Secondly, under the simple assumption of prices being set immediately after wages, the real wage is equal to the price-determined real wage and hence is invariant over the cycle to the extent that the price-determined real wage is flat. Once lags in price- and wage-setting reflecting costs of adjustment are introduced in a more realistic model, the flatter the PRW, the less variation will there be in real wages over the cycle for any given bargained real wage curve. Reasons for nominal inertia in prices, i.e. why they are not reset continuously, were canvassed briefly in Chapter 16 and will not be discussed again here. The theoretical task is to show the way in which a range of different product market situations imply a price-determined real wage for the economy and why firms take the complementary output and employment decisions.

As noted in Chapter 6 above, there are a number of theoretical explanations that have been put forward to explain the apparent flatness of the price-determined real wage curve. The evidence on this is by no means all in yet. Here we set out the most prominent contenders in more detail than was appropriate in Part II. First, there is the case of monopoly, where the profit-maximizing firm sets price where marginal cost equals marginal revenue. The shape of the price-determined real wage implied by this condition then depends on how marginal costs and the elasticity of demand vary with changes in output. The PRW will be downward-sloping if marginal costs are increasing and the elasticity of demand is constant. However, a flat PRW arises *either* if marginal costs are fairly flat and the elasticity of demand is constant, *or* if marginal costs are increasing and the elasticity of demand rises to the correct degree with output. Empirical evidence and theoretical arguments have been put forward in support of each combination.

A second set of arguments in favour of a flat PRW come from theories that take explicit account of the limits on rationality imposed by the uncertainty of the environment in which the firm operates. Normal cost pricing, where the firm sets the price as a mark-up on expected unit labour costs at a standard level of capacity utilization, is frequently rationalized this way. Although the normal cost pricing (NCP) hypothesis arose from inferences based on observation, attempts have been made to develop theoretical foundations for it. One idea is that NCP is an example of firm behaviour consistent with *bounded rationality*. In conditions of uncertainty, the use of a rule of thumb such as mark-up pricing may appear to firms to be their optimal course of action. It is argued that, even if firms have a good idea of their marginal costs, they lack sufficient information about the demand curve facing them to calculate marginal revenue. Alternatively, the idea of near rationality (Akerlof and Yellen 1985) can be invoked once again: the losses from inertial price-setting are small relative to the outcome from strict profit maximization.

The second section of the chapter is a digression. What happens if the price-determined real wage does in fact slope downwards? The section briefly outlines the macroeconomic implications of a *downward-sloping* price-determined real wage. We show that, if the PRW does slope downward, this does not affect two of the basic features of the imperfect competition model: (1) there is still a unique equilibrium rate of unemployment, and (2) the product market does not clear; i.e., firms are demand-constrained. However, it is more difficult to render a downward-sloping PRW consistent with the evidence that prices are unresponsive to changes in aggregate demand. This is the reason we have used a flat PRW throughout the book.

In the third section, we move to consider oligopolistic theories, showing briefly how a price-determined real wage curve can be derived, and then going on to illustrate the usefulness of oligopolistic models for analysing price-setting in the open economy.

In the final section of the chapter, we turn to the relationship between the firm's price and employment decisions and the aggregate relationships between prices, wages, and employment. We present an explicit comparison between the partial equilibrium relationships for an individual firm and the equilibrium for the firm sector as a whole. This helps to clarify the notion of the demand constraint on the firm sector under imperfect competition.

18.1   Microeconomic Arguments for a Flat Price-Determined Real Wage

18.1.1   Imperfect Competition with Marginal Cost equals Marginal Revenue Pricing

Let us first take the case of monopoly. The monopoly firm maximizes profits when the extra revenue from a rise in output of one unit equals the extra cost associated with producing that additional unit. To focus on price-setting, we explain the *identical* argument in terms of a unit increase in price. The additional revenue from a unit increase in price comprises two elements: first, the increase in revenue on each unit sold because of the higher price received ($+y$); and second, the fall in revenue associated with the reduced sales caused by the higher price ($P(\mathrm{d}y/\mathrm{d}P)$). The reduction in costs associated with the price increase is equal to the lower wages that need be paid as the result of lower output ($W(\mathrm{d}E/\mathrm{d}y)(\mathrm{d}y/\mathrm{d}P)$). The profit-maximizing monopolist equates this marginal revenue with the associated marginal cost:

$$y + P(\mathrm{d}y/\mathrm{d}P) = W(\mathrm{d}E/\mathrm{d}y)(\mathrm{d}y/\mathrm{d}P).$$

Multiplying through by $\mathrm{d}P/\mathrm{d}y$ gives

$$y(\mathrm{d}P/\mathrm{d}y) + P = W(\mathrm{d}E/\mathrm{d}y).$$

Hence $P[1 + (y/P)(\mathrm{d}P/\mathrm{d}y)] = W/(\mathrm{d}y/\mathrm{d}E)$.

Defining $\varepsilon = |(\mathrm{d}y/\mathrm{d}P)(P/y)|$, the absolute value of the price elasticity of demand, and noting that $\mathrm{d}y/\mathrm{d}E$ is the marginal product of labour which we will call MPL,

$$P(1 - 1/\varepsilon) = \frac{W}{MPL}.$$

We can now write the pricing equation as

$$P = \left(\frac{1}{1 - 1/\varepsilon}\right) \frac{W}{MPL}.$$

[price equation; monopoly]

Thus, in the case of the monopoly, the mark-up on *marginal costs* is $1/(1 - 1/\varepsilon)$. Numerical examples with a constant demand elasticity, ε, help illustrate the price equation. For example, if the elasticity of demand is 2, then price will be twice marginal cost; a lower elasticity of demand ($\varepsilon = 1.5$) means that price is three times marginal cost. This confirms our intuition that the less responsive is demand to a rise in price (the lower is the value of ε), the higher is the profit-maximizing price. As the value of the elasticity of demand rises towards infinity, we move towards the case of perfect competition where price is set equal to marginal cost: the mark-up is 1. At the other limiting case where the elasticity of demand tends towards 1, the mark-up tends towards infinity. The reason is clear: with $\varepsilon = 1$, total revenue is always the same irrespective of prices, so the monopoly maximizes profits by producing a vanishingly small amount so that costs are virtually zero; the price therefore tends to infinity.

By rearranging the price equation, we can deduce the economy's price-determined real wage curve:

$$w^P = (1 - 1/\varepsilon)MPL.$$
$$\text{[price-determined real wage (PRW)]}$$

In Fig. 18.1, we depict a standard downward-sloping marginal product of labour curve and show two different price-determined real wage curves reflecting different values of the elasticity of demand. When $\varepsilon = 2$, the price-determined real wage will be 0.5 of the marginal product of labour ($\frac{1}{2}MPL$); with $\varepsilon = 3$, $w^P = \frac{2}{3}MPL$. The lower is the elasticity of demand, the greater is monopoly power and therefore the lower is the price-determined real wage at each level of employment.

The price-determined real wage is downward-sloping in the case of a constant elasticity of demand and a downward-sloping marginal product of labour. There are two reasons why the PRW could be flat. (1) It is simple to see that if both ε, the elasticity of demand, and MPL, the marginal produce of labour, are constant, the price equation reduces to that of our standard case of mark-up pricing and the PRW is therefore flat. (2) If the marginal product of labour is downward-sloping but the mark-up falls in the level of employment (or output), then it is possible that the loss of monopoly power at higher output could just offset the fall in the real wage because of the declining marginal product of labour producing a flat PRW. The following summary of recent research into the slope of the marginal

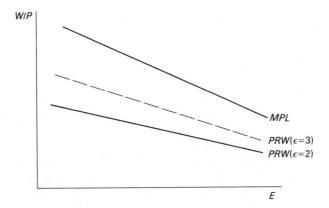

Fig. 18.1 Relationship between marginal product of labour, price elasticity of demand, ε, and the price-determined real wage

cost curve and counter-cyclical mark-ups follows closely the assessment by Blanchard and Fischer (1989: 463–8).

The Slope of the Marginal Cost Curve

There is a long tradition of economic argument which seeks to explain why the imperfectly competitive firm's marginal cost curve is fairly flat. The facts taken as requiring explanation are summarized in Okun's law: firms are able to supply rising output with constant increases in employment. Attempts to explain this frequently hinge on why it may be rational for an imperfectly competitive firm to operate with excess capacity. More recently, formal arguments have been proposed to account for the existence of excess capacity as a tool of entry deterrence (e.g. Dixit 1980; Fudenberg and Tirole 1983).

However, while the theory is poorly developed, the 'facts' of the matter are themselves in dispute. Recent empirical work by Bils (1987) seeks to demonstrate the existence of rising marginal costs. The proponents of rising marginal costs point to the additional costs of overtime work as output is raised and to the higher costs of bringing into use older vintages of equipment to meet the additional demand. In other words, it is argued that excess capacity will exist in the form of *less efficient* and therefore higher-cost equipment. Nevertheless, Blanchard and Fischer conclude that, apart from Bils's work, 'most empirical studies are consistent with the notion that marginal costs are roughly constant or perhaps even declining' (1989: 465).

The Behaviour of the Mark-up

As mentioned in Chapter 6 above, one way of explaining a declining mark-up as output rises is to provide reasons for a pro-cyclical elasticity of demand. Bils's argument (Bils 1989) is based on the idea of investment by the firm in customer loyalty through the pricing decision. Customer loyalty confers monopoly power on the firm in relation to its old customers. He suggests that as demand rises there is an increase in the number of potential customers for the firm: the proportion of new to old customers rises. In an attempt to gain these new customers, the benefit of which will persist, the firm lowers its price. Thus, the mark-up falls as the level of demand rises. A different argument (Rotemberg and Saloner 1986) is that it is the degree of *collusion* between imperfectly competitive firms that falls as output rises. Lower collusion means lower mark-ups. The idea is that as demand rises the incentive for firms to deviate from the collusive solution by price-cutting increases because there is a larger potential gain in demand. Evidence in favour of either of these hypotheses appears mixed.

18.1.2 Normal Cost Pricing

To present a macroeconomic model based on imperfect competition in Part II, a simple yet plausible pricing hypothesis was adopted. This hypothesis was normal cost pricing (NCP), where a constant mark-up is added to normal unit costs. For simplicity, we assume that labour is the only variable input. The ith firm sets its price as

$$P_i = (1 + \mu)(W_i/\overline{LP}),$$

where μ is the markup and is $\overline{LP}$ labour productivity at normal capacity utilization. We generalized this pricing rule across the economy by assuming that all firms were identical:

$$P = (1 + \mu)(W/\overline{LP}),$$

which, on substituting $m = \mu/(1 + \mu)$ and rearranging, led to

$$w^P = \overline{LP}(1 - m).$$
$$\text{[price-determined real wage (PRW)]}$$

The short-run predictions of the model (the short run being defined as the period for which normal capacity utilization remains fixed) are that changes in aggregate demand have no effect on prices and that increased wages produce increased prices in proportion. The result is a horizontal price-determined real wage curve at the aggregate level.

The original idea of mark-up pricing as a general explanation of price-setting under imperfect competition for manufacturing firms came from an empirical study of 58 firms conducted by Hall and Hitch and published in 1939. They found that in practice businesses do not set prices according to marginalist principles, i.e. so as to equate marginal cost with marginal revenue. Furthermore, simple marginal cost pricing suggests frequent price variations—whenever cost or demand conditions change. Instead, observation suggested that prices were rather rigid in spite of variations in demand and marginal cost. The Hall–Hitch survey provoked a number of attempts to explain these observations. Since the initial study, a wealth of much stronger objective evidence has been put forward to support the existence of normal cost pricing. The best known study for the UK is that of Coutts *et al.* (1978).

Let us look a little more closely at the normal cost pricing principle. As stated earlier, for the ith firm a mark-up is added to the cost of production at a normal rate of capacity utilization:

$$P_i = (1 + \mu)(W_i/\overline{LP}).$$

The mark-up, μ, includes the capital cost per unit of output. Capital costs are fixed, so actual capital cost per unit will decline as the volume of output rises. For NCP purposes, however, unit capital costs are also assessed at normal capacity utilization.

A firm using normal cost pricing reacts to the divergence between demand and its current output level by altering only its sales, not its price. Its immediate reaction is to alter its stocks, and this prompts a change in output. This is exactly the type of quantity adjustment we first encountered in Part I under conditions of fixed prices. The firm reacts to a change in its normal costs (as the result for example of a wage increase) by raising its price. The level of the mark-up, μ, in a sector is dependent on the market power of the sector and will reflect the entry and exit conditions prevailing in the industry.

18.1.3 Conclusions

A number of hypotheses have been put forward to account for the observation that prices do not seem to respond much to changes in output, given the money wage. Of course, it may turn out to be the case that one hypothesis is appropriate to some industries in the economy, while another fits the behaviour in other industries.

18.2 Analysis with a Downward-Sloping Price-Determined Real Wage Curve

For completeness, it is useful to point out how the basic imperfect competition macroeconomic model operates when the price-determined real wage is downward-sloping. The accompanying box provides the details of the modifications to the analysis.

Macroeconomic Analysis with a Downward-Sloping PRW

We have seen above that, under conditions of imperfect competition, declining marginal productivity of labour in the absence of an offsetting pro-cyclical elasticity of demand means that the PRW will be downward-sloping. Because of the familiarity of the notion of marginal cost equals marginal revenue pricing and declining marginal productivity, it is useful to examine the implications for macroeconomic analysis of the resulting downward-sloping price-determined real wage. Note that a downward-sloping price-determined real wage produces the prediction of *counter*-cyclical real wages—a prediction inconsistent with the stylized facts presented in Chapter 16.[1]

---

[1] At least, if it is assumed that prices adjust faster to wage increases than wages adjust to price increases.

It is easy to show there is a unique equilibrium rate of unemployment. Figure 18.2 depicts the labour market diagram with the upward-sloping bargained real wage curve and the downward-sloping price-determined real wage curve; the inflation quadrant is drawn beneath. From the diagram it is clear that there is a unique equilibrium rate of unemployment at U_N; inflation will be constant. We now consider a lower unemployment rate, U_0. As in the standard analysis, a positive gap has opened up between the bargained real wage and the price-determined real wage. However, the analysis of the path of inflation associated with the higher level of employment deviates slightly from the standard one because the real wage changes.

Previously, with a horizontal PRW, we had a price equation:

$$P = (1 + \mu)(W/LP),$$

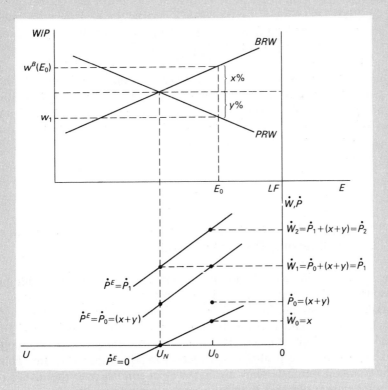

Fig. 18.2 Inflation analysis with a downward-sloping PRW

which, with constant LP and μ, resulted in the equation for price inflation of

$$\dot{P} = \dot{W}.$$

With a downward-sloping PRW—owing to falling MPL—the pricing equation is

$$P = \frac{1}{1 - 1/\varepsilon} \frac{W}{MPL},$$
[price equation; monopoly]

and therefore with a constant ε, price inflation will be equal to

$$\dot{P} = \dot{W} - M\dot{P}L.$$ [price inflation equation]

Assuming inflation of zero at the equilibrium rate of unemployment, money wages rise by $x\%$ to take the real wage up to the bargained real wage at U_0. As is clear from the diagram, prices must rise by more than $x\%$ in order to be consistent with profit maximization on the PRW. Prices will rise by $x + y\%$, taking the real wage down to w_1. In the following period, with unemployment still at U_0, unions secure money wage rises of last period's inflation (assuming simple adaptive expectations) plus a rise of $x + y\%$ to take the real wage up to the bargained real wage at U_0. Prices will then rise by exactly the same amount to return the real wage to w_1. Just as with the horizontal PRW, inflation rises continuously as long as the economy is kept at a rate of unemployment below the equilibrium through the use of an accommodating monetary policy.

18.3   Oligopolistic Pricing, the Price-Determined Real Wage, and Open Economy Pricing Behaviour

Once *oligopolistic* considerations are introduced, there are additional reasons for expecting prices to be insensitive to demand variations. In markets with few producers, it has been suggested that the interaction between firms could explain the divergence of pricing behaviour from standard marginalist predictions. In simple terms, the group of oligopolists seeks to expand the profits in the market in which they operate. This is their common interest. They are however in conflict over the division of the total market between them. In such a situation, the use of price cuts to enlarge one firm's market share would present the clear danger that *all* firms will retaliate to protect their own share. The result is a reduction of total profits. For reasons such as these, greater price rigidity might be expected than is predicted by the marginal cost criteria.

If firms are aware of their interdependence, simple maximizing strategies are insufficient as a means of modelling pricing decisions. We begin this section with the standard Cournot–Nash model of oligopoly. This is used to provide an introduction to the notion of interdependence, and a price-determined real wage curve is easily derived. However, since Cournot oligopolists choose the level of output rather than the price, we turn to the more appropriate Bertrand–Nash model where the oligopolists are price-setters producing differentiated goods. We show how price is set as a mark-up on unit costs, and thus at the aggregate level we have a price-determined real wage curve that emerges straightforwardly from the Bertrand model.

The Bertrand equilibrium produces an outcome for the firms inferior to the joint profit-maximizing position (this is also true of Cournot), and it is argued that in practice, where the price-setting game is repeated many times, firms would find a way of keeping to the joint profit-maximizing price. There are complications involved in working through such a 'repeated game', and to avoid going into these, we will make use of recent literature to sketch a simple game which mimics the operation of the repeated game. Once again, a mark-up pricing solution emerges. This model can be thought of as a modernized kinked demand curve theory. We find that prices are rigid in the face of changes in demand. For both Bertrand–Nash and the modernized kinked demand curve model, the emphasis is on the application to open economy pricing behaviour of the model. For a more detailed background to the analysis of oligopoly using game theory, see Tirole (1988), especially Part II, 'Strategic Interaction', and Chapter 6, 'Dynamic Price Competition and Tacit Collusion'.

18.3.1 The Cournot–Nash Model

A simple way of motivating the Cournot model[2] is to think of an industry consisting of two identical fishing boats which leave in the morning to make their catch and return in the evening to place the fish on the market. There is no communication between the boats, and the problem facing each one is to decide how many fish to catch given knowledge of the market demand for fish and knowing that the other boat faces the same problem. The problem facing each boat can be modelled as a one-shot prisoner's dilemma (refer back to Section 9.3). The pay-offs in terms of profits to each boat from following strategy 1 (the joint profit-maximizing one of catching few fish) and strategy 2 (the Cournot solution, where many fish are caught) are as follows:

---

[2] This example is from J. Friedman (1983).

		Player B	
		Low catch	High catch
Player A	Low catch	10 10	15 2
	High catch	2 15	5 5

Clearly, the dominant strategy involves minimizing the risk of ending up with profits of only 2—this would occur for boat A if they decided to catch few fish while boat B brought in a huge haul. B's large catch would push down the market price and A would be left with few fish to sell at the depressed price. Thus, both players will adopt the strategy of catching many fish and they will end up with less than the maximum amount of profits.

Let us look at the price that emerges from the Cournot solution and see how to derive a price-determined real wage curve. The market demand for the goods will depend simply on the price of the good relative to the general price level, and we denote this relative price by p. Thus, for the two firms, $p = F(q_A + q_B)$, where q_i is the output of the ith firm. To simplify, let us linearize this function:

$$p = \alpha - \beta(q_A + q_B).$$

Each firm chooses its output to maximize profits on the assumption that the output of the other firm is fixed. In other words, just as in our fishing example, outputs are chosen simultaneously. Real profits of firm A, assuming constant unit labour requirements, τ (identical for each firm), and a common wage, are

$$\pi_A = q_A p - \tau w q_A = \alpha q_A - \beta q_A^2 - \beta q_A q_B - \tau w q_A,$$

where p is the industry price relative to the general price level and w is the money wage relative to the general price level.

Thus, by differentiating π_A with respect to q_A and setting equal to zero, we deduce that the profit-maximizing output for A is given by

$$\alpha - 2\beta q_A - \beta q_B = \tau w.$$

Since both firms are identical, output of both will be the same when both are profit-maximizing. Hence

$$q_A = q_B = q \Rightarrow \alpha - 3\beta q = \tau w$$

or

$$q = (\alpha - \tau w)/3\beta.$$

We can work out the price implied by this level of output by substituting combined output, $2q$, back into the demand curve:

$$p = \alpha - \beta[\tfrac{2}{3}(\alpha - \tau w)/\beta] = \tfrac{1}{3}\alpha + \tfrac{2}{3}\tau w. \quad \text{[pricing equation]}$$

Thus we have a price equation showing the link between the relative price level and the real wage. If we now imagine that the economy consists of many similarly organized industries setting identical prices, relative prices will be equal to 1. This defines a price-determined real wage. Thus, setting $p = 1$ gives $1 = \tfrac{1}{3}\alpha + \tfrac{2}{3}\tau w$. Hence

$$w^P = \tfrac{3}{2}(1 - \tfrac{1}{3}\alpha)\,\tau^{-1}.$$
$$\text{[price-determined real wage curve]}$$

However, it is clear that the Cournot setup is unsatisfactory for the modelling of price-setting, since for Cournot it is quantities that are chosen by the firms; the price simply emerges when the output is placed on the market.

18.3.2 The Bertrand–Nash Model

To consider the Bertrand model, we assume that each producer sells a differentiated product and perceives a demand curve for its output which depends inversely on the price it sets relative to the average price level and directly on the price its rival sets. So as to be able to extend the results to look at open economy pricing, let us identify one firm as the domestic firm and the other as the foreign firm. The foreign firm's price and output are indicated by * and we set the exchange rate equal to one for simplicity. For the domestic firm in the ith industry, demand is

$$q_i = \alpha - \beta P_i/P + \Gamma P_i^*/P.$$

The domestic firm's nominal profits are equal to

$$\Pi_i = P_i q_i - W\tau q_i$$
$$= P_i \alpha - \beta P_i^2/P + \Gamma P_i^* P_i/P - W\tau\alpha + \beta P_i W\tau/P - \Gamma W\tau P_i^*/P,$$

where for simplicity we assume that the domestic and foreign firm have the same nominal wage, W, and unit labour requirement, τ. To find out the domestic firm's profit-maximizing price, we differentiate Π_i with respect to P_i and set equal to zero:

$$\partial\Pi_i/\partial P_i = \alpha - 2\beta P_i/P + \Gamma P_i^*/P + \beta W\tau/P = 0.$$

Thus,

$$P_i/P = (\alpha/2\beta) + (\Gamma/2\beta)(P_i^*/P) + (\tau/2)(W/P).$$

Now, we can imagine two different situations about the determination of P_i^*. The first is where $P_i^* = P^*$ is determined externally quite independently of P_i. The second is the Bertrand model proper which will be set out later.

In the first case, if all domestic firms are in the same situation so that $P_i = P$, we multiply the above equation by P:

$$P = (\alpha/2\beta)P + (\Gamma/2\beta)P^* + (\tau/2)W,$$

and rearranging,

$$P = [\beta/(2\beta - \alpha)]W\tau + [\Gamma/(2\beta - \alpha)]P^*. \quad \text{[price equation]}$$

Let $b = \beta/(2\beta - \alpha)$ and $c = \Gamma/(2\beta - \alpha)$. The price equation is

$$P = bW\tau + cP^*.$$

The price set by the domestic firm depends both on domestic costs, $W\tau$, and on the price set by the foreign firm, P^*. The pricing equation can be rearranged to derive the price-determined real wage, which will depend inversely on price competitiveness, $\theta (\theta \equiv P^*e/P)$:

$$w^P = \frac{(1 - c\theta)}{b\tau}. \quad \text{[price determined real wage]}$$

Secondly, we look at the Bertrand analysis itself. The logic is analogous to the Cournot model, except that the domestic firm and its foreign rival each set their *price* on the assumption that the other's will not change in consequence. The equilibrium pair of prices, $\bar{P}$ and $\bar{P}^*$, is defined by $\bar{P}$ maximizing the domestic firm's profits given $\bar{P}^*$, and $\bar{P}^*$ maximizing the foreign firm's profits given $\bar{P}$.

We already know what price, P', the domestic firm will set to maximize its profits contingent on an arbitrary foreign price, P'^*:

$$P' = bW\tau + cP'^*.$$

Mutatis mutandis, the foreign rival will set

$$P''^* = bW^*\tau^* + cP'',$$

to maximize its profits against an arbitrary domestic price, P''. The prices of the two companies are in equilibrium against each other when these two price equations both hold and when

$$P' = P''(= P) \text{ and } P'^* = P''^*(= P^*).$$

To find the equilibrium pair of prices, P and P^*, we have to solve the two simultaneous equations:

$$P = bW\tau + cP^*$$

$$P^* = bW^*\tau^* + cP.$$

Solving for P and P^*,

$$P = \left(\frac{b}{1 - c^2}\right)W\tau + \left(\frac{cb}{1 - c^2}\right)W^*\tau^*$$

$$P^* = \left(\frac{b}{1 - c^2}\right)W^*\tau^* + \left(\frac{cb}{1 - c^2}\right)W\tau.$$

To derive the price-determined real wage curve for the domestic economy, assuming all domestic firms behave similarly, we divide both sides of the first equation by W, and multiply and divide the second term on the right-hand side by τ:

$$P/W = \left(\frac{b}{1 - c^2}\right)\tau + \left(\frac{cb}{1 - c^2}\right)\tau\frac{W^*\tau^*}{W\tau}$$

$$= \left(\frac{b\tau}{1 - c^2}\right)(1 + c\theta_W),$$

where θ_W is defined as $(W^*\tau^*/W\tau)$. This measures *international competitiveness* in terms of relative unit labour costs (refer back to Section 11.5). Rearranging and remembering that τ, unit labour requirements, is the inverse of labour productivity,

$$w^P = \left(\frac{LP}{b}\right)\left(\frac{1 - c^2}{1 + c\theta_W}\right)$$

[price-determined real wage]

   A diagrammatic presentation of the pricing reactions of the two firms helps clarify the analysis. Figure 18.3 has the domestic price, P, on the vertical axis and the foreign price, P^*, on the horizontal. The 45° line is shown. Along this line foreign and domestic prices are equal; competitiveness is one. The price equation for the domestic firm tells us the price that will be chosen by the domestic firm at each level of the foreign price. When drawn in P–P^* space, this is the domestic firm's reaction function denoted by R (domestic firm) in Fig. 18.3. It has a slope of less than 45°. To construct the domestic firm's reaction function, we find where the isoprofit contours are tangential to vertical lines marking the price chosen by the foreign firm. At P^*_L, the profit-maximizing price for the domestic firm is shown by point A. If the domestic firm set a higher price, such as at point a, then the loss of demand outweighs the revenue gain; if a lower price is set (such as a point a'), then the gain in demand is outweighed by the revenue loss. If the foreign firm were to set a high price, P^*_H, then the domestic firm would choose point B: it pays the domestic firm to raise its price but not by as much as the rise in the foreign price. With a higher price, the domestic firm reaps a revenue gain; by not raising its price by as much as its competitor, this gain is augmented by a competitive advantage as the domestic firm takes some of the foreign firm's market.
   The reaction function for the foreign firm (R (foreign firm)) is

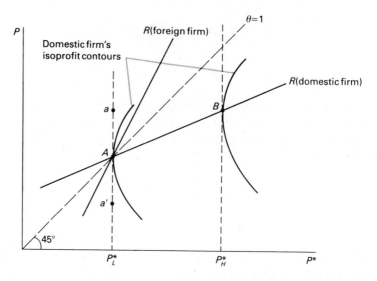

Fig. 18.3 Bertrand–Nash model: reaction functions of domestic and foreign firms
Bertrand–Nash equilibrium is at A (assuming identical costs)

constructed in exactly the same way. If the foreign and domestic firms
happen to have the same unit costs, then the Bertrand–Nash equilibrium
where the two reaction functions intersect will occur on the 45° line. This is
indicated by point A in Figs. 18.3 and 18.4. The domestic and foreign

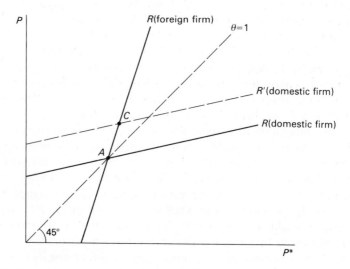

Fig. 18.4 Bertrand–Nash model: domestic cost increase produces new
Bertrand–Nash equilibrium at C; domestic firm's price competitiveness falls
$(P > P^*)$

prices will coincide. Let us now consider a rise in domestic costs. This shifts the domestic firm's reaction function upward to R' (see Fig. 18.4). There is a new Bertrand–Nash equilibrium at point C with the domestic firm's price higher than that of its rival: the domestic firm's price competitiveness has been eroded because, although its rival also raises its price, it does not do so by the same extent. The foreign firm takes the opportunity to increase its share of the market.

Thus, the domestic firm is faced with a deterioration of its price competitiveness (and hence there is a rise in the share of imports of the domestic economy) and with some deterioration in profitability, since from the pricing equation the rise in domestic costs is not fully passed on. We therefore have pricing behaviour that is a hybrid of the two extremes of mark-up pricing and world pricing discussed in Chapter 11. Pure mark-up pricing is the case where a domestic cost rise is fully passed on in the price level and therefore the consequences are entirely reflected in lower price competitiveness. With 'world pricing', the domestic firm does not pass on higher domestic costs at all, since it sticks to the price set on the world market. Higher domestic costs in this case are reflected purely in lower profits.

18.3.3 A Modernized Kinked Demand Curve Model

In its original formulation, the kinked demand curve model[3] (Sweezy 1939) was not a model of price-setting at all; rather, it was an attempt to explain the rigidity of the prices of manufactured goods in the face of changes in demand and in costs. The model proposed that there was a kink in the demand curve facing the oligopolists at the existing price. The theory did not entail an explanation of the level of the existing price. The demand curve was more elastic to the left of the kink than it was to the right of the kink. This reflected the assumed oligopolistic behaviour: in the face of a price rise by the ith firm, no rivals would follow and the ith firm would lose a great deal of its market share; in the face of a price fall by the ith firm, all other firms would follow suit so as to maintain their market share, with the result that the ith firm would gain few additional sales.

A modernized version of the kinked demand curve model (e.g. Bhaskar 1988) provides a model of price-setting that mimics a repeated Prisoner's Dilemma game and results in a kinked demand curve at the chosen price. We will present a very simple example with identical firms to show how a *collusive joint profit-maximizing* solution can be sustained. The model is interesting not only because it supplies a more satisfying explanation of the existence of a kinked demand curve, but also because, when applied to the open economy, it provides a way of explaining from a microeconomic standpoint the kind of world pricing hypothesis that we used in Section

[3] For a survey of the original theory of the kinked demand curve see Reid (1981).

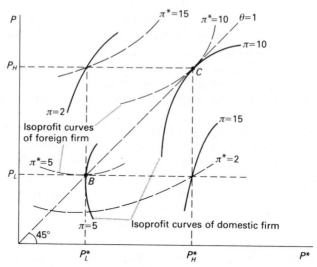

Fig. 18.5 The Bertrand–Nash equilibrium (B) and the collusive equilibrium (C)

11.5. In contrast to Bertrand, where a rise in domestic costs produces a combination of lower price competitiveness and lower profits for the domestic firm, the kinked demand curve illustrates why the burden may fall entirely on profits.

We sketch the argument using diagrams. Figure 18.5 depicts the isoprofit curves of two firm, one domestic and one foreign. As before, we assume that initially costs are identical. The Bertrand–Nash solution is shown by point B, where isoprofit curves are tangential to vertical price lines. For illustrative purposes, profits of each firm at point B are 5. As is clear from the isoprofit lines, the joint profit-maximizing position for the pair of firms will occur at point C. At C, the isoprofit curves are tangential, indicating that this is a Pareto optimum for the pair. Assume, to simplify the argument that the two duopolists can set the price at only either P_H or P_L. As argued earlier, and as can be deduced from the matrix below, this

		Foreign firm (*)	
		P^*_H (high price)	P^*_L (low price)
Domestic firm	P_H (high price)	10 10	15 2
	P_L (low price)	2 15	5 5

collusive solution will not be an equilibrium in a one-shot game. (The high price–high price outcome is the analogue in the price-setting game to the low quantity–low quantity outcome in the Cournot game discussed above.) In order to sustain a collusive outcome, it is necessary to move to the context of repeated games. The basic idea is that when a game is repeated it is possible for conventions to arise which operate to sustain the collusive outcome. Using the profit pay-offs indicated, we can illustrate the idea as follows. One firm can say: I will punish any deviation from the high price strategy by playing low for one period after you play low, *as long as* you play high the next period. You will quickly work out that it is not worth your while to deviate from the high price strategy even for one period. If you deviate for one period, then your returns are: 10, 15, 2, 10, 10, etc. If you deviate for any longer, I will play low price and we will each be stuck with 5 until you return to high and take the one-period dip in profits to 2. Clearly, it is rational for each player to secure the stream of 10, 10, 10, etc., by *always* playing high. This is a punishment strategy of the kind discussed by Abreu (1988). A similar example is discussed in Tirole (1988).

Let us now consider the implications of a rise in domestic costs. Higher domestic costs shift the isoprofits curves of the domestic firm to the right (see Fig. 18.6). The domestic firm would like the common price in the market to rise to P'_H (point D), but it cannot enforce this since its lower

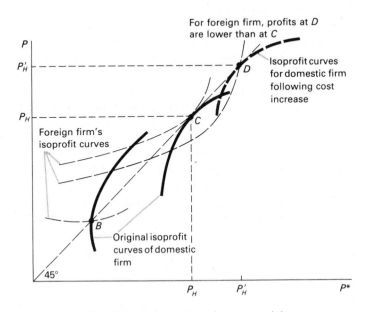

Fig. 18.6 Kinked demand curve model
Domestic costs rise but domestic firm leaves price unchanged; domestic firm suffers profit squeeze

cost competitor will stay at P_H. (The foreign firm's profits are lower at D than at C—see the isoprofit lines.) Thus, the domestic firm will leave its price unaltered at P_H and will suffer losses in profits associated with the higher costs. We now have a situation in which the lower cost firm (the foreign firm) is the price leader in the sense that the prevailing price in the market is its optimal price. Should it now encounter a cost increase, it will raise its price and hence the common price will rise. Thus, we have the interesting prediction that a rise in costs in the low cost economy—the price leader—will result in a rise in the common price, while a rise in costs in the *higher* cost country will be reflected entirely in profit squeeze.

18.4 Comparing Partial Equilibrium for the Firm with the General Equilibrium of the Firm Sector

In reconciling familiar concepts from microeconomics with apparently similar concepts in macroeconomics, great care must be taken. In this section, we highlight the relationship between the price-determined real wage curve—an aggregate concept—and the firm's demand-for-labour curve. The crucial difference between the two is that the price-determined real wage curve is defined as the real wage implied by price-setting behaviour *when all firms are pricing in line with each other* (assuming identical firms). By contrast, the firm's demand-for-labour curve shows the level of employment associated with each real wage *when the firm's price is out of line with that of other firms*. This is the sense in which the comparison is between the general equilibrium of the firm sector (all firms have adjusted their prices) and the partial equilibrium of the individual firm when the prices and outputs of all other firms are held constant.

The relationship between the two concepts is made clearest by looking explicitly at an individual firm, i. To reduce the number of subscripts, let us denote the output of the individual firm by q and its employment by e. The output of firm i will depend both on the relative price set by firm i (i.e. on P_i/P) and on the level of real aggregate demand in the economy as a whole, y^D. Similarly, employment in firm i will depend on its output and hence on relative prices an aggregate demand. Thus we write the expression for total profits (total revenue minus total costs) in real terms (π_i) as

$$\pi_i = (P_i/P) \, q(P_i/P, y^D) - (W_i/P) \, e[q(P_i/P, y^D)].$$

The profit-maximizing condition of marginal revenue equals marginal cost is therefore

$$q + (P_i/P) \, [\partial q/(\partial P_i/P)] = (W_i/P)(\mathrm{d}e/\mathrm{d}q)[\partial q/(\partial P_i/P)].$$

Rearranging, we get

$$P_i/P = [(de/dq)/(1 - 1/\varepsilon)](W_i/P),$$

where $\varepsilon = |[\partial q/\partial(P_i/P)] [(P_i/P)/q]|$, the absolute value of the price elasticity of demand. Let us now assume that the elasticity of demand is constant (i.e. is constant and identical across firms). We also assume for simplicity that the marginal product of labour, dq/de is constant and denoted by LP. Thus,

$$P_i/P = [1/(1 - 1/\varepsilon)][(W_i/P)/LP].$$

Since all firms are identical, $P_i = P$ and

$$W_i/P_i = (1 - 1/\varepsilon)(LP) = W/P.$$

This defines a horizontal price determined real wage curve (see Fig. 18.7).

Note that the firm maximizes profit by producing $q = q(P_i/P, y^D)$, even though the marginal product of labour exceeds the real wage, so that it *appears* that it would pay the firm to produce more. If it did produce more, however, it would not be able to sell the additional output at the price that was chosen to maximize profits. This helps to clarify the difficulties with Malinvaud's combined use of perfect competition and rationing of firms (refer back to Section 5.3). Malinvaud assumes perfect competition and thus bewilders us by also claiming that firms will ration themselves. Here we explain explicitly why it is not in the interest of firms to expand, *even though* the marginal product of labour exceeds the real wage. Once imperfect competition is adopted, the explanation for 'rationing' is straightforward.

Now, let us focus on the individual firm's demand for labour. The firm's employment function is $e = e(q)$, where $q = q(P_i/P, y^D)$, and therefore

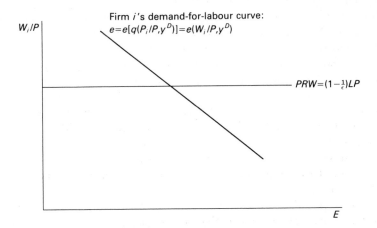

Fig. 18.7 The economy-wide PRW, and the firm's demand-for-labour curve at a given level of aggregate demand, y^D

$$e = e[q(P_i/P, y^D)].$$

Demand for its output depends negatively on the price differential between the ith firm and the economy's average, and positively on aggregate demand. Substituting

$$P_i/P = [1/(1 - 1/\varepsilon)][(W_i/P)/LP]$$

into the employment function shows that employment in the ith firm will depend negatively on the real consumption wage, W_i/P:

$$e = e[q(\lambda W_i/P, y^D)],$$

where $\lambda = 1/[(1 - 1/\varepsilon)LP]$.

Thus we can draw a negatively sloped demand-for-labour curve for the individual firm in the labour market diagram (see Fig. 18.7). The reason the firm's demand-for-labour curve slopes downward is *not* because of declining marginal productivity—we have assumed constant productivity; rather, it is downward-sloping because a higher money wage in the ith firm leads to a higher price there according to the pricing equation above. Thus, prices in the ith firm are above those elsewhere, which reduces demand for ith firm goods; hence employment is lower. The higher ith firm wage combined with an unchanged economy-wide price level means that a higher real consumption wage is associated with lower employment in the ith firm. Hence the ith firm's demand-for-labour curve is downward-sloping (see Fig. 18.7). Of course, in aggregate, if all firms are identical, then the relative price term in the output demand, and hence in the labour demand equation, drops out. Employment in the firm sector as a whole then depends only on the level of real aggregate demand. Once all firms are in equilibrium, they must be on the PRW—at the intersection of the firm's demand-for-labour curve and the PRW.

This brings us to the third relationship between the real wage and employment which concerns firms: the EAD curve. The EAD shows how much employment is needed to produce the output to meet aggregate demand. Like the price-determined real wage curve, it is an aggregate relationship which holds for the firm sector as a whole. If a higher real wage in the economy produces a higher level of aggregate demand, through the effect of higher real wages on the aggregate propensity to consume, then the EAD will have a positive slope. It will be negatively sloped if the detrimental effect of higher real wages on profitability and investment outweighs any positive consumption effect (refer back to Section 6.4). Throughout most of the book, it has been assumed that the EAD is vertical.

If we now put all three curves together in one diagram (Fig. 18.8), we can see how they relate to each other. For illustrative purposes, we assume a positively sloped EAD. The firm's demand-for-labour curve is indexed by the level of aggregate demand, y_0^D. It is clear from what has been said

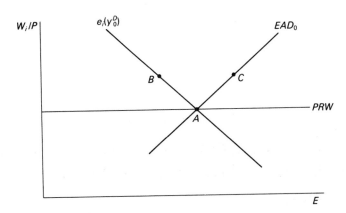

Fig. 18.8 Relationship between firm's demand-for-labour curve and PRW and EAD

A: if W rises and P responds; B: if W_i rises and P_i responds, but all other W and P remain unchanged; C: if W rises but P remains unchanged

before that, with all prices and wages identical, there is a unique position for the economy: this is at the intersection of the demand for labour, the EAD and the PRW curves, at a point such as A. Now, consider point B. A point such as B on firm i's demand-for-labour curve will be observed if W_i rises relative to the average wage W, and P_i responds. In other words, we have the case where wages and prices in the ith firm rise relative to the economy's average. The fact that i's relative price rises means that demand for ith firm goods declines (at the fixed level of aggregate demand) and employment in the ith firm falls. This is a partial equilibrium effect. As soon as we assume an economy-wide wage increase, i.e. a rise in W, then all prices will rise and the economy remains at point A.

A point such as C on the EAD would occur in the case where both W_i and W had risen but prices had not yet responded. In other words, there is a rise in real wages in the economy which pushes up aggregate demand and hence raises the demand for output. In an economy in which prices are set very soon after wages, we would not expect to observe such a situation.

18.5   Conclusion

The material in this chapter has helped to show how price-determined real wage curves are constructed for the standard situations of imperfect competition, and why it is not unreasonable to see the PRW as constant as output varies. We have also shown why it is rational for firms to produce at the level they do, even though they would like to produce more at the given real wage.

19

The Shifting Equilibrium Rate of Unemployment: Hysteresis and Other Explanations

In the middle of the 1980s, an empirical puzzle developed which required explanation. The estimates made by econometricians of the equilibrium rate of unemployment[1] in a number of the OECD economies appeared to be rather close to the actual rates of unemployment recorded.[2] Table 19.1 shows estimates of equilibrium rates of unemployment and compares them with actual unemployment. As actual unemployment rose, the equilibrium rate of unemployment appeared to follow in line. Another way of saying

Table 19.1 Actual and estimated equilibrium unemployment (NAIRU)

	Actual unemployment (%)		Estimated NAIRU	
	1976–80	1981–83	1976–80	1981–3
France	5.3	7.3	5.3	6.9
West Germany	3.7	6.7	3.7	5.3
Italy	7.1	9.4	8.9	7.7
UK	5.5	10.8	4.6	9.5
EEC	5.4	8.8	5.3	7.3
	Actual unemployment (%)		Estimated NAIRU	
EEC				
1966–70	2.4		2.6	
1971–75	3.2		5.3	
1976–80	5.4		5.3	
1981–83	8.8		7.6	

Source: Layard *et al.* (1986: 47–8).

[1] For a clear explanation of how these estimates are made, see Fallon and Verry (1988: 288–90).

[2] e.g. Layard *et al.* (1986); Coe and Gagliardi (1985).

this is that, although an initial rise in unemployment was associated with falling inflation, inflation subsequently stabilized.

Figure 19.1 shows OECD unemployment and inflation rates for the decade 1978–88. Although unemployment has remained fairly constant since 1982, continuously falling inflation has not been observed. This finding produced a range of responses from economists. Those who had always been sceptical of the empirical relevance of the concept of an equilibrium rate of unemployment concluded that it was indeed a useless concept. A second and perhaps more illuminating response was the use of the notion of *hysteresis* to account for the phenomenon of the equilibrium rate of unemployment tracking the actual rate of unemployment. As we will see shortly, we have already come across the idea of hysteresis in the discussion of the fixed exchange rate open economy, where an expansionary policy that lowered actual unemployment would also reduce the equilibrium rate of unemployment to the new level of unemployment.

Before we enter into a full discussion of hysteresis, it is necessary to deal with an obvious alternative explanation for the rise in the equilibrium rate of unemployment with actual unemployment in the 1980s. Such an explanation relies on the occurrence of exogenous changes which shifted the bargained real wage upward and or the price-determined real wage downward. If such exogenous changes occurred, then governments would have been forced to reduce aggregate demand so as to keep inflation stable. Actual unemployment would have risen in line with the equilibrium

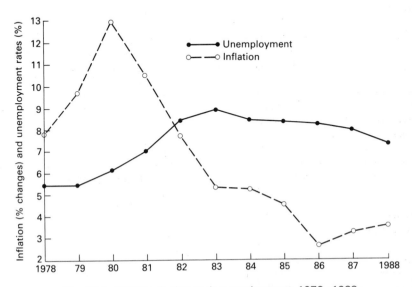

Fig. 19.1 OECD inflation and unemployment, 1978–1988
Sources: OECD, *Historical Statistics*; OECD, *Economic Outlook*

rate of unemployment. The major exogenous reasons for a rise in the equilibrium rate of unemployment, which it is generally agreed did explain a higher NAIRU in the mid-1970s, were (1) an increase in the power and militancy of unions, and (2) an increase in the price of oil as a result of decisions of the OPEC cartel. Let us look at each explanation in turn.

1 *Union power.* It is widely accepted that the decade from the mid-1960s to the mid-1970s saw a major increase in union power and militancy. Indicators of this phenomenon frequently cited are strike statistics and union membership. Both sets of data confirm a rise in union militancy across the major OECD economies. This can be represented by an upward shift in the BRW curve. Table 19.2 presents data on union density and strikes for the four large European economies. The wave of union militancy in the early 1970s is reflected in the high level of days lost in strikes in 1967–71. Union membership density increased over the 1970s.

2 *OPEC oil price rise 1973–4.* As discussed in Section 15.3, a rise in the price of an imported material will have the effect of shifting down the price-determined real wage curve if profit margins are to be maintained.

Both these effects are depicted in Fig. 19.2, and the implied rise in the equilibrium rate of unemployment is clear. Of course, the second effect was exacerbated for most OECD economies by the second OPEC shock in 1979. However, this two-pronged explanation does not make sense from the perspective of the 1980s. The equilibrium rate of unemployment went on rising in the 1980s (for the UK, at least up until 1986), in spite of the fact that union power increased no further and the OPEC price rises were reversed.

Table 19.2 Strikes and union membership density

| (a) Strikes (working days lost p.a. per 100 employees in industry) | | |
	1967–71	1977–80	1981–3
France	350	25	19
West Germany	8	10	—
Italy	161	165	147
UK	60	132	37

| (b) Union density (% non-agricultural wage and salaried employees) | | |
	1970	1979	1984/5
France	22	28	28
West Germany	37	42	42
Italy	39	51	45
UK	51	58	52

Source: (a): *Employment Gazette*, June 1989 and earlier issues; (b) Freeman (1988: 66, Table 1).

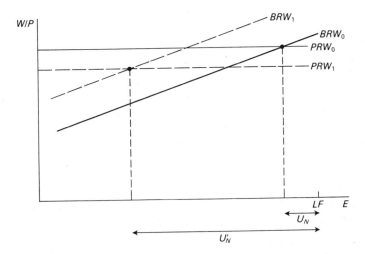

Fig. 19.2 Effect of increased union power (BRW$_0$ to BRW$_1$) and higher oil prices (PRW$_0$ to PRW$_1$) on the equilibrium rate of unemployment

1   *Union power.*   Union power has declined in most OECD countries in the 1980s, though by different degrees. This is reflected to some extent in data on both strikes and union membership (see Table 19.2). The cross-country differences reflect governmental and employer strategies, as well as different rates of unemployment. In consequence, we focus on the decline in union power in the UK, though the structural economic factors at work apply to other countries as well. Although some of the decline in the UK is simply a reflection of the higher unemployment over this period (a move down the bargained real wage curve to the left), that is not a sufficient explanation. There are other exogenous reasons for a reduction in union power. First, the gradual movement of employment from urban–industrial centres with strong union networks to small towns has resulted in a diminution of union power. This has been intensified by other structural changes in the labour market, such as the increased proportion of women in employment, the shift from blue-collar to white-collar workers, from full-time to part-time work, from large to small plants, and from employment in manufacturing to services. To make an extreme comparison, part-time women workers in a service sector industry in a small town are less likely to be organized by a strong and militant union than full-time blue-collar male workers in manufacturing in a traditional industrial area.

A second exogenous factor weakening unions has been the effect of the growth of international competition and of the openness of economies, which has had the effect of strengthening employer resistance to wage claims. An increase in the short-term pressures on firms from financial institutions may have had a similar effect.

Thirdly, in a number of economies, of which the UK is the leading example, the government has changed the structure of bargaining in the public sector. More generally, the government's legislative programme towards industrial relations has had some success in realizing its goal of reducing the power of unions in both public and private sectors.

For all these reasons, there is little dispute that the 1980s have seen a weakening of unions which cannot be accounted for solely by a move down a given bargained real wage curve. These developments can certainly play no part in explaining the *rise* in the equilibrium rate of unemployment.

2   *Oil price rises.*   The OPEC price rises of 1973 and 1979 have been reversed in the 1980s—again suggesting that the equilibrium rate of unemployment should have been reduced.

It seems therefore that the two explanations that were applied successfully to account for the rise in the equilibrium rate of unemployment in the 1970s lack credibility in explaining the rising NAIRU of the 1980s. Other exogenous variables that have been put forward, such as mismatch in the labour market, have not been convincingly demonstrated to have been significant causes of the rise in the equilibrium rate of unemployment. It was these findings that led researchers to investigate the possibility that cutbacks in aggregate demand could themselves have had the effort of raising the equilibrium rate of unemployment. This idea has been labelled 'hysteresis'.

19.1   The General Idea of Hysteresis

Although the familiar English word 'history' does not derive from the same root as the word 'hysteresis', it gives the right idea as to the meaning of the latter. As scientists have used the term, it means that the equilibrium of a system depends on the actual history of the system. In our context, the equilibrium rate of unemployment depends on the actual history or path of unemployment. In shorthand, the equilibrium rate of unemployment is *path-dependent*. This has important policy implications since it means that, if the government pushes up unemployment, it will affect the equilibrium rate of unemployment i.e. the rate of sustainable unemployment at which the economy can operate.

This is a long-winded way of making the point that there may be mechanisms in the economy which mean that a rise in unemployment increases the equilibrium rate of unemployment, either by shifting the bargained real wage curve upward or by pushing the price-determined real wage curve downward. The idea is that this effect is a medium-run phenomenon—it does not occur instantaneously. Furthermore, it is important to distinguish between two different conceptions of a hysteresis process. First, there is the position which we shall refer to as 'pure hysteresis', in which there is no unique *long-run* or underlying equilibrium rate of unemployment at all. Changes in aggregate demand shift actual unemployment around, and with a lag this shifts the equilibrium rate in line. The case of pure hysteresis presents the extreme alternative to the model of the New Classical macroeconomics: not only does government demand management policy affect unemployment in the short run, but it also determines the path of the equilibrium rate of unemployment.

The second and much less extreme view is that, while there is a unique underlying equilibrium rate of unemployment, changes in actual unemployment can shift the medium-run equilibrium rate of unemployment. At a medium-run equilibrium rate of unemployment inflation is constant, and only gradually, through the operation of other economic forces, will the equilibrium rate revert to its long-run level. In this case, the economic system displays hysteresis in a looser sense; more generally, there is *persistence* in unemployment. If unemployment is shifted away from the long-run equilibrium rate, it can take a very long time for it to return; in the intervening years, rates of unemployment away from the long-run equilibrium will be observed *with constant inflation*.

There are many different channels through which changes in aggregate demand may bring about changes in the equilibrium rate of unemployment. Three examples from the literature are:

1   the 'insider–outsider' effect;[3]
2   the relationship between short-term and long-term unemployed in the pool of unemployed;[4] and
3   the role of capacity scrapping.[5]

It is useful to sketch the working of each of these mechanisms as a way of introducing the idea of hysteresis. Looking at the insider–outsider model first, two groups of workers are identified. The insiders are those currently employed who are in a strong bargaining position because their possession of firm-specific skills means that the firm cannot simply sack them and replace them with new workers. Insiders are presumed to be interested in maintaining their own employment and increasing their real wage; they attach virtually no importance to the creation of employment for those who are currently unemployed. This means that the bargained real wage depends on the level of actual employment. If employment is high, the number of insiders is high and therefore, in order to preserve their jobs, the bargained real wage curve is low. Conversely, if employment is low,

---

[3] Lindbeck and Snower (1986), Blanchard and Summers (1986).
[4] Layard and Nickell (1986).
[5] Sneessens and Dreze (1986), Soskice and Carlin (1989), van der Klundert and van Shaik (1989).

there are few insiders and a high real wage is consistent with maintaining *their* employment; thus the bargained real wage curve is high. If aggregate demand is reduced, the lower number of insiders will not bargain for wage reductions to give employment to ex-insiders: they will simply set the wage consistent in equilibrium with their remaining employed. Because of the monopoly power of the insiders, the higher level of unemployment has no effect on subsequent wage-setting. The economy will be stuck at a new higher equilibrium rate of unemployment. This is a model of pure hysteresis.

The second explanation for hysteresis focuses on the role of the long-term unemployed in the labour market. This differs importantly from the insider–outsider model in that a unique long-run equilibrium rate of unemployment remains. The medium-run NAIRU will change with changes in the long-term unemployed as a proportion of total unemployment, but there remains a unique long-run equilibrium rate of unemployment. The logic of the argument, which will be spelled out in detail below, is that the higher the proportion of long-term in total unemployment, the less impact will any given level of unemployment have on the bargaining power of the union. The long-term unemployed are viewed as having in effect withdrawn from participation in the labour market (both for psychological reasons and because of progressive loss of relevant skills), and hence exert significantly less pressure on wage-setting.

There is empirical evidence that a rise in unemployment which persists has the effect of raising the proportion of long-term unemployed. The result is that union bargaining power is increased at each rate of unemployment: the bargained real wage curve shifts upward. This creates a new equilibrium rate of unemployment at higher unemployment, which we shall refer to as a *medium-run* NAIRU. However, the conclusions to be drawn are rather different from those coming from the insider–outsider model. In particular, it is argued that the new higher equilibrium rate of unemployment owing to the rise in the proportion of long-term unemployed is not a long-run phenomenon. The explanation is based on the empirical finding that in the long run there is an equilibrium relationship between the percentage of total unemployment that is long-term and the overall unemployment rate.

For each percentage of long-term unemployment, there will be a bargained real wage curve relating the real wage to the actual rate of unemployment. But only one rate of unemployment on each BRW will be sustainable in the long run; the equilibrium relationship between the percentage of long-term unemployed and total unemployment tells us which one it is. By joining together the points on each of the bargained real wage curves, a long-run BRW is generated. With a unique intersection with the price-determined real wage, there is therefore a unique long-run NAIRU.

The third explanation that has been adduced to account for hysteresis derives from the effect of a fall in aggregate demand on capacity utilization and through this to investment. It is suggested that the lower investment induced by lower rates of capacity utilization leads in the medium run to a rundown in the size of the capital stock. Thus rates of capacity utilization begin to rise again. At *very* high rates of capacity utilization, there are reasons to suspect that profit margins are widened. If each firm is aware that its competitors will be unable to take advantage of a price rise by holding their own price unchanged and expanding output because they lack the capacity to do so, then price increases at high rates of capacity utilization may occur. To the extent that this is the case, the equilibrium rate of unemployment will be shifted up as prices respond to the shortage of capacity in the economy. We would expect to observe concurrently high actual unemployment, high rates of capacity utilization, and a high equilibrium rate of unemployment. However, we will see that, just as in the case of long-term unemployment, the shift in the equilibrium rate of unemployment brought about by capacity scrapping will not last indefinitely. Eventually, capacity utilization will return to 'normal' and a unique long-run equilibrium rate of unemployment will be defined.

Each of these arguments is symmetrical with respect to the direction of change of aggregate demand. Although the examples have been presented in terms of the effect of lower aggregate demand in raising the equilibrium rate of unemployment, the logic of each argument is that raising demand would have the effect of reducing the equilibrium rate of unemployment. In the insider–outsider model, the number of insiders would be increased and this would have the effect of reducing their militancy since there are more jobs to protect. With a lower proportion of long-term unemployed, the medium-run equilibrium rate of unemployment will be reduced, because at any rate of unemployment there will be a higher proportion of the unemployed exerting active pressure in the labour market. Finally, in the capacity scrapping case, higher demand would raise levels of capacity utilization and induce more investment, which would have the medium-run effect of lowering the equilibrium rate of unemployment.

The possible existence of hysteresis phenomena brings back into focus the debate between Keynes and the classics. With a unique equilibrium rate of unemployment, Keynes's analysis appeared to be of central importance only for the short run. In other words, Keynesian intervention is required only in so far as it is necessary to ensure that the level of aggregate demand is appropriate for keeping the economy at the equilibrium rate of unemployment. Expanding demand beyond the level consistent with the NAIRU would eventually be associated with rising inflation. Hysteresis suggests however that Keynesian policies may have a medium-run effect in shifting the equilibrium rate of unemployment itself. Nevertheless, there is a major debate which concerns the long-run nature of the shift in the equilibrium rate of unemployment. In the sketch of the models above, it was suggested that, in both the long-term unemployment case and the case of capital scrapping, the medium-term equilibrium rate of unemployment can be shifted down by an expansionary policy but there is a unique long-run equilibrium rate of unemployment.

To conclude our introduction to the idea of hysteresis, it is useful to point out once again the implications of the existence of hysteresis for the relationship between unemployment and inflation. When there is a unique equilibrium rate of unemployment, we have a vertical long-run Phillips curve reflecting the fact that only when unemployment is at the equilibrium rate of unemployment is inflation constant (see Fig. 19.3). Inflation in this case (assuming simple adaptive expectations) is equal to last period's inflation plus a positive function of the extent to which the equilibrium rate of unemployment exceeds actual unemployment.

$$\dot{P} = \dot{P}_{-1} + f(U_N - U),$$

with $f(0) = 0$ so that $\dot{P} = \dot{P}_{-1}$ if and only if $U = U_N$. When hysteresis exists, many rates of unemployment may be equilibrium rates. Generally, to move to lower unemployment, there will be a rise in inflation, which will then stabilize. Thus, inflation is equal to last period's inflation plus a negative function of the *change* in the rate of unemployment:

$$\dot{P} = \dot{P}_{-1} + g(\Delta U).$$

Following the more detailed look at the three examples of hysteresis outlined above, there are three further routes through which the path of actual unemployment can affect the equilibrium rate of unemployment or the sustainable rate of unemployment, which are relevant to the open economy.

19.2 The Insider–Outsider Model: Pure Hysteresis

The insider–outsider model was developed by Lindbeck and Snower (1986)

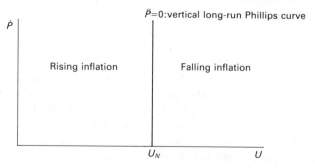

Fig. 19.3 The $\dot{P}$–U relationship with a unique equilibrium rate of unemployment

and Blanchard and Summers (1986).[6] As emphasized above, it rests on the monopoly power conferred on employees as the result of the firm-specific skills that they possess. This power exists because of the substantial costs that are attached to the training of new workers in these firm-specific skills.[7] The strength of insiders enables them to reject any outside influence by national unions to bargain for objectives that the insiders do not want. It is typically assumed that the objectives of insiders are (1) to maintain their own employment and (2) to increase their real wage—with objective (1) taking precedence over (2)—and (3) to attach no importance to creating employment for those who are currently unemployed.

A Monopoly Model: a Simple Example of Pure Hysteresis

A simple model of hysteresis will be presented which comes close to the model in Blanchard and Fischer (1989: 453–4). We begin by showing that, *if*

1 insiders act as monopolists (because they are so strong),
2 they maximize the utility of the representative employed worker, and
3 there is no labour turnover,

then we have a pure hysteresis model; that is, a rise in unemployment induced by a sustained cut in aggregate demand creates a rise in the equilibrium rate of unemployment. The first step in getting to this result is to construct indifference curves. The important difference with the analysis of the union in Chapter 17 is that members of the union—employed and unemployed—are not chosen at random for employment. In this case, i.e. with the union comprising only the insiders, there is a new set of indifference curves for each level of employment (for, say, the ith firm). As Fig. 19.4 illustrates, indifference curves begin from the current level of employment; any point on indifference curve $A'A'$ is preferred to any point on AA, and any point to the left of E_0 is inferior to any point to the right. If the current level of employment were to be higher, say at E_1 in Fig. 19.4, the curves would shift to the set of broken curves based on the dashed vertical line above E_1.

Moving to the constraint facing the insiders, as with the monopoly union, the relation between the real wage, W_i/P, and employment, E_i, is the demand-for-labour curve which will shift with the level of aggregate demand:

$$E_i = \alpha(P_i/P)(y^D/LP),$$

---

[6] Empirical support for a hypothesis such as the insider–outsider one was found first by Gregory (1986) for the Australian economy.

[7] The power will be reinforced if the acquisition by new workers of these skills depends—as it typically does—on the co-operation of existing workers.

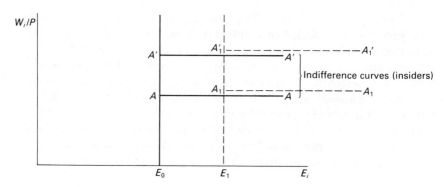

Fig. 19.4 Indifference curves for the insiders at employment level E_0

where y^D is aggregate demand and $\alpha(1) = 1/n$, where n is the number of firms. Thus, employment in the ith firm depends inversely on the firm's price relative to the average price level P. When $P_i = P$, the ith firm secures $1/n$ share of total demand in the economy.

The ith firm sets prices as a mark-up on average costs:

$$P_i = (1 + \mu)(W_i/LP).$$

Substituting the pricing equation into the employment equation gives

$$E_i = \frac{\alpha[(1 + \mu)(W_i/P)(1/LP)]}{LP}y^D$$

[firm's demand-for-labour curve]

Clearly, given this demand-for-labour curve and employment at E_0, the utility of the representative worker is maximized at A, where the demand-for-labour curve intersects the vertical line above E_0 (see Fig. 19.5). The highest indifference curve attainable is $v = v_0$, by the

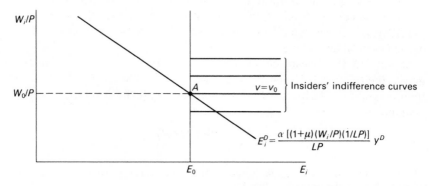

Fig. 19.5 Insiders maximize utility by choosing highest W_i/P subject to all insiders remaining employed

insiders choosing the real wage W_0/P. In short, on any demand-for-labour curve, we will be at the real wage that results in everyone currently employed being hired (or at least believing that they will be hired). *But*, if all firms act identically, then there is only one possible real wage, the PRW. Thus actual employment for each of the i identical firms will be determined by the demand-for-labour curve at the PRW.

Let us begin with the economy at an equilibrium rate of unemployment, U_N, and show that a fall in aggregate demand produces a rise in the equilibrium rate of unemployment to U'_N. Looking at Fig. 19.6, the insiders numbering E_0 initially (i.e. when demand is y_0^D) choose point A. Aggregate demand falls to y_1^D, shifting the demand-for-labour curve for the ith firm to the left. The E_0 insiders in each ith firm now choose point B to maximize their utility. When there is low demand, and since they have no interest in the unemployed, the insiders go for the highest real wage attainable, i.e. consistent with just maintaining $E = E_0$. All groups of insiders do the same. The result, of course, is that all wages and prices rise by the same amount; therefore the real wage remains at its initial level and employment falls from A to B'. Now we must check that B' is also an equilibrium rate of unemployment. Let us assume that the real wage at B is 5% below the real wage at A.

Table 19.3 depicts the path of inflation. In period 0, with aggregate demand at y_0^D and pre-existing inflation of 10%, actual wage and price inflation is 10%. In period 1, demand falls and money wages rise by only 5%—i.e., the insiders accept an expected fall in real wages of 5% with expected price inflation of 10%—as the insiders set the wage at point B in Fig. 19.6. Firms immediately raise prices by 5% as well. Thus, real wages

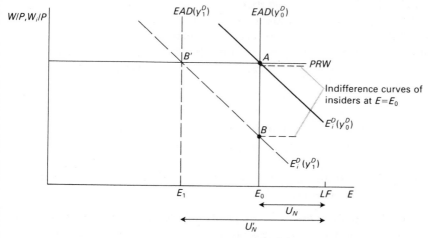

Fig. 19.6 Pure hysteresis arising from the behaviour of insiders

Table 19.3 Pure hysteresis: constant inflation at both low and high unemployment

Period	$\dot{W}$	$\dot{P}$	$\dot{P}_{-1}$	Real wage	Aggregate demand (y^D)	Employment
0	10	10	10	PRW	y_0^D	E_0
1	5	5	10	PRW	y_1^D	E_1
2	5	5	5	PRW	y_1^D	E_1
3	5	5	5	PRW	y_1^D	E_1

everywhere remain constant, demand in all firms falls, the firms lay off workers, and unemployment rises to U'_N. In period 2, with insiders now numbering only E_1 and demand at y_1^D, wages are set equal to expected inflation (to secure point B'). The number of insiders in each firm has been reduced in size and they have set the wage so as to maintain employment of E_1. This implies the choice of point B'. Prices rise in line and the economy remains at B'. The situation with constant inflation of 5% can continue indefinitely—as long as aggregate demand remains unchanged. There is a new equilibrium rate of unemployment, U'_N, at the lower employment level, E_1.

This example gives a clear illustration that there is a fall in inflation associated with a *rise* in unemployment, but not with a lower *level* of unemployment. The central mechanism driving the result is that the group of insiders has been *reduced* as a result of the unanticipated fall in aggregate demand, with the result that U'_N is also an equilibrium rate of unemployment. A smaller group of insiders produces less moderation in the system than was the case when there were E_0 workers. The E_1 workers are concerned only not to put their employment at risk.

The argument in relation to a rise in aggregate demand is exactly symmetric. The E_1 workers accept an expected real wage rise when aggregate demand rises from y_1^D to y_0^D. But the actual real wage does not rise and employment rises to E_0. There is a new lower equilibrium rate of unemployment.

19.3 The Long-Term Unemployed and Shifting Medium-Run Equilibrium Rates of Unemployment

The model of hysteresis based on the role of the long-term unemployed rests on two assumptions.

A1   The higher the percentage of long-term unemployed in total unemployment, the less impact any given level of unemployment will have on the bargaining power of the unions.

This proposition is illustrated in Fig. 19.7(a), where the BRW is indexed by the proportion of long-term unemployed in total unemployment, LT. The bargaining power of unions rises because employers are not keen to hire the long-term unemployed. This is because the latter have often lost work skills which they had, and have lost confidence in their own abilities and social skills. Employers (often wrongly) attribute the fact that they are long-term unemployed to their having been assessed and found wanting by other employers. In addition, the unemployed may have withdrawn from active search for employment. Thus, the pool of workers that employers seriously consider employing will be much smaller than total unemployment, if there are many long-term unemployed. And what is important for union bargaining power is the former group.

A2   There is an equilibrium relationship between the proportion of long-term unemployed, LT, and actual unemployment.

This is an empirical relationship and will differ across countries. High

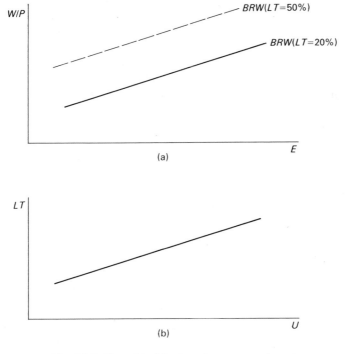

Fig. 19.7 The role of the long-term unemployed
(a) BRW shifts upwards as proportion of long-term unemployed rises.
(b) Empirical relationship between proportion of long-term unemployed (LT) and the unemployment rate

unemployment in the 1980s appears to be associated with high durations of unemployment rather than with a high inflow into the pool of unemployed. The explanation for this is presumably related to the attitudes both of employers and of the long-term unemployed themselves. As noted above, employers are nervous of employing the long-term unemployed. Similarly, the longer a person has been unemployed, the less effort is put in to looking for work. If a person fails to get work initially, then the probability of exiting the unemployment pool falls and that of long-term unemployment rises. The relationship between the level of unemployment and the proportion of long-term unemployed is illustrated in Fig. 19.7(b).

The implications for the equilibrium rate of unemployment of this pair of assumptions can be seen most vividly by combining the panels of Figure 19.7. This is done in Fig. 19.8. The equilibrium relationship between the share of long-term unemployed and the unemployment rate implies a unique relationship between these two variables and hence between the bargained real wage and the unemployment rate. Thus, there is a long-run bargained real wage curve, LBRW, superimposed on the bargained real wage curves indexed by the share of long-term unemployed. In the long run, only one point on each BRW(LT) curve can be maintained. As noted in the introduction, we now have a situation in which there are medium-run and long-run equilibrium rates of unemployment.

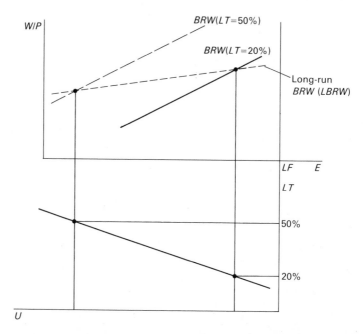

Fig. 19.8 The long-term unemployed: defining the long-run BRW

Let us follow through the implications of a deflation of demand by the government. It reduces demand from y_0^D to y_1^D, and this is indicated in Fig. 19.9 in the leftward shift of the EAD curve. In the immediate aftermath of the fall in demand, if we assume that the proportion of long-term unemployed is initially fixed at 35%, the value of the bargained real wage drops from w_0 to w_1. (Of course, in the very short run the proportion of long-term unemployed will actually fall because there are more new people in unemployment. In this case, w^B may fall to w_2.) At point b, w^B is considerably below the PRW. This means that money wages rise by significantly less than expected inflation: $\dot{W} < \dot{P}_{-1}$. Inflation will be falling because of the negative gap between the PRW and the BRW of $(c'' - b)$ at E_1. As time passes, the proportion of long-term unemployed will rise—in the example in Fig. 19.9, from 35% to 45% (45% is the equilibrium percentage of the long-term unemployed when $U = U_1$ as shown by the LBRW)—and the gap between the bargained real wage and the price-determined real wage narrows (to $c'' - c$). This reflects the decline in the influence of the total number of unemployed on wage-bargaining as a higher proportion of the unemployed cease to be active in the labour market. Money wage inflation will now fall much more slowly.

U_1 is not an equilibrium rate of unemployment, but it can be seen from Fig. 19.9 that there is a new equilibrium rate of unemployment now where the new bargained real wage curve (BRW(45%)) intersects the PRW curve. This new equilibrium rate is U_2.

But U_2 is not a *long-run* equilibrium rate. If the government wanted constant inflation, then reflating the economy to U_2 would be only a

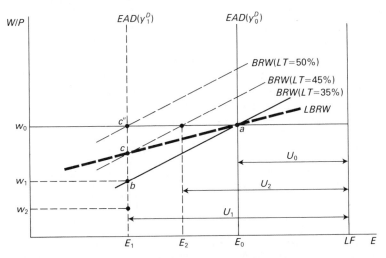

Fig. 19.9 Long-term unemployment and medium-run hysteresis

medium-run solution. For once unemployment has fallen to U_2, a proportion of long-term unemployment of 45% is no longer the equilibrium share. At U_2, the share of long-term unemployed steadily drops, moving the equilibrium rate steadily back to U_0. Thus, unlike the insider–outsider model, the hysteresis is not a permanent phenomenon.

The importance of the long-term unemployment model lies in highlighting the mistakes that the government may make if it is unaware of the effect of long-term unemployment on wage bargaining. Mistakes are likely to be particularly serious if the LBRW is close to horizontal or, worse, is downward-sloping at high unemployment rates. It can be seen from the construction of the LBRW curve in Fig. 19.8 that there is no pre-ordained reason why the LBRW should be downward-sloping; if the relation between LT and U becomes steeper as unemployment rises, it is possible for the LBRW to be a shallow U-shape, as in Fig. 19.10. Indeed, Layard and Nickell show empirically that this may be the case (1987: 143–6). In the example in Fig. 19.10, if the government deflates aggregate demand below y_1^D, say, to y_2^D, it can be seen that increasing inflation will result, perhaps wrongly causing the government to deflate yet further.

19.4 Hysteresis and Capital Scrapping

This third route to hysteresis focuses on the effect of changes in capacity utilization on pricing decisions.[8] We present a simple model which produces results consistent with observations for a number of European economies in the 1980s: rising capacity utilization as unemployment rises, and a rising equilibrium rate of unemployment as unemployment rises. An example of the patterns is shown for the UK in Fig. 19.11. The hysteresis mechanism works through changes in the capital stock. Unlike the bulk of this book, where, as is typical in macroeconomics, the capital stock has been held constant, here changes in it are critical.[9]

Central to the capacity scrapping argument is the proposition that, at very high rates of capacity utilization, firms push up their profit margins. This is the result of the assumption by each firm that, when they are all faced with a capacity constraint, it is safe to make use of the opportunity

---

[8] A simpler model of hysteresis based on the erosion of the physical capital stock is that low investment from the mid-1970s has meant that there is insufficient capital to employ all of the labour force at current real wages. Such an explanation seems to ignore the extent of substitutability between labour and capital in the short run through the use of additional shifts, etc. Bruno and Sachs (1985) give several compelling historical counter-examples to the absolute capital shortage thesis, pointing out for example the rapidity with which full employment was attained in many economies after the Second World War in spite of reductions in civilian capital stock.

[9] The argument as to the effects of changes in aggregate demand on capacity utilization and investment and the way that this produces medium-run hysteresis is outlined in a simple way here. For a more formal model, see Soskice and Carlin (1989).

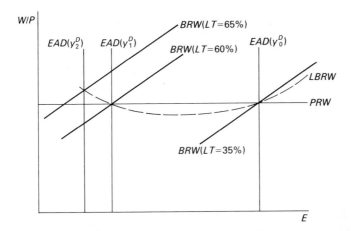

Fig. 19.10 The consequences of a long-run bargained real wage curve which is downward-sloping at high rates of unemployment

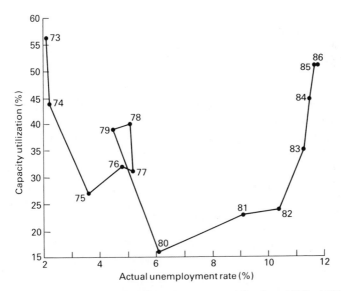

Fig. 19.11 UK unemployment and capacity utilization, 1973–1986

Capacity utilization shows 100 minus the percentage of respondents stating that they are working below full capacity.

Sources: Capacity utilization from CBI Industrial Trends Survey results for October each year, reported in *National Institute Economic Review*: unemployment rate from OECD, *Economic Outlook*

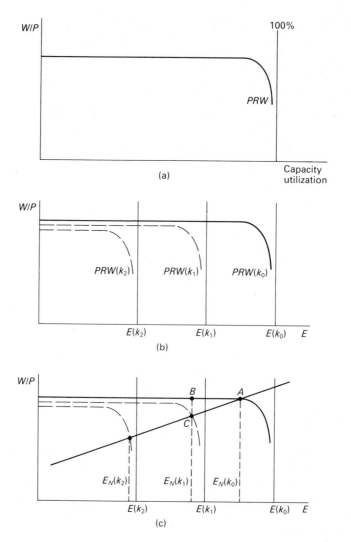

Fig. 19.12 Capacity utilization, the level of the capital stock, and equilibrium rates
of unemployment
(a) The PRW and capacity utilization
(b) PRWs at different levels of capital stock
(c) Equilibrium rates of unemployment, which vary with the level of the
capital stock

for widening profit margins. Figure 19.12(a) illustrates the relationship
between the price-determined real wage and the rate of capacity
utilization. The dip in the PRW close to full capacity utilization is due to

the rise in the mark-up of P over W, and hence there is a fall in the price-determined real wage. For simplicity of exposition, we will assume that capacity utilization and employment can be measured along the same, horizontal axis.

The second component of the story is that, for each *level of the capital stock*, there will be a different level of employment at which capacity utilization is at its maximum. For example, when the capital stock is large, k_0, a high level of employment, $E(k_0)$, will be associated with full capacity utilization (see Fig. 19.12(b)). Similarly, with a low capital stock, k_2, a much lower level of employment, $E(k_2)$, will fully utilize the capital stock. The price-determined real wage associated with each level of the capital stock is shown.

The bargained real wage is now added to the model (Fig. 19.12(c)). From the diagram, three different levels of employment at which the price-determined real wage is equal to the bargained real wage can be read off, each of which is associated with a different level of the capital stock. Thus, there are three possible equilibrium rates of unemployment. To put the model into action, we assume that investment is a function of the rate of capacity utilization. Suppose that the economy is initially at point A in Fig. 19.12(c), i.e. at an equilibrium rate of unemployment with constant inflation. Introduction of a restrictive demand management stance on the part of the government produces a drop in capacity utilization and a rise in unemployment. The economy moves from A to B and is characterized by falling inflation as the result of the diminution of union bargaining power associated with the rise in unemployment. The lower level of capacity utilization depresses investment, and firms will allow their capital stock to decline. Eventually the capital stock will fall to the level k_1. With this much lower capital stock, the level of output demanded will require a high rate of capacity utilization and firms will respond by pushing up their profit margins; inflation will cease falling since the bargained real wage and the price-determined real wage are now equal at point C. Thus, equilibrium unemployment has followed actual unemployment upward. Any reversal of the demand management stance will lead to renewed investment and to an increase in the size of the capital stock; the economy can eventually move back to point A and remain at A with constant inflation.

To this point, we have a pure hysteresis model. However, there is one particularly unsatisfactory aspect of it. Inspection of Fig. 19.12(c) reveals that the equilibrium rates of unemployment occur at *different* rates of capacity utilization. For example, point A is much further away from full utilization of the capital stock k_0 than is point B from full utilization of k_1. This is inconsistent with a long-run equilibrium since it can be assumed that firms will have some *specific* target rate of capacity utilization. It is likely, for example, that firms will have an optimal amount of so-called *strategic spare capacity* based on entry considerations (e.g. of the kind discussed by

Dixit 1980). This suggests that the investment rule should be more specific; namely, for a given capital stock, k_1,

if $E > \bar{E}(k_i)$ then increase the size of the capital stock;
if $E < \bar{E}(k_i)$ then scrap capital,

where $\bar{E}$ denotes the level of employment associated with operating with the desired strategic spare capacity. In Fig. 19.13(a), the level of employment when there is the desired margin of spare capacity, SSC, is shown by $\bar{E}(k_o)$, and $\widetilde{E}(k_o)$ is the level of employment when all capacity is being used. SSC is assumed independent of k, so $\bar{E}(k) = SSC + \widetilde{E}(k)$.

In Fig. 19.13(b), the full model is shown. Now it is clear that there is a *unique* level of employment at which the economy is in competing-claims equilibrium and also at which firms have their desired rate of capacity utilization, in the sense that they are operating with exactly their strategic spare capacity. There will be a medium-run equilibrium rate of unemploy-

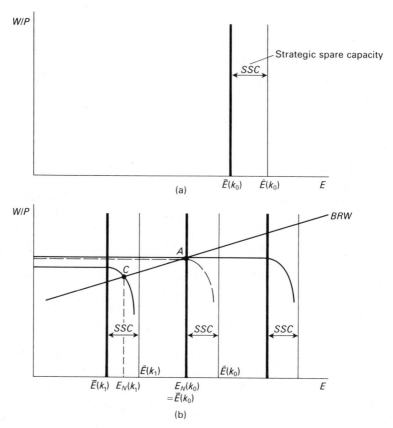

Fig. 19.13 Capital scrapping: unique long-run equilibrium rate of unemployment

ment at $E_N(k_1)$ as the result of the processes described above. The effect of depressed demand lowers capacity utilization and leads to capital scrapping; this produces a fall in the capital stock to k_1 and results in the widening of profit margins, since with such a low capital stock, virtually all of the existing capacity will be required to produce the level of output demanded, and this provides the opportunity for firms to boost their prices. Inflation will stop falling. However, this is not a long-run equilibrium for the economy, because at point C firms are operating with *less than* their desired spare capacity. Thus, they will be raising investment so as to get back their desired strategic spare capacity. The capital stock will begin rising again, and falling inflation will appear once more. Only when the capital stock is at the level of k_0, where the equilibrium rate of unemployment *coincides* with the operation of firms with their optimal strategic spare capacity, is the economy in long-run equilibrium with constant inflation and an unchanging capital stock (point A).

Thus, in the full model of capital scrapping, we have a result that is analytically similar to that of long-term unemployment: while there is no unique equilibrium rate of unemployment in the medium term, there is a unique long-run rate of unemployment. Meanwhile, the economy can be characterized for lengthy periods of time by the persistence of unemployment—i.e. by unemployment away from its long-run equilibrium rate and yet with constant inflation.

Conclusion

Using a simple model, we have shown how hysteresis can result from the relationship between businesses' pricing behaviour and capacity utilization. This form of unemployment persistence is a possible explanation for the twin observations of a return to 'normal' levels of capacity utilization in 1979 and 1985 in the UK despite the presence of continuing rises in unemployment over the period as a whole, and the apparent tendency of the equilibrium rate of unemployment to move upward with the actual rate of unemployment over this period. The implications for the capital stock and for unemployment of following a deflationary demand management policy over an extended period in an economy that is characterized by wage- and price-setting of the type assumed here have been illustrated. We have shown the path of the equilibrium rate of unemployment in the medium run and the presence of a unique long-run equilibrium rate of unemployment.

As a link to the previous arguments about hysteresis, it is possible that, from the labour market side, a process very similar to the one described in this section may occur as a result of the decline in the stock of marketable skills in the economy during a prolonged period of deflation.

19.5   Actual, Equilibrium, and Sustainable Unemployment in the Open Economy

19.5.1   Standard Fixed Exchange Rate Argument: Unemployment Persistence

In the analysis of the fixed exchange rate open economy in Part III, we dwelt at length on the non-uniqueness of constant inflation (or equilibrium) rates of unemployment. To recap, let us assume that the economy is currently experiencing constant inflation at the world rate of inflation. By definition, it is at an equilibrium rate of unemployment. Suppose that there is a fall in aggregate demand as the result for example of the adoption of a more contractionary fiscal stance. At higher unemployment, wage inflation will begin to fall, reflecting the lower bargaining power of the unions. Price inflation, being a weighted average of wage inflation and the world rate of inflation, will fall more slowly than wage inflation, but will fall relative to the world rate. Hence real wages will fall—with money wage inflation below price inflation—the underlying mechanism being the fall in the price-determined real wage as the real cost of imports rises (owing to world price inflation being above domestic price inflation). Thus, the price-determined real wage will shift downward. Eventually, the price-determined real wage will be equal to the lower bargained real wage at the higher unemployment rate. As the gap between the PRW and the BRW narrows, wage inflation and price inflation gradually move back up to the world price inflation rate. In other words, following a burst of disinflation associated with the lower level of aggregate demand, inflation returns to the constant rate of world inflation.

As discussed in detail in Part III, the underlying long-run constraint on the rate of unemployment in the fixed exchange rate open economy is set by the current account. However, the economy can be moved away from this minimum sustainable rate of unemployment through the effect of demand shocks. Because the price-determined real wage curve shifts when domestic inflation moves out of line with world inflation, the fall (or rise) in inflation is only temporary. Thus, unemployment can stay away from the long-run minimum sustainable rate of unemployment (fixed by current account balance) for lengthy periods of time.

Under flexible exchange rates and perfect capital mobility, the same phenomena will occur unless the value of the expected exchange rate is tied to a real variable such as a specific level of competitiveness or current account balance. *If* the expected exchange rate is tied to a real variable, then there is a unique rate of unemployment associated with constant inflation, and any deviation of unemployment from this rate will be accompanied by rising inflation fuelled by a depreciating exchange rate (or falling inflation fuelled by an appreciating exchange rate). Rising or falling inflation will operate to drive the economy back to the equilibrium rate of unemployment. In this case, the existence of persistence or hysteresis in the unemployment rate will depend on the existence of other mechanisms, of the type discussed elsewhere in this chapter and in Chapter 16.

19.5.2 Entry and Exit in Export Markets: a Case of Hysteresis in the Minimum Sustainable Rate of Unemployment

If it is the case that it is more difficult to enter an export market than to exit from one, and if a period of time at low competitiveness results in the exit of a number of exporters from the market, then a return to the previous level of competitiveness will not see a return to the same balance of trade position. Because of the asymmetry between entry and exit, a period of time at the original level of competitiveness, although resulting in the re-entry of some exporters, will leave the economy with a lower number in total. In other words, the minimum sustainable rate of unemployment will have been increased.

Figure 19.14 gives an example of such a process. Initially the economy is at point A on the balance of trade line associated with n_0 exporters. The government deflates the economy. A simple example would be the case of overshooting discussed in Chapter 15 above: the government implements a tight monetary policy, which in the presence of sluggish wage and price adjustment produces an appreciation of the exchange rate greater than would be necessary for equilibrium. In Fig. 19.14, the economy moves from point A to point B. Suppose that the economy remains at B for two years and that, as a result, a number of exporters withdraw from their overseas markets: it is simply not profitable for them to continue selling

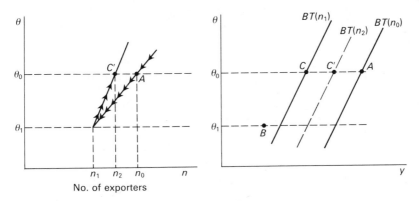

Fig. 19.14 Entry and exit in export markets
The permanent effects on the sustainable rate of unemployment of a period of overvaluation of the real exchange rate

abroad with a real exchange rate equal to θ_1. The left-hand panel of the figure depicts the relationship between the level of the real exchange rate (competitiveness) and the number of firms exporting. It is assumed that the number of firms responds with a lag to the level of the real exchange rate, e.g., θ must remain at a particular level for—let us say—two years before the number of exporters changes. Thus, after two years at point B, the number of exporters drops to n_1 and the BT line shifts to the left to $BT(n_1)$.

We then suppose that the overshooting of the exchange rate unwinds and, in addition, the government eases its monetary stance so that the real exchange rate returns to its original level of θ_0. In the short run, the highest level of output the government can achieve consistent with current balance is shown by point C—a level much lower than was originally possible, i.e. when there were n_0 exporters.

In the longer run, if θ_0 is maintained, firms will be attracted back into export markets. But—and this is the long-term problem of deflationary monetary policies—it is much harder to enter an export market than to leave one. This means that a simple reversal of the real exchange rate will not attract as many firms into export markets as had previously left. As the left-hand panel of Fig. 19.14 indicates, the number of exporters will rise but only to n_2. Thus, the balance of trade line will eventually shift to $BT(n_2)$. The government would then be able to move to a lower level of unemployment than C consistent with trade balance; but, because of the problems of re-entering foreign markets, the original position of A is unattainable.

Obviously, this is only the barest sketch of an argument and lacks a microeconomic model of firm entry and exit behaviour. However, it provides an illustrative story of the possible existence of hysteresis in the sustainable rate of unemployment, and is one way of explaining how '[a] period of overvaluation or undervaluation . . . changes the industrial landscape in a relatively permanent fashion' (Dornbusch 1987a: 9). The experience of the UK manufacturing sector as a result of the sharp real appreciation of sterling in 1979–80 appears to reflect the kind of effects outlined above. In the early 1980s there was a sharp rise in the number of company liquidations, especially in the export sector (Landesmann and Snell 1989). Between 1980 and 1985, the UK share of exports in total OECD manufacturing exports fell from 11% to 8%.

19.5.3 The Effects of Foreign Debt Accumulation

In discussing the current balance in this book, we have given only passing attention to interest payments. The current balance consists of the balance of trade in goods and services together with the balance of interest payments by the domestic economy on assets owned by foreigners and interest receipts on foreign assets owned by domestic residents. If the domestic economy owns fewer foreign assets than foreigners own domestic assets, there will be a net outflow of interest (and other earnings). Assume a fixed exchange rate (of $e = 1$), and hence $r = r^*$; and call the net external debt of the domestic economy D^x; then the economy will have to pay r^*D^x to foreigners each year. Thus, equilibrium on the current account will require a surplus on trade in goods and services of r^*D^x to balance the interest payments of r^*D^x.

What are the implications for the BT line—or, more accurately, the current balance or CB line, as we should now call it? Clearly, the higher is either r^* or D^x, the further left will be the CB schedule in the Salter–Swan diagram. This reflects the fact that, given θ and y^*, and hence exports, output will have to be reduced so as to reduce imports to pay for r^*D^x. In Figure 19.15, $D_1^x > D_0^x$, and hence $CB(r^*D_1^x)$ is to the left of $CB(r^*D_0^x)$.

Now, the punch-line is this—and it goes in the opposite direction to the argument of the last subsection:

1 the external debt, D^x, increases by exactly the deficit on the current account, or decreases by the surplus; so

2 the current balance (CB) schedule will automatically move if the government runs either a deficit or a surplus on the current balance;

3 if the government chooses an expansionary aggregate demand policy and hence runs a deficit, the current balance schedule shifts inwards as the external debt rises; so short-term expansion and a current balance deficit (as the French government under Mitterrand found out in

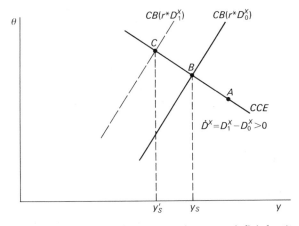

Fig. 19.15 The implications of running a current account deficit for the sustainable rate of unemployment

1981–2[10]) implies longer-term deflation; and deflation now implies greater current balance freedom in the future.

By running the economy at point A, with a current deficit, the sustainable rate of unemployment is shifted upward as the current balance line shifts to the left—e.g. to $CB(r^*D_1^x)$. With the structure of wage- and price-setting given by the competing-claims equilibrium line (CCE) as shown, running a deficit at point A produces a *fall* in the sustainable level of output from y_s (point B) to y_s' (point C). Hence there is a rise in the sustainable rate of unemployment.

Note again that this example of the interaction between current levels of activity and long-run sustainable ones runs in the *opposite* direction to the examples discussed previously. Here, the choice of *lower* unemployment in the short run, through the use of expansionary demand management, has the effect of *raising* the sustainable rate of unemployment (Alogoskoufis (1989)).

19.6   Conclusions

It is very important to re-emphasize here that research on explaining the persistence of unemployment in the high unemployment economies is far from complete.[11] We have differentiated between two different kinds of explanation for the observed persistence; on the one hand, some have argued that exogenous 'push' factors have pushed up the bargained real wage curve and or pushed down the price-determined real wage curve with the result that equilibrium unemployment has risen. In order to prevent accelerating inflation, governments have had to restrain demand and allow actual unemployment to rise in line with the equilibrium rate. With this explanation, high (equilibrium = actual) unemployment will persist until the bargained real wage curve is shifted downward or the price-determined real wage curve is shifted upward. Let us take the case of the downward shift in the PRW consequent on the first OPEC price increases of 1973. Such an exogenous deterioration in the terms of trade increases the equilibrium rate of unemployment *unless* there is an immediate *downward shift* in the bargained real wage curve. Experience suggests that such a readjustment of bargaining objectives did not occur swiftly in many countries. Of course, eventually, bargaining behaviour may adjust to the new objective circumstances and the equilibrium rate of unemployment will gradually fall. In the meantime, unemployment will persist.

[10] See Sachs and Wyplosz (1985) for details.
[11] See Alogoskoufis and Manning (1988) for a recent attempt to survey the acceptability of several of the hypotheses discussed above. Gordon (1988) reviews the issues and comes down much more firmly in support of the existence of the hysteresis explanation than do Alogoskoufis and Manning.

Policy prescription under such circumstances points to the adoption of incomes policies or the introduction of changes in bargaining structures. Supply-side policies that have a favourable effect on productivity may also be helpful in shifting the PRW. Similarly, supply-side fiscal measures may be indicated.

On the other hand, it has been argued that rises in *actual* unemployment have themselves brought about the upward shift of the bargained real wage curve (e.g. insider–outsider; long-term/short-term unemployed models) and therefore have caused a rise in equilibrium unemployment. The pure hysteresis version of this type of argument suggests that unemployment will persist at high levels until actual unemployment is reduced. Falling actual unemployment will feed through to a fall in equilibrium unemployment and will allow the economy to operate at lower unemployment with stable (if somewhat higher) inflation. There is a difference between the pure hysteresis model (insider–outsider), where only a fall in actual unemployment will affect the equilibrium rate, and the long-term/short-term unemployment and capacity scrapping models, where, although high unemployment will persist, there will be a gradual and possibly very slow return of the economy to the underlying long-run equilibrium rate of unemployment.

The policy prescription is for governments to introduce policies that stimulate demand in the economy and raise employment. Specific measures to provide jobs for the long-term unemployed would be particularly helpful if the persistence is due to the role of long-term unemployment.

Unanswered Questions and Future Directions of Research

This book has attempted to make the main recent developments in unemployment and inflation theory accessible to undergraduate economists who have already taken an introductory macroeconomics course. Because many of the recent developments have appeared only in journal articles with a substantial mathematical content, this book may also be useful to economically educated readers and practising economists who do not have the time to immerse themselves in the literature. While the purpose of the book has been to simplify models in the literature and to present them within a unified, systematic model throughout, a key development of the imperfect competition analysis in the future will be a generally accepted model at a suitably high level of sophistication.

There is no question as to the importance of these new developments. *First*, they represent an increasingly dominant approach to analysis, in Western Europe and perhaps also in the USA—as witnessed for example by the graduate text of Blanchard and Fischer.

Second, they represent the creation of an alternative to the New

Classical macroeconomics with what is beginning to be described as 'New Keynesianism'.[12] Hence the analytic door to the justification of aggregate demand management by government, which had been closed by the New Classical approach, is reopened. This applies both to the traditional Keynesian short run and arguably—as we have seen in the discussion of hysteresis in this chapter—to the medium and long run as well.

Third, by contrast to earlier Keynesian analysis, they are based on clear microeconomic foundations. These are derived from imperfect competition in both product and labour markets. As discussed in previous chapters and summarized below, however, important theoretical lacunae remain. None the less, the 'New Keynesianism' has a micro-theoretical robustness that previous versions lacked. The microfoundations are themselves in areas of exciting intellectual developments—industrial organization and wage-bargaining theory—in part because of the power of modern game theory. This suggests that New Keynesian analysis will provide a framework for much further development.

Fourth, the New Keynesian analysis, rooted in imperfect competition, is impressively better than the New Classical model at explaining the major stylized macroeconomic facts of advanced industrialized economies, in particular the existence of involuntary unemployment.

The New Keynesian analysis is, however, very far from complete. There remain major areas of debate to be resolved. Among the most important 'problem' areas in the theory of employment and inflation are the following.

1 *The relationship between the imperfect competition model and rational expectations*. To explain why, if there is a unique equilibrium rate of unemployment, the economy adjusts only slowly towards it, New Keynesian analysis invokes adaptive expectations and/or staggered price- and wage-setting. In the real world, prices and wages are indeed set at intervals, and inflation expectations are usually formed adaptively. But theoretical explanations of these real world phenomena are still far from satisfying.

2 *Exchange rate expectations*. Great progress has been made in the past decade in our understanding of foreign exchange markets. But answers to the fundamental question of how expectations of the nominal exchange rate are determined remain elusive. Perfectly competitive financial markets bear resemblance to co-ordination games for which many equilibria exist—as Keynes noted long ago. This leads to theoretical problems, even with fixed exchange rates. A key assumption of our analysis of open economies is that governments cannot generally run current account deficits for an extended period of time (unless they are the

---

[12] 'New Keynesianism' is *not* synonymous with 'neo-Keynesian', 'post-Keynesian', or 'new Cambridge' approaches.

counterpart of a stable long-term capital inflow). Without doubt, govern-ments believe this to be the case, but there is no good theoretical explanation of it.

3 *Hysteresis/persistence of unemployment.*   As we have seen in this chapter, a major dispute concerns this issue. It is clear from the earlier discussion, in which the main types of hysteresis argument have been set out, that there is no agreement on whether long-run hysteresis exists; nor can it be ruled out that other 'hysteresis-type' models will be developed in the future. As suggested by the discussion of the policy implications of the different explanations for unemployment persistence, this is a most critical area of future research.

References

Abreu, D. (1988), 'On the theory of infinitely repeated games with discounting', *Econometrica*, 56: 383–96.

Ackley, G. (1978), *Macroeconomics: Theory and Policy*, Macmillan, New York.

Akerlof, G. A. and Yellen, J. (1985), 'A near-rational model of the business cycle with wage and price inertia', *Quarterly Journal of Economics*, supplement, 100: 823–38.

—— (eds.) (1987), *Efficiency Wage Models of the Labour Market*, Cambridge University Press.

Alexander, S. S. (1952), 'Effects of a devaluation on a trade balance', *IMF Staff Papers*, 2: 263–78.

Alogoskoufis, G. (1989), 'On fiscal policies, external imbalances and fundamental equilibrium exchange rates', Centre for Economic Policy Research, DP no. 322.

Alogoskoufis, G. and Manning, A. (1988), 'On the persistence of unemployment', *Economic Policy*, 7: 427–69.

Artis, M. J. (1984), *Macroeconomics*. Oxford University Press.

Ball, L., Mankiw, N. G., and Romer, D. (1988), 'The New Keynesian economics and the output–inflation trade-off', *Brookings Papers on Economic Activity*, 1: 1–65.

Bank of England (1982), 'Measures of competitiveness', *Bank of England Quarterly Bulletin*, 22: 369–75.

Barro, R. J. (1974), 'Are government bonds net wealth?' *Journal of Political Economy*, 82: 1095–1118.

—— (1989), 'The Ricardian approach to budget deficits', *Journal of Economic Perspectives*, 3: 37–54.

Barsky, R. and Solon, G. (1989), 'Real wages over the business cycle', National Bureau of Economic Research Working Paper no. 2888.

Begg, D. K. H. (1982), *The Rational Expectations Revolution in Macroeconomics: Theories and Evidence*, Philip Allan, Oxford.

Bhaskar, V. (1988), 'The kinked demand curve: a game-theoretic approach', *International Journal of Industrial Organisation*, 6: 373–84.

Bils, M. (1987), 'The cyclical behaviour of marginal cost and price', *American Economic Review*, 77: 838–55.

—— (1989), 'Pricing in a customer market', *Quarterly Journal of Economics*, 104: 699–718.

Blanchard, O. J. (1986), 'The wage–price spiral', *Quarterly Journal of Economics*, 101: 543–65.

—— and Fischer, S. (1989), *Lectures on Macroeconomics*, MIT Press, Cambridge, Mass.

—— and Kiyotaki, N. (1987), 'Monopolistic competition and the effects of aggregate demand', *American Economic Review*, 77: 647–66.

—— and Summers, L. (1986), 'Hysteresis and the European Unemployment Problem', *NBER Macroeconomics Annual*, 15–77.

Blanchflower, D. and Oswald, A. (1989), 'The wage curve', LSE Centre for Labour Economics, Discussion Paper no. 340.

Blinder, A. S. and Solow, R. M. (1973), 'Does fiscal policy matter?' *Journal of Political Economy*, 81: 319–37.

Bosanquet, N. (1983), 'Tax-based incomes policies', in D. Robinson and K. Mayhew (eds.), *Pay Policies for the Future*, Oxford University Press.

Bowles, S. (1985), 'The production process in a competitive economy: Walrasian, Hobbesian and Marxian models', *American Economic Review*, 75: 16–36.

Branson, W. H. and Rotemberg, J. (1980), 'International adjustment with wage rigidity', *European Economy Review*, 13: 309–32.

Bruno, M. and Sachs, J. (1985), *Economics of Worldwide Stagflation*, Basil Blackwell, Oxford.

Buiter, W. H. (1977), 'Crowding out and the effectiveness of fiscal policy', *Journal of Public Economics*, 7: 309–28.

—— (1980),'The macroeconomics of Dr Pangloss: a critical survey of new classical macroeconomics', *Economic Journal*, 90: 34–54.

—— (1985), 'A guide to public sector debt and deficits', *Economic Policy,* no. 1: 13–60.

—— and Miller, M. H. (1983), 'Changing the rules: economic consequences of the Thatcher regime', *Brookings Papers on Economic Activity*, 2: 305–79.

Calmfors, L. and Driffill, J. (1988), 'Bargaining structure, corporatism and macroeconomic performance', *Economic Policy*, 6: 13–61.

Cagan, P. (1987), 'Hyperinflation', in J. Eatwell *et al.* (eds.), *The New Palgrave Dictionary of Economics*, Vol. 2: 704–6.

Carlin, W. and Soskice, D. (1985), 'Real wages, unemployment, international competitiveness and inflation: a framework for analysing closed and open economies', mimeo, Oxford University.

Chick, V. (1977), *The Theory of Monetary Policy* (rev. edn.), Basil Blackwell, Oxford.

Christ, C. (1968), 'A simple macroeconomic model with government budget constraint', *Journal of Political Economy*, 76: 53–67.

Clower, R. (1965), 'The Keynesian counter-revolution: a theoretical approach', in F. H. Hahn and F. P. R. Brechling (eds.), *The Theory of Interest Rates,* Macmillan, London.

Coe, D. T. and Gagliardi, F. (1985), 'Nominal wage determination in ten OECD countries', OECD ESD Working Paper no. 19.

Coutts, K., Godley, W., and Nordhaus, W. (1978), *Industrial Pricing in the United Kingdom*, Cambridge University Press.

Dernberg, T. F. (1989), *Global Macroeconomics*, Harper & Row, New York.

Dixit, A. (1980), 'The role of investment in entry deterrence', *Economic Journal*, 90: 95–106.

Dornbusch, R. (1976), 'Expectations and exchange rate dynamics', *Journal of*

Political Economy, 84: 1161–76

—— (1980), *Open Economy Macroeconomics*, Basic Books, New York.

—— (1987a), 'Exchange rate economics: 1986', *Economic Journal,* 97: 1–18.

—— (1987b), 'Purchasing power parity', in J. Eatwell *et al.* (eds.), *The New Palgrave Dictionary of Economics*, Vol. 3: 1075–85.

—— and Fischer, S. (1980), 'Exchange rates and the current account', *American Economic Review*, 70: 960–71.

Eatwell, J., Milgate, M. and Newman, P. (eds.) (1987), *The New Palgrave Dictionary of Economics* (4 vols.), Macmillan, London.

Fallon, P. and Verry, D. (1988), *The Economics of Labour Markets*, Philip Allan, Oxford.

Faxen, K.-O. (1982), 'Incomes policy and centralised wage formation', in A. Boltho (ed.), *Growth & Crisis in the European Economy,* Oxford University Press.

Flanagan, R. J., Soskice, D. W., and Ulman, L. (1982), *Unionism, Economic Stabilization, and Incomes Policies*, Brookings Institution, Washington DC.

Fleming, J. M. (1962), 'Domestic financial policies under fixed and floating exchange rates', *IMF Staff Papers*, 9: 369–79.

Freeman, R. B. (1988), 'Labour market institutions and economic performance', *Economic Policy*, 6: 63–80.

Friedman, B. M. (1978), 'Crowding out or crowding in? Economic consequences of financing government deficits', *Brookings Papers on Economic Activity*, 3: 593–641.

Friedman, J. (1983), *Oligopoly Theory*, Cambridge University Press.

Friedman, M. (1953), 'The case for flexible rates', *Essays in Positive Economics*, Chicago University Press.

—— (1957), *A Theory of the Consumption Function*, Princeton University Press.

—— (1968), 'The role of monetary policy', *American Economic Review*, 58: 1–17.

—— (1974), *Unemployment versus Inflation: An Evaluation of the Phillips Curve*, Institute for Economic Affairs Occasional Paper 44, London.

Fudenberg, D. and Tirole, J. (1983), 'Capital as a commitment: strategic investment to deter mobility', *Journal of Economic Theory*, 31: 227–50.

Goldstein, M. and Khan, M. S. (1985), 'Income and price effects in foreign trade', in R. W. Jones and P. B. Kenen (eds.), *Handbook of International Economics*, Vol. II, Elsevier, Amsterdam.

Goodhart, C. A. E. (1975), *Money, Information and Uncertainty,* London, Macmillan.

Gordon, R. J. (1988), 'Back to the future: European unemployment today viewed from America in 1939', *Brookings Papers on Economic Activity*, 1: 271–312.

Greenwald, B. C. and Stiglitz, J. E. (1988), 'Examining alternative macroeconomic theories', *Brookings Papers on Economic Activity*, 1: 207–60.

Gregory, R. G. (1986), 'Wages policy and unemployment in Australia', *Economica Supplement*, 53: S53–74.

Grubb, D., Jackman, R. A., and Layard, R. (1983), 'Wage rigidity and unemployment in OECD countries', *European Economic Review*, 21: 11–39.

Grubb, D., Layard, R., and Symons, J. V. (1984), 'Wages, unemployment and incomes policy', in M. Emerson (ed.), *Europe's Stagflation*, Oxford University Press.

Gurley, J. G. and Shaw, E. S. (1960), *Money in a Theory of Finance*, Brookings Institution, Washington, DC.

Hall, R. and Hitch, C. (1939), 'Price theory and business behaviour', *Oxford Economic Papers*, 2: 12–45.

Herin, J., Lindbeck, A., and Myhrman, J. (eds.) (1977), *Flexible Exchange Rates and Stabilization Policy*, Westview Press, Boulder, Col.

Hicks, J. R. (1974), *The Crisis in Keynesian Economics*, Basil Blackwell, Oxford.

Hoover, K. D. (1988), *The New Classical Macroeconomics*, Basil Blackwell, Oxford.

House of Commons, Committee on the Treasury and Civil Service (1981), *Third Report*.

Isard, P. (1977), 'How far can we push the "Law of One Price"?' *American Economic Review*, 67: 942–8.

Jackman, R. (1984), 'Money wage rigidity in an economy with rational trade unions', in G. Hutchinson and J. Treble (eds.), *Recent Advances in Labour Economics*, Croom Helm, London.

—— and Layard, R. (1986), 'The economic effects of a tax-based incomes policy', in D. Collander (ed.), *Incentive-Based Incomes Policies*, Ballinger Press, Cambridge, Mass.

—— Layard, R., Nickell, S., and Wadwhani, S. (1989), 'Unemployment', unpublished manuscript.

Johansen, L. (1982), 'A note on the possibility of an international equilibrium with low levels of activity', *Journal of International Economics*, 13: 257–66.

Kalecki, M. (1971a), 'The mechanism of the business upswing', in M. Kalecki, *Selected Essays on the Dynamics of the Capitalist Economy*, Cambridge University Press.

—— (1971b), 'Class struggle and distribution of national income', in M. Kalecki, *Selected Essays on the Dynamics of the Capitalist Economy*, Cambridge University Press.

Keynes, J. M. (1936), *The General Theory of Employment, Interest and Money*, Macmillan, London.

Kravis, I. B. and Lipsey, R. E. (1978), 'Price behaviour in the light of balance of payments theories', *Journal of International Economics*, 8: 193–246.

Kydland, F. E. and Prescott, E. C. (1982), 'Time to build and aggregate fluctuations', *Econometrica*, 50: 1345–69.

Laidler, D. and Parkin, M. (1975), 'Inflation: a survey', *Economic Journal*, 85: 757–8.

Landesmann, M. and Snell, A. (1989), 'The consequences of Mrs Thatcher for UK manufacturing exports', *Economic Journal*, 99: 1–27.

Layard, R. (1982), 'Is incomes policy the answer to unemployment?' *Economica*, 49: 219–39.

—— and Nickell, S. (1985), 'The causes of British unemployment', *National Institute Economic Review*, 111: 62–85.

—— and —— (1986), 'Unemployment in the UK', *Economica*, 53: S121–166.

—— and —— (1987), 'The labour market', in R. Dornbusch and R. Layard (eds.), *The Performance of the British Economy*, Clarendon Press, Oxford.

——, Basevi, G., Blanchard, O., Buiter, W., and Dornbusch, R. (1986), 'Europe: the case for unsustainable growth', in O. Blanchard, R. Dornbusch, and R.

Layard (eds.), *Restoring Europe's Prosperity*, MIT Press, Cambridge, Mass.

Leijonhufvud, A. (1967), 'Keynes and the Keynesians: a suggested interpretation', *American Economic Review*, 57: 401–10.

—— (1968), *On Keynesian Economics and the Economics of Keynes*, Oxford University Press.

Lindbeck, A. and Snower, D. (1986), 'Wage setting, unemployment and insider outsider relations', *American Economic Review*, 76: 235–9.

Lucas, R. E. (1972), 'Expectations and the neutrality of money', *Journal of Economic Theory*, 4: 103–24.

—— (1975), 'An equilibrium model of the business cycle', *Journal of Political Economy*, 83: 1113–44.

Maddison, A. (1987), 'Growth and slowdown in advanced capitalist economies', *Journal of Economic Literature*, 25: 649–98.

Malinvaud, E. (1977), *The Theory of Unemployment Reconsidered*, Basil Blackwell, Oxford.

Martin, A. (1990), 'Sweden: restoring the social democratic distributive regime', Harvard European Centre, Occasional Paper Series.

Marx, K. (1976), *Capital*, Vol. 1, Penguin, Harmondsworth.

McDonald, I. and Solow, R. (1981), 'Wage bargaining and employment', *American Economic Review*, 71: 896–908.

McKinnon, R. I. (1984), 'An international standard for monetary stabilisation', Institute for International Economics, Washington DC.

Meade, J. E. (1951), *The Theory of International Economic Policy*, Vol. 1: *The Balance of Payments*, Oxford University Press.

Modigliani, F. and Brumberg, R. (1954), 'Utility analysis and the consumption function: an interpretation of cross-section data', in K. K. Kurihara (ed.), *Post-Keynesian Economics*, Rutgers University Press, New Brunswick, NJ.

—— and Tarentelli, E. (1977), 'Market forces, trade union action and the Phillips curve in Italy', *Banca Nazionale del Lavoro Quarterly Review*, no. 120: 3–36.

Muellbauer, J. and Portes, R. (1978), 'Macroeconomic models with quantity rationing', *Economic Journal*, 88: 788–821.

Mundell, J. E. (1958), *International Economies*, Macmillan, London.

Muth, J. F. (1961), 'Rational expectations and the theory of price movements', *Econometrica*, 29: 315–35.

Nash, J. F. (1953), 'Two-person cooperative games', *Econometrica*, 21: 128–40.

Nickell, S. J. and Andrews, M. (1983), 'Unions, real wages and employment in Britain 1951–79', *Oxford Economic Papers*, 35, suppl.: 183–206.

OECD (1989), *Economic Survey of Sweden 1988/89*, Paris.

Okun, A. M. (1981), *Prices and Quantities: A Macroeconomic Analysis*, Brookings Institution, Washington, DC.

Oswald, A. J. (1985), 'The economic theory of trade unions: an introductory survey', *Scandinavian Journal of Economics*, 87: 160–93.

—— (1987), 'Efficient contracts are on the labour demand curve: theory and facts', LSE Centre for Labour Economics, DP no. 284.

—— and Turnbull, P. (1985), 'Pay and unemployment determination in Britain: what are labour contracts really like?' *Oxford Review of Economic Policy*, 2: 88–97.

Patinkin, D. (1987), 'Keynes, John Maynard', in J. Eatwell *et al.* (eds.), *The New*

Palgrave Dictionary of Economics, Vol. 3: 19–41.

Phelps, E. S. (1970), 'Money–wage dynamics and labour market equilibrium', in E. S. Phelps *et al.* (eds.), *Microeconomic Foundations of Employment and Inflation Theory*, W. W. Norton, New York.

—— (1972), *Inflation Policy and Unemployment Theory*, Macmillan, London.

Phillips, A. W. (1958), 'The relation between unemployment and the rate of change of money wage rates in the United Kingdom, 1861–1957', *Economica*, 25: 283–99.

Pigou, A. C. (1933), *The Theory of Unemployment*, Macmillan, London.

Pohjola, M. (1989), 'Corporatism and wage bargaining', mimeo, WIDER, Helsinki.

Radcliffe Report (1957), *Committee on the Working of the Monetary System: Report*, Cmnd. 827, HMSO, London.

Reid, G. C. (1981), *The Kinked Demand Curve Analysis of Oligopoly*, Edinburgh University Press.

Rotemberg, J. and Saloner, G. (1986), 'A super-game-theoretic model of price wars during booms', *American Economic Review*, 76: 390–407.

Rowthorn, R. E. (1977), 'Conflict, inflation and money', *Cambridge Journal of Economics*, 1: 215–39.

—— and Wells, J. (1987), *Deindustrialisation and Foreign Trade*, Cambridge University Press.

Rubinstein, A. (1982), 'Perfect equilibrium in a bargaining game', *Econometrica*, 50: 207–11.

Sachs, J. (1980), 'Wages, flexible exchange rates and economic policy', *Quarterly Journal of Economics*, 94: 731–47.

—— (1985), 'The dollar and the policy mix: 1985', *Brookings Papers on Economic Activity*, 1: 117–85.

—— and Wyplosz, C. (1985), 'The economic consequences of President Mitterrand', *Economic Policy*, 2: 261–322.

Salop, S. (1979), 'A model of the natural rate of unemployment', *American Economic Review*, 69: 117–25.

Salter, W. (1959), 'Internal and external balance: the role of price and expenditure effects', *Economic Review*, 35: 226–36.

Sargent, T. J. and Wallace, N. (1976), 'Rational expectations and the theory of economic policy', *Journal of Monetary Economics*, 2: 169–83.

Sawyer, M. C. (1982), *Macroeconomics in Question: The Keynesian–Monetarist Orthodoxies and the Kaleckian Alternative*, Wheatsheaf, Brighton.

Schelde-Andersen, P. and Turner, P. (1980), 'Incomes policy in theory and practice', *OECD Economic Outlook—Occasional Studies*, July.

Shapiro, C. and Stiglitz, J. (1984), 'Equilibrium unemployment as a worker discipline device', *American Economic Review*, 74: 433–44.

Sneessens, H. and Drèze, J. (1986), 'A discussion of Belgian unemployment combining traditional concepts and disequilibrium econometrics', *Economica Supplement*, 53: S89–119.

Soskice, D. (1978), 'Strike waves and wage explosions, 1968–70: an economic interpretation', in C. Crouch and A. Pizzorno (eds.), *The Resurgence of Class Conflict in Western Europe*, Macmillan, London.

—— and Carlin, W. (1989), 'Medium-run Keynesianism: hysteresis and capital scrapping', in P. Davidson and J. Kregel (eds.), *Macroeconomic Problems and Policies of Income Distribution*, Edward Elgar, Aldershot.

Stevenson, A., Muscatelli, V., and Gregory, M. (1988), *Macroeconomic Theory and Stabilisation Policy*, Philip Allan, Oxford.

Swan, T. (1960), 'Economic control in a dependent economy', *Economic Record*, 36: 51–66.

Sweezy, P. (1939), 'Demand conditions under oligopoly', *Journal of Political Economy*, 47: 568–73.

Taylor, J. (1979), 'Staggered wage setting in a macro model', *American Economic Review*, 69: 108–13.

Tirole, J. (1988), *The Theory of Industrial Organization*, MIT Press, Cambridge, Mass.

Tobin, J. (1958), 'Liquidity preference as behaviour towards risk', *Review of Economic Studies*, 25: 65–86.

—— (1972a), 'Inflation and unemployment', *American Economic Review*, 62: 1–18.

—— (1972b), 'The wage–price mechanism: overview of the conference', in O. Eckstein (ed.), *The Economics of Price Determination*, Federal Reserve Board, Washington, DC.

—— (1980), *Asset Accumulation and Economic Activity*, Basil Blackwell, Oxford.

Trevithick, J. (1978), 'Recent developments in the theory of employment', *Scottish Journal of Political Economy*, 25: 107–18.

van der Klundert, T. and van Shaik, A. (1989), 'Unemployment persistence and loss of productive capacity: A Keynesian approach', Center Tilburg University, D.P. Series no. 8905.

Wallich, H. C. and Weintraub, S. (1971), 'A tax-based incomes policy', *Journal of Economic Issues*, 5: 1–19.

Walters, P. (1985), 'Distributing decline: Swedish social democracy and the crisis of the welfare state', *Government and Opposition*, 9: 356–69.

Williamson, J. (1983a), *The Open Economy and the World Economy*, Harper and Row, New York.

—— (1983b), *The Exchange Rate System*, Institute for International Economics, Washington, DC.

Zeuthen, F. (1930), *Problems of Monopoly and Economic Welfare*, Routledge, London.

Index